NATURES PAST

RNED

NATURES PAST

The Environment and Human History

Paolo Squatriti, Editor

THE UNIVERSITY OF MICHIGAN PRESS
Ann Arbor

Published in the United States of America by
The University of Michigan Press
Manufactured in the United States of America
⊗ Printed on acid-free paper
2010   2009   2008   2007   4   3   2   1

A CIP catalog record for this book is available from the British Library.

Library of Congress Cataloging-in-Publication Data

Natures past : the environment and human history /
Paolo Squatriti, editor.
        p. cm. — (The comparative studies in society and history book
    series)
    Includes bibliographical references.
    ISBN-13: 978-0-472-09960-3 (cloth : alk. paper)
    ISBN-10: 0-472-09960-4 (cloth : alk. paper)
    ISBN-13: 978-0-472-06960-6 (pbk. : alk. paper)
    ISBN-10: 0-472-06960-8 (pbk. : alk. paper)
    1. Human ecology—History.   2. Environmental degradation—
History.   3. Conservation of natural resources—History.
4. Environmental policy—History.   I. Squatriti, Paolo, 1963–
GF13.N38   2006
304.2—dc22   2006021900

Acknowledgments

Editors probably accumulate more debts of gratitude in the long process of assembling for publication a collection of essays than authors of monographs do. In editing *Natures Past* I have certainly had occasion to draw heavily on the resources of patience and forbearance and intellectual generosity of many people. My thanks most obviously go to the ten authors, whose patience was saintly, but they at least could be imagined to act out of enlightened self-interest, with the publication of their work as a reward. Alongside them, my debts are deepest to Ray Grew, who tirelessly answered disparate (and desperate) questions and asked the right ones himself at the right times, without ever being obliged to. If *Natures Past* grew from an idea into a conference and a book, it is also due to the support and energy of Tom Trautman and David Akin. At the 2003 conference that definitively launched the project, valuable contributions came from the intellectual vigor of Stuart Kirsch, Maria Montoya, John Knott, and Phil Deloria. Finally, this book benefited greatly from the intelligent copyediting of Mary Hashman, to whom I am grateful.

At the end of September 2006, as the proof of *Natures Past* finally became available, I learned of the death of Nick Howe, who had contributed so much acumen and decency to the venture. The only consolation for this sad loss is the thought that the memory of his presence in the landscape he loved is preserved in his words, here and elsewhere.

Grateful acknowledgment is given to *Comparative Studies in Society and History* (*CSSH*) for permission to reproduce the following articles in revised form:

"Distribution Fights, Coordination Games, and Lobster Management" by James Acheson and Jack Knight, revised from a paper that originally appeared in *CSSH* 42:209–38.

"Fruit Trees and Family Trees in an Anthropogenic Forest" by Nancy Lee Peluso, revised from a paper that originally appeared in *CSSH* 38:510–48.

"Colonialism and Forestry in India: Imagining the Past in Present Politics" by K. Sivaramakrishnan, revised from a paper that originally appeared in *CSSH* 37:3–40.

"Naming the Stranger: African Cultural Adoption of Maize" by James McCann, revised from a paper that originally appeared in *CSSH* 43:246–72.

Grateful acknowledgment is also given to *Comparative Studies in Society and History* (*CSSH*) for permission to reproduce the following article in original form:

"In Search of Natural Identity: Alpine Landscape and the Reconstruction of the Swiss Nation" by Oliver Zimmer, which originally appeared in *CSSH* 40:637–65.

Material in chapter IX has appeared in Ted Steinberg, *American Green: The Obsessive Quest for the Perfect Lawn* (New York: W.W. Norton, 2006)

Contents

Illustrations

Introduction

Natures Past and Present
Environmental Histories

Paolo Squatriti

A focused interest in past ecological relationships, in how people have fit into ecosystems over time, is actually quite a new thing. Environmental history, the umbrella label for this kind of intellectual pursuit, is a typically late twentieth-century invention. Indeed, as a formal discipline (or subdiscipline or interdiscipline), the study of the dialectical relationship between humans and the physical environments they inhabit is hardly thirty years old. Environmental history may have had multiple beginnings and a long prehistory in the writings of people who saw how "netted together" ecosystems are even before Darwin asserted the principle;[1] yet the historians who banded together in 1976 to found the American Association for Environmental History felt like mavericks and pioneers, misunderstood by their "mainstream" colleagues who studied past religions, or labor relations, or war and politics, or even gender, technology, and the family.

A marked sense of alterity and of standing apart from the rest of the historical profession has thus distinguished the practitioners of environmental history since the 1970s. This sense of distinctness, of being a chosen group whose long peregrination through the wastelands of neglect has defined its identity, remains vigorous even now that other scholarships have begun to recognize the value of what environmental historians do and environmentally inclined historians are included in the activities of the major professional organizations.[2] Distinguished environmental historians still feel that their concerns do not receive sufficient attention and recognition and readily take on the role of "marginals" whose contributions to the community of scholars are misunderstood or simply excluded. For example, Ted Steinberg's fine chapter in this volume opens with an expression of disappointment over a history of American suburbanization that did not consider some of the environmental dimensions of the issue. To a considerable extent, the "otherness" of environmental history, whether perceived by its adepts or by its more passive readers, is based on some genuine eccentricities in this mode of historical production. Some, at least, of the distance between environmental history proper and its broader audience depends on the sense of unfamiliarity generated by the different cultural assumptions of those "inside" and "outside" the field. *Natures Past* is, among other things, an attempt to bridge the chasm between orthodox environmental history and other approaches that are fellow travelers in the project of understanding the place of human communities in past biophysical environments.

Whether or not the belief that environmental sensibilities and concepts get short shrift except among specialists is wholly misplaced, its persistence is an intriguing component of environmental history, especially as practiced in North America.[3] The notion that others who are engaged in the evocation of past times have missed the point that environmentally minded scholarship makes, like the feeling that environmental history is a special and separate branch of that engagement, has had considerable repercussions on both the consumption and the production of what environmental historians write. It is probably fair to say that few scholarly cultures are quite as self-conscious and self-reflexive as environmental history. Environmental historians like to define what is peculiar to and distinctive about their practices, so an enormous number of position papers, reviews of the "state of the question," and general manifestos have typified environmental history's rather short life on earth. Other kinds of historians are less prone to compose how-to manuals and quite categorical statements of what is and what is not legitimate practice or authentic environmental history.[4]

Behind this distinctive urge to delineate precisely environmental history's boundaries may lie the discipline's mixed genealogy. Environmental historians have worked hard to set their pursuits apart from those of progenitors, beginning with 1800s environmental mystics like Henry Thoreau or doomsayers like Ralph Waldo Emerson, whose contribution was one of sensibility and orientation. They have distanced themselves from history influenced by the French *Annales* school and its insistence that *everything* has a recountable past, from frontier scholars who followed Frederick Jackson Turner's intuition about the "conquest" of wilderness in American history, from intellectual historians who chronicled shifting ideas about environmental relations since ancient Greece,[5] and from others who have discussed the reciprocities between past people and environments.[6] Even as environmental historians may recognize affinities with these other, older ways of thinking, the relationship between these historians and the progenitors can turn testy, and historical geographers sometimes consider the development of environmental history in North America as a kind of usurpation. The *Journal of Historical Geography,* for instance, differs little in focus from *Environmental History* or *Environment and History,* the main academic journals associated with orthodox environmental history; and one of the earliest, most lucid blueprints for doing environmental history, Ian Simmons's *Environmental History: A Concise Introduction* (London, 1993), is the work of a geographer, though some of his chapters deal head-on with historical sources and methods. Yet as *Natures Past* helps to show, the reiterated "births" of environmental history, its dynamic family relationship with numerous other fields of inquiry, are in fact sources of this sort of history's enduring strength and attraction. Outside the United States, the creators of ecologically aware history are seldom trained as environmental historians and their highly heterogeneous intellectual preparation produces some excellent hybrids. Genuine interdisciplinarity is attained when botanists or meteorologists become historians and when historians try their hand at some "hard" science; it has been so at least since Lucien Febvre wrote *A Geographical Introduction to History* in 1925.

This volume reflects some of the potential that environmental history's multidisciplinarity produces. Within the covers of this book, an anthropologist teaches of how North Atlantic fishers and lobsters reached an understanding, in the course of a century and a half, based on local economic and ecological realities; meanwhile, a student of German nationalism applies his knowledge of placeness to some steep landscapes in western Europe to show that environmental facts interacted with cultural and political needs in the seventy-five years after Germany's unification, just as they do today, to fashion a Swiss collective sense of belonging in a specific topography; and anthropologically informed forestry reveals that trees have meanings to Indonesian people that affect forest cover, even as the life cycles and botanical characteristics of some trees induce these meanings. The point is that environmentally inclined study of the past brings out some of the fantastic complexity of people's location in nature. It does so best when a systematic omnivorousness and methodological ecumenicity are given free rein, delivering a better, richer comprehension of past ecological dynamics and of the past tout court. Environmental history's impure genealogies have advantages.

If environmental history has yet to take its place as one of the protagonists of history writing, that may also be because other historical discourses do not speak its same language. This is not just a matter of C. P. Snow's two cultures and the fairly obvious fact that environmental histories tend to resound with more biological, geological, or meteorological jargon than most humanists can stand.[7] After all, most historical lexicons are technical and have the capacity to exclude nonspecialists. What renders the environmental historical dialect distinctive, instead, are the rhetorical conventions and ideological underpinnings that support much environmental history. Few social historians, or specialists in the history of technology or commerce or whatever else, capable as they are of using arcane vocabulary, are animated by the urgent sense that their research touches upon the decisive issue of their time. Environmental historians, who are often also committed, upstanding environmentalists, tend to see manifold connections between the history they study and the dangers the past few generations of human activity are thought to have created for the earth's biodiversity. For although even historians of the ancient Mediterranean are not immune from it, this cast of mind, and the attendant rhetorical devices, is more prominent among chroniclers of *modern* ecological changes.[8] Vulnerable nature, a victim of modern people's unfair treatment, in effect a subaltern creature of the modern political economy, calls for paladins, and environmental historians respond, nature's champions. In consequence, some of the most celebrated monographs of environmental history adopt a chiding tone and use past cataclysms as the rods with which to chastise profligate and environmentally callous people today.[9] The mantle of the prophet is environmental historians' national costume, and their national idiom is the fervent warning of the ineluctable fate that awaits all who fail to repent and amend their unsustainable ways.

Its millenarian flavor can render orthodox environmental history unpalatable, enough to justify its exclusion from conventional historical narratives that prize academic skepticism, detachment, and irony. Millenarianism also deprives certain accounts of how people and ecosystems interacted of their interest, for millenarian reconstructions of the past are teleological and all phenomena are reduced to predictable demonstrations of the teleologists' theory (in this case, environmental disaster comes, like the retribution of the righteous God, for unsustainable human activity).[10] Indeed, this lachrymose vision of how past environmental relations have worked is pervasive enough that some critics have even given it a name (the "standard environmental narrative"), though they doubt it is as common as it used to be even a few years ago.[11] Overall, the authors of *Natures Past* eschew catastrophist language and ideology, reminding us, because it is easy to forget, that environmentally inclined scholarship has more than one voice in the early twenty-first century.[12]

One tonality that has not crept into the environmental historical choir has been the interpretative package associated with heightened awareness of the social and cultural construction of understanding. By and large environmental historians have resisted the lure of poststructural intellectual postures popular over the past two decades. Other kinds of history have been more pliant, and this hesitation too sets environmental history apart. It may be as McNeill thinks, that the more scientifically inclined environmental historians cannot bear to jettison hard-earned knowledge of the physical world, so they cleave to the idea that the nature they study and, a bit more questionably, represent is real. Thus the "social construction of nature just isn't all that important,"[13] and it is a lonely voice in environmental historical publications that calls for more contextualization in history of the ecological sciences so central to environmentally conceived reconstructions.[14] This positivism is all the more problematic when the sources upon which environmental historians base their accounts are textual, or representations of reality just like the parliamentary records political historians might use, or the texts analyzed by historians of Islam or Judaism or minorities or colonialism or whatever else. As Nicholas Howe indicates in his chapter in this volume, the subtle analysis of literary constructions need not lead away from the reconstruction of the lay of the land. His point—that representations of landscape contain the ideology *and* the landscape of whoever did the representing, in Anglo-Saxon Wessex or southwestern American trailer parks—is replicated in a different context by Oliver Zimmer, whose subtle awareness of the ideological underpinnings of landscape discourses also confirms the potential synergies between historical approaches sensitive to geographical facts and ones where the "literary turn" of late twentieth-century Anglophone academia is more prominent.

Though the whiff of old-fashioned "history as it actually was" may cling to environmental history, in other respects this scholarship proves itself able to engage contemporary theoretical approaches (and anyway, in the endless cycle of academic theorizing, old-fashioned approaches seem to be making a comeback). The moral engagement of many environmental historians, their passionate sense that the past really matters and helps to unmask the crucial imbalances in social and ecological relations in contemporary contexts, gives their narratives magnetism and power. It renders the discipline more attractive because it is more "relevant." Even if such relevance comes from parroting the Green movement rather than informing it, to be in a dialogue with any kind of movement at all is a privilege of few contemporary historians or academics. Moreover, environmental history's commitment to exposing the often frightening repercussions of recent historical processes allows it to intersect with many current interpretative theories. The parallel moral concerns in much recent scholarship on modern colonialism might explain the interesting compatibility between environmental and colonial historiographies, applied, outside North America, especially to south Asia. K. Sivaramakrishnan's contribution to *Natures Past* participates in debates about both modern Indian history and forest history. It is a call for moderation, for less explicitly engagé approaches to the history of the subcontinent's forests. He seeks to trace an alternative course for an environmental colonial history that is neither nostalgic and nationalist nor simplistic about subaltern resistance to colonial manipulations of the wooded landscape.

It is perhaps not evident in *Natures Past,* yet it is noticeable that, to date, the most prolific producers of environmental history have been Americanists. Whether because of some deep-seated predisposition planted in the historiography of North America by Turner's famous notion of a frontier between a more and a less humanized landscape or because the quicker, thicker modernization of North America's economy produced precocious ecological angst, Americanists got a head start in environmental history. Whereas many historians of the American environment cite Rachel Carson's *Silent Spring* (1962) as their inspiration, only from the mid-nineties did the ecological history of other hemispheres attract wide attention, including from their denizens, and the European Society for Environmental History was founded only in 2001.[15] Still today, it is predominantly among U.S. historians that one finds those who "do" environmental history actually trained in the discipline. As a result, the skills and issues valued in the historiography of North America have received disproportionate emphasis in the study of past environmental interactions: not everywhere do frontier issues matter, or conservationist ideologies, or massive industrial pollution. Understandings of what is relevant in environmental history that are less than ecumenical have limitations. They contribute to marginalizing the discipline.

American historical preoccupations, and models, reveal some drawbacks when they are exported from their habitat. In many other parts of the world, it is difficult to conceive of wilderness as a historical (as opposed to a prehistorical) phenomenon. The colonialist discourse equating the Garden of Eden with the New World instead remained a vibrant part of American history, and in the 1990s indignant repartees followed from one scholar's suggestion that America's wilderness was a culturally specific, and ideologically loaded, construct.[16] And just as there are troubles with the transplantation of the wilderness dogma, there are fewer suitable subjects for ecological hagiography in Europe and Asia than the sainted Native American offers to Americanists. Most prelapsarian tribes vanished from the Old World long ago.[17] James Acheson's skillful evocation of the long coevolution of fishing practices, politics, and lobster behavior helps gauge the degree to which environmental virtue, even in the Americas, has to be worked at; Maine's coastal waters are not wilderness and have not been for a long time. Indeed, they were becoming a textbook demonstration of the "tragedy of the commons" as rapacious predators vied with each other, using ever more formidable technologies, to get their fair share of the available resources. Precisely because of its humanization, and the forms its transformation into a managed resource has taken of late, maritime Maine offers an interesting counterpoint to Edenic ideas of the Americas, and the consequent fall from grace, that have been endemic in U.S. environmental historiography.[18]

In general, the modernist concerns of American historiography, and hence of the environmentally minded history that it inspires, do not match the sources and scholarship traditions of other places. This too can create unease among students of the "deep past" who seek inspiration and ideas in a discipline overwhelmingly focused on the industrial economies of the past (at most) two hundred years. In the pages that follow, Peter Perdue's chapter about the Qing dynasty administrators who worried about agrarian practices and their ecological costs is a lesson in the relevance of early texts to contemporary political and environmental debates. Perdue patiently recreates various geographical situations from the bureaucratic accounts their governors left behind and proves that the authors' elite training predisposed them to ecological sensitivities that sound positively modern. "Sustainability," it turns out, has early Chinese progenitors.

On the other hand, the preoccupation with natural processes and transformations that take far longer than an American presidential election or, say, the integration of an immigrant group into one or another midwestern urban context, can give environmental history added appeal outside the confines of American history. After all, environmental historians have a greater facility for the *longue durée* than most other historians do; theirs is the one "history from the ground up" that can actually deal with time frames that are almost geological. Hence Asian and other societies that have produced historical records over thousands of years are well positioned to allow scholars to uncover the "deep" and slow-moving environmental dimensions of their past. Richard Hoffmann, by addressing the secular imprint left by large human agglomerations on astonishingly vast hinterlands, suggests that urban metabolism had ecological consequences, deep ones, on medieval European landscapes. His time frame is a mere few centuries, but he conveys the idea very effectively that environmental change is a human tradition, not a modern deviation. Likewise, James McCann tracks the five-century journey of a new plant as it made itself at home in many parts of Africa or, to use the terminology of environmental history, as a new agroecosystem emerged.[19] To do so, he relies on unusual sources, on linguistic traces, as well as on the genetic characteristics of maize from different parts of the New World. The ecological implications of this long adaptation, the other plants maize replaced, the soils maize rendered cultivable, the populations maize could sustain, the new pests that surely traveled with the new cultigen—in sum the new equilibria between economies and ecosystems maize evoked as it established itself—are all stories McCann hints at.[20] In describing the arrival of maize in Africa, he evokes the slow, sometimes almost invisible, transformation of environments whose outcome is plainly visible today.

The primacy of the modern period in environmental history reflects a latent belief in the distinctiveness of human interactions with ecosystems since the advent of modern industry and technologies.[21] Timescales that doggedly isolate the modern from the premodern (an unfortunate and revealing formulation) both reflect and accentuate the environmental anxiety that has energized environmental history for the past quarter of a century.[22] The belief that modernity introduced a rupture in humanity's environmental involvement is related to the messianic component in the environmental historical tradition, its conviction that capitalism and the commodification of nature are root evils of modern life, with unprecedented ecological costs.[23] The belief is misguided because it is ahistorical and forgetful of thousands of years of dramatic, if not always rapid, changes in the lands people inhabited. Uncovering environmental change in remote times need not defuse current alarm over greenhouse effects or Aral Sea desertification any more than tracing the coevolution of human and other communities in places far removed from Turner's frontier, and from industrial technology, does. Hoffmann's creative application of a set of ideas developed in very late modern times to much earlier evidence points beyond the fact that before modernity human communities had an impact broader than they (and hitherto us) imagined, at the less obvious fact that, with a little imagination, the impact can be measured.[24] The clever use of diverse types of evidence, including urban archaeology, renders modern parameters applicable to northern and Mediterranean Europe's cities during their late medieval moment. This is a sign of how porous an environmental perspective makes the barriers between modern and previous periods. Perhaps it is also a portent of how environmental perspectives will undermine the Weberian paradigm according to which modernity, and environment-transforming capitalism, brought radical innovation to an essentially stable world system in which, as J. R. McNeill argues in his chapter about malaria, people were much more vulnerable to natural forces than they have become in modern circumstances.[25]

How powerful modern economic trends really have been in the transformations of ecosystems over the past two centuries is, however, fully visible in the chapters by Nancy Lee Peluso, Ted Steinberg, and James Acheson. While Steinberg and Peluso lean toward more culturally inflected understandings of why specific vegetations prevailed in the United States and Indonesia, respectively, Acheson privileges the political; but all three reflect on the all too human drive to turn pieces of nature into property and the repercussions possession had. In West Kalimantan, collective forms of ownership, within the same lineage, and a graded system of rights to arboreal resources fashioned a specific kind of woodland. The esteem people felt for the fruits of some trees determined the allocation of rights. But as Peluso deftly points out, the trees' rates of growth and their fruits' rates of maturation were equally efficacious determinants. The interaction of culture, modern (colonial and postcolonial) ideas of property, and botany created shifting outcomes in this Indonesian province during the 1990s and thereafter. Similarly, American ideas of propriety, aggressive marketing, and grasses' different characteristics conspired to establish the "front lawn" (and the "back" one too) as one of the outstanding landscape features in the modern United States. Unfortunately, West Kalimantan collective entitlement did not take root together with Kentucky Bluegrass, and American extended families do not gather to mow the lawn or carry off the resulting mulch. However, where the asset in question is less terrestrial, off Maine's coast, modern Americans can and do manage resources communally. Acheson describes the negotiations whereby "wild" lobsters become individual fishers' property, according to rules the entitled fishers accept and following the biological rhythms that lobsters' growth and reproduction set. Thus modern Maine lobster fishing, Bornean durian husbandry, and American lawn mowing reflect not only economic imperatives and market pressures but also ecological constraints and how cultural expectations filter the two.

With this in mind, the uncritical acceptance of canonical chronologies, the subdivisions of past time that gained currency in Western writing during the Renaissance, begin to look threadbare and beset by limitations. Even in European historiography, for which the subdivisions were manufactured, the times are changing. For instance, the old distinction between ancient and medieval history (or slave and feudal modes of production) is now softened by the burgeoning field of late antique studies, whose students wonder about the half millennium after 200 AD or so, leapfrogging over the chronological barriers erected by

Gibbon and Pirenne, who located the end of Rome in the fourth or seventh centuries. Meanwhile the first light of modernity, the Renaissance, has lost glamour, but its substitute, early modern times, no longer means what it used to mean, namely, the period between the fifteenth and nineteenth centuries; major surveys now call the period 1000–1348 early modernity or altogether ignore the fissure between medieval and modern periods.[26] Some archaeologists have proposed the ninth century as the beginning of the modern way of doing things in Europe, including, presumably, dealing with environments.[27]

Environmental historians are less stuck in this antediluvian (or really Petrarchan) way of dividing up past time. To some extent it is thanks to the hegemony of U.S. history within their field of endeavor: ancient and medieval are useless chronological labels for Americanists. Nevertheless, environmental historians' commitment to the more recent segment in the Petrarchan tripartite arrangement, to modern times as somehow set apart from and more significant than preceding times, belies a basic acceptance of the chronological canon. Perhaps the desire to dramatize recent developments justifies the urge to privilege the modern period's ecological changes over everything that happened before modernity. Still, to insist on the uniqueness of the modern brings in its wake the surrender of the liberating potential that so many environmental processes—which move to rhythms difficult to corral within categories like ancient, medieval, and modern—might have for historical practice. *Natures Past* includes essays from different sides of the chronological divide precisely to avoid the impoverishment of historiographical presentism and to participate, however tangentially, in the recent telluric shifts that have begun to redraw chronologies. Surely this is one trend to which environmental history has a lot to offer.

Just as how we slice up past time into bits to examine matters and determine what we find and what we expect to find, so too our geographical frames of reference bear reflection. *Natures Past* attempts to escape the chronological provincialism, or modernist bent, that excludes so much from our understanding of the human place in nature. It also seeks more geographical ecumenicism in the pursuit of such understanding. Many traditional concerns of environmental history, such as changes in vegetation cover or in climate or the absorption of industrial waste, are slow processes that affect vast territories. In fact sometimes they are only legible against enormous geographical backdrops. Certainly deforestation during the second millennium AD or climate shifts like the "Little Ice Age" are modifications on such a scale that they are easier to evaluate correctly as "Eurasian" developments than as components in national, or even microhistorical, accounts. The geographical frameworks adopted, lately, by historians curious about Europe's "takeoff" in the sixteenth through nineteenth centuries and their eagerness to squirm out of the nation-state, still the ecological niche of most who study the past, should encourage environmentally minded historians, many of whose concerns transcend national borders and categories.[28] Thus, geographical deprovincialization and willingness to trace transformations across national and regional boundaries, as James McCann does in his discussion of maize in Africa and as J. R. McNeill suggests for his Atlantic world, might well align other sorts of history with the environmentally informed reconstructions in useful ways. The will to see synoptically and to recognize environmental change as something that has swept through every recess of the earth in ways that humble human structures like the nation-state is a way of seeing well attuned to twenty-first-century circumstances.

Natures Past is a sign of the interest of the journal *Comparative Studies in Society and History* (*CSSH*) in the lively environmental historical debates of the past thirty years or so. It includes six essays that originally appeared in the journal's pages, for the most part in the 1990s. It also incorporates four new essays, written for the volume. Following *CSSH*'s by now standard practice in compiling thematic collections of essays, the journal sponsored a conference, held at the University of Michigan in October 2003, to enable the various authors to meet, trade notes, try ideas, and discuss each other's findings, perhaps finding inspiration or novel perspectives to include in the revised essay submitted for publication.[29]

The result is a cosmopolitan and genuinely interdisciplinary, not to say heterogeneous, assemblage that ranges widely in time, geography, and methodology, as this introduction has attempted to show. Under the capacious umbrella of environmental history, *Natures Past* brings disparate discourses into dialogue. Its range demonstrates the ecumenical potential held by the study of people's past interactions with their ecological settings: pretty much anywhere one looks, and through whatever lenses, if one looks carefully, an environmental history worth pondering will emerge. For, whatever else the human condition is, it certainly entails a web of environmental relations, and these are as dynamic and varied as the people and ecosystems that constitute them. Thus whether one examines eighteenth-century land management in China in ways familiar to intellectual historians, the capacity of insects to shape the course of human events in the colonial Atlantic in the best environmental determinist mode, or the imaginative construction of place in Anglo-Saxon England and interwar Switzerland with the utensils of landscape history, or even if one looks at the emergence of the lawn fetish in the twentieth-century United States as an integrated cultural history, one is confronted with people dealing creatively with their natural surroundings and the latter dealing out mutable conditions to people. This ongoing interchange, the currently orthodox conception of environmental relations, mirrors the ever-shifting, unstable complexities that natural scientists are increasingly prone to identify in the ecosystems they probe.[30] Given the marvelous interdependence and complexity of ecological phenomena, ecumenicism and interdisciplinarity recommend themselves as the best means of advancing our understanding of how people have lived their environments.[31]

NOTES

1. A. Crosby, "The Past and Present of Environmental History," *American Historical Review* 100 (1995): 1182.

2. In the American context, when Alfred Crosby's account of how the environmental-historical leopard got its spots appeared in the centennial issue of the *American Historical Review,* surely environmental history had arrived.

3. For example, R. White, "Environmental History," *Pacific Historical Review* 70 (2001): 110–11.

4. A modest sampling includes V. Winiwarter, "Approaches to Environmental History," in J. Loszlovszky and P. Szabó, eds., *People and Nature in Historical Perspective* (Budapest, 2003), 3–22, or her *Was Ist Umweltgeschichte?* (Vienna, 1998); C. Merchant, *Columbia Guide to American Environmental History* (New York, 2002); R. White, "Environmental History," *Pacific Historical Review* 54 (1985): 297–335 and 70 (2001): 103–11; and D. Worster, ed., "Doing Environmental History," in *The Ends of the Earth* (New York, 1988), 289–307. *Environmental History* 10, no. 1 (2005), airs the opinions of various specialists on the state of the field, but such evaluations consistently pepper the pages of the journal (and those of its competitor, *Environment and History*).

5. Terence Glacken, *Traces on the Rhodian Shore* (Berkeley, 1967).

6. The decline of academic historical geography in the United States created the space that environmental historians could fill. See M. Williams, "The Relation

of Environmental History and Historical Geography," *Journal of Historical Geography* 20 (1994): 3–21, for a defensive overview.

7. D. Worster, "The Two Cultures Revisited," *Environment and History* 2, no. 1 (1996): 3–14. It is odd that the archaeologists whose increasingly laboratory-based techniques and investment in material culture predispose them for cross-pollination with environmental history have such a low profile in the field. Paleoecological analyses have the potential for destabilizing canonical histories: S. Cohn's *The Black Death Transformed* (London, 2002) deconstructs the holy cow of bubonic plague in the major environmental catastrophe for European people's last millennium.

8. J. Hughes, *Pan's Travail* (Baltimore, 1994).

9. D. Worster's *Dust Bowl* (New York, 1979) and *Rivers of Empire* (New York, 1986) are prime examples.

10. J. Diamond's *Collapse: How Societies Choose to Fail or Succeed* (New York, 2005) fits in this set.

11. See Sivaramakrishnan's chapter in this volume.

12. W. Cronon, ed., *Uncommon Ground* (New York, 1995), already sounded this note in the late twentieth century; it has garnered a following among U.S. specialists in the last decade.

13. McNeill, "Observations on the Nature and Culture of Environmental History," *History and Theory* 42 (2003): 17; see also Crosby, "The Past and Present," 1188–89.

14. S. Ravi Rajan, "The Ends of Environmental History," *Environment and History* 3, no. 2 (1997): 245–52. Instead, gender receives some attention from environmental historians: M. Leach and C. Green, "Gender and Environmental History," *Environment and History* 3, no. 3 (1997): 343–70; Carolyn Merchant's research centers on the intersection of gender and environment.

15. R. Grove, *Green Imperialism* (Cambridge, 1995), famously studied colonial conservationism. The frameworks of colonial studies provided context for much work: A. Crosby, *Ecological Imperialism* (New York, 1986); M. Gadgil and R. Guha, *This Fissured Land* (Berkeley, 1992). There was self-conscious environmental history in Europe before the European Society for Environmental History: see, for example, P. Brimblecombe and C. Pfister, eds., *The Silent Countdown: Essays in European Environmental History* (Berlin, 1990) and the remarkable R. DeLort and F. Walter, *Histoire de l'environnement européen* (Paris, 2001).

16. W. Cronon, "The Trouble With Wilderness," appeared with three rejoinders in *Environmental History* 1, no. 1 (1996): 29–46.

17. The lands down under offer more fertile fields for American-style environmental historical ideas: E. Pawson and S. Dovers, "The Challenges of Interdisciplinarity: An Antipodean Perspective," *Environment and History* 9, no. 1 (2003): 53–76. Subaltern Studies also perceive much ecological virtue in precolonial landscapes and in the peasant resistance movements of south Asia, ironically replicat-

ing, thereby, Western, and especially American, notions of past ages of gold and of noble savagery.

18. R. White, "'Are You an Environmentalist or Do You Work for a Living?'" in Cronon's *Uncommon Ground,* 171–85, nicely traces the drawbacks in America's "romanticism of inviolate nature."

19. D. Worster, "Transformations of the Earth," *Journal of American History* 76 (1990): 1093ff.

20. Jean Andrews, "Diffusion of MesoAmerican Food Complex to Southwestern Europe," *Geographical Review* 83 (1993): 194–204, offers a nice comparison.

21. J. McNeill, *Something New Under the Sun* (New York, 2000).

22. McNeill, "Observations," 43. The contributors to *Time-Scales and Environmental Change,* ed. T. Driver and G. Chapman (London, 1996), remind us that involvement in the really "deep past" of millions of years ago erases the modern/premodern distinction.

23. F. Uekoetter, "Confronting the Pitfalls of Current Environmental History," *Environment and History* 4, no. 1 (1998): 36–39.

24. In European contexts, the arrivals of modernity (the Renaissance) and of "real" environmental change are considered coeval: see, for instance, K. Thomas, *Man and the Natural World* (London, 1983).

25. From a quite different perspective, Nicholas Howe achieves a similar dissolution between modern and premodern times when he combines some of the landscapes he knows, from the seventh to twenty-first centuries, into a harmonious whole in chapter 7 of this volume.

26. D. Levine, *At the Dawn of Modernity: Biology, Culture, and Material Life in Europe after the Year 1000* (Berkeley, 2001), 1–2 passim; D. Nicholas, *Urban Europe, 1100–1700* (Houndmills and New York, 2003). Perhaps the environmental perspective on Mediterranean history in P. Horden and N. Purcell, *The Corrupting Sea* (Oxford, 2001), led to the authors' jettisoning of established chronologies.

27. R. Hodges, *Towns and Trade in the Age of Charlemagne* (London, 2001). C. Sonnlechner, "The Establishment of New Units of Production in Carlongian Times," *Viator* 35 (2004): 21–48, proposes an intensification of ecological change in the same period on the European continent.

28. V. Lieberman, *Strange Parallels* (Cambridge, 2003); E. Jones, *The European Miracle* (Cambridge, 2003).

29. Oliver Zimmer chose to leave his 1996 essay unchanged.

30. "Climax species" and related ideas implying ecological optima and potentials for stability have lost credence in the last decades. Linear development, not cycles, now enjoys more natural-scientific favor (though climatologists have their doubts). For a stimulating introduction to these issues, see D. Botkin, *Discordant Harmonies* (Oxford, 1990).

31. My thanks to Ray Grew and John McNeill for suggesting useful amendments to this introduction.

1 Distribution Fights, Coordination Games, and Lobster Management

James Acheson

ONE OF THE MOST important issues in resource management is understanding under what conditions people will conserve the resources on which their livelihood depends. In all too many cases, overexploitation is the rule. All around the world, fish stocks, forests, grasslands, air, soils, wildlife, and water quality have been seriously degraded by human beings. Environmental disaster is not inevitable, however, for in many cases those who are dependent on resources, and their governments, have acted to generate effective rules to manage those resources at sustainable levels (Anderson and Simmons 1993; Berkes 1989; McCay and Acheson 1987; Ostrom 1990; Pinkerton 1989; Ruddle and Akimichi 1984).

One of the most successfully managed resources in the world is the Maine lobster fishery, where catches are currently at record high levels despite decades of intense exploitation. While the cause of these high catches is uncertain, there is a consensus that the good fortunes of the lobster industry are due both to effective regulations and to favorable environmental circumstances. In this chapter, focus is on the way the formal regulations came into being, but the role of the environment should not be forgotten.

There are two ways for groups to obtain needed regulations. They may cooperate to provide informal agreements, which Taylor calls a "decentralized" solution (1990, 225), or they may appeal to the state to provide such rules (i.e., a "centralized" solution). The Maine lobster

industry has done both. In this chapter I describe the political processes resulting in the production of the most important formal regulations (centralized solutions) in the Maine lobster industry. Although it is not my focus here, it should be kept in mind that the industry has also developed rules informally (see, e.g., Acheson 1975, 1988, 2003).

The story of Maine's lobster-fishing regulation is more than one hundred years old. In the 1870s and 1880s the industry lobbied for the first size regulations and rules to protect the brood stock; in 1933 the double gauge measure was passed, protecting both juvenile and large, reproductive-sized lobsters; in 1948 the all-important Maine-style V-notch law passed; in 1985 the escape vent law came into being; in 1999 the zone management law was passed that permitted fishermen in each zone to impose trap limits on themselves. These laws have tremendous support in the Maine lobster industry. They are judged so effective that in 1998 the Atlantic States Marine Fisheries Commission was persuaded to adopt the V-notch and double gauge laws for the inshore area from Cape Cod to the Canadian border. The Canadians are seriously thinking of adopting these measures as well. In a world in which many of the world's marine resources are being exploited to economic extinction (*New York Times* 1992; McGoodwin 1990, 1–4), the story of how this conservation legislation came into being has an importance that extends far beyond the northwest Atlantic.

In this chapter, essentially I argue that these conservation regulations were put into place over the course of the past 120 years by political processes that do not fit neatly into any one theoretical mold. Complicating the picture are the complex and changing roles played by factions in the lobster industry, government bureaucracy, and the Maine legislature.

Questions about the generation of conservation rules take us into the middle of one of the most important debates concerning social life—namely, how do norms and institutions come into being, and how do they change? While the generation of norms and institutions has never been the primary focus of attention for any social science discipline, the problem has been approached by people from virtually every such field over the course of several decades. In the 1960s and 1970s, anthropologists were making key contributions to this field, as seen in the work of Barth (1981), Bailey (1969), Heath (1976), and Kapferer (1976). More recently, the most seminal work has been done by political scientists,

economists, and sociologists interested in rational choice theory and the closely related field of institutional economics. My analysis draws most heavily on the insights and concepts of the rational choice literature.

Theoretical Issues

Several important theoretical commitments lie behind my analysis. First, and perhaps most important, the production of norms is seen as rooted in the rational decisions of individuals. That is, individuals pursue a variety of interests and goals, and the choices they make are designed to achieve their aims most efficiently. In many situations the outcomes for an individual are dependent on the choices and rewards of others. People choose to establish norms because norms make it possible to gain the benefits of coordinated activities and joint ventures. Conversely, individuals will tend to change norms or defect from them when it is in their best interest to do so.

Second, the simple fact that norms will bring about collective benefits does not guarantee that such norms will be provided. The problem was first framed by Mancur Olson (1965), who pointed out that, even if rules or other public goods would benefit all, they would only be provided if "special incentives" existed. The essential problem was what Olson described as the "free rider problem." That is, there is no incentive for an individual to help to produce a public good since that individual will have the benefit of the public good regardless of whether or not that person contributed to its production. Since it is rational for every individual to "free ride" on the efforts of others, the public good is not produced. Everyone has acted rationally, and yet they are all worse off than if they had cooperated. Either rewards or sanctions are necessary to overcome the tendency to become a free rider.

Recent rational choice theorists prefer to phrase the problem in terms of a collective action dilemma (Elster 1989, 17; Taylor 1990, 223). The collective action dilemma is a situation in which there is a divergence between the interests of the individual and those of the society. In the absence of rules, rational action by the individual will bring suboptimal results or even disaster for the collectivity. In collective action dilemmas, it is not rational for individuals to cooperate even though cooperation would bring positive results for all. Moreover, Coleman (1990, 251) points out that in collective action dilemmas the activities of one person

produce externalities for others. That is, individuals are permitted to foist some of the costs of their activities onto others. It is the existence of externalities that brings the demand for norms.

Collective action dilemmas have received a good deal of attention from social scientists because they describe so many of the most vexing problems plaguing humanity. Taylor underscores the importance of the concept by saying that all "politics is the study of ways of solving collective action problems" (1990, 224).

Marine fisheries present a classic collective action problem. In the absence of rules concerning property rights, fishermen are capable of imposing very large externalities on each other. In addition to the problems of gear conflict and gear congestion, there is the issue of subtractability. That is, the fish one person catches from the common pool are not available to others. Moreover, the damage that can be done to the environment (e.g., breeding stocks, nursery grounds, and migration routes) by shortsighted fishing practices can have serious consequences for everyone who seeks to exploit these same stocks in the future. Even though a rule controlling exploitative effort would help protect the brood stock, produce larger catches and income, and lower prices for the consumer, such rules are provided only with difficulty, since it is in the interest of the individual fisherman to avoid being constrained.

In most fisheries the conditions necessary to produce norms restraining exploitive activities have been largely absent. The failures to solve these collective action problems have been documented in great detail in the literature on common property resources (Baden and Hardin 1977; McGoodwin 1990). What is unusual about the Maine lobster industry is that it is one of the few fishing industries that has been able to solve most of the collective action problems it has faced.

Over the course of the past few years, a large body of literature has been developed concerning the generation of rules and institutions. One theme in the literature concerns the prerequisite conditions that are conducive to collective action. The emphasis is on the characteristics of groups and resources that are likely to give rise to rules and institutions (Ostrom 2000a, 2000b). These scholars argue that a large number of variables play a role in making it possible for groups to generate rules to manage common-pool resources informally, but they do not agree on what those variables are. However, there is a consensus that small, homogenous groups with a strong sense of community and high depen-

dence on the resource will find it easiest to devise management rules (Agrawal 2002).

Another body of theory has been developed on the mechanisms by which rules are generated, which focuses on the types of interactions between people that give rise to rules and norms (e.g., North 1990; Sugden 1986; Lewis 1969; Knight 1992). These interactions can be modeled as different types of games. There are three such mechanisms described in the literature: social conventions, negotiations over distributional benefits, and competitive selection.

Social Conventions

According to this theory, norms are social conventions that emerge as a result of the need to coordinate activities. The proponents of this theory assume a coordination game in which all actors have equal power. All actors would prefer a cooperative solution, because such a solution gives higher outcomes than an outcome that does not involve cooperation. In a pure coordination game, "a coincidence of interest predominates" (Lewis 1969, 14). A good example of a social convention is driving on one side of the road. Equally good results can be had from a rule specifying that everyone will drive on either the right or the left. Bad results in the form of a high collision rate will follow from a failure to agree on one or the other.

If only one equilibrium or solution exists, it would presumably be relatively easy for the parties to recognize this fact and establish it as the rule. If two or more solutions are available, the actors might enter into an agreement to select one of them. If they cannot do this, the actors will seize on any salient information in their environment to aid in selecting one of the available solutions. Over a period of time, some of the actors focus on one solution and the others emulate them, which in time establishes a convention (Sugden 1986, 73). Once the convention is established it will tend to be self-reinforcing, since no actor can better his or her own position by defecting from it (Knight 1992, 99).

Negotiations over Distributional Benefits

This body of theory explains the production of norms as an aftereffect of strategic conflict over assets and rewards. It shares with the social conventions model the ideas that humans stand to gain greatly from

coordinating activities and that rules are necessary if those gains are to be realized. However, this perspective emphasizes the distributional effects of rules. Rules rarely distribute rewards equally; they often result in parties or groups gaining differential rewards. In some cases people are fully aware of this and consciously maneuver to create rules that will give them a distributional advantage. In other cases, rules are generated as the unplanned by-product of a struggle over rewards or of attempts to resolve conflicts over rewards. In both cases, the goal of actors is to attain a reward; rules are created to facilitate that goal.

The rules are created through a process of negotiation. The parties involved have different amounts of power in the negotiations because they have different assets. The actors with more assets have a distinct advantage in the negotiations because they are in a position to accept more risk, because they have more withholding power, and because people are less willing to sanction them if they violate a norm. Consequently, the rules that result from negotiation sessions are apt to favor the more powerful; the less powerful have no option but to accept those rules since they cannot do better (Knight 1992, 128). If the creation of a rule is the result of a centralized, collective decision-making process, the rule will reflect the asymmetries in the actors' resources. That is, we would expect those with more resources to succeed in negotiating the establishment of a rule beneficial to themselves.

If the norms come about via an informal or "decentralized" process, we would expect a different sequence of events to occur. Over time, actors with more resources will be able to resolve negotiations in ways favorable to themselves. Others with similar resources will be able to do the same, establishing a pattern. As people recognize that they are dealing with someone with superior resources, they will adjust their strategies to achieve their own best outcomes. In time, they will alter their strategies to converge on a particular outcome, thus establishing a norm.

Exchange and Competitive Selection

The third approach sees norms as emerging from voluntary contracts to facilitate exchange. This approach is most closely associated with what has become known as the "New Institutional Economics." It has been used to explain the emergence of a large number of organizations and institutions, including firms, markets, property rights, contract law, and torts (Acheson 1994; North 1990; Williamson 1985). The essence of the idea is that when two people perceive that they can benefit from an exchange, they must agree on the terms by which that exchange will take place, including rules guaranteeing the compliance of both parties and the sanctions that will be imposed if either party reneges on their duties toward the other. These contracts become norms and institutions guaranteeing the fruits of cooperative enterprises.

Contracts are beneficial because they lower transaction costs, meaning they reduce the cost of getting the information necessary to negotiate an agreement, negotiating the exchange, and enforcing the exchange. The rules embodied in contracts can benefit both parties even though they are engaged in a prisoner's dilemma interaction.

Institutional change results from changes in prices. When the price of technology, information, enforcement, or production changes, the parties to an exchange may decide that they can do better with a new contract. Sometimes they can negotiate a new contract within existing norms. In other cases, negotiating a contract may necessitate changing or ignoring more basic norms or structural principles upon which the contracts depend (North 1990, 86).

The exchanges into which one chooses to enter and the contracts governing them are selected with a goal of overcoming high transaction costs. These choices produce a range of organizations.

The kinds of organizations that prevail in the long run depend on relative efficiency. Competition will drive out of existence those organizations that are inefficient; successful organizations provide maximum joint benefits for those involved in the exchanges and an efficient use of resources for the society. Alchain (1950) first used these concepts in his model of evolutionary competition: less profitable firms will be driven out by more efficient and more profitable firms. More recently, much the same argument is found in the work of Douglass North (1990). This argument rests on the assumption that competition produces norms that are in the long-run best interests of individuals and the larger society.

The Biology and Technology of Maine's Lobster Industry

Throughout its history, the Maine lobster industry has been an inshore trap fishery. The typical lobster fisherman has a boat about thirty-five feet long equipped with a diesel or gas engine, which he operates alone or with one helper. Today, the average fisherman fishes with about 570 traps made of wood or wire and baited with fish remnants. Each trap is equipped with funnel-shaped nylon "heads," which make it easy for lobsters to climb into the trap but difficult for them to find a way out. The traps are connected to a wood or Styrofoam buoy by a "warp line." The buoys are painted with a distinctive combination of colors registered with the state (Acheson 1988, 84–90). Each day, fishermen sell their catches to one of the eighty private dealerships or seventeen cooperatives that are located in harbors along the coast (115–32).

The lobster fishery is highly territorial. All along the Maine coast, the fishermen from each harbor have a marine "territory" in which they place traps. People placing traps outside the territory of their harbor are likely to be sanctioned by the surreptitious destruction of their lobster traps (Acheson 1988, 2003). This means that lobster fishermen place their traps in a very restricted area—usually under one hundred square miles—that they defend against outsiders.

Lobsters' size is a key element in the fishery's management. Lobster biologists and fishermen measure lobsters on the carapace—from the eye socket to the back of the body shell. It takes approximately seven years for a lobster to grow from larval stage to a carapace length of 3.25 inches—the current minimum size that can be legally harvested in Maine. During the earliest larval stages, they float through the water column for a period of several weeks before settling to the bottom. Adolescent-phase lobsters are between 1.57 and 3.54 inches (carapace length) and forage actively at night but hole up during the day since they are subject to predation by large fish. Lobsters in the reproductive phase (over 3.54 inches carapace length) are subject to far less predation and migrate considerable distances. They are most abundant in deep water and offshore areas (Skud and Perkins 1969). Very large lobsters (over 5 inches carapace length) have no natural enemies and may live as long as one hundred years (Cooper and Uzmann 1971).

In the Gulf of Maine, most female lobsters do not mature sexually until they are over 3.15 inches (late adolescent phase), and 50 percent are not mature until they reach 3.5–3.7 inches carapace length (reproductive phase) (Krouse 1972, 1973). Fecundity increases with size. When females first become mature at 3.25 or 3.50 inches they can extrude a few hundred eggs. A single large female (over 5 inches carapace) can extrude as many as one hundred thousand eggs. For this reason, some of the most important lobster conservation regulations (e.g., the oversize measure and the V-notch) seek to preserve these large, reproductive-sized lobsters. Lobsters molt several times a year early in their lives but only once a year or every other year, usually in the summer months, once they are mature. Lobsters mate right after mature females have molted, when their shells are soft and they are defenseless. Once the eggs are extruded from the lobster's body they remain attached to her abdomen for a period of nine to eleven months until they hatch. Lobsters in this reproductive stage are called "berried" or "egged" lobsters.

Lobster catches have varied considerably over the course of the twentieth century. Since 1988, catches have been high (between thirty and fifty-six million pounds), but in the 1920s and 1930s, they varied between five and seven million pounds (Maine Department of Marine Resources 1995; Acheson 2003). The reason for these changes in the size of the lobster stock is a matter of debate among lobster scientists, but it is certain that a very large number of variables affect lobster stock size. Some of these factors can be affected by management (e.g., fishing effort and technology); others are ecological factors that cannot be controlled or influenced much by the people in the fishery (e.g., water temperature, disease, and food supply). As suggested at the beginning of this chapter, the large supply of lobsters is almost certainly the result both of effective regulations and of favorable ecological factors such as high August water temperatures (Acheson and Steneck 1997; Alden 1989). Although the focus here is on the development of the regulatory apparatus, it should not be forgotten that catches could drop, perhaps dramatically, if certain ecological factors change. Such a drop could be experienced even though the regulations are very effective.

Minimum Size Limit and Protection of Egged Females, 1870–90

Until the middle of the nineteenth century lobsters were caught for local consumption, but no commercial lobster industry existed (Martin and Lipfert 1985, 9–11). The commercial development of the industry had to await two technical developments in the 1840s: the invention of the lobster smack, a sailing vessel with a circulating seawater tank, allowing shipment of live lobsters to the cities along the North Atlantic coast, and the invention of canning (Cobb 1901, 243–44; Martin and Lipfert 1985, 13).

After 1840, the commercial lobster industry expanded rapidly. Untold millions of live lobsters were shipped to destinations such as Boston and New York. The first lobster cannery was established in 1842, and by 1880, there were twenty-three plants in Maine packing lobster (Rathbun 1887, 690). In this period, the vast majority of lobsters caught were canned.

In the 1840s and 1850s, lobsters were plentiful and the size was very large (Martin and Lipfert 1985, 43). However, by the late 1860s there were clear signs of trouble. The catch was the same, but the numbers of fishermen and traps had increased markedly, resulting in a clear reduction in both the average size of lobsters caught and the catch per unit of effort (Cobb 1901, 244, 255–56; Herrick 1911, 367–69; Rathbun 1887, 701–8). After 1880, catches declined to the point where the operation of some of the canneries had to be curtailed early in the season for a lack of lobsters to pack (Cobb 1901, 256). These changes caused widespread anxiety in coastal communities, where it was feared that the lobster industry "was crashing" (Martin and Lipfert 1985, 43).

Everyone concerned with the industry agreed that something should be done to protect the resource, but the solutions proposed by the canners and live lobster industry differed significantly (Rathbun 1887, 725). The fishermen and dealers engaged in the live lobster trade blamed the canners. There can be no denying that canning was very wasteful. Canners made a practice of transporting lobsters in "dry smacks," which killed a lot of the catch (Cobb 1901, 250). It took about five pounds of raw lobster to get one pound for packing. Moreover, although the canneries took all sizes of lobsters, they preferred small ones, because they could be had at a cheaper price per pound. Several reports indicate that canners regularly processed lobsters weighing as little as half a pound or less (Cobb 1901, 256; Martin and Lipfert 1985, 42).[1] Such practices were detrimental to the live lobster industry. Since the stock-in-trade of the fresh lobster dealers and fishermen were large "dinner"-sized lobsters destined for restaurants in the large cities of the East Coast, it was in the interests of this part of the industry to protect small lobsters until they grew to a size where they could be sold on the "live market."

Thus the battle lines were drawn between the canners and the live lobster industry. The laws that ultimately emerged were the result of a twenty-year struggle for control of the resource. Much of the ammunition for that battle was supplied by European lobster biologists, who recommended that the problems in the lobster industries of their own countries could be cured with various types of regulations on size, season, and protection of breeding stock (Rathbun 1887, 711–25).

Interestingly, it was the canners who lobbied the Maine legislature for the first "conservation laws" to defend their interests (Judd 1988, 605). In 1872 a law was passed forbidding the taking of "berried" (i.e., egg-bearing) females (Legislative Document 1872). In 1874, the canners lobbied the legislature again, with the result that fishing for lobsters less than 10.5 inches (head to tail) was prohibited from October 1 to April 1 (Laws of Maine 1874). These so-called conservation laws were designed to curtail the activity of the fresh lobster industry but did little to change the practices of the canneries. The law prohibiting the capture of egged females did not affect the canners since they used lobster too small to extrude eggs, while the seasonal size minimum left the canneries free to take all sizes of lobsters during the summer canning season and made the state responsible for protecting the lobsters when the canneries were processing vegetables. Not too surprisingly, the devastation to the resource continued.

The canners may have won the first battle, but they were to lose the war. After 1870, the live lobster trade expanded enormously because of the market expansion facilitated by the arrival of the railroads, which allowed long-distance shipment of iced lobsters, and the development of the lobster pound (a fenced-in portion of the ocean) where live lobsters could be stored for months. As increasing numbers of fishermen supplied the live market, their dependence on the canneries decreased, especially in the western part of the coast, where access to rail service was better. The political power of those involved in the fresh lobster market grew correspondingly.

Those in the live lobster trade knew that the existing legislation worked to the benefit of the canners and did nothing for conservation. They wanted a law prohibiting the canneries from slaughtering millions of small animals, so that the lobsters could grow to a size at which they could be sold in the live trade. One fisherman called the existing laws a "farce" and called for a "law to protect the small and soft lobsters the entire year" (Rathbun 1887, 727). Many echoed his sentiments, and the legislature was soon besieged with requests and petitions from fishermen's groups for legislation to protect small lobsters.

In 1879, it became illegal to can lobsters from August 1 to April 1 (Laws of Maine 1879). Four years later, to catch any female lobster "in spawn or with eggs attached, or any young lobster less than nine inches in length" between April 1 and August 1 was proscribed (Laws of Maine 1883). These pieces of legislation changed the distribution of the lobster catch considerably, since they made it illegal to take the small and cheap lobsters on which the canners depended, effectively reserving the lion's share of the catch for the live lobster industry.

The canners and the fishermen along the eastern coast, who sold to the canneries, fought back. They opposed the minimum size measure and repeatedly petitioned the legislature to allow canning to continue unencumbered. Their propaganda claimed that it was the pounds—not canning—that were causing the depletion of the resource.[2]

The live lobster industry continued its assault unabated. In 1885 its lobbying efforts resulted in a law effectively reducing the canning season to three and a half months (Laws of Maine 1885); and in 1889 the law was changed so that lobsters as small as 9 inches in total length could be taken only from May 1 to July 1 (Laws of Maine 1889). These laws made canning so unprofitable that the canneries began to close (Cobb 1901, 256–57). Many went to Canada. In 1895, the legislature passed a law increasing the minimum legal size to 10.5 inches at all times of year; this law apparently forced the last of the canneries from the state (McFarland 1911, 233; Judd 1988, 606). It was widely accepted by the press and public that the canneries were responsible for the worrisome decline in lobster stock. Their exit from the state was not mourned by many. Even the fishermen who supplied the canneries seemed to assume that the demise of canning in Maine would see resurgence in the lobster stock (Martin and Lipfert 1985, 45).

Although both canners and the fresh lobster industry lobbied for legislation to reserve much of the catch for themselves, the rules they put in place were designed to protect juvenile lobsters and egg-bearing females. To this day, efforts to conserve the lobster still depend on size regulations and protection of the breeding stock.

The Fight for the Double Gauge, 1915–33

The end of canning and the passage of these first conservation laws did not see an improvement in the prospects of the lobster industry. Catches continued to decline. From 1900 to 1920, the average catch was 13.2 million pounds—close to half of what it had been in 1889 (Maine Department of Marine Resources 1995). Both fishermen and biologists recognized that the industry was not what it had once been (Cobb 1901, 241; Rathbun 1887, 707).

The consensus among biologists was that additional regulations were needed, over and above the 10.5-inch minimum size limit and the prohibition against catching gravid females that had been passed in the 1880s (Kelly 1990, 3). As early as 1910, the biologist George Field argued that catches would not begin to rise until the larger, more prolific breeding stock was protected (Martin and Lipfert 1985, 51). However, most people in the industry were strongly opposed to raising the minimum size, seeing clearly that such an increase would cut their catches by increasing the number of lobsters that had to be thrown back and would produce large lobsters that would have to be sold at such high prices that Maine would be effectively closed out of many of the national and international markets. In retrospect, it is hard to argue with the reasoning of either side.

The biologist Francis Herrick proposed a compromise solution, namely, a double gauge law specifying both a minimum size to protect small lobsters and a maximum size to protect larger, proven breeding stock. This would focus all fishing on lobsters that were large enough to make a good meal (i.e., dinner-sized lobsters) but were small enough so that they could not usually extrude eggs. Herrick originally thought the minimum should be 9 inches and the maximum 11 inches (Herrick 1911, 382).

Lack of consensus resulted in the legislature doing little beyond changing the way lobsters were measured, thereby retaining in effect the 10.5-inch minimum gauge. Lobsters were to be measured on the carapace rather than in terms of total length. Thus a 10.5-inch lobster (total length) became a 4.75-inch lobster (total back shell length) (Laws of Maine 1907). Fishermen continually agitated against these legal measures since both laws outlawed the vast majority of the lobsters they caught (Acheson 1992, 155). In future years, this would become known as the "poverty gauge" (Acheson and Steneck 1997).

In 1915 conditions in the industry were serious enough that the legislature appointed a commission to study lobster regulation (Legislative Record 1915a). Dr. Francis Herrick was called to testify and strongly urged the commission to recommend a double gauge law for the long-run welfare of the industry and the state (Legislative Record 1915b; Martin and Lipfert 1985, 55). The commission recommended passage of the double gauge law, but after representatives from coastal counties talked with their constituents, no bill favoring the double gauge was sent to the floor of the legislature (Legislative Record 1915c).

The basic cause of the impasse was a conflict of interest between industry factions. In general, fishermen from the western counties wanted to lower the minimum size from 4.75 inches on the back shell (10.5 inches total body length) to 9 inches total body length. They found allies among dealers and hoteliers who wanted to increase their share of the national markets, where small or "chicken" lobsters from Massachusetts and Canada had proven all too popular. However, most of the fishermen along the central and eastern parts of the coast did not favor a small gauge, since they believed it was nothing more than a ploy by the dealers to import large amounts of small Canadian lobsters and undercut the price received by Maine fishermen (Correspondence of the Commissioner 1933a). They couched their case in terms of conserving the reproductive stock.[3] Only a disaster would break this impasse.

In 1919 catches declined sharply, and they remained at record low levels throughout the 1920s and well into the 1930s.[4] Once the Depression began, prices for lobster fell drastically even though catches were very low. The incomes of fishermen were so low that 32 percent of those in the industry went out of business between 1928 and 1932 (Acheson 1992, 157–60; Correspondence of the Commissioner 1933b; Maine Department of Marine Resources 1995). The disastrous conditions continued for years (Correspondence of the Commissioner 1931a, 1931b, 1931c, 1933c). The fishery was not to recover until after World War II.

Horatio Crie, who was the commissioner of sea and shore fisheries and a very able politician, played a key role in all of the attempts to alleviate the situation. First, Crie and industry leaders attempted to get higher prices for lobsters by initiating an advertising campaign and by introducing three bills in the U.S. Congress levying tariffs on imported Canadian lobsters (Correspondence of the Commissioner 1931d, 1933d, 1933e). When these efforts failed, Crie and his ally in the legislature, Senator Look, turned their attention to passing a double gauge law (Correspondence of the Commissioner 1933f). Crie pointed out that the double gauge law would protect small lobsters, conserve the large reproductive-sized lobsters, and allow Maine fishermen to catch smaller, more marketable lobsters than the current law allowed. It would also, he argued, keep out 40 percent of the Canadian lobsters that were currently flooding the U.S. market (Elton 1933a). In short, Crie argued that the double gauge law would be good for both conservation and sales.

In 1933 Crie began a whirlwind campaign to rally support for the double gauge law. He announced his support in all the coastal newspapers; he sent letters explaining his position to fishermen and the congressional delegation (Correspondence of the Commissioner 1933f, 1933g); and he had his wardens try to get fishermen to sign petitions favoring the double gauge (Correspondence of the Commissioner 1933h).

But no consensus emerged. A questionnaire that Crie sent to all lobster license holders revealed that the industry was badly split on the issue (Elton 1933b). Judd (1988, 622) reports that "1,166 respondents favored the double-gauge law, and 1,068 were satisfied with the existing limit." Most of the support came from the western coast; most of the opposition was from the east (Acheson 1997, 12).

The debate became nastier, and the correspondence reveals a good deal of bitterness and frustration on all sides (Correspondence of the Commissioner 1933h). In the regular session of the legislature efforts to reduce the legal minimum size to nine inches (overall) and to establish a double gauge law were both voted down (Elton 1933a, 8).

In December 1933, the Maine legislature met in special session to deal with a number of issues concerning the deepening economic crisis. Another double gauge bill was proposed as the solution to the lobster industry's problems. On December 11, 1933, Commissioner Crie spoke in favor of the bill, emphasizing the need to preserve the industry by protecting the large, reproductive animals. He promised that "if a double gauge measure is passed . . . you will see the lobsters continue to increase from year to year and no one will ever have to feel disturbed about the depletion of the lobsters on the Maine Coast so long as a double gauge measure is enforced" (Correspondence of the Commissioner 1933i, 2).

A few days later, with almost no publicity or debate, the Maine legislature narrowly passed the bill (Elton 1934). It provided for a 3-1/6-inch minimum and a 4.5-inch maximum carapace measure. It was truly a radical piece of legislation, one of the few double gauge laws in the world (Legislative Document 1935),[5] and it remains the backbone of lobster conservation efforts in Maine to this day.

Reaction in the industry was decidedly mixed. Some groups went on record as favoring the law (*Portland Sunday Telegram* 1933). The opponents were so unhappy that they decided to try to have it overturned by a referendum, but they did not obtain enough signatures to have it put on the ballot (Correspondence of the Commissioner 1934). The opponents of this law remained bitter for decades, convinced that Crie had sold out their interests to the dealers.

Economic conditions played a role in the passage of this legislation. The industry and legislature were more willing to consider radical solutions after years of economic decline. However, the bill would likely not have passed into law were it not for Crie's political entrepreneurship. His open advocacy of the bill, his enlistment of support from key legislators, and his speech to the legislature before the final vote were all crucial factors. Most important were his lobbying efforts with the industry. In the last analysis, the double gauge law passed because of a coalition among the proponents of the bill in the industry, Commissioner Crie, and powerful members of the Maine legislature, such as Senator Look, who were concerned with marine resources. When this coalition went into action in 1931, twenty years of gridlock gave way in less than eighteen months. In essence, Crie and Look had negotiated a deal in which they gave their support to an industry faction favoring a smaller minimum size limit to increase markets in exchange for that faction's support of a maximum size measure protecting the more prolific large lobsters.

The Escape Vent, 1978

From 1976 to 1978, there was a great deal of interest within the bureaucracy and the industry in establishing an escape vent law. Such a law would specify that a space be built into each trap, by one means or another, to allow the small, sublegal lobsters to escape from the traps before they were hauled up. This would reduce the amount of time it took fishermen to clean out their traps. It also would reduce the numbers of lobsters killed or mutilated, since small lobsters are eaten by larger lobsters in the traps and by large fish after they are thrown overboard on their way back to the bottom; molting lobsters also are eaten by any hard-shell lobster in the trap. In addition, lobsters tend to hang on to the traps and regularly have claws pulled off by fishermen who are attempting to remove them and throw them overboard. An escape vent would reduce the numbers mutilated in this way.

By the mid-1970s, the escape vent was an idea whose time had come. Massachusetts and Newfoundland had recently established escape vent laws (Martin and Lipfert 1985, 109). In the United States, state and federal biologists were very interested in reducing mortality on sublegal lobsters. In the mid-1970s the entire research staff of the Maine Department of Marine Resources (DMR) became strong advocates (Krouse and Thomas 1976). Spencer Appolonio, who was commissioner at that time, recalls that "Cecil Pierce of Southport developed a plastic vent. We [the DMR biologists] tried it out in a tank, and it clearly worked." Within a year, a proposal for an escape vent became part of the proposed "American Lobster Management Plan," written by the Northeast Marine Fisheries Board in conjunction with the New England Regional Council (*Maine Commercial Fisheries* 1978).

Some fishermen, at least, saw virtue in escape vents. A few scattered along the coast had already been placing escape vents in their traps. "Highliner" (highly successful fisherman) Jimmy Brackett of Pemaquid Harbor said that "one of the secrets of success was to have one lathe on the bottom of the trap with a large space" to reduce the amount of work cleaning out small lobsters from traps and to increase the catch of legal-sized lobsters. Eddie Blackmore, past president of the Maine Lobstermen's Association (MLA), recalls, "After I had escape vents in all my traps I was saving an hour a day pulling [hauling traps] and two to three gallons of gas."[6] In the debate that followed, some of these men became the strongest advocates of the escape vent.

In 1976, Representative Greenlaw of Stonington introduced a bill in the legislature (Greenlaw 1978) mandating an escape vent. This produced a good deal of discussion in the industry and the legislature. Greenlaw withdrew the bill in the face of opposition led by Representative Bonnie Post (Owls Head), who, speaking for the fishermen in her district, argued that the escape vent was something that fishermen should do for themselves and that, in any case, the issue needed more study before it should be enacted into law. Post then tried to get the DMR to carry out additional studies on the efficacy of the escape vent but with little success. In the meantime, a consensus emerged in the industry supporting the idea of an escape vent. Blackmore strongly endorsed the idea, and the MLA worked for the bill on the local level.

In the next session of the legislature, Representative Post introduced an escape vent bill. During the hearings that were held up and down the coast, it became apparent that the bill had enemies in the industry but a good deal of strong support as well. DMR biologist Ken Honey, who moderated many of these hearings, recalls that there was scattered opposition, especially along the eastern part of the coast, but no well-orchestrated attempt was made to scuttle the bill. It passed in the legislature over moderate opposition in 1978 (Laws of Maine 1978) and went into effect in 1979. Twenty years later, the escape vent has tremendous support in the industry. Eddie Blackmore said that this "is probably the best single thing we have done in the past fifty years."

In retrospect, the escape vent law passed so expeditiously because it had solid support in the industry, the DMR, and the legislature's Marine Resources Committee. For its rapid passage, it is perhaps unique in the history of the industry.

The V-Notch, 1917, 1948

The current V-notch law allows any fisherman who catches an egg-bearing female to cut a notch in one of the side flippers on her tail. Such V-notched lobsters may never be taken, since they are considered proven breeding stock.[7] Many lobster fishermen consider this the most important conservation measure in force today. In their view, it has resulted in a very large brood stock, which ensures an adequate number of eggs in the water. It has tremendous support in the industry at present.

In 1915 and 1917, there was a general consensus that additional conservation laws were needed to increase the lobster stock. While the legislature refused to pass the double gauge law, there was a consensus that the preservation of the industry depended on protection of the breeding stock. In response, the legislature established a program whereby egged lobsters would be purchased by the state, whose officers would punch a hole in their tails and release them (Legislative Record 1917). Fishermen were forbidden to take lobsters with punched tails (Kelly 1990, 3).

Fishermen were not allowed to sell the berried lobsters they caught to the state. Only pound owners could do so (Maine Commission of Sea and Shore Fisheries 1926, 16). The biologist Leslie Scattergood said, "This law was passed primarily to stop pound owners from scrubbing the eggs from lobsters that had extruded eggs while they were in the pounds." Because pound owners had bought these lobsters from fisher-men, they considered themselves entitled to sell them, even after they had extruded eggs. Thus, the "punched-tail" law or "seeder program" was an effort to bribe pound owners to obey the law. By the mid-1930s, however, the seeder program had expanded to the point where the state of Maine was purchasing "60,000 pounds of seed lobster, from the fishermen through dealers, at market prices" (Maine Department of Sea and Shore Fisheries 1936, 11). These lobsters were punched so that they could not be taken again. Most were released where the warden had pur-chased them, but others were used in the hatchery at Boothbay Harbor.

There have been only a few minor changes in the laws concerning egged lobsters from 1917 to the present. In 1948, the law was changed to state that egged lobsters would be marked by cutting a V-shaped notch in the tail rather than being marked by a round hole punched in the tail. In addition, egged lobsters could only be purchased from people licensed by the commissioner, a change designed to aid enforcement efforts (Laws of Maine 1947).[8] After 1973, the law specified that the V-notch was to be placed in the "right flipper next to the middle flipper" (Kelly 1990, 4).

The big change in the V-notch program took place on the informal level when increasing numbers of lobster fishermen took advantage of the law to conserve the resource by voluntarily cutting notches in the tails of the egged lobsters they had caught. MLA past president Eddie Blackmore considered the young veterans returning from World War II responsible for the change: "We decided that if we were going to keep it [the fishery] going, we needed to do something to replenish the supply." One of the primary ploys they used was to take advantage of the V-notch law by *voluntarily* cutting notches in the tail flippers of egged lob-sters. Former commissioner Vinal Look points out, "There was never a law that stated that fishermen could not cut V-notches in the tails of egged lobsters." It became increasingly popular to do so. It is one of those cases, perhaps rare, where a formal law was turned into an informal norm.

People interested in the industry are not unanimous about the current V-notch law. Lobster fishermen have long considered this law the most important conservation measure in force today, since it ensures not only that egged females are returned to the water but that they are protected so they may breed again. In their view it has resulted in a very large brood stock, which ensures that there is an adequate number of eggs in the water. One fisherman once said, "If you do away with that [V-notch] law, you do away with the industry. It is that important." Some scientists agreed. A study by Bayer, Daniel, and Vaitones (1985) reinforces the idea that the V-notch program is doing a good deal to maintain the breeding stock by ensuring that a high proportion of the females that have borne eggs are returned to the water to breed again.

However, federal and state scientists disagreed. They argued that the V-notch did not increase the number of eggs; and, even worse, they thought cutting notches in the tails of lobsters was a source of infection. As a result, throughout the 1970s and 1980s, the federal and state bureaucracies worked for passage of the federal fisheries management plan, which would abolish the V-notch and double gauge laws. In order to save these measures, in 1985 the leadership of the Maine lobster industry entered into an unusual compromise, with the bureaucrats offering assent to an increase in the legal minimum size, which most fishermen strongly opposed, if the federal government (i.e., the Regional Fisheries Management Council) would maintain the V-notch and oversize laws. It was a compromise in which both sides got the legislation they believed to be most essential. But it should be noted that the Maine fishermen, including the leadership of the MLA, believed so strongly in the V-notch program that they were ready to sacrifice greatly to maintain it (Acheson 1989, 212–13).

In an effort to buttress their arguments in favor of the V-notch program, the MLA has undertaken an annual V-notch survey since 1982. This survey consistently shows that "over 60% of egg-bearing females had a V-notch." Such results suggest that the V-notch program is working to save a very large number of breeding females (*Lobster Bulletin* 1995, 3).

Finally, in 2000, lobster scientists working for the federal and state governments admitted what most fishermen had been convinced of for decades—namely, that the V-notch and oversize laws were effective in conserving the resource. But this change of heart does not remove the fact that for decades the federal and state scientific establishment had tried its best to have both laws rescinded. They would have succeeded had the industry not opposed their efforts so strenuously (Acheson 1997, 15–21).

Trap Limits and the Zone Management Law, 1995

The number of traps increased astronomically beginning in the 1950s. This escalation was made possible by the advent of the hydraulic trap hauler, which allowed fishermen to use more traps than they had previously, and a 1953 law that allowed use of multiple traps on a line (Kelly 1990, 11). Once some people in an area began to use more gear, others were forced to follow suit or see their share of traps on the bottom decline. In some areas, particularly in Casco Bay, people who were using three hundred traps in the late 1960s were using over two thousand in the 1990s.[9]

Shortly after the trap escalation began in the 1950s, people in the lobster industry began calling for a trap limit (i.e., a ceiling on the number of traps a license holder could use). The proponents argued that a trap limit would confer benefits on all. One would catch as many lobsters if everyone were restricted to the same number of traps, and there would be substantial savings, in that fewer traps would have to be built, baited, and tended. Moreover, fishing a smaller number of traps, it was argued, would permit fishermen to use smaller and less costly boats that could be operated by a single person rather than larger vessels requiring crews of two and three people. Perhaps most important, a trap limit would also alleviate the problems of trap congestion and gear tangles, which had become very severe.

Such a large number of lobster fishermen saw benefits in the limits that at least one trap limit bill was introduced in almost every session of the Maine legislature since the mid-1950s. All attempts failed until 1995.

Efforts to establish a trap limit always foundered on two issues. First, there is a strong feeling that a trap limit will do no good unless it is coupled with a limit on licenses ("limited entry"). The logic is that a trap limit will not relieve congestion if new fishermen can still come into the industry, bringing with them thousands of new traps. However, limited entry has always been received with ambivalence by the legislature, because this practice would exclude young people from the lobster fishery, one of the few employment possibilities available in many coastal towns (Acheson 1975, 663–65).

Second, and more important, although the majority of fishermen agreed that there should be a limit on traps, no one agreed on what the limit should be. Part of the problem was that the average number of traps fished varied widely from one part of the coast to another. A trap limit that would be acceptable to people in eastern Maine, where six hundred traps was considered a large number, would be completely unacceptable in an area such as Casco Bay, where fishermen commonly had over eighteen hundred traps. Moreover, within each town the so-called full-time fishermen generally fish far more traps than the part-timers, who have other jobs. Thus, attempts to introduce trap limits engendered two sources of conflict: between different areas of the coast and between full-time and part-time fishermen in any single harbor (Acheson and Wilson 1996). This resulted in a lack of consensus in the industry and a general lack of support for any trap limit proposal in the legislature.

Moreover, the conflict over trap limits is exacerbated by the fact that such limits have severe distributional effects. Trap limits do not constrain all fishermen. They force those fishing over the allowable maximum to reduce the number of traps they fish, which is likely to affect the "big" fishermen but may not force the "small" fishermen to make any changes at all. In the process, however, the percentage of traps that small fishermen have on the bottom is increased relatively, giving them a higher percentage of the catch. From this perspective a trap limit is a means by which small fishermen can constrain big fishermen and lower the latter's proportion of the catch.

Yet the pressure on the legislature to pass such a bill was unceasing (Acheson 1975, 666). Representative David Etnier said, "I would go to Five Islands and places in my district and all I would hear is, 'Why don't you do something for us? Why can't we get a trap limit?'"

By the 1990s, other forces and ideas were gaining momentum that were to result in a trap limit in the aftermath of other legislation. For the past two decades, a sizeable body of literature has been produced to document the local-level conservation rules found in a large number of fishing communities (Anderson and Simmons 1993; Berkes 1989; McCay and Acheson 1987; Ostrom 1990; Ruddle and Akimichi 1984). Such work gave rise to a growing interest in comanagement (governance structures in which the authority to manage fisheries is shared by government and industry groups) (Pinkerton 1989). In 1993, after a session on comanagement at the Maine Fishermen's Forum, organized by Jim Wilson of the University of Maine, the idea began to float around the Maine fishing industry. In 1994, Robin Alden became commissioner of marine resources in Maine. She had become increasingly interested in comanagement because she was convinced that if fishermen had management authority they would impose on themselves those conservation rules that they believed were effective in conserving resources and that were in their own best interests. This would foster a sense of stewardship and reduce enforcement costs. She immediately began to lobby for comanagement in the DMR, with industry members, and with members of the legislature. By the spring of 1995, the legislature's Joint Standing Marine Resources Committee was holding hearings on a number of issues, including trap limits and comanagement.

Late in the spring of 1995, the legislature passed a trap limit law (Legislative Document 1995, 782) as part of a broader comanagement law for the lobster industry, which has become known as the "zone management law." This law stipulated a twelve-hundred-trap limit. It further said that the coast would be divided into zones, which would be managed by councils composed of lobster license holders. Fishermen in these zones could impose on themselves, with a two-thirds vote, rules to limit the number of traps a person could fish (below the statewide twelve-hundred-trap limit), the times when fishing is allowed, and the number of traps on a line.

The passage of the zone management law was somewhat surprising. Even close observers of the industry, such as MLA executive director Paton White, admitted they were not sure "how and why it got passed." Certainly it was not a law for which they had lobbied. The industry was interested in comanagement, but industry leadership had lobbied for a trap limit combined with limited entry, and what emerged from the legislature had zones and no limited entry provision.

What influenced the legislature to pass this law? One factor was a conviction that comanagement should be tried; but another was that the Marine Resources Committee had been frustrated for decades by its inability to pass an acceptable trap limit bill (Sonnenberg 1991). The zones are a mechanism for coming to grips with one of the major stumbling blocks for trap limits—namely, strong disagreements about how many traps would be permitted—by allowing different areas of the coast to establish their own limits.[10]

The commissioner certainly had a strong influence on the legislation that emerged. She lobbied for comanagement and a trap limit and against limited entry. It is clear now that members of the Marine Resources Committee used the strong support for a trap limit in the lobster industry as a springboard to frame a comanagement bill that gave fishermen of each zone the right to pass some regulations on themselves, including a more restrictive trap limit than the twelve-hundred-trap limit for the state as a whole.

Response to the zone management law was decidedly mixed in the industry. Once the law was passed, the leadership of the MLA became enthusiastic supporters of the law and worked hard to see it implemented. Others were much less enthusiastic. A group of fishermen from eastern Maine filed a lawsuit that was later judged to have no merit (*Bangor Daily News* 1996). Some part-time fishermen (with other jobs) were fearful that the full-time fishermen would pass laws restricting the time when fishing could be done (e.g., prohibiting fishing on Saturdays or after 4:00 p.m.), which would force them from the industry. Many full-time fishermen all over the state were leery of the law, since they believed it would favor the part-time fishermen, who would have a majority of votes.

By May 1997, the zones had been established, zone council members had been elected, and the zone bylaws had been written. The first order of business the zone councils took up was trap limits. By the summer of 1998, all seven of the zones had held referendums in which very restrictive trap limits were established. Some zones passed very restrictive trap limits by a wide margin. Zone E, for example, passed a six-hundred-trap limit, with 82 percent of those voting opting in favor of this limit.

The fishermen with large numbers of traps were unhappy. Fully aware that a trap limit affected only big fishermen and that fishermen with small or medium-sized "gangs" of traps did not have to reduce the number of traps they fished, they also knew some of the small fishermen were increasing the number of traps they fished. To make things worse, fishermen were moving out of the failing groundfishery (cod, haddock, hake, and pollock) and making lobster their primary target species. The distributional effect of all of these events was enormous. The trap limit reduced the percentage of all traps that big fishermen had on the bottom and increased the percentage used by small fishermen or ex-groundfishermen. Of course, this had a huge effect on the incomes each group earned from the lobster fishery. In the Casco Bay area, for example, there were full-time fishermen who had to reduce the number of traps they fished by 70 percent, while the total number of traps used in the zone increased.

The relationship between full-time and part-time fishermen is never good. Yet the passage of the trap limit law created an unusual amount of bitterness on the part of the big fishermen, who felt that the small and part-time fishermen had conspired to produce a law for their own benefit at the expense of the full-timers.

The full-time fishermen responded by lobbying successfully for two laws to counter some of the effects of the trap limits. One was a trap tag freeze, which essentially permitted lobster license holders fishing under eight hundred traps to purchase only one hundred more trap tags than they were issued in 1998 and which limited the speed with which part-time fishermen could expand the number of traps they fished. In addition, the full-time fishermen wanted to reduce entry into the industry. If big fishermen were to reduce the number of traps they fished, small fishermen should not build up their trap numbers much and the numbers of new-comers who could enter the industry should be curtailed. The argument advanced in favor of these laws was that both would reduce fishing effort. But everyone knew that they were designed to recoup the losses the trap limits delivered to the big fishermen (Acheson 2003, 107–14).

Rational Choice Theory and the Mechanics of
Lobster Conservation Laws

As is the case with all institutions, lobster conservation regulations allow people to attain benefits that they could not attain by acting alone. However, norms are not produced automatically even in cases where everyone would benefit from them. In the literature on rational choice theory three different explanations exist for the emergence of norms. I argue that only two of these three are applicable to the production of regulations in the Maine lobster industry in the past 120 years.

Distribution Fights

Knight has hypothesized that most institutions come about as a by-product of conflict over resources in which there are multiple equilibria and asymmetrical power relationships (1992, 123–32). The party able to establish a norm favoring itself is the one with the greatest share of the resources (132). This explanation is applicable to the generation of three of the most important lobster conservation laws. The first minimum size measure and prohibition on taking egged females, the double gauge law, and trap limits all came about as by-products of negotiations over distributional rewards.

The first size regulations and prohibitions against taking egg-bearing females were instituted during the course of a battle between the canners and the live lobster industry over control of the lobster supply. These rules do conserve the resource; but they could also be formulated in ways that would give either the canners or the live lobster industry an advantage, by rules resulting in lobsters of a size advantageous to one section of the industry or the other. At first, the canners succeeded in persuading the legislature to pass seasonal rules and size regulations to constrain the live lobster industry and reserve the catch for themselves. After 1879, the live lobster industry succeeded in lobbying for laws that ultimately made it impossible for the canners to stay in business. The live lobster faction won because they had more support in the public, the press, and the legislature.

The same overriding distributional concerns dominated the long battle for the double gauge law. Fishermen in the western part of the coast, dealers, and hotel owners wanted smaller, cheaper lobsters (i.e., nine-inch lobsters) to expand their markets. Many fishermen, especially those in the eastern part of the state, feared that lowering the gauge would result in a flood of imports from Canada, undercutting the Maine price to the benefit of the dealers. Neither side had the resources to gain an advantage until Commissioner Horatio Crie and members of the Marine Resources Committee formed a coalition with the industry faction wanting a smaller gauge, in exchange for their support for the double gauge.

In the case of both the first conservation laws of the 1870s and 1880s and the double gauge law, fishermen in the eastern part of the state were pitted against those in the west. In this contest those in the east were at a distinct disadvantage, since there are fewer fishermen east of Penobscot Bay. More important, there are only two counties along the eastern coast but six in the west. Since this disparity gives fishermen from the western part of the coast more influence in the legislature, they were able to force through rules in their favor.

The trap limit is the result of twenty-five years of conflict over distribution of the resource. Essentially, trap limits are devices used by fishermen using smaller numbers of traps to constrain the efforts of people with more gear. Large-scale fishermen resist such constraints, especially when trap limit rules would result in a higher proportion of the catch going to the hated part-timers. The zone management law was an innovative way of dealing with this distributional problem. By allowing different zone councils to set their own regional trap limits, the law minimized conflict among demands coming from different regions of the state, with their different fishing practices.

In the case of all three of these laws, there were multiple solutions to the problem (i.e., multiple equilibria), each of which would benefit one industry faction more than another by allocating to it an increased part of the catch. People in the industry were, of course, fully aware of this fact and fought strenuously in the legislative arena for laws that would benefit them. The faction that ultimately succeeded was the one that had the most resources, in terms of numbers of votes and power in the legislature. In every case, this meant forming a coalition with agents of the government, who had their own agendas. The laws that emerged were compromises incorporating features desired by powerful industry factions to gain control over the lobster resource and others that agents of the government were able to insert in the bill (e.g., the double gauge law and the zone management law, with the attendant trap limit).

The processes by which these three lobster regulations have been generated serve as a reminder of one of the most basic axioms of the new institutional economics and rational choice theory, namely, that regulations are rarely neutral; they usually help some people more than others. "Individuals realize this, and . . . they attempt to change institutions to serve their ends more effectively" (Ensminger 1992, xiii).

In the lobster industry, negotiations over distributional rewards are scarcely friendly. One consultant hired to give expert advice on the effect of several proposed regulatory changes in 1986 was clearly appalled by the atmosphere surrounding negotiations concerning lobster legislation, calling it an "adversarial struggle" (Botsford, Wilen, and Richardson 1986, 53–55). However, conflict is almost inevitable, given the nature of the incentives involved. All three of these distributional contests can be modeled as iterated prisoner's dilemma games. The dominant strategies of the factions are different; the stakes are relatively large; and there is strong motivation to defect from a norm. But there are also solutions that entail cooperation as a rational self-interested strategy. Under such conditions, the task is to develop procedures that will make these cooperative strategies more attractive than defection. In such an atmosphere sweet words and reason will gain little, while persuading the legislature to support one's bill pays handsomely.

Social Conventions

The escape vent law and the V-notch law came about as the result of an entirely different process. The interactions that generated these rules are best modeled as pure coordination games of the type described by Lewis (1969) and Sugden (1986). In such games, there is a "coincidence of interests" among the actors (Lewis 1969, 14). Such games may have multiple equilibria, but one of them is preferred by everyone. Moving to this solution benefits everyone.[11]

At the time they were enacted, both the escape vent and the V-notch laws were widely perceived as equally benefiting everyone in the industry and serving the cause of conservation as well. By passing these laws, the legislature helped fishermen as individuals, moved the industry as a whole closer to Pareto optimum, and satisfied bureaucrats concerned with their public trust responsibilities. The process by which these laws were passed was far less acrimonious than that resulting from the distribution battles described previously.

Beyond these similarities, the circumstances surrounding the passage of the escape vent law and the V-notch program were quite different. The escape vent law came about through formalization of an existing practice; the V-notch law took advantage of a formal law to build a conservation program by decentralized means.

Support for an escape vent law came about very quickly in the 1970s since the bureaucracy and the Marine Resources Committee of the legislature were well disposed toward it. Many people in the industry supported the proposal, influenced by the fact that some "highliners" had tried escape vents and found them advantageous. In a sense, the passage of this law was tantamount to the formalization of an informal practice. Many laws are, in fact, generated in this fashion (Knight 1992, 85).

The V-notch program is an informal institution building on the possibilities presented by a formal law. The original law was designed to save a few thousand seed lobsters. Fishermen saw the possibilities inherent in this situation and proceeded to V-notch very large numbers of the egged lobsters they caught in the interest of conservation. Their voluntary activities have made the program far more effective than its originators ever dreamed in 1917.

Exchange and Competitive Selection

We argue that none of the lobster conservation laws were produced by a process of exchange and competitive selection. No law was the result of a deal or deals resulting in contract. Certainly there is nothing in the history of this legislation to suggest that competition forced less efficient types of contracts to extinction. Once rules were established, they tended to remain.

The Development of Maine Lobster Regulations:
The Analysis

The historical data on lobster legislation support the contention that a number of other factors have had a marked influence on the development of regulations in the Maine lobster industry. While all of them have been discussed by rational choice theorists and others interested in the production of norms, they fall into no well-integrated theoretical mold. We suspect, however, that some of the following factors play a role in influencing fisheries regulations and resource management policy more widely.

Preconditions Favoring the Development of Rules

The social organization of the lobster industry is one that favors both the development and enforcement of rules. First, a good deal of evidence suggests that groups will be more likely to develop rules to manage resources if they are homogenous, since any rule that is devised will affect all members of such groups equally (Agrawal 2002, 62–63, 68; Ostrom 1990, 188). The lobster industry is relatively homogenous technologically and socially. All lobster fishermen must fish for lobster with wire traps, virtually all of the boats in the fishery are under forty feet long and have one- or two-person crews, and the ancillary equipment on board is relatively standard (i.e., trap haulers, lobster storage tanks, and electronic navigational equipment). Moreover, the vast majority of the license holders in the fishery come from "Yankee" families that have lived in these coastal communities for generations (Acheson 1988). Only a small proportion of lobster fishermen come from other backgrounds. The importance of heterogeneity is underscored by the fact that the industry had difficulty agreeing on rules when heterogeneity resulted in different factions with different interests. For example, it was very difficult to get trap limits because of the difference in trap numbers used in different parts of the coast. This problem could only be overcome by dividing the coast into zones with the power to make different trap limits. Even then, a stumbling block for trap limits was the fact that full-time and part-time fishermen want different limit levels.

There is also strong evidence that people who are more dependent on the resource are more motivated to devise conservation rules (Agrawal 2002, 62–63, 68; Ostrom 1990, 188). The vast majority of coastal communities in Maine are very dependent on the lobster resource. Lobster is not only the most important fishery, but in most small towns outside of York and Cumberland counties (Maine's most industrialized), there are few economic alternatives.

In addition, the strongly territorial system of the lobster industry gives fishermen an incentive to conserve the resource. People will not generate conservation rules if new entrants will gain the benefits of their efforts (Ostrom 1990, 90). The territorial system keeps new entrants at bay. Moreover, no set of rules—formal or informal—will last unless they are enforced, and the territorial system eases the problem of enforcement. The territorial system ensures that all of the fishermen exploiting an area know each other, if not personally then at least by reputation. Within a given territory, fishermen are continually monitoring each other's behavior. Anonymity is impossible. This ability to monitor each other makes it difficult to violate either formal or informal rules without being noticed.

The Role of the Industry, Science, and
Government in Generating Legislation

In the past 120 years, regulations of the Maine lobster industry have been the result of interactions between several different interested parties, including factions of fishermen, state and federal officials, and scientists. Conservationists are latecomers to the game. Without question, fishermen have had more influence over legislation than any other group. Vinal Look, former commissioner of the DMR, said that "the legislature has never passed an important regulatory bill without substantial support from the industry." This means that, if we want to understand the genesis of lobster regulatory legislation, we must focus primarily on the strategic choices of various groups of fishermen and the process of negotiation among them.

While industry lobbying was the foremost factor producing all lobster-conservation legislation, the government was very active in the process and pursued its own ends. Indeed, its presence in the debate changed everything. First of all, it added two new players to the mix, the legislature and the DMR. The legislature and the DMR often have different goals, but they have one dominant interest that distinguishes their actions from those of the industry. The oceans are owned by the public and held in trust by the government, which has the responsibility to conserve the resources of the ocean. It is a responsibility the legislature and the DMR have taken very seriously. Although the legislature is always careful to assess public support and the interests of their constituents, in the last analysis, conservation has been a primary emphasis. This is, perhaps, only to be expected. Governments have an interest in promoting economic growth, both to increase state revenues and to build political consensus facilitating the exercise of power (Knight 1992, 191). The industry has also been interested in conservation, especially in recent decades. But for industry members, conservation is of less importance than distributional issues.

Second, the introduction of the government changed outcomes. To be sure, neither the DMR nor the legislature could dictate rules that had little or no industry support. But agents of the government could and did enter into coalitions with various industry factions to get the support needed to pass certain pieces of legislation. In these cases, government agents had enough power to alter bills in ways that met their own agenda. The double gauge law, for example, was the result of a coalition between Commissioner Horatio Crie and a faction of the lobster industry in the western counties that wanted a smaller minimum gauge. Neither could have attained their goals in the absence of the other. Commissioner Crie was able to use industry support for a smaller minimum size measure to get a double gauge law, which protected both juvenile and reproductive-sized lobsters.

Sixty years later, Commissioner Robin Alden and her allies in the legislature were able to use strong industry support for a trap limit to fashion the zone management law. This gave the industry a trap limit embodied in a comanagement law.

Scientists played a decidedly secondary role in the generation of conservation legislation. Pronouncements by scientists concerning industry problems were certainly not enough to swiftly advance remedial legislation. Richard Judd (1988, 598) points out that "there was no simple one-to-one correlation between biological necessity and conservation law." However, scientists have been a primary source of management ideas and data. The original size limit laws, the laws protecting egg-bearing females, the double gauge law, and the escape vent law originated with European scientists. Sometimes it took decades for these management ideas to be enacted into law. The double gauge was proposed by biologists just after the turn of the century, but no law was enacted until 1933. The idea of a trap limit had been bandied around for over thirty-five years. Ideas of scientists were eventually incorporated into laws, but only after powerful factions in the industry realized they could be used to further their own agenda. This underlines how scientific facts are often little more than ammunition that can be seized on by contestants in distributional fights at convenient moments.

Political Entrepreneurship

Political entrepreneurs played a crucial role in the development of some of the most important lobster conservation laws. The double gauge law would not have been passed were it not for Commissioner Crie; and MLA past president Eddie Blackmore lobbied hard for the passage of the double gauge and the escape vent laws. Similarly, Commissioner Alden was a strong supporter of comanagement. These people wielded no unusual power, nor could they provide rewards. Rather, they were critical in changing people's attitudes toward legislation by pointing out to various groups the benefits to be gained. In this regard, Taylor argues that the ability to change attitudes is the most important function of political entrepreneurs (1990, 233–34). It was difficult to effect such change among the fishermen, but the Maine entrepreneurs stubbornly promoted their very clear solution to a particular problem until it gained acceptance: for both Horatio Crie and Eddie Blackmore, this literally took years.

Path Dependency

The development of lobster conservation laws reveals a high degree of path dependency. Choices that were made in the nineteenth century opened some avenues for regulation and closed off others. In the late nineteenth century, it became axiomatic among biologists and fishermen that the key to conserving the lobster resource was the preservation of lobsters in critical parts of their life cycle, namely, juvenile and repro-ductive-sized lobsters. This became part of the ideology of the industry (Geertz 1973). The first rules in the 1870s accomplished these goals by a minimum size measure and a prohibition against taking egg-bearing females. These laws set a precedent that has not changed to this day. All of the important legislation that followed was built on the principles of protecting the breeding stock (i.e., the 1917 seeder program, the 1933 double gauge law, and the V-notch program) and protecting the juve-niles (i.e., the escape vent and the increase in the legal minimum size). Majeski (1990, 278–79) makes a strong case that humans use precedent-based reasoning in attempting to solve problems. Such reasoning oper-ates to extend existing norms into new situations and certainly appears applicable to lobster legislation. Once it was widely accepted that stock was to be conserved by protecting lobsters in important parts of their life cycle, the industry and legislature never varied from this solution. Given this worldview, it was to be expected that, when the New England Regional Fisheries Management Council sought to do away with the oversize measure and the V-notch rule in the 1980s, the industry opposed it vehemently. These proposals violated what most fishermen consider the most important principle behind effective management.

Moreover, acceptance of the idea of conserving the lobster by pro-tecting them during delicate parts of their life cycle precluded the use of other kinds of regulations widely used to manage fisheries. In the 1970s, the National Marine Fisheries Service financed a survey to explore the kinds of regulations fishermen would accept. The survey clearly showed that the industry would be very opposed to a moratorium on fishing, limited entry, a tax on traps, or any kind of quota (Acheson 1975). All of these measures attempt to conserve the resource by cutting fishing effort, a principle the Maine lobster industry regards as ineffective and ill-advised.

The success of past legislation in conserving the resource led inevitably to increased lobbying for a trap limit in the 1990s. In supporting the double gauge, the escape vent, and the V-notch laws, lobster fishers are forgoing current catches to attain larger and more certain catches in the future. The conserved lobsters are in a common pool. As Hechter points out, "Once individual assets are pooled in a central place, however, another free-rider problem occurs: how is it possible to stop a depositor from taking more than her fair share or from consuming the entire fund?" (1990, 246). In the lobster industry, the solution to this problem is the trap limit, which is designed to prevent fishermen with many traps (known as "hogs") from gaining an unfair share of the common pool.

Developing a Conservation Ethic

Since the 1930s, the lobster industry has undergone a fundamental cultural change, developing a conservation ethic. In the 1920s and the 1930s, there was less interest in conservation legislation and more opposition to rules to conserve the lobster. The maximum size measure was not passed until 1933, almost thirty years after it was first proposed, and then only over the very strong objections of half of the industry. In addition, those rules that were passed were systematically violated (Correspondence of the Commissioner 1931e).

Through the MLA the lobster industry was advocating legislation to conserve the lobster by the 1980s. The MLA leadership led the fight for the escape vent in the 1970s; and in the 1990s they lobbied for a trap limit, which ultimately led to passage of the highly successful zone management law. At the federal level, MLA past president Eddie Blackmore worked very hard to ensure that the Maine legislature and New England Regional Fisheries Management Council retained the V-notch law and oversize measure.[12] In 2000, the leadership of Lobstermen's Associations in Maine and Massachusetts led the successful fight for Amendment 4 to the federal lobster plan, which would extend the V-notch program and oversize laws to federal waters in Massachusetts and New Hampshire (Acheson 2003). In short, over the past eighty years, the industry has transformed itself from a "pack of bandits" into one of the most conservation-minded fishing organizations in North America.

How did this change occur? A good deal of work will need to be done to answer this question fully. However, I believe that the outline is clear. Ideology, rules, and changes in catches, along with biological, technical, and organizational factors, affected each other in an interactive way to produce what we call the conservation ethic, a massive shift in the culture of the industry. In the late nineteenth and early twentieth centuries, the lobster conservation rules were extensively violated, and violations of these laws were condoned both by people in coastal communities and by the courts. The painful experience of the lobster bust of the 1920s and 1930s altered people's perceptions of conservation laws. Many became convinced that cheating was doing a good deal of damage to the resource and that compliance with the rules would result in collective benefits. An increasing number of people began to obey the rules and to report flagrant violators (Acheson 1997, 8–10). Arguments in favor of conservation were buttressed by the modest increases in landings that occurred in the late 1930s and early 1940s.

After World War II, many (but not all) returning veterans became convinced that conservation would benefit the resource. They wanted to make a living in the lobster industry and did not want it to return to the dismal conditions of the 1930s. Eddie Blackmore, past president of the MLA, stated, "Many people came back from the war and wanted to go fishing. We knew that if we took care of it [the fishery] it would be there." Beginning in the 1940s, fishermen increasingly became convinced that protecting the breeding stock enhanced the fishery and that to accomplish this they should support the V-notch program. The popularity of V-notching grew continually from the late 1940s onward.

Success fed on success. During the 1950s, 1960s, and 1970s catches were very stable, averaging twenty million pounds, three times what catches had been in the lobster bust years of the 1920s and 1930s. The stable catches hardened the conviction of many fishermen, including industry leaders, that their view of the ocean was correct and that the lobster conservation laws were effective and were playing a key role in producing relatively high catches and incomes for them. This conviction, in turn, led to increased efforts to sanction those who violated the law. "Bandits" now had an unsavory reputation in coastal communities, and fishermen increasingly felt justified in helping the wardens get evidence against them. Taking "shorts" (undersized lobsters) was now viewed by most as a crime, not a necessity.

The increased faith in conservation regulations led to the development of further regulations. In 1978, the industry supported legislative initiatives for the escape vent law and likewise in 1995 for the zone management law. The high lobster catches experienced from the late 1980s on have buttressed belief in the effectiveness of the conservation laws and in the fishermen's view of the ocean that make such laws seem so sensible. Many lobster fishermen now are convinced that the success of the industry is due, in great part, to their own effort in supporting passage and enforcement of conservation laws.

In summary, changes in practice, values, catches, and the view of the ocean all worked to reinforce each other over the course of decades in a way that has allowed this industry to get the legislation it wanted (and some it initially did not) and to ward off less desirable rules. The rules that have solved the collective action dilemma for the lobster industry are the result of a seventy-year-long process in which stable and higher catches have buttressed faith in lobster conservation laws and reinforced a view of the ocean and the lobster on which those laws are based. This faith in conservation, in turn, has led to passage of more laws and increased support for enforcement efforts. Once the upward spiral began, technology, biology, and the social organization of the industry contributed to it. The selective gear (i.e., traps) and the biology of the lobster made it possible to put juveniles and breeding-sized lobsters back in the water without harm, bolstering stock sizes, while the harbor gang organization made it easy for fishermen to monitor each other and aided enforcement of the rules.

When catches remained stable for decades, lobster fishermen became relatively sure that the resource would be there in the future and that the conservation laws would be enforced by the wardens and obeyed by other fishermen. Under these conditions, the need to take the resource as fast as possible recedes and the temptation to disobey the law flags.

Attitudes toward the future change. Knowing that the resource will be there makes it more sensible to think in terms of long-term conservation. After all, those who sacrifice to conserve the resource today will themselves reap the rewards, along with future generations. The discount rate, in short, becomes lower.

Events in the lobster industry are not unique. Axelrod argues that norms evolve over time in a process in which success plays a crucial role. "This approach is based on the principle that what works well for a player is more likely to be used again while what turns out poorly is more likely to be discarded" (1986, 1097). The lobster industry demonstrates how those who faced a catastrophic loss in the "bust" came to recognize some of the problems, made sequential changes, learned from their mistakes, and gradually developed a highly successful industry over the long run.

This suggests that the most critical question facing resource management is how to foster a sense of stewardship among users of natural resources. It will involve structural changes to ensure that those who bear the sacrifices of conservation legislation will gain the benefits. It will also mean some more difficult changes in values and attitudes.

NOTES

Data on which this chapter is based were gathered in the course of a project entitled "Case Studies in Co-Management" sponsored by the University of Maine Sea Grant. Special thanks are due to Jack Knight, who commented extensively on an earlier draft of the chapter.

1. The smallest lobster that can be taken currently must be 3.25 inches on the carapace and weigh about 1.25 pounds.

2. Lobsters in pounds suffer mortality due to cannibalism, particular on lobsters that have the misfortune to shed, and to disease, especially gaffkemia. But pound owners try to minimize such mortality on lobsters they own.

3. To read some of the testimony and debate, one would have thought that the lifeblood of the industry was lobsters thirteen inches and over.

4. In the years between World War I and World War II, catches ranged between five million and seven million pounds in most years, one-fourth of what they had been in the 1890s (Maine Department of Marine Resources 1995). The causes of this decline are complex, and there is little consensus on them (see Acheson and Steneck 1997).

5. The double gauge law appears in Maine Public Law, 1933, c. 2, sec. 89. It was amended in 1935 (Laws of Maine 1935).

6. This and other quotes throughout the chapter derive from my conversations with informants.

7. The V-notch will last through several molts and serves to protect egged females for a period of several years. This rule is thought to be especially effective in conserving the largest females, which may not extrude eggs every year but are capable of producing over one hundred thousand eggs every other year.

8. Apparently some unscrupulous dealers and fishermen continued to scrub the eggs off berried females and sell them. When caught with egged lobsters in their possession they would claim they were saving them for the seeder program.

9. The average number of traps fished by Maine lobster fishermen was 475 in 1996.

10. In April 1995, many people were called to testify before the Marine Resources Committee of the Maine legislature, including myself. I urged the committee to consider a zone management bill and to try giving more management responsibility to fishermen. Several other people had similar messages. Together these people had some influence on the bill.

11. In this sense the establishment of the escape vent and the V-notch laws is not really a collective action problem as defined by Elster (1989, 24–27), where rational action (i.e., defection) by an individual can lead to a Pareto inferior outcome.

12. This is one of the strangest episodes in the annals of fisheries management. Federal scientists wanted to increase the minimum gauge to 3.5 inches, which they argued would allow a much higher percentage of female lobsters to reach a size where they could extrude eggs. They also wanted to do away with the V-notch and oversize laws, both to achieve regularity uniformity (Maine was the only jurisdiction to have such rules) and because the scientists argued they were ineffective. The industry was very much opposed. In its view, a 3.5-inch minimum size would produce large lobsters, which would mean ceding the market for small or "chicken" lobsters to the Canadians, who had a smaller gauge. More important, the industry believed that the V-notch and oversize laws were effective management tools. Ironically, in 2000, the scientists came to agree that these laws were far more effective than they originally thought.

II Fruit Trees and Family Trees in an Anthropogenic Forest

Ethics of Access, Property Zones, and Environmental Change in Indonesia

Nancy Lee Peluso

> Landscapes are culture before they are nature;
> constructs of the imagination projected onto wood,
> water, and rock. . . . But once a certain idea of
> landscape, a myth, a vision, establishes itself in an actual
> place, it has a peculiar way of muddling categories, of
> making metaphors more real than their referents; of
> becoming, in fact, part of the scenery.
>
> (Schama 1995)

SETIPA MOUNTAIN RISES behind Bagak Sahwa, on the south side of the paved trunk road between the city of Singkawang and the town of Bengkayang. On the other side of the road, a wide strip of irrigated rice fields meanders along a river that stretches north to meet the Selakau River. Bagak, a hamlet of more than one hundred single-family houses, is laid out on a line lazily perpendicular to the trunk road, aiming toward Setipa's peak. The mountain and the hamlet are buffeted by a mile-wide strip of forest that winds around the mountain's foothills. The village forest consists of tropical trees in mixed stands of mostly fruit and rubber, scattered bamboo clusters, and tangling vines slithering forth from the edges of cleared footpaths. The forest is dotted with an occasional patch of swidden hill rice or a broad-leafed cluster of banana. After the first half mile, the tangles and thorns are left behind; the forest takes on a park-like quality. Open expanses under a layered canopy of tall trees make it easy and relatively cool to walk from one giant fruit tree to the next.

Wrapping around the hillside, the park forest contains hundreds of three-, four-, and five-generation durian trees, many of them triple arm-spreads around, the emergents in the tightly closed canopy. Because their planters have passed on, some trees are remembered now by the planters' names: Nek Bantakng, Nek Limo, Nek Suhotn, Nek Rawoh, and Nek Garakng. Beside some of them are the trees planted by their living children and grandchildren: Si Anyap and Si Sulam. Other trees called *Si* were planted by men or women who died young—before receiving the honor of being called Nek (grandparent).[1] Some trees are named for the peculiar shape or taste of their fruit: Si Jongkup is named for its bottle-shaped fruits. A level below these trees in the multi-storied canopy is the progeny of fruit trees planted at the same time as the durian: tangy *langsat,* creamy *angkaham,* and sweet mangosteen. Up and down the slopes of Setipa and adjacent hills, these trees planted by Bagak hamlet's Salako ancestors have stood as witness to and subject of the village's history.

The Transformation of Property and Access Conventions

This chapter examines the transformation of property and access conventions in an anthropogenic forest in West Kalimantan, a province in Indonesian Borneo. Although both property rights and landscape are treated as processes that may react to transformations in one another, they cannot be linked in a linear or determinist fashion. Rather, the mutual constitution of property and landscape processes needs to be understood as part of what Hart (2002) has called "socio-spatial trajectories," dynamic layerings or convergences of history, meaning, and conjuncture.

Two main aspects of this anthropogenic forest are examined. One is the creation and management of forest landscapes by forest-dwelling peoples. I show how swidden cultivators have not only deforested but also afforested or reforested their lands rather autonomously, that is, without government, nongovernment organization, or project sponsorship or encouragement. This is perceptible only by looking at landscape change over a relatively long period—in this case, about one hundred years. Examining only a moment in a landscape process, such as the burning of a forest patch to make a swidden or the extraction of forest products, obscures the long-term effects of local management processes. A second aspect of this anthropogenic forest is its demonstration that nature reserves created by government agencies or other outsiders can interrupt local forest and land management schemes and cause unanticipated, yet connected, changes outside reserve boundaries. Such interruptions, which ignore local management processes, may lead local people to find ways to alter the species composition of those "reserved" spaces as a means of contesting their appropriation. In other words, they represent what Sivaramakrishnan (this volume) has pointed to as a pattern in instances of "resistance"—that the form of resistance emerges and operates in tension with the efforts to take control.[2]

Focusing on property rights and access to forest resources, my examination of social relations in these forests pursues three themes. The first is the ways in which politics and discourses alter both the landscape and the ways people gain access to the landscape's resources. To untangle these processes of change, I examine how certain resources have represented or generated power, wealth, and meaning to those who control or have access to them (Shipton and Goheen 1992; Peters 1992). I focus particularly on the ways shifting fields of power, production relations, and cultural meanings of various resources have generated different relations between land and trees across generations. A second theme is spatial and temporal fluctuations in individual and collective property relations in long-living trees, which constitute "temporal and spatial zones" of access, control, and management. The third theme is the changing forms of resource access and what I call an "ethic of access," specifically, how this ethic has somewhat tempered the potentially harsh consequences of broader trends toward privatization, individuation, and commodification of resources.

These social and ecological developments are not a unique artifact of a single village's history and experience: they are being experienced in other parts of West Kalimantan (Ex 1992; Salafsky, Dugelby, and Terborgh 1993; Padoch 1994; Peluso and Padoch 1995). They resemble the anthropogenic forests and agroforestry systems of East and South Kalimantan and other tropical agroforestry production systems (e.g., Lahjie and Seibert 1988; Potter 1987; Colfer et al. 1993; Leaman, Razali, and Sangat-Roemantyo 1991; Peluso 1992b; Weinstock 1983; Tsing and

Tsing 2003; Colfer and Soedjito 1995). Such managed forest ecosystems appear in other parts of Indonesia and the tropics in general (Alcorn 1981; Posey 1985; Denevan and Padoch 1987; Hecht, May, and Anderson 1988; Michon and Michon 1994; Sather 1990; Balee 1989; Leach 1995). Bagak's case, then, contributes to knowledge of forest landscapes and the roles of local people in creating, maintaining, and altering them (Posey 1985; Hecht and Cockburn 1989; Padoch 1994; Schama 1995).

Much of my discussion of resource tenure and meaning centers on durian trees (*Durio zibethanus*), placing this fruit tree in the context of contemporary villagers' management of other fruits, rubber, and agricultural land. Demand for the fruit all over the island of Borneo— throughout Southeast Asia in fact—guarantees brisk sales wherever there are roads or rivers to transport it. Durian is an important component of both the social fabric and the physical landscape. The tree's biological characteristics of longevity and high productivity affect property relations and illustrate the importance of time as well as space in the study of agrarian change. By scrutinizing changes in, and contestation of, property relations through the trees' many productive generations, we gain a bird's-eye view of social changes in the landscape and their meanings.

Resource Tenure, Zoning, and Environmental Change

We still barely understand the relationships between multiple forms of tenure in agrarian resources and the roles of property and political economy in shaping agrarian landscapes (Fortmann 1988, 11). We do know, however, that any explanation of environmental change is complicated by property relations, themselves inflected by conflicting sources of legitimate authority like customary and formal legal systems (Moore 1986; Fortmann 1990; Bromley 1991; Peluso 1992c, 1993a), negotiated systems of meaning (Dove 1986; Posey 1989; Peluso 1992a; Shipton and Goheen 1992; Peters 1992), and an individual's position in society, that is, membership and relative power in various social networks (Blaikie 1985; Berry 1989; Okoth-Ogendo 1989). Both cultural and political-economic processes and institutions influence access to resources (Moore 1986; Berry 1989; Bromley 1989, 1991). How resource access and control affect, and are affected by, power, wealth, and meaning will shape that resource's management (Peters 1992).

Like most social relations, property relations are dynamic: they shift as power relations and contexts do (Moore 1986). A dynamic view of property thus compels a focus on *process* rather than simply on the institutions, social structures, or bundles of rights and responsibilities that are particular *outcomes* of processes and negotiations. This study of property as process requires multilayered analysis. Political ecologists in fact study both local histories and the historical layers of political economy that affect local practice (Smith 1984; Blaikie and Brookfield 1987; Neumann 1992; Peluso 1992b; Bryant 1992). Changing governments and policies, market opportunities or structures, and individuals or groups in power match changes in the customary practices and local contexts that guide decision making and the practice of everyday life, including local resource management. How things change, as well as why, is a central political-ecological concern.

The sheer number of species in tropical forests multiplies the complications of studying property relations and farmer decision making. The range and diversity of agroforestry products are as vast as the tenure arrangements for each. To take a single example, there are many ways to carve up the bundle of rights to a tree, as Louise Fortmann (1985) has aptly shown. The largest bundles of rights include those to own or inherit, to plant, to use, and to dispose of a tree. Each of these rights can be subdivided; many of them interact with other factors. Tree tenure may determine or be determined by land tenure, or forms of access to these two resources may be independent (see also Ribot and Peluso 2003). Different users might have concurrent rights to use different parts of the tree, and these uses may not always be compatible. Changes in land rights may lead to changes in tree rights or vice versa. In addition, rights holders like state institutions, households, and individuals operate at different scales and often concurrently derive different sorts of benefits (or pay divergent costs) from their access to trees and land. Whether a tree was planted or grew spontaneously can make a difference in rights, as can a product's intended use for subsistence or sale (Fortmann 1985).

One other influence on tree tenure bundles, to add to Fortmann's list, is a tree's natural characteristics. Factors such as the length of time it grows and produces fruit, nuts, or other products influence people's ability to manage a tree. So do a tree's reproductive strategies, that is, the number of seeds the mother tree produces, the manner of harvesting (whether the fruit is harvested by humans or left in the forest for other creatures), the survival rate of seedlings, and the intensity of management (Peters 1994). Biological characteristics also play roles in inheritance patterns. Date palms, for example, can be inherited indefinitely because new sprouts continually emerge from mother trunks (Leach 1988). Natural characteristics often affect the value placed on the tree and the meaning of access to it. The tree's potential life span also affects access to the land where it grows—alone or with other trees—as will whether it is planted with others of the same or different species and the range of characteristics and management practices.

Long-living trees can teach a lesson about the notion of zoning. Zoning need not be only a spatial category, in which separate spaces are set aside for crop production, reserve forests, economic forests, or other types of management. Any tree left to grow for a long time affects access to the land in which it is planted for a longer time than field crops. Zoning has both intentional and accidental temporal dimensions. Mixed-age stands of trees—a forest or a plantation—can encompass many temporal zones simultaneously, for different species and particular individuals will live longer than others.

The fruition of certain resources is often guided by an "ethic of access" (Peluso 1992a, 1992c), particularly when resources represent deeply felt cultural practices. An ethic of access is similar to the notion of a subsistence ethic (Scott 1976) but different when the social meaning of the resource is more highly valued than its commodity value. An ethic of access can be driven by more than economics or subsistence rights and serves social, political, and ritual purposes as well, representing kinship, power relations, and ritual harmony. However, like other aspects of resource tenure, the ethic of access is a moment in a temporal zone of a larger property process. Its meaning is rooted in the experience of history and in historical memory, but its present meaning and realization are also affected by contemporary social, political, and environmental factors. Always, the ethics of access to particular resources are influenced by the physical characteristics of a resource, especially its longevity and divisibility, the type of use of a resource (whether for subsistence or commercial purposes), and the social meaning of the resource beyond economic value. As motivators for behavior and as indicators of change, ethics of access and their relations to actual practice can help us analyze changes in resource management. In this chapter I will show that responses to change are reflected in the practices that transform the landscape and in the means of allocating access to resources whose value, meaning, and accessibility have changed. I use the term "access" in a broader sense than "property," although both resource access and property rights are key social relationships that influence—and are influenced by—the commodity and production characteristics of the resources under consideration (Ribot and Peluso 2003).

Bagak's Landscape Today

Bagak is one of the two hamlets (*dusun*) in Bagak Sahwa village (*desa*). Located entirely on the south side of the main road, the hamlet is flush against the hillside forest that borders the Gunung Raya Pasi Nature Reserve. In the early 1990s, the whole village had a population of approximately eleven hundred people in 258 households; 114 of these households fell within Bagak's jurisdiction.[3] The village is one of seventeen in subdistrict Tujuhbelas, in Sambas district, on a well-paved road running from the coastal city of Singkawang inland toward Bengkayang and the international border with Sarawak, Malaysia.[4] Begun as a footpath, this road was widened and hardened in the 1920s and 1930s by the Dutch colonial government and paved by the Indonesian government in 1963.

Over the eighty years prior to my first visit in 1990, this hamlet of Salako[5] Dayaks has moved and been sedentarized by the spontaneous and planned settlement of other villages and the fixing and formalization of administrative village borders by successive colonial and national governments. The administrative village territory is bounded to the south by the relatively small (three thousand hectare) nature reserve created by the Dutch in 1932 as a watershed protection area for Singkawang. To the east of the village lie the agricultural lands of adjacent villages and special transmigration settlements for retired police and air force officers established in 1968 after the Confrontation with Malaysia and subsequent regional unrest and military activity.[6] To the west of the village are a Catholic mission church and school established in 1916. To the north are extensive rubber plantation lands established on the administrative village lands of Maya Sopa. Some Salako from Bagak moved there in the 1930s, but the bulk of these lands are worked by several thousand transmigrants resettled there from Java by the Indonesian government in the late 1980s and early 1990s. This transmigration area occupied some of the land that had been converted from swamp forest to agriculture by Chinese settlers after the eighteenth century.

Bagak Sahwa today consists of some twenty-seven hundred hectares of land, according to official village statistics. This land was once heavily managed, farmed, and occupied by the ancestors of Bagak villagers, but now one-third (nine hundred hectares) is formally under the jurisdiction of the nature reserve, as part of the Ministry of Forestry's Department of Forest Protection and Nature Conservation (PHPA). The reserve includes some of the ancestral longhouses and many previous agroforestry sites of Bagak residents' grandparents. Contemporary conservation regulations require villagers to acquire permits from the forestry department to enter the reserve, although villagers generally ignored or were ignorant about this and local foresters do no enforcing of entry. Foresters tried to restrict certain forest uses such as swidden cultivation and hunting, which, although rare, still occurred in the 1990s. Foresters were quite lenient about people collecting fruit from trees planted within the reserve's boundaries.

In addition to some farming of irrigated rice fields located north of the road in Sahwa, Bagak villagers practice a complex, long-rotation form of land management: a kind of cyclic swidden-fallow agroforestry (Denevan and Padoch 1987; Padoch and Peters 1993). After the harvest of swidden field crops—rice, corn, cassava, and vegetables—and perhaps a second or third year's crop of groundnut or cassava, a swidden fallow is generally planted in rubber, fruit, or mixtures of rubber and fruit. Such gardens are managed subsequently for both the planted tree species and the volunteer trees that sprout in the interstices and are protected during slash weeding (Padoch and Peters 1993). Because the trees are kept in place for a long time and their products are used, for example, for food, fuel, or medicinal purposes, the swidden fallows become managed forests; this has been the fate of most hillside land in Bagak. Some swidden fallows are purposefully left alone, without planting economic trees, allowing them to revert to successional forest cover in order to save the land for future field-crop cultivation. An alternative or intermediary land use is to plant a low-management but high-production crop such as banana. At any given time, each household manages numerous plots under different types of tree and field crops for consumption or sale.

Until the introduction of rubber in the 1920s (see subsequent discussion), the landscape managed by Salako Dayaks consisted largely of swidden field crops and their multiaged fallows and was dotted with managed fruit forests planted in former living sites and some uncut or very mature hill dipterocarp forest. Mature forest not converted to swiddens or forest gardens was tapped for timber, resins (copal), gaharu, and other subsistence and commercial products. Rice self-sufficiency[7] was crucial to local people when markets were few and food supply more local; numerous large swiddens provided the family's food and dominated a "young" landscape. People were strongly connected to their fruit forests, so much so that when fruit forests grew too large to permit sufficient swidden cultivation, the village moved rather than cut the trees. In Bagak in 1991, for example, only a third of the villagers planted any swiddens at all; the average size of these was a meager one-third hectare. Economic trees dominated the landscape. "Rubber," in the words of one local woman, "has become our daily rice," and windfall profits accrue in good years to those with fruit to sell. Throughout the 1990s, the extensive lowland fields that were once among the most productive of wet rice in the region were only partially farmed. Some of this land is loaned out or rented to other smallholders.

The precise amount of land under particular land uses at any moment in time is not clear, because of annual changes in some land uses, because government land-use categories are not consistent with local terms, and also because statistics are unreliable. In 1990, the village head estimated that nearly half of the 1,800 hectares of village land outside the nature reserve were managed forests of one sort or another. More than 800 hectares of these managed forests contain mixed stands of rubber, durian, langsat (*lansium domesticum*), rambutan (*Nephelium lappaceum*), angkaham, cempedak (*Artocarpus spp.*), and other planted fruits, along with self-sown species used for timber, fuelwood, and thatch. Self-sown rattan, bamboo, and medicinal plants are also protected. Of another 296 hectares of fallows set aside for planting in hybrid rubber, 208 hectares were planted as part of a government program between 1981 and 1988.[8] The remaining cultivated land is largely in annual crops, with some 200 hectares of irrigated fields, although not everyone who owns these plots has enough time or labor to plant paddy rice. In August 1990, the village head estimated that some 350 hectares were cultivated or fallowed swiddens.[9] The remaining productive land consists of relatively mature secondary growth in fallow and is not managed intensively.

The social implications of such a landscape structure—primarily managed forest gardens with little land for growing rice—have been profound. Before government restrictions on their movement, these villagers would likely move to a new spot, where they could make new swiddens and continue to harvest rubber and fruit from these gardens. Today, however, they are stuck in place and closed in on all sides. A short foray into the landscape history of Bagak will demonstrate how these changes came to be.

Bagak's Landscape Yesterday: A Short History

> In former days . . . it was not the land that was
> important but trees and their fruit. It was quite common
> for people to have [what is now called] "a garden"
> together, Mr. A with Mr. B., because they liked to plant
> their trees next to each other.
>
> (Nek Manap, *kepala adat*, Bagak Sahwa)

The ancestors of the Bagak Dayaks lived in longhouses near the upper slopes of Setipa Mountain just outside what is today the Gunung Raya Pasi nature reserve, in an area called *Ngidupm*. Living in the mountains allowed them to farm, hunt, and raise animals while defending themselves from their enemies. Not an aggressive headhunting group, these Salako did not make war in order to expand their resource territories, although they responded to war parties' depredations with counterattacks. Villagers claim that their ancestors have occupied Setipa for several hundred years.[10] The villagers moved their longhouse sites short distances, sometimes when the trees near the longhouse had grown too large, sometimes when illness struck the occupants, sometimes when agricultural land grew scarce. When they left a site, additional durian and other fruit trees were planted in the space left by the uprooted (and reused) house structures. The site was henceforth called a *timawokng,* meaning "a former living site."[11] On the surface, they look like fruit forests. As we will see, they were and are highly social forests.

While the Dayaks practiced swidden cultivation in the dry hills, the swampy lowlands to the north were farmed by Hakka-speaking Chinese.[12] Several settlements made up predominantly of ethnic Chinese were later integrated into Bagak's administrative territory, including sites in the hamlet now called Sahwa, and part of a settlement called Patengahan—which appears on Dutch topographic maps from as early as 1850. Local grave sites indicate that Chinese settlement here may have begun as early as 1740, soon after the Chinese began mining gold for the Sultan of Sambas at nearby Montrado and Buduk (Chew 1990; Jackson 1970; Heidhues 2003). Chinese associated with local political organizations of miners, called *kongsis,* cut the lowland forest and dug canals to drain the swamps and plant rice and vegetables.[13] On drier land, some raised pigs (Heidhues 2003).

The Agrarian Act passed by the Netherlands East Indian government in 1870 prohibited Chinese and other "non-native" peoples from owning land. In dismissing the role of these people in converting forest to productive irrigated agriculture, the Dutch looked at race and not practice, ignoring some of their own criteria for recognizing land rights: continuous cultivation and the conversion of unproductive forest to production of crops. The Chinese could only acquire usufruct rights to the land, though written agreements were effectively long-term leases.[14] Although they did not formally own the land, the Chinese continued to alter it, improve it, and make it productive. Chinese planters also leased rights from the Dutch colonial government to the drier lands along the road through Patengahan, where they built houses and eventually planted rubber gardens and some fruit trees. They were the first non-Europeans in the area to grow rubber on a large scale, perhaps the first crop in the area with solely commercial value and no local use.[15]

Land under native cultivation and tenure (which would have included any land being farmed by Salako and other Dayak groups) was considered unfree state land or customary territory and subject to a separate legal treatment.

The Salako of Bagak generally maintained control of their forest and land resources, except for occasional tribute payments to the Malay Sultan of Sambas. The community sold or bartered agroforestry products with Malay traders or local Chinese shopkeepers who came to the longhouses seeking them; they sold fish, *illipe* nuts (from the tengkawang tree, an oilseed pressed and used for cooking oil at the time), savory preserved durian (*tempuyak*), and fresh fruit. Some longhouse dwellers walked over nineteen kilometers to Singkawang market, selling directly to the Chinese in the *pasar* (marketplace) for higher prices.

In 1920, the Dutch colonial state initiated plans to turn the upper slopes of the Gunung Raya Pasi complex, including Setipa Mountain, into a nature reserve, a watershed protection area for the growing city of Singkawang. The initial line for the reserve border was drawn where a water catchment device was to be constructed, encompassing all of the village's current and former living sites and the sites of their ancestral forests and lands as well. The longhouse occupants had to move off the mountain and forfeit their ancestral rights to farming in that area. No trees were cut down, however, so people could continue to collect fruit and rubber. Nevertheless, people were unhappy with the government's plans. Dutch officials worked with local leaders to convince people that they had no choice but to move from Setipa to the lower-lying areas near Chinese rubber and fruit gardens. Eventually people moved out of longhouses into single- and double-family dwellings large enough to accommodate extended families.

The villagers' unhappiness with the new spatial arrangements caused some families to remain on the mountain (inside the reserve) until nearly 1940, eight years after the nature reserve was officially established; they moved only when the Dutch controller threatened to jail them. The head of the settlement continued to negotiate with the Dutch to change the reserve boundaries and accommodate the claims of local people who had planted trees or converted land there. Though it is not clear when, the Dutch eventually moved the reserve boundary above the old longhouse sites, restoring a good deal of the people's territory, in a victory for the locals.

The villagers have always also challenged the reserve's border in less organized, informal ways. Villagers still harvest durian, langsat, rambutan, angkaham, cempedak, and other fruits planted in the reserve by their ancestors. During the Japanese occupation (1942–45), the Indonesian revolution (1945–49), and the early years of Indonesian independence, villagers made swiddens within the reserve boundaries and planted rubber and fruit in the fallows. Yet with the brief return of the Dutch in the late 1940s, some were jailed for having made swiddens within the reserve boundaries. Nevertheless, in the 1950s government surveillance of this and other forests was slight. By planting more trees within the borders, people were also staking their claims in their continued access to, if not control of, the hillside's upper slopes, thus renegotiating old territorial and resource claims. They also hunted deer and collected the products of various self-sown species such as bamboo shoots, candlenut, and rattan within the borders of the reserve. As late as 1976, local people working on the construction of the permanent border markers were able to move the boundary back by another one hundred meters. The unofficial buffer zone they created on the border between the nature reserve and the village's fruit and rubber gardens provides an example of how local people have asserted their claims to the reserve through everyday practices.

The intervention of the colonial state in the arrangement of the village's social and productive space did more than superimpose a new set of rules about land and forest use. Real and imaginary boundaries were imposed for the first time on the villagers' access to the lands and on land uses they had always preferred.[16] This intervention and past events created the preconditions for a landscape dominated by trees.

The change in spatial arrangements, and the growing need to buy some food, helped spark Salako interest in planting rubber. After people were denied legal access to the extensive tracts of reserve and secondary old growth on the mountain, it became difficult for everyone to find enough swidden land to produce their families' food. Nearly half of the old longhouses' population chose to move north of Sahwa, and, rather than settle in what became the hamlet of Bagak, they joined a village near some swidden fallows they had farmed in the past. A few of those who stayed experimented with planting irrigated rice in the fields near the Chinese, but eventually most gave up—the time and labor demands of wet rice production interfered too much with their other productive activities. Rubber was much less labor intensive, and its Chinese planters were doing well. By the 1930s, they could exchange rubber for government-issued coupons to buy food and other supplies on credit. After moving out of the reserve and losing access to agricultural land, and when the price of rubber began to rise, the villagers' interest in it increased. Rubber's biological characteristics also made it an attractive crop: latex could be collected and marketed in virtually all seasons except the rainiest weeks or the very driest days. Uncollected latex did no harm to the tree's productivity. Until Indonesia's Confrontation with

Malaysia, it could be carried, with no risk of spoilage, to the Malaysian border of Sarawak and sold or exchanged for goods there. Latex could also be sold to shopkeepers or middlemen along the Singkawang road, which the Dutch widened again in the 1930s.[17] Rubber trees increased the value of the villagers' land and increased the diversity of a household's economic options. When the first Dayaks moved down from Setipa, none yet planted rubber. Gradually, it became popular, and by 1991, 85 percent of the villagers owned productive rubber trees.[18] As late as the mid-1960s, however, Chinese rubber production still dominated the local market. The current village head claims that when he arrived in 1965, Chinese smallholders were producing most rubber exported daily from Bagak.

The Republic of Indonesia was formed in 1950, and Bagak's villagers became Indonesian citizens. But independence from colonialism did not change their immediate environment: the Catholic mission, the nature reserve, nearby settlements and agriculture, and the road still bounded their own settlement. By the mid-1960s, many people were no longer able to produce their year's supply of rice on their own land and had to buy it. Rubber and fruit trees dominated the landscape, filling in more and more swidden fallows. The marketing of forest and agroforestry products assumed a more important role in household subsistence strategies. In theory, legal pluralism preventing the Chinese from owning land had ended, but in practice this had little effect. National and international politics playing out in West Kalimantan distracted from abstract issues of land transfer and legal change.[19]

Perhaps such stresses on land and changes in production contributed to local people's willingness to participate in the eviction of Chinese farmers from the lands they and their ancestors had transformed and managed—in spite of the strongly held local belief that labor invested in land and tree management imparted rights. In 1968, the Indonesian army, assisted by local Dayaks, violently drove the Chinese from agricultural areas to urban centers such as Singkawang and Pontianak and all along the road between them.[20] People who lived through these events in Bagak said that the Chinese from Patengahan or Bagak were evicted without violence but were still unable to return. Approximately 150 hectares of paddy lands, plus productive rubber and fruit gardens, left behind by evicted Chinese were taken over by local Salako and others and eventually became part of the administrative village of Bagak Sahwa.

Important changes in the landscape and in the distribution of formal rights to control resources began to emerge at this time—once again, largely because of the ways the state intervened in the allocation, formalization, and enforcement of property rights in *land*. Some people had moved onto the land that the Chinese had left behind, claiming a plot with a simple wooden placard. Some informants said that when it became clear that the Chinese would not be allowed to return, they worked with people from the subdistrict office and the army to establish their claims. Some described a kind of informal group of officials who divided the irrigated fields among local families who wanted some. In 1991, the village head (appointed in the 1960s) told me that as soon as he took office, he reallocated much of the claimed land because many people had taken very large shares while others received nothing. Other people refused to take any of this land; one villager called it "the land filled with tears." Claims could be made official at the agrarian office, but not everyone sought formal land title.

Starting in the late 1960s, transmigration settlements designated specifically for retired Indonesian police and army families were established in and around the village's borders. These settlements inserted into the landscape were symbols of the Indonesian state's violence. In the 1970s, the settlements of Patengahan and Sahwa were combined with Bagak into a single administrative village called Bagak Sahwa, while other small settlements in the area were combined into administrative units by the Village Authority Act of 1979.

New landscape transformations resulting from national government interventions and global dynamics began to cover over the pre-Indonesian history of Bagak. The early 1980s saw a second surge in rubber planting, when a World Bank–funded government project for smallholder production of high-yielding rubber (PPKR) was introduced. Land and tree tenure relations created on project land were new. Village or *adat* land converted to high-yielding rubber production changed its status from customary land (*tanah adat*) to a kind of state property, while people maintained rights to the produce of the high-yielding rubber trees. Thus, while landed property was becoming equally important to ownership of trees in village forests, individually owned plots of trees were gaining in importance on lands converted (at least temporarily) to state property.[21] Once the loans were paid off, the land was to be privatized in an individual (i.e., not adat) sense, and the owner was to receive a land title. Where rubber was once a means by which people could make relatively long-term individual claims on a piece of family or village land, PPKR rubber now became a way for the state to temporarily reclaim land from the villagers. As the authorizer of the land titles, the state also permanently changed villagers' relation to that land and to other villagers who farmed it. A new scale of jurisdiction was produced through these practices.

Easy access to the urban markets of Singkawang and Pontianak, facilitated by the paving of the road in the 1960s and the advent of Japanese motorcycles and vans in the 1970s, added incentives for planting trees. Beyond the changes brought on by rubber, the places where fruit trees were planted changed. Durian trees were no longer found only in former living sites but were taking over swidden fallows and invading rubber gardens (themselves planted in swidden fallows). By 1991, some 97 percent of sample households had planted durian trees in swidden fallows; at least 41 percent had planted durian in or just next to their rubber gardens. Durian stems occupied 71 percent of the total basal area of old and medium-aged fruit forests (Charles Peters, personal communication, 1994).[22]

In sum, over the past century, changes in regional political ecology reconstituted Bagak Sahwa as a place. People became fixed within administrative village borders, as territorialized subjects. The nature reserve and fluctuating enforcement of its borders were superimposed on older land usages. Two forms of rubber, introduced at two different times, each had a different impact on the structure and ownership of the landscape. The eviction of nearly seventy Chinese families led to the appropriation of some 150 hectares of irrigated rice land and some rubber and fruit gardens. Along with the improvement and expansion of transport facilities, such changes fostered a booming market for fruit. Each of these changes modified patterns of access to and valuation of resources. We have seen here how particular historical events both shaped and were constrained by environmental and political changes in Bagak. Property rights and access to terrestrial resources were created, shifted, pushed, and pulled by actors with varying degrees of power and authority.

Fruit Trees and Family Trees

Bagak villagers' ethics of access have affected resource control in their area through spatial and temporal zones of ownership and use. The differences in the biological characteristics of specific trees and field crops play an important role in the extent, intensity, or duration of zoning, thus illustrating how ecological and sociological processes interact within a landscape.

Inheritance Ethics

For villagers resident in Bagak, land and trees still provided the most important sources of household income through the 1990s. Individual or household rights to resources have generally been recognized by members of the community based on two different sorts of considerations: kinship, through bilateral inheritance, and the investment of labor in resource production or management.[23] Inheritance alone is not enough to guarantee equal shares of fruit or forest products if those rights are not actually acted upon and earned. Participation in the harvest of most fruits and forest products is both a right by inheritance and a conveyor of rights by dint of labor investment. Labor also imparts rights, for example, through the clearing of brush from old fruit or rubber gardens to make a swidden, to provide a tree or a cluster of trees more light or space, to facilitate the harvest of fruit or latex, or to plant a tree. On commonly held land, activity around the trees, or the planting of them, ties up and creates temporal zones of essentially privatized rights.

In principle, both male and female children share equal rights to inherit their parents' resources, although primary rights to household resources remain within the household unit and usually pass to the child who stays in the household and takes care of elderly parents. The household, or the husband and wife plus resident children and any elderly parents or others, manages a set of land-based resources in addition to any cash savings or movable property. Some of this property is inherited, some accumulated by household members who labor for wages inside or outside the village. Land-based resources include inherited lands under cultivation and in fallow, inherited durian and fruit trees, rubber gardens, and other lands cleared or trees planted by household members. When people lived in longhouses, the household unit was defined as all those living in one of the house's apartments (*bi'ik*). After they married, children generally built their own bi'ik—attached either to one set of parents' longhouse or to another one nearby. Whichever child remained within the apartment to care for the parents in their old age would inherit primary rights to the household's resources. This child's spouse would move into the apartment; after having children, the pair would eventually take over as coheads of the household. When the parents died, the new household head usually managed the household's resources and divided access to these inherited resources among his or her siblings. A larger share of these resources generally went to this person, as compensation for the cost of caring for the parents.[74]

Although most families in Bagak today live in single-family homes, the concept of primary rights going to the child who resides with the aging parents remains. As discussed later, however, primary rights are not meant to exclude other siblings from gaining access to the productive resources of their parents and grandparents. Perhaps for this reason, local people refer to the primary rights holder simply as "the person in charge" (*yang kuasa*).[25] As used in Bagak, the term implies that other kin have rights that are administered, but not monopolized, by the one in charge. The person in charge of the inherited trees may be male or female, eldest or youngest. The youngest is the most common among the Salako of Bagak simply because they are generally the last to marry.

This inheritance system shapes the distribution of resources in several ways. First, because inheritance is bilateral and marriage is not restricted by class or status group qualifications, descent groups overlap. Bilateral inheritance hypothetically prevents one or several descent groups from dominating land and other resources such as long-living trees. Bilateral inheritance means that an individual is a member of many different descent groups at the same time and has some rights of access to the fruit of trees planted by ancestors common to the descent group. Each person has four grandparents and thus at least four immediate descent groups. Each couple has thus a potential claim on the trees of eight people in their grandparents' generation. People also have rights to the trees planted by their grandparents' parents and grandparents. Durian trees last as long as 150 to 200 years, covering many generations of claimants.

At marriage, a couple's families decide which family they will live with, meaning whose land will they work and eventually inherit. The choice is based on which side has land or trees available to pass on, a condition directly related to how much labor their ancestors invested in clearing forest, making swiddens, and planting trees. These practices do not preclude one family borrowing land from the other or taking part in a different fruit tree harvest. In practice, though these guidelines are followed, there is a great deal of fluctuation.

In addition, the inheritance principle grants greater rights to one of the children in a household—the one who continues the household and cares for aging parents. This individual gains the right to manage (*ngurus*) the household's resources, which generally means deciding how access to these will be allocated. In practice, such decisions can be made collectively, by a group of siblings, or even by a sibling who does not live in the original household. As described later, allocation may entail rotating access to fruiting trees on a seasonal, weekly, daily, or other basis. It may involve temporarily or permanently dividing up the rights to particular trees among living siblings. Thus, there are underlying disparities in principles and practices. The rules both of intergenerational inheritance and of the ethic of access articulate a relatively egalitarian allocation of access to resources. In practice, however, having one member of a descent group in charge of the tree gives him or her greater power over the resource and greater control over entitlement for everyone, including subsequent generations. While custom dictates that grandparent trees have a different inheritance status than the trees planted by parents (see subsequent discussion) some people told of cases in which the rights to the fruit of grandparent trees were taken over by a single sibling. The individualization of control over these trees does not diminish the ethic of access to them—other grandchildren of the planters often adamantly retain a claim to the fruit for their own consumption as opposed to sale. The person in charge is expected to allow them to collect fruit for a night or two if that claim is exercised.

Women are somewhat less frequently in charge of family trees than men. A survey of inheritance transactions for all the durian trees in two of the oldest *tembawangs*—former living sites, replanted with trees— (Timawokng Anjauh and Gantekng Raru) and a sample transect through three medium-aged tembawangs (Timawokng Rumoh, Pagukn Batu, and Sirarok Atas) showed 183 inheritance transactions in the lives of durian trees growing within the transects. Primary rights were descended 38 percent of the time to female children and 62 percent of the time to male children or nephews. Local people explained this discrepancy by noting that, in previous generations, most women did not travel to old tembawang, fearing headhunters. In looking at gendered differences in married couples' living arrangements, I found that half of the village sample of forty households lived on the land of the wife's family and half on that of the husband's family.

Other practices could prevent the monopolization of family resources by a single heir. For example, parents sometimes allocated the trees before they died, saying that this would either prevent sibling discord or ensure that a favored grandchild, niece, or nephew received a specific tree. In some cases, sibling cohorts agreed to maintain equal access to the trees and to share in the trees' management.

In other cases, the person in charge refused access to siblings, and the rest of the family was too embarrassed to publicly pursue a solution. Access could also be practically lost when someone moved so far away that collecting fruit or cultivating a swidden became impractical. Some rightful heirs withdrew from the coheirs' pool when they had their own trees—a common, almost expected, practice. The circumstances behind such changes in the claims on grandparent trees varied (see subsequent discussion).

Zoning, Temporal and Spatial

Fruit is the most complicated of the three main landscape components (swiddens and fallows, rubber, and fruit). It is becoming even more so as regional political ecology and property relations change. Many trees produce fruit for three to five human generations, but durian may produce through seven or more, as mentioned previously. With each generation, basic mechanisms of access change, as more people have inherited rights to a tree's fruit. Leaving the village does not necessarily eliminate one's rights of access to ancestral fruit trees; children or grandchildren can return to their natal village or travel to others during the durian season to share fruit with their siblings or other kin (compare Appell 1970). In the 1990s, however, such journeys were becoming relatively rare. Moreover, any harvest shares imparted to visitors would likely be restricted to collecting fruit for consumption—that is, not for sale—as the visitor seldom had helped manage the tree or even cleared brush before the harvest.

The temporal or intergenerational zoning of rights works roughly as follows: while alive, the tree planter (and spouse) has exclusive/private rights to the fruit. The fruit is collected and sold by the owner or some-one he or she designates: unsold fruit is consumed with other household members, guests, and family members in other households. Profits from the sale of any fruit belong to the household or the planter. After one spouse passes away, the other is in charge of allocating access to the fruit, again generally sharing the annual harvest with other members of the household and immediate family.

After the tree planter and spouse have passed away, all the children collectively inherit rights to the tree's fruit, with one child retaining pri-mary rights, as described earlier. Once tree rights pass to the third gen-eration, the tree is called a *panene'an* (grandparent tree) and the guide-lines change. All the grandchildren of the planter—a coheir's group of cousins—have equal rights in principle. Many local informants insisted that rights to the fruit of panene'an trees were never to be monopolized by an individual, even though someone might be in charge. The same rule of nonmonopoly was to hold true for the fourth, fifth, and sixth generations of heirs. One reason given for this differentiation between the children's and grandchildren's generations was that the investment in parental care had been compensated by favored resource access in the children's generation. Grandchildren were seen to have equal rights.

Depending on age, the conditions of a person's access to different trees changed. Tree planters (and their spouses) were exclusive owners; the children of the tree planters were sibling coheirs; grandchildren and great-grandchildren constituted larger coheir groups. In practice, of course, not all heirs demanded access to all their family trees at the same time. Young couples and individuals tended to depend on the efforts of parents and grandparents, inheriting or sharing in their parents' fruit and often sharing access to grandparent trees. As they grew older, they tended to harvest fruit primarily from trees they planted themselves.

Thus adults bore various responsibilities for future generations. They were expected to plant enough trees to become independent of the grandparent trees (without forgoing their rights in them). Even if they pulled themselves out of the descent group pool, adults may still join in a few days of the harvest of favorite trees to enjoy a particularly deli-cious fruit, to sample a variety of durian flavors in a season, or simply to have the fun of gathering with cousins. But by planting new trees, they created the grandparent trees of the future. Ancestors' fulfillment of their obligations was visible in the number of trees or sites to which descendants had rights.

How access was divided among coheirs depended in part on biology and ecology. Resource abundance depended on the species, the tree's productivity in a particular site, and the fruit's value. Some fruits, such as rambutan, mangosteen, or rambai, are freely picked and eaten by village children.[26] The fruit from trees that must be climbed and for which there is a good market is generally divided equally among all claimants, sometimes with an extra share for the tree climber. This is the case for rambutan, langsat, angkaham, and coconut. Some families distribute these picked fruits among all coheirs, present at the harvest or not; others require a physical presence when the tree is climbed. This may depend on whether there is enough fruit (that season or ever) for the heirs to sell it.

The Case of Durian

Its unique longevity and other biological properties, as well as its social meanings and economic value, make durian special. When durian reaches its peak of ripeness (and flavor), it drops from the tree. At that point, it must be eaten, processed, or sold, because as the days pass, it rapidly loses flavor, quality, and value—all indicated by the intensity of the fruit's sweet-pungent aroma. A single mature tree can produce as many as five hundred or more fruits, while young trees "learning how to fruit" in their first years may produce as few as fifteen. In Bagak durian fruits are never plucked from the trees; they must drop. The head of custom (*kepala adat*) in Bagak told me in the early 1990s that people who plucked their durian used to be fined. Picking durian before it was ripe affected the reputation of the entire village's durian—such news traveled to the marketplaces of Singkawang and elsewhere.

Seasonality is also important in allocation. Not all trees in a single site ripen at once. A single tree's fruit drops over a period of approximately seven to twenty-one days. Moreover, durian trees follow local forest masting patterns, making productivity variable from year to year, with a great harvest generally taking place every four years or so. Variations in tree and seasonal productivity mean that the durian season in a village lasts three months or more.

The durian tree's multigenerational longevity, the uncertainty of a tree's production schedule, the need to harvest fruit as it falls, and the fruit's high desirability for both subsistence and commerce have all affected harvesting rules, practices, and expectations. First and most important, a coheir must be present at the harvest, that is, when the fruit drops from the tree. This entails building a temporary shelter near the tree in which family members will wait for several weeks. During a productive durian season, much of the village moves up to the hillsides and mountains where the trees that they and their ancestors planted grow. They carry the fruit down the hillside by the basketful or sell fruits to carriers who make daily rounds through the forest gardens. Before the durian harvest, coheirs may have helped clear brush from the base of the tree where the fruits would drop to seal a claim to a harvest share. Claimants might also send a proxy to do this work—a child, a nephew or niece, a wage laborer, or a person with whom they agree to split their share.[27]

The number of trees that a descent group holds affects the allocation of access. When an ancestor planted only a few trees, the descendants are likely to rotate access in a system called *baboros*. Baboros has diverse forms, all of which involve alternating responsibility for waiting until fruits drop. Participants may take turns, each waiting for a few days; some may wait during the days, others the nights, or all may wait together and divide the day's or night's take equally. Babaros can be seen as a short-term temporal zoning strategy. When an ancestor planted lots of trees in many, often scattered, places, it is more likely that the children or grandchildren will divide up access spatially, rotating access to different sites from one year to the next. When trees were planted far from each other, it may be physically impossible for the whole group to harvest all the falling fruit together. Sometimes the same descendant family would harvest a particular plot year after year.

Because it has many meanings, durian crystallized a special ethic of access. Durian trees' longevity has made them into evidence of human settlement: wherever durian trees are found, settlements have existed at one time or another (Padoch and Peters 1993; Sather 1990). Although when people moved away they might plant many kinds of fruit trees in the gaps left by the house structure, they always seem to have planted durian, at least in the last three hundred years of these Salako. Clusters of durian trees provide a history of a village's movement across space and through time—more spatial-temporal zoning. These sites, the former living sites of longhouses, are known as *timawokng*—the Salako word for tembawang (see Padoch and Peters 1993).

The village's social history is connected to its old durian trees by more than geography.[28] Unlike other trees, durians are named after the planters; after something that makes the fruit unique such as the flavor, texture, or shape of durian fruit; or after an unusual geological feature of the landscape near the durian tree, all of which mark its spot in the landscape. Frequently the tree is named after some event that occurred nearby. For example, one durian tree is named for a squabble between two brothers over the division of the fruits, one throwing his share down the hill in disgust at the arrangement. People working on a hot day took water from a spring near another durian tree and named that one to remember their thirst. Social history has thus been inscribed in the landscape. As one farmer said of his ancestors' histories, "We couldn't write their names in a book so we remember them by the trees they planted." Whether or not they have inherited rights in particular trees, villagers share a collective interest in these trees—a claim to the history.

The naming of trees has some parallels with the naming of people—a practice that changes through a person's life. Newborns are not named right away but wait until their personality or an experience suggests a name. A person is not considered "complete" until he or she has had children. Traditionally, parents' names change with the birth of a first child—their childhood name is replaced by the name "Mother of So and So" or "Father of So and So." Similarly, a durian tree is named only after it has begun to bear fruit and that fruit has some sort of characteristics or experience. After having grandchildren, a person's name changes to "Grandparent of So and So." And just as people are called by different names or honorifics in different stages of life, a tree can have different honorifics attached, depending on the planter's status at death or the number of generations that tree has endured.[29]

The durian harvest is an occasion for recognizing family ties. Durian trees are especially enduring representations of kinship because the fruit's superior value and taste require waiting together for maturation, because the trees endure through numerous human generations, and because access to family resources is negotiated through participation in the harvest, as mentioned earlier.[30] To refuse a sibling or a cousin fruit for consumption is considered very bad form and likely bad luck—the trees might not bear fruit ever again. Since a tree's harvest may extend over three to four weeks, groups of siblings, cousins, young married couples, and children wait together to share the fallen fruits on the spot or divide them up for sale. Any durian opened for consumption will be joyfully shared by all present, including passersby and guests of the coheirs, all of whom feel free to comment on the texture, taste, or quality of the fruit. As falling durian fruits know no time of day, waiting in the pondok at night has its own special thrills. The oldest trees are located in the oldest longhouse sites, and harvesters often see or hear spirits while they wait. Few are willing to stay alone in a pondok at night.

The oldest durian trees in Bagak grow in the vicinity of the warriors' ancestral burial grounds. Each one of these trees bears a name, but villagers cannot explain their meanings because the stories disappeared with the people whose ancestors planted them, and they may have been planted before these villagers' ancestors moved to the area now called Bagak. These trees are considered the property of the whole village. When their ancestors first occupied this territory, the durian trees were part of the landscape and provided the new settlers with fruit. For this reason, their fruits have since been slated for newcomers, visitors, or others who lack access to durian, whatever the reason. So strong are the feelings about the role of these trees in the village's social history that, even after they fell or were felled, they were still talked about in the present tense in the 1990s.

Other customs render even privately owned durian a common resource under specific circumstances. For example, anyone can eat another's unguarded durian that happens to fall just at the moment he or she is passing by, whether or not the lucky person has inheritance rights to it. Similarly, if a fruit falls when someone is passing, that person is compelled to share in its immediate consumption. Not making or accepting an offer to share or failing to follow ritual procedure for refusing can lead to fatal accidents, especially poisonous snake bites, cutting oneself with a bush knife, or falling out of fruit trees.[31]

The durian trees' longevity and the complicated inheritance patterns they evoke impose complex constraints on farmers' land-use decisions. Land under trees that live for five to seven generations is clearly taken out of field-crop production for a century or more. In the past, friends and family planted durian trees near one another so that their children's children would wait together for the fruit to drop and remember their ancestors together. The coinheritance of grandparent trees could prevent one cousin from felling the durian trees for individual benefit, whether for access to the land or for wood. However, when one person plants many trees in a single area, he or she ties up whole tracts of land, a practice that is becoming more and more common. Planters bequeath a whole plot—not just individual trees—to children and grandchildren.

These changes in some ways enable people to take advantage of the market. Durian yields are erratic but highly profitable. A good durian harvest can earn the tree owner hundreds of thousands of rupiah in one or two months' time.[32] In 1991, for example, Bagak, like much of the region, had a bumper crop of durian and other fruit. On a single day (February 10) at the end of this season, I counted some ten thousand fruits being sold out of the hamlet (Peluso and Padoch 1995). The following two years were generally poor or mediocre production years. Another bumper crop came in 1994. Of those in the 1991 sample who would venture estimates of the income from durian they sold, their average income was Rp. 338,200, with one person reporting Rp. 1,000,000 in cash returns. As a benchmark, hulled rice cost approximately Rp. 700 per kilogram in the marketplace at the time, compared to a village price of Rp. 300–500 for a single durian. For some families, these windfalls accounted for as much as half of the year's cash income.[33] These sales figures do not account for the durian consumed or given away or for the durian made into savory *tempuyak,* durian preserved in jars. In good years, like 1994, many people reported selling ten or more kilograms of tempuyak at Rp. 1,000–1,500 per kilogram.

Rice and Rubber—A Comparison

Rice and rubber are the other important components of Bagak's physical and social landscape. They are also imbued with specific values affecting the bundles of rights associated with them. In former days, self-sufficiency in food production was highly valued, largely of necessity. Prior to the turn of the twentieth century, minimal restrictions on agricultural expansion, movement of settlements, and the availability of extensive areas of forest for planting hill rice meant that access to land for swiddens was not a constraint. A preference for hill rice, and the capacity to produce a lot of it, meant that people rarely bought rice.

As we have seen, many factors shaped the nature and role of swidden production in Bagak. Contrary to what might be expected, the acquisition of irrigated rice land left behind by the Chinese evicted in 1968 was of minor importance to actual food production at the time. Local people claim that the rice yields were extremely low during the first twenty years after they took over these lands from the Chinese; if anything, people could only produce enough from these fields to feed their families for a couple of months. Many people did not even bother to plant, given the poor yields. Nevertheless, the irrigated fields represented reserve lands for future production—a luxury common when swidden fallows and forest were more accessible. Then, years of bad harvests and the repeated failures of seeds provided by a government anxious to induce swiddeners to plant irrigated rice drove local people to plant traditional varieties (those the Chinese used to plant), and better harvests occurred between 1991 and 1993. However, on average, harvested rice lasted most families only a few months.

How irrigated fields will be inherited is a question the next generation will answer: these fields had been farmed by Chinese farmers for some two hundred years and were not part of the traditional Salako resource reserve.[34] However, initial trends indicate (unsurprisingly) that irrigated plots are sometimes allocated to a single child, sometimes reserved for the person who continues the household, and sometimes divided between two or more children. Instead, swidden fields (fallows) were inherited collectively by the descendants of the forest clearer. As with trees, primary rights in swidden fallows went to the child who continued the parents' household. Like other resources, however, land evoked certain ethics of access. In the case of land for swiddens, the primary rights holder was expected to allow other kin access to old swiddens from old fallows not actively cultivated. Such land was considered "borrowed," and payments were rarely if ever made for the rights of access. The language of borrowing implies an owner or a primary rights holder that differed from the user—even if the user was a grandchild of the clearer.

Borrowing land to plant trees was generally not allowed. It was recognized that this would shift the lines of inheritance and would change the primary use of the land from field crop production. One informant claimed that although much of the hillside was being converted to tree production, Salako adat *required* certain plots be retained for rice production. Borrowing implied a single season of planting, maybe more, but did not imply permanent transfer of rights. Some families tried to control how long a plot was in fallow before it could be recultivated by themselves or borrowers; these rules, however, changed as the population grew and they were less able to move away

Despite these customs and practices, swidden rice production has declined overall and yields from swiddens have declined as swidden sizes have shrunk. In 1990 and 1991, rice from both swiddens and irrigated fields yielded enough to feed the people who had produced it for an average of four months. Only 58 percent of the village sample cultivated swiddens in 1990–91; all who did cultivated one swidden field of an average size of less than 0.40 hectares. In 1994, 41 percent of the villagers planted swiddens averaging 0.42 hectares. From their swiddens in 1991, villagers reported an average yield of approximately 250 kilograms of paddy (unhulled rice, cleaned only of stems). Since irrigated rice yields have varied greatly and tend to be quite low, many people try not to depend on them.

Rubber is the newest component in the local agroforestry system and is the only one of these three major land uses intended specifically and exclusively for sale, since rubber trees have no local use except unproductive trees cut down as firewood. Rubber has none of the social or ritual meaning attached to durian or rice. Neither the community nor descent group forms emotional attachments to rubber gardens. Rubber trees are not named, and the latex is not shared by the descent group. Some of these practices are attributable to the rubber tree's relatively short span of production and life (about forty years). Also rubber cannot be divided except in arrangements between two parties (owner and tapper) for share tapping, and it has no subsistence or ritual or use. More important, rubber is simply a commercial product and lacks an embedded ethic of access. Yet by the 1990s rubber had become the primary source of that regular income people used to purchase food and other subsistence items.

Villagers have access to two kinds of rubber: what they call "local rubber" and high-yielding rubber. About 85 percent of sample households owned some kind of rubber trees in 1991; and, at the time of the survey, 76 percent regularly collected rubber from them. The sample's average yield per collection day was 6.15 kilograms of crudely processed rubber (sheets). People had different methods for collecting latex: some collected it from local rubber trees on alternate days so the tree could produce enough latex, while others collected it every day. Some owned enough trees to have two collection routes, collecting from half their trees on one day and the other half on the next. On very rainy or very dry days, people tended not to tap local rubber. Water from a hard rain could overturn the latex collection cups; and on very hot, dry days, the latex dried up. In 1991, just over a third of the sample owned productive high-yielding trees; average daily yields from these were approximately 6.75 kilograms.[35] The high-yielding varieties have been bred to allow for daily tapping—the latex runs even on very dry days.[36] People tend to collect rubber year-round, with breaks during the rice harvest and highly productive fruit seasons. In a year of unusually good fruit production, rubber generally provided only one-half of the total family cash income from agriculture. In average or poor fruit production years, rubber provided nearly all of it.

When a coheir of a swidden fallow decides to grow rubber, the land is taken out of the cropping cycle for the thirty years or so that rubber takes to mature and produce. Before actually planting the rubber, the cultivator clears the secondary growth (which can be quite dense even after a few years' fallow) in the swidden fallow. Rights to these rubber trees inhere to the planter and his or her household. If the planter dies, rubber gardens generally pass to a single child or, if the planter had many trees, to several. Most people talked about rubber as a short-term use of the land. Unlike durian, rubber trees will die or stop producing within the span of an adult's lifetime (twenty to forty years). In principle, when a rubber garden stopped producing, the land was to be returned to the descent group's pool. The rights to clear and replant it would be revested in the grandchildren and great-grandchildren of the original forest clearer, just like any swidden fallow.

In practice, many swidden fallows planted in rubber have been effectively privatized. Even if the land were to return to the descent group after the rubber trees stopped producing, the thirty to forty years over which rubber occupied land of the descent group constitutes a much longer time than that taken by rice and vegetables or banana or other fallow vegetation. Planting rubber in effect altered the temporal zoning of land rights.

The financial dependence on rubber may explain its importance and popularity in the local landscape. As it became clear that rubber was replacing rice as the main way of providing for a family's subsistence, it seemed to become more difficult for a person holding primary rights to swidden fallows to deny a kinsperson access to those fallows for growing rubber. Thus, while no particular ethic of access attaches to latex and rubber trees, there is one for land on which the trees are planted. The notion of subsistence rights underlying the attachment of rights to land seemed to prevail. The social relations centered on rubber, therefore, were configured via the property rights and ethics associated with rice and land. Associations with fruit trees except durian also played a role. Like fruit, rubber lasts a long time and ties up resource access across considerable zones of space and time. But like land planted in rice, land under rubber produces something—latex—that is controlled by only one person or household. Thus while rubber comes from trees, its year-round availability and its replacement of rice in many swiddens fallows make it, in practice, much more like rice than fruit. Rubber has indeed replaced rice as the daily "staple" of the household.

In sum, over some sixty years, managed forests of economic trees have been gradually taking over the swidden fallows of Bagak. In the past, such reforestation would have led people to move to a new spot to farm rice and continue to collect tree products. But the new political and economic setting has made village migration impossible.

Not all tree species have as great a significance in the local economy or the social fabric as rubber and durian. But the two are different, and they differ as well from rice production. Rubber rarely stays in the ground through more than two generations; it is planted exclusively for commerce and has no use value, but it has become the basis of the household economy. On the other hand, the most valued and valuable of the fruits, durian, lasts five to seven human generations and is both locally consumed and sold. Durian fruit and trees have deep social meanings to descendants of the planters and to the community as a whole, constituting perhaps the most important visible evidence of the community's settlement history. Hill rice, the main product of swidden fields, is in decline and may disappear entirely from this landscape except as the occasional interim use between generations of economic trees. How irrigated rice land will fit into this picture remains to be seen.

Commodification and the Individuation of Rights in Durian

> Selling your durian trees is like selling your own grandfather.
>
> (Pak Po'on, Bagak Sahwa)

The market boom in fruit and the increasing reforestation of the landscape have led to two major changes in durian management. First, many families have permanently allocated panene'an trees to individuals. Second, people are opening up tracts of land—old fallows, old rubber gardens, and sometimes the edges of the nature reserve—to plant durian and other fruit and to explicitly claim the land for their descendants. Yet the trend toward individualization of durian rights is not absolute, as households and extended families vary in the types of tree tenure arrangements that they maintain, and some descent groups still rotate access to fruiting trees among their members.

We have seen that social and biological factors shape the distribution of access to descent group trees. Four considerations seem to weigh heavily on distribution decisions: the number of trees that the descent group holds, the relative yields of various trees, the productivity of the trees allocated in previous years, and the other resources to which each of the coheirs has access. When market demand is as great as it is for durian, which must be sold immediately after it falls, and when market access is easy, all members of a descent group worry about the smallest wastage. An individual's available time to harvest fruit becomes more important to allocation decisions.

At the time of year when access rights are discussed, many trees' actual yields are unknown. People talk in August through October about the winds, the flowers, and the relative dryness in relation to the upcoming durian season. Yet these signs can deceive, and actual yields may diminish through unforeseen circumstances, such as heavy winds or rain. Durian yields fluctuate each year, although some trees produce nearly every year. Usually older trees with many branches produce a great deal of fruit, but at some point their productivity wanes. Some years nearly the whole village has highly productive harvests; others produce nothing for anyone; still other years offer bumper harvests in mountain gardens and nothing in the flatlands. Even within the same section of village forest, variation is common. Productivity depends both on the site's characteristics and on the owners' management (see Padoch 1994). Despite attempts by families to balance access to the fruit of panene'an trees, some villagers find they have no fruit to sell in certain years.

The changes in durian management have affected temporal and spatial landscape zones. Temporal changes are most evident in the distribution of third-generation or older durian trees because the third generation is the first that in principle holds the rights to fruit in common. In

1991, more than one-third of the sample families reported having private rights to panene'an trees, citing reasons such as grandparents and parents wanting to avoid disputes among children and grandchildren. Discussions with sample villagers in 1996 indicated that 68 percent had privatized all their panene'an trees, but only 42 percent of sample households said they were the private rights holders—meaning that in the course of privatization, 26 percent had lost access to panene'an trees. Only 12 percent of the sample said that they had not privatized any panene'an trees.

Privatization of trees also had spatial effects, imparting different values to land according to the number, productivity, and value of its trees. Increasingly, people cleared fallows with the intention of planting some kind of forest garden immediately after the rice crop: some 47 percent of those who planted swiddens in 1993 and 42 percent of those in 1994 planted trees in the fallows immediately after the rice and vegetable harvest. While rubber, densely planted to facilitate latex collection, secured some sort of territory for an individual or a household, a durian tree, which used to be planted next to others' individual trees, only tied up small spaces for multiple generations of descendants. At the individual or household level, durian's space was more of a temporal zone; the spatial zoning was longhouse-wide, as trees were planted when people moved away in the spaces once occupied by family apartments. However, as durian trees begin to be planted in swidden fallows of one-third to one hectare, the trees' temporal zone has come to occupy larger spaces. They are still not planted as a monocrop—they tend to be clustered with langsat, rambutan, or other fruit trees—but the durian's longevity and value, as explained above, make it dominant.

Grandparent durians usually are assigned to individuals in three ways: the descent group may agree to distribute its commonly held trees among individual members, a grandparent may designate specific trees or clusters of trees to individual grandchildren, or individuals may usurp the descent group's authority and assume de facto possession of a grandfather tree, usually by planting young trees around the panene'an trees or simply by building a shelter there year after year during the durian harvest, without consulting the group. This is essentially a territorialization strategy (Peluso 1993b) but one carried forth with the descent group's implicit consent. In several cases where this had happened, other family members explained the group's failure to exercise their collective claims as an effort to avoid public discord. It may also be seen as a more general acceptance of individualization or privatization. The appropriation of descent group–held swidden fallows and fields by planting plots of rubber through one or more production cycles is part of a similar trend.

Individualization of descent group rights is not universal, though it is a major trend in Bagak. Some families insist that the grandchildren and great-grandchildren of a tree planter are violating important customary principles by privatizing access to grandparent trees (Peluso and Padoch 1995). Indeed, when I first started asking about the privatization of panenen'an trees, several of my key informants insisted I was wrong. They refused to believe it—until people concerned confirmed it.

Whether or not descent groups have individualized rights to grandparent trees, nearly all villagers express the feeling that individual control of trees makes management easier and avoids potential disputes, suggesting that the past saw many more disputes than are discussed at present. Perhaps desire for a certain independence from the group motivated the planting of one's own trees. Although they did not give up their rights in the trees, they took themselves out of the descent group's rotation of commonly held resources. When their children established households in the future, they could still make claims on that rotation.

Among the families following the old practices, panene'an trees still serve two types of redistributive purposes. The first type is a dynamic, ongoing redistribution of access to village or descent group resources between age groups. Young couples had always depended on panene'an until their parents' or their own durian trees bore fruit. The second type is a redistribution that aids the weaker, less diligent, or less clever farmers, who benefit from continued access to the trees and fruit of their ancestors. Yet lifetime dependence on the fruits of the ancestors comes at a price. Most villagers regard such long-term dependence as both a sign of laziness and a handicap to children and grandchildren. And, more practically, today's farmer who fails to plant trees deprives future grandchildren of fruits to enjoy.

Durian has long been a commodity sold by Bagak villagers and their predecessors who lived in the mountains before the establishment of the nature reserve. The commodification of durian thus began before the paving of the road and the growth of nearby cities. Yet these earlier commodifications did not transform the landscape or the ethics of access to durian and farmland in such radical ways—not until it became politically impossible for the village to move as a unit.

In some ways, rubber began the major landscape transformation. The ecology and biology of rubber—particularly its capacity to produce year-round for market—gave it an edge over seasonal durian or other fruits. Chinese farmers were producing rubber in gardens along the Singkawang-Bengkayang road between the early twentieth century and their eviction in 1967. Salako tended to mix their rubber with fruit trees, but more rubber trees were needed to produce enough latex for the household's needs. Rubber provided the necessary cash for the family's subsistence when sedentarization and political-economic change caused the decline in rice production. Durian harvests, if they occurred at all, were limited to one time of the year; the fruit could not be stored except as tempuyak, a preserve with much lower value than fresh durian.

The increasing ecological and economic importance of trees in the landscape has increased the value of the land on which they are planted. Whoever cleared forest for swiddens always obtained for themselves and their descendants rights to that land in perpetuity; but the planting of trees has a different effect.[37] Although it was not uncommon in the past for someone to plant a cluster of three to six fruit trees (*kompokng*) and thus to occupy a piece of land, the notion that a garden (*kabotn*) consisting of a relatively large unit of land would be valuable because fruit trees are planted there is new.

Because of the spatial and temporal dimensions of its production, rubber was the first tree crop to transform land rights. It influenced later processes for planting and claiming garden land under durian. Once rubber became the subsistence base for virtually the whole village, other changes in the local and regional political ecology led to the spread of durian. Durian, other fruits, and local rubber varieties grew well together in mixed gardens (people sometimes referred to them as "friends"). The burgeoning urban markets for fruit, the village's location on a main road, the propensity of their ancestors to plant durian, and the perseverance (and luck) of the village leaders who refused to contract village land to encroaching plantations (which would have meant cutting at least some durian trees) have given Bagak durian a premium place in the market. Moreover, durian production is becoming a territorial endeavor.

Conclusion

The biological properties of the trees and crops in this West Kalimantan landscape have intersected with resource tenure practices there to produce change. The case advances our understanding of landscape processes, for the experience of Bagak confounds the stereotypical interpretation of "forest conversion" and agricultural intensification in the tropics. The usual evolutionary model assumes a natural forest that is cut and burned for field crop production. Intensification of agricultural production is seen to involve increasing labor or capital and technological inputs per unit of land and an emphasis on commercial or subsistence field agriculture. These intensifications are generally linked to increases in population and sedentarization (e.g., Geertz 1963; Boserup 1981; Dove 1985) and are often imposed by state authorities. In contrast to this pattern, as population and sedentarization increase in this West Kalimantan village, villagers are moving away from field crops toward more extensive production from forests and agroforests. The villagers' extensive and intensive tree planting was stimulated not only by the farm land scarcity brought by enforced sedentarization and their loss of legal rights to ancestral lands appropriated for a nature reserve; it was also engendered by the increased market access that resulted from road construction, urbanization, and the improved market conditions.

These contemporary management activities, in fact, build on traditional practices, preferences, and property rights, even though sedentarization and the introduction of new tree crops altered both the contexts and effects of these practices. As a result, the composition of the landscape and the balance between private and group rights to the resources in it are changing. Bagak's case strongly suggests that forest products—not unmanaged extraction or deforestation—have been important elements of landscape management here for hundreds of years, even though the meanings and values of these resources may differ from those of many years ago. This indicates that the "extractive economies" literature, which tends to underplay purposive forest and agroforestry management, is excessively negative (see, e.g., Bunker 1985; cases in Nepstad and Schwartzman 1992; Dove 1996, but compare Hecht, May, and Anderson 1988; Hecht and Posey 1989; Padoch 1994; Michon and Michon 1994).

The unintended outcomes of government interventions at Bagak are

also surprising. Government land management policies, sedentarization, changes in regional markets, and national political events initially
caused hardship for Bagak: new sorts of spatial land-use zones arose
and legal and illegal land uses got redefined, often bringing widespread
degradation and poverty. Bagak villagers, however, created a new and
well-managed social and ecological landscape. They built on components of their earlier land-use system (mixed fruit forests), adding other
economic components (rubber gardens), reinterpreting access rights to
the nature reserve after their lands were expropriated, and altering
modes of access to various local resources and land in response to political-economic change. The new, forested landscape had new temporal
and spatial zones of property rights, a product of explicit and implicit
negotiations between local residents and governments.

Since they were forced to move down the mountain, every generation
of villagers has contested the boundaries of the nature reserve in new
and different ways, yet the conditions of exclusion have always helped
shape the forms of contestation and resistance. Resistance is thus in a
dynamic tension with the forms of control. Forced by the Dutch to
abandon their "traditional" landscape, the Salako had to move from living in longhouses to single-family homes, albeit often ones large enough
to accommodate some extended family members. Similarly, villagers
were slowly pushed by the changing context to reconceptualize both the
extent of their territory and the importance of land rights rather than
rights in trees or crops. The current Bagak landscape thus serves as a living record of a village's history of conflict and negotiation with government, with thousands of former Chinese residents, and with those
settled in and around the relatively new village borders.

It is not unusual to recognize that prices, policies, and legal systems
affect formal property rights. At Bagak, clearly a tree's biological characteristics also influence property rights. The long-lived durian trees'
social value extends beyond economics, biology, and even the claims of
the tree planter's descendants, because the entire village views the trees
as markers of settlement history and territorial extent. The shorter life of
the rubber tree, and its production exclusively for cash, brought different kinds of changes to the distribution of private and commonly held
land across the landscape. Thus Bagak illustrates the relationship
between nature and cultural or political economic practice.

More importantly, however, this case shows how a historically grounded set of meanings attached to a resource can critically mediate both exclusionary and incentive-based rights structures. Property rights in durian trees multiplied with each succeeding generation. Although some rights holders had greater control over these resources than others, the notion that all descendants retain *some* claims to fruit contradicts the stereotyped linear procession of property relations from open access to common property to private property (Bromley 1989).

Although intensification of land management and improvement of market access have driven privatization, the social meanings of these resources and their links to the villagers' collective and individual histories have created a tension, and some people resist the divisive aspects of commodification. Yet this ethics of access could not survive all pressures. Around the time of the agrarian unrest in the 1960s and 1970s, a new ethnicized or racialized ethic of access was brewing.[38]

Zoning has both temporal and spatial aspects. These are best illustrated by the analysis of property rights in long-living trees but can also be understood or analyzed through an examination of the larger set of resource tenure arrangements that people are engaged in at different points in their lives. The ethic of access worked to regulate this temporal zoning as well: through everyday practices, the ethic shaped the redistribution of access between various age groups.

Bagak teaches us that dynamic processes of resource access and landscape construction are more rewarding concepts than notions of property and landscapes as inert objects. If landscape is an artifact of human consciousness and therefore subject to multiple interpretations, visions, and memories (Schama 1995), it becomes ever more important to understand how the meanings and value of landscape shape access to it, as well as landscape's very social physical forms.

Epilogue: Ten Years Later

Revision, ten years after writing this essay, afforded a chance to consider the ways subsequent developments in Bagak and its environs corresponded to the patterns in property rights and resource access originally recorded. This naturally created profound challenges, for two major political changes occurred after the fieldwork that informed this essay. These affected the nature of access to resources in the Bagak landscape, as well as the ability of local people, journalists, and researchers to talk about those and earlier changes. Here I can address only a few of the new developments.

Indonesia's political regime was transformed in 1998, with the fall of President Suharto, the dictator who had held Indonesia under his thumb for thirty-two years. Since then, the freedom of speech that suddenly characterized everyday life transformed field research in Indonesia. Freedom of speech changed what could be said about current and past events, as well as what could be researched and how it could be written up. When this essay was originally written (1994 through mid-1996), talking openly or writing about ethnic conflict was forbidden by law. This made the collection of social history a tightrope walk, particularly in areas where there had been political violence. In some regions, like Sambas in West Kalimantan, certain groups were under constant suspicion and surveillance. Indonesian police had called the district a place where "the Chinese problem" warranted formal and informal policing. The pursuit of any in-depth research on the few rural Chinese still living where I worked, including research on their turbulent history, posed security and ethical problems for me as well as anyone who agreed to interviews. This prevented me from collecting detailed oral accounts of the evictions and their effects on landholding patterns discussed briefly previously. Only indirectly (e.g., through questions about the sources of the lands held by Bagak residents surveyed) could I put together a partial picture of ethnic divisions in village land use and property before the "Chinese Demonstrations." When Suharto lost power and Reformasi took root, this situation changed dramatically. Moreover, in 2003, Mary Somers Heidhues's book on the history of the West Kalimantan Chinese was published.

The second change was brought on by the two major instances of ethnic violence that wracked the western districts of West Kalimantan in 1996–97 and 1999, culminating in the forced eviction or flight of virtually all Madurese from rural Sambas and Pontianak districts. Only a few Madurese families had lived in the village of Bagak Sahwa, and I knew of only one Madurese man who had married a Dayak woman in the Bagak hamlet on which my research focused. Thousands more Madurese who lived in surrounding villages, however, were forced to leave. Both violent upheavals were inscribed on the landscape through racialized redistributions of land, a development that has had a deep effect. Without going into detail here, a couple of claims from my 1996 essay deserve reconsideration in the wake of the violence and political changes.[39]

Ethnic Violence, State Power, and Property Rights

The history of the Dayak-Madurese violence is complex, but the longer-term history of the former Chinese residents discussed previously helps to explain it.[40] In the 1950s, the early years after the formation of the Republic of Indonesia, descendants of these early Chinese occupants continued to work their families' smallholdings. Since some Chinese residents of West Kalimantan were citizens and others were not, a confusing variety of relations with the new Indonesian state prevailed (Coppel 1983; Heidhues 2003). The unclear legal status of their land was confused by the changing political situation. But the independent nation-state wanted to eliminate the legal pluralism associated with colonialism and feudalism (Lev 1985). The Basic Agrarian Law was passed in 1960, changing the legally pluralist land laws based on racial identities to a unitary legal system that was meant to provide access to land for any citizen of Indonesia. In practice, there was little time to work out its actual implementation in West Kalimantan or to figure out which of the thousands of Chinese smallholdings, many clustered in rural Singkawang and Sambas, could be issued titles, which would require citizenship.

Other national-level concerns pushed aside these everyday concerns. From 1963 to 1966, West Kalimantan province was a primary staging area for the Confrontation with Malaysia. Communists and other insurgents from Sarawak were trained by the Indonesian Armed Forces in West Kalimantan—at the time the Indonesian Communist Party was a legal and active party. However, in 1966, General Suharto rose to power and ended the Confrontation with Malaysia. At the same time he initiated an internal war on the newly minted enemies of the state, the very communists who had fought for Indonesia during the Confrontation with Malaysia.[41] Anti-Chinese violence, in large part orchestrated by anticommunist Indonesian troops stationed in West Kalimantan, struck the province in late 1967. As mentioned previously, the upshot of the violence was the eviction of between fifty thousand and one hundred thousand people from rural West Kalimantan, most of whom had lived in Sambas, Pontianak, and Sanggau districts. Most were forced to move to urban centers in West Kalimantan or elsewhere in Indonesia.

The Suharto government claimed that the land of the evicted Chinese was state land, under lease, and therefore should return to state administration. Practically speaking, this was difficult, if not impossible, as hundreds of people in the districts involved were claiming the land—as troops had told them they could and should in the buildup to the evictions. Because the government wanted the locals' continued support in the search for "communist guerrillas" still hiding in the forests, it issued special certificates—but not formal land titles—to verify that local people had been given rights to these appropriated lands.[42]

In Bagak, the experience with the newly acquired irrigated rice land was mixed. Some farmed it; some tried and gave up because it required more labor or capital than they had available; some did not farm it. At the same time, migrants were streaming into Sambas, both spontaneously and sponsored by Indonesian government resettlement programs. Outside Bagak, some of the extensive lowlands were converted to rubber plantations for transmigration (government-sponsored migration) projects. Spontaneous migrants, many of them from Madura or Madurese from East Java, came to fill the jobs opening up as development proceeded, especially in road building, construction, and farming. They also sought land to farm, to graze cattle, or to build houses or shops on. In what seemed a lucky accident, those from Java and Madura were most familiar with sawah cultivation and less inclined to swidden farming. Some of these people bought, rented, or borrowed land from Bagak villagers who did not want to work their sawah.[43] Still, in the 1970s not all Madurese were newcomers to the region. Some had come as early as the turn of the century. Some of these, in Bagak and elsewhere, were allocated land after the Chinese evictions, and some of the newcomers bought or borrowed land from their Madurese friends and family who preceded them. In Bagak, most (if not all) Madurese landholders had converted their initial land occupation certificates to formal land titles and had strong legal documentation of their holdings

Violence erupted twice in the late 1990s, once for several months and once a few weeks. In 1996–97 it involved Dayaks and Madurese; in 1999, Malays and Madurese were first involved, with Dayaks joining the fight against Madurese later. While people on all sides were killed and lost property, Madurese collectively suffered the most. Tens of thousands of Madurese fled or were expelled by Dayaks and Malays, not only from the rural areas of Sambas and Pontianak districts but from some of the key urban areas as well (except Pontianak, the capital of the province). The expulsions of the Madurese, like those of the Chinese thirty years earlier, were followed by the claiming and reclaiming of the land left behind, which had now experienced two violent repossessions.

Madurese who fled in 1996–97 were given grants and subsidies to rebuild their houses. Yet the conditions prevailing after the violence of 1999 have precluded their return.[44] In some areas, exiles have little hope of getting compensation for lost land or other resources (e.g., cattle and crops) and property.[45] This was not the case in Bagak, where some Madurese had bought land to farm or to build houses on and sold the land when they left. On a return visit in 2004, I was told that these Madurese had sold their land to a variety of buyers—to private buyers, the forest service, and the local church group.

In sum, in this section of the province, violence has a long history, often involving government provocateurs (Heidhues 2003). My short history of landscape change was constrained by the New Order's policies, sometimes without my recognizing it, and was therefore less engaged with reflections on ethnic subjectivities in the regional landscape—or the racialized nature of the landscape. For instance, after the Chinese expulsions, government officials changed hundreds of place names and maps to eliminate or "Indonesianize" as many Chinese or Chinese-sounding names as possible. Salatiga on the road to Anjungan is a famous example of this; once, in the heyday of Chinese agricultural achievement, it had sported a Chinese name. The maps that I was using during my years of field visits, therefore, had themselves been "cleansed" and used as part of the government effort to rewrite history. This practice was later repeated in the aftermath of the Dayak-Madurese and Malay-Dayak-Madurese violence when locals changed the names of places where they had evicted whole villages of Madurese, including Salatiga.

Violence, the Market, and Ethics of Access

The local history of violence and its aftereffects brings up the question of how race or ethnicity cuts into the "ethic of access." Does such an "ethic" only apply to fellow Salako or other Dayaks, and, if not, how could such violence ever take place? I think that ethnicity or race alone does not explain how and under what conditions such an ethic works.

Rather, both the nature of the resource—its commodity or use values, its ecological properties, its meanings, its engagements in local histories—and the social relations among people seeking access are much more relevant to any invocation of ethics of access. These ethics of access are not general principles about living in the world but represent only specific parts of larger—and shifting—property and access relations.

In Bagak, anyone who wished to lease a tree or set of trees could do so—lessors during the years I did research were of Chinese, Malay, Salako or other Dayak, Javanese, Sundanese, Madurese, and even Sumatran backgrounds. These were commercial transactions, like buying and selling fruit, also unconstrained by racial identity per se. Locals liked to talk about how many different people came and enjoyed Bagak durian. Likewise, access for consumption or subsistence was not explicitly ethnicized or racialized. When someone without local family came to visit and live in the village, they were included also through temporary access to durian trees at harvest time. If they married in, they enjoyed a family's grandparent trees. If none was available or the visitor was a trader, a government official, or a visiting researcher, certain trees were set aside specifically for them. Of course, the closer a family relationship or friendship, the more likely they shared access (and management). Similarly, though an ethic of access enabled someone who had moved to a different settlement to come and enjoy the durian from a tree planted by a great-grandfather or great-uncle, it rarely occurred. Vicariously, however, the existence of these distant trees and their storied fruits was valued. This was evident in the ways people referred to them: "His grandfather planted durian in that [faraway] place." "He still has a *tembawang* there." "His durian is originally from that tembawang."

Ethics of access applied primarily to resources for consumption or subsistence. Over the time when I observed directly, and likely for much of the historical period addressed in the essay, ethics of access pertained mostly to fruit, particularly durian. Practices and ideas associated with this ethic enabled people who had no fruit at a particular time in their lives, or in a slow season, or when they were newcomers or visitors to gain access to the harvest of the most celebrated fruit in these managed forests. Norms about whether someone could share in the joyful, on-the-spot consumption of a freshly fallen fruit included anyone who happened to be passing when a durian fell, a sign—perhaps from the ancestor who planted the tree, if not from the tree itself—that the passerby was being invited to share this fruit and to simultaneously share in all or some of the meanings that eating it together with a group of people could have. Yet even with durian, these practices or this ethic did not—in Bagak at least[46]—extend to automatic shares in commercial harvests. Access to durian was rotated within descent groups among siblings and cousins and grandchildren whether they intended to sell the fruit or consume it. The rotation was guided by ethics of access that inhered to the descent group, born of the descent group's historical practices and the number and productivity of the grandparent trees that they had inherited. If someone who gained access to a grandfather tree collected enough fruits to sell, they were free to do so. Durian, thus, could be consumed or sold. If the arrangement was between kin, the end use might not even be considered. If it was a transaction involving the visitors' trees, the arrangements also did not matter. People would give pause, however, to allocate long-term access to a commercial user of a tree without payment of a fee—whether that person was Chinese, Madurese, Javanese, or Dayak.

Consider, in comparison, that the same kind of an ethic of access seemed not to apply to rubber, the other major local tree crop in the 1990s. Rubber differed from durian because its exclusive use was commercial. It was not just the dominance of exchange value, though it was in part the *absence* of consumption or subsistence uses. Moreover, the pattern of planting rubber in small plots, with many trees close to each other to facilitate the harvest of latex, generated a different geography of production, even when these plots were small and mixed in or surrounded by fruit trees. The land was therefore tied up in a different way. When durian was more frequently planted in plots—never as a monocrop but as a dominant tree in a proscribed area, a former swidden—for mostly commercial purposes, the claim on the land involved also changed qualitatively.

Ethics both affected and were affected by shifting relations between private and collective property rights. Rights of access to the fruits did not permit any individual to cut grandparent trees without the consent of the descent group or the person in charge of the tree. But even beyond the bounds of descent group affiliations, or even village residence, ethics of access enabled the sharing of resources, particularly for consumption.

In this sense, the ethic of access to fruit for consumption in Bagak in the 1990s can be compared to other moral economies involving capitalist transformations and access to food for subsistence (Thompson 1963; Scott 1976; Greenough 1982; Watts 1983). The difference here is that fruit is not a staple food and loss of access to it is less likely to lead to starvation than loss of access to grains. Further, though it is about consumption, in Bagak the ethic is also about social inclusion and historical memory and about maintaining a well-balanced spiritual environment—specifically avoiding the unstable and dangerous state known as *kemponan*. Thus both the nature of the resource and the social relations that constitute its production affect the "ethics" of resource management and allocation practices.

Were land disputes more likely to lead or be connected to violence than disputes over access to trees? Ethics of access to land—specifically to swidden land—used to be more important, but again, given the recognition of land rights in perpetuity to forest clearers, these were ethics that operated primarily *within* descent groups. Borrowing land was generally a transaction between cousins or other kin within a geographically limited space, save when a descent group was uninterested in farming a piece of land or when immigrants sought it.[47] Disputes could occur over different interpretations of the agreement by which land was loaned or rented, whether or not it involved family. But these small-scale disputes, while sometimes bitter and protracted, seemed not to produce violence, at least in Bagak. Thus access to land was not enough in and of itself to explain the violence and violent evictions on the scale discussed previously, even though land redistribution was an effect of the ethnic wars. But this area was not an area of land shortage, and cultivation of wet rice was not a priority for Salako. Speaking in retrospect, people claimed the violence and evictions were about government or cultural politics rather than access to land.

In Bagak, Madurese had not taken over all the Chinese land left behind—and there were over a hundred hectares. Once the Chinese were gone, local Dayaks and others claimed some of their land. Because of inequities in the ways land was claimed at first, some large plots were redistributed by a new village head. In an interview many years later, a village leader explained his actions by invoking a kind of ethic of access—the need for everyone in the village who wanted some of that valuable land to get it—since they had all gone through the traumas of the evictions. He also gave land to Madurese, Malays, and Salako from outside the village who had once moved away.

Some Dayaks inadvertently referred to an ethic of access in discussing misunderstandings around some of the land transactions with Madurese—in those cases when land was not actually sold. The lending of land, for example, is seen as a means of giving someone a chance to subsist while they develop new ways of making a living. As with access to fruit from grandparents' trees, access to borrowed land should not go on forever. One man said, "We let them come and farm, to borrow land, but they did not respect their hosts; they took over more and more land; they did not respect our ways." While neither this view nor an ethic of access can explain or justify the massive violence that occurred, it demonstrates in a small way a style of thinking about resource access that can have much larger effects and implications.

E. P. Thompson (1975) famously called the sources of conflict over access to land, forests, and wildlife in eighteenth- and nineteenth-century England struggles over "power and property right." The people whom I studied in West Kalimantan are similarly—and endlessly, it seems—engaged in struggles in which power and property right are constantly being reinvented. The memories of earlier struggles are inscribed within their landscapes, and I have been engaged in an ongoing process of deciphering the clues that I find scattered about. The search has strengthened my belief that present and past constitute each other through the shifting sands of memories, claims, and practice.

NOTES

1. The term *nenek* in the Salako language is used to refer to both grandmother and grandfather. *Nek* refers to a parent or grandparent, while *Si* is used for someone who died young without having children.

2. See also Peluso 1992a.

3. Most of the data reported here were collected from in-depth interviews and participant observation gathered when I stayed in the village, on six separate occasions, between August 1990 and April 1996. I conducted further research on several two to three week visits from 1997–2004.

4. These administrative geographies have been changed since 2000. Bagak Sahwa is now part of East Singkawang, a section of the administrative city of Singkawang and thus technically not a part of either Tujuhbelas or Sambas. Sam-

bas district has been divided into two *kabupaten,* and just to the east of Bagak's border the new district of Bengkayang begins.

5. I spell Salako (the ethnic group) and Selakau (the river) differently because of differences in practice. The Salako claim that their origins lie along the Selakau River. On Indonesian maps, the river is called Selakau.

6. The Confrontation with Malaysia was a period of conflict between Malaysia (mostly Sarawak) and Indonesia (mostly the provinces of Kalimantan) that lasted from approximately 1963 to 1966.

7. Or rice mixed with cassava and maize.

8. This is part of the Program Pembangunan Karet Rakyat (People's Rubber Development Program, or PPKR), in which smallholders are allocated one hectare or more of land and took loans of Rp. 4–6 million (US$2,000–$3,000) to plant rubber trees that would yield within five years. These 296 hectares include the more than 100 hectares that partially burned. These trees were largely planted as required by the World Bank in neat monocultural rows 2.5 by 8 meters apart. Some farmers, however, have innovated by planting the occasional pineapple plant or *cempedak* tree in the midst of their rubber.

9. Since 1990, many of these fallows have been planted to fruit and rubber.

10. A Dutch map published in 1890 shows a longhouse called "Bakak" as well as two other longhouses, Pasar and Gambar, in these hills. Three longhouses big enough to be mapped indicate a long residence. Oral histories collected by Simon Takdir (unpublished paper, 1998) place the Salako in these hills as early as the 1820s.

11. See also Padoch and Peters 1993; Padoch 1994; Sather 1990.

12. Hakka is a subgroup of the Han Chinese who migrated to West Borneo primarily from mainland Guangdong. Their original places of origin in China are disputed (Yuan 2000). In China, as in Borneo, they tended to be agricultural pioneers: "sometimes with the help of local . . . people, [they] farmed less fertile areas, and migrated readily to new sites—hence the name Hakka, which means 'guest people'" (Heidhues 2003, 31). Hakka also refers to their "dialect" group, which in 1930 included more than half the Chinese in West Borneo but earlier constituted a strong majority in the region. See Heidhues 2003, 37–43, for comparative descriptions of Hakka in West Borneo in China.

13. On kongsis, Chinese mining and farming, see Jackson 1970; Yuan 2000; and Heidhues 2003.

14. These lease rights were called *Huur Overencomst* (or H.O.). Some twenty-five thousand of these were recorded in Sambas in the 1920s (Cator 1936; Heidhues, 2003). Still, the reach of the colonial state in these directly ruled, so-called Chinese districts was only hegemonic on paper, and thousands more hectares of unrecorded land must have been under cultivation by the tens of thousands of Chinese farmers in Western Borneo (Ozinga 1940; Cator 1936).

15. Tradition has it that local Malays were first to acquire and plant it, but Chinese production soon surpassed Malay production and jump-started Dayak production.

16. The Dutch planned to let the watershed go back to "undisturbed" forest. This colonial intervention differed from previous ones: the Chinese had moved into a part of the landscape—the lowland—that was not at the time exploited by the people of Bagak. Similarly, when the Malays exacted tribute in the form of forest products, they did not move into the village and take over the territory within which these products grew. Even the missionaries were not interested in evicting local people from lands on which they depended psychologically and physically. For the first time, these Dayaks were squeezed between state-appropriated and controlled land and Chinese cultivators in the irrigated lowlands.

17. The road had apparently been widened early on to facilitate Dutch military operations against Chinese mining kongsis in the first half of the nineteenth century and, after falling into disrepair, was cleared again to facilitate European settlement for plantation production. The latter effort lasted only about fifteen years at the end of the nineteenth century.

18. This contradicts the case study presented by Dove (1988), who maintains that swidden production was a means of resisting external control. Perhaps because of Bagak's proximity to the market, external access was considered less important.

19. In particular, attacks on Sarawak were launched from West Kalimantan, with this part of the province a major staging ground. The area became highly militarized between 1963 and 1966. With the fall of Sukarno and the rise of Suharto, the Confrontation with Malaysia also ended. However, violence against alleged enemies of the new regime manifested itself in a pogrom against the Chinese. See Coppel 1983; Heidhues 2003; Peluso and Harwell 2001; Davidson and Kammen 2002.

20. Social and political relations at that time have been difficult to reconstruct from fieldwork and oral histories alone. Moreover, research on ethnic conflict was strongly discouraged by the Indonesian government. Without archives from this period, it is impossible to tell the nuanced story this tumultuous period in local social relations deserves.

21. In reality, the bank (People's Bank of Indonesia, or BRI) owned the trees until the loans were paid off—a legality that benefited local people when more than half the trees burned in the 1994 fire.

22. The basal area is the area of a cross-section of trees at breast height.

23. In Western philosophy, of course, John Locke saw labor as the critical creator and confirmation of property rights.

24. This pattern is common among many Dayak subgroups throughout Kalimantan and Sarawak: Swidden lands cleared by the parents or other previous residents and the cash crop trees they planted or protected go to the child who tends the parents. In some Borneo societies, land and other resources are instead returned to the community's common pool when the household heads (husband and wife) pass away (Appell 1970). Rubber trees do not usually last more than two generations and therefore are not subject to the complex inheritance rights associ-

ated with fruit trees, especially durian. See also Sather 1990; Geddes 1954; Schneider 1973; Pringle 1970; Dove 1985; Weinstock 1983.

25. While *yang kuasa* can also be translated as "the one with the power" or "the powerful one," the connotation of this translation is too strong.

26. In this, children can be said to have specific access rights to fruit, as in 1930s Southern California, where a "child's culture" assigned claims on fruit growing in people's yards to children (Aschmann 1988).

27. See Peluso and Padoch 1995.

28. Peter Brosius (n.d.) makes a similar point for the Penan of Sarawak, whose conception of the landscape revolves around the social-historical events that took place along rivers, forest paths between rivers, at the base of certain trees, and so on.

29. See note 1.

30. Illipe nut trees in some areas also represent common ancestry to coheirs but because most trees only fruit in cycles of four years or more and because the nuts are not consumed en masse and on the spot, the experiences (and the memories) are qualitatively different. Illipe nut trees are not named. The low prices of illipe nuts, the uncertainty of their markets, and the usefulness of their wood for construction have caused many Bagak villagers to cut them down. Few illipe nut trees remain on village lands or in the buffer zone between the village and the reserve.

31. This state of danger is called *kemponan* and is commonly accepted throughout Borneo as an outcome of refusing any food, cigarettes, or a betel chew. Individuals may also be put into the state of kemponan if they go into someone's house and are not offered such refreshment (Robert Sulis Ridu, personal communication, 1996).

32. In the mid-1990s, one U.S. dollar equaled approximately two thousand rupiah.

33. Income from other fruits—particularly langsat and angkaham—varied and was not reported systematically.

34. Some Salako families had tried making small sawahs near the Bagak River, but even today they often lie fallow because they require much labor and produce small returns.

35. For various reasons most participants in the scheme have not attained the productivity goals.

36. In heavy rain it is impractical to tap even these high-yielding varieties of rubber trees.

37. Land rights for forest clearance and swidden cultivation are well documented for Borneo; see, for example, Geddes 1954; Freeman 1955; Appell 1970; Weinstock 1983; Padoch 1983; Dove 1985, 1988; Rousseau 1990.

38. See Peluso and Harwell 2001 for a discussion of the violent changes in land access in the 1960s and 1990s. Davidson and Kammen (2003) provide a thorough account of the 1960s violence but deal less with its legal and land distribution ramifications.

39. I am completing a book that deals extensively with representation and re-interpretation of social-environmental history, using the various Bagak and western West Kalimantan narratives as a starting point.

40. See the "Bagaks' Landscape Yesterday" section of this chapter. See Peluso and Harwell 2001 and Peluso 2003a and 2003b for more extensive treatments of local violence; see Davidson 2002; Suparlan 1998; Heidhues 2003; and Davidson and Kammen 2002 for other analyses of the region's violence and its effects.

41. The Indonesian Communist Party, legal under Sukarno, was the largest Asian party outside China. For discussions of some of the dynamics in West Kalimantan, see Coppel 1983; Davidson 2002; Davidson and Kammen 2002; Heidhues 2003; Peluso 2003a.

42. Recently, however, as decentralization is redrawing district and city boundaries, these certificates have not been accorded full recognition and owners are being denied compensation when their land is taken for state projects.

43. The legal procedures involved in these land transfers were probably never very clear. In 1976, years after the Chinese land had been distributed, government certificates issued, and some land transferred again to newcomers (whether lent, rented, or sold), the Department of Agrarian Affairs recommended that these lands become "objects of land reform" (Anonymous 1970). To my knowledge, no one in the village knew of this, nor did it seem to matter.

44. At a recent meeting in Jakarta on the current conditions of internally displaced persons in Indonesia, it emerged that Sambas Dayaks and Malays continue to adamantly reject the possibility of Madurese returning. Only in a few cases have local people committed to protect resident Madurese in their villages who are said to have "adapted" to Dayak custom. But since killings and evictions were generally carried out by people from distant villages it is difficult to promise absolutely that Madurese families can be protected.

45. In the aftermath of the violence, many Madurese exiled from the district have said they had purchased land from Dayaks, for which they wanted but did not expect to receive compensation (Glenn Smith, Helene Bouvier-Smith, Latief, personal communication, 2004). Many Dayaks, on the other hand, claim that the land transfers in question were not intended to be permanent but rather short-term arrangements, that is, borrowing or renting. It is hard to ascertain the actual meanings of these arrangements. Though the practice of loaning land was common, the use of terms such as "borrowing" (*pinjam*), "buying" (*beli*), or "renting" (*sewa*) is frequently ambiguous.

46. Compare, however, with the practice in Ta'e, where Christine Padoch carried out research (Peluso and Padoch 1996).

47. As we saw, people of other ethnicities sometimes married into Salako descent groups—Chinese, Javanese, Sundanese, or even Madurese. Intermarriage with Malays generally entailed conversion to Islam (*masuk Melayu*) and loss of access to family resources.

III Histories of Colonialism and Forestry in India

K. Sivaramakrishnan

Preface: Revisiting an Argument after a Decade

W HEN I FIRST STARTED writing this essay in 1992, environmental history in South Asia was in its infancy. The bold and, in places, overtly controversial grand narrative that people still use as a point of departure for detailed, if contrapuntal, studies had not yet been published. I refer, of course, to *This Fissured Land* by Madhav Gadgil and Ramachandra Guha. Both of these pioneers of environmental history in South Asia recognized the value of long duration studies to understand and explain environmental transformation and related social change. Their work constituted a credible historical narrative of disruption and displacement of rural lives and livelihoods in India by the forces of war, disease, empire building, and, lastly, European, especially British, colonial domination in the nineteenth and twentieth centuries. *This Fissured Land* was available by the time I was revising this essay for publication. Even before that book, the work of Vandana Shiva (1988, 1991) had rehearsed some of the arguments Gadgil and Guha (1992, 1995) would make. And Shiva was more polemical, less concerned with evidentiary bases, and sweeping in her characterization of long periods of history and whole civilizations. Though varied in their sophistication, these works shared a powerful vision of Indian pasts before the time of colonial domination. What intrigued me was that this shared vision of precolonial India and its rural life had also persuaded the people they wrote against—colonial officers charged with expropriating India's villagers and forest dwellers, as well as national development planners charged with orchestrating India's progress in postcolonial times.

What puzzled me, if the scholarly record is to be trusted, has remained an enduring enigma for the field of South Asian environmental history. From Marxists to New Age Utopianists scholars have hastened to trace, and insist upon, the transition from harmony to disruption, justice to inequity, and prosperity to misery that marked the advent of first colonial rule and then modernity in the Indian subcontinent. This consensus is what Paul Greenough (2001) has memorably recounted as the standard environmental narrative.[1] He not only goes on to list the fallacies in causal connections and temporality that this narrative propagates but also points to its vegetal bias and the consequent neglect of the zoological environment in the standard narrative.[2] Yet Greenough's article, published ten years after it was written, has been somewhat overtaken by the march of environmental history in South Asia.

Historical scholarship produced in the last decade has enriched our understanding of how land, water, forests, wild animals, and occasionally the atmosphere were experienced, managed, and changed in South Asia over the past two hundred years at least. This has led the eminent environmental historian Mahesh Rangarajan to comment that "the past is only now beginning to intrude more clearly on deliberations about the future" (2002, 135). He notes, and I would agree, that early work was driven by the clarity provided by a moral imperative. The task was to write a nationalist environmental history, and it was also to add to the record of colonial infamy the evidence pertaining to the despoliation of nature and destruction of tribal culture carried out by the British. Environmental history emerged in this context out of either the invention of antique civility or the desire to document social movements that fought against expropriation of ancestral lands and traditional lifeways.

When Rangarajan talks about the past intruding more clearly in the present, he is actually alluding to recent colonial scholarship's movement away from narratives of rupture and dislocation to studies of continuities and changes with more complex articulations. By the mid-1990s environmental history passed into the hands, chiefly, of historians, and it also moved from the western Himalaya (the base of both Ramachandra Guha's and Shiva's regional expertise) to the Indo-Gangetic plain and, to a lesser extent, to the Deccan plateau of south-central India. This change of scene implied that canopy-dominant tree species went from pine, oak, and deodar to teak and sal (*shorea robusta*).

Contiguous forest tracts became smaller and resembled more the patch-work landscape of farm field, pasture, and forest that is the subject of much recent work.[3] Scholars were now dealing with areas that had been home to the rise and fall of empires based on sophisticated agrarian economies in which forests, waterways, and wild animals had been well integrated for the supply of food, fodder, irrigation, protein, sport, and the symbolic purposes of kings and commoners alike.

Another important effect of a change of scene was that evidence was now available, particularly in South India, on the long history of Euro-pean engagement with the tropical environments of South Asia. This began probably when Vasco Da Gama and his men came to the Mal-abar coast. Richard Grove (1995) documents the prolonged British encounter with peninsular and coastal India, both along the Coroman-del and the Malabar coasts. A theme that Grove develops in his study on a British empire scale, and that I was able to pursue with more assiduity in one part of the country, is the way in which India in particular became the laboratory and field research station where many aspects of silvicul-ture, horticulture, arboriculture, soil sciences, forest hydrology, and entomology were experimentally developed in the nineteenth century.[4] In the late eighteenth and early nineteenth centuries amateur British sci-entists in India made serious contributions to meteorology, tropical medicine, geology, and cartography, as well as botany, zoology, and ethnology.[5] The availability of these colonial scientific accounts is important for my argument because it meant that environmental his-tory, by the late 1990s, was no longer easily written as another episode in the history of colonial domination and indigenous resistance—that is, as a subtheme of liberal or Marxist nationalist historiography.

The precolonial past that was invented from at least Henry Maine onward and was represented in the works to which I have alluded has not been investigated from the perspective of environmental history as much as has the colonial period. The chief problem is one of adequate sources in vernacular materials. The rare scholar with the capacity and materials to write environmental histories of the precolonial past (Guha 1999) also finds it hard to orient analyses away from the seductive or oppressive framework (depending on whether you support or oppose the ideas) presented by Shiva or Gadgil and Guha. Thus Sumit Guha (2002), writing yet again on the question of the commons in precolonial western India, cannot resist taking another potshot at the usual target.

He notes, "Shiva and her fellow thinkers . . . characterized . . . all pre-modern regimes as prudent and balanced resource users. Writers like Shiva are distinctly cavalier with evidence, and one searches in vain for any tangible historical material of how earlier communities were constituted, or how they actually managed their resources" (Guha 2002, 183). As Sumit Guha goes on to point out later in the same article, despite repeated criticism Shiva's presentation of the past remains entrenched in many quarters, not least of which is the government, where the approach paper to the ninth national five-year plan, for the period 1997–2002, regurgitated the same ideas in the section on what needs to be done in the arena of forest management.

In my own work, almost all of which was completed only after this article was written, I have fluctuated between stressing continuities between periods—precolonial, colonial, postcolonial—and the ruptures that did occur when colonial state formation went into high gear in the 1880s and later when India's developmental democratic state launched social engineering on a vast scale in the Nehruvian era. After all, the Indian Forest Act of 1927 remains in force, even if lately seriously compromised by a spate of legislation that has, largely in the name of consolidating the enterprise of nature conservation and environmental protection, made it the least draconian of legal instruments available to the national government in the twenty-first century. But full adult franchise has also brought remarkable changes to India in the past fifty years. Since 1995, constitutionally mandated *panchayat* (local government) elections are among the most avidly contested polls, and democracy is a very vibrant and serious business in rural India.

In sum, the growing and thickening flow of environmental history in South Asia has meant that older topics such as forests, pastures, irrigation, urban ecology, health, and pollution and the new complexities of transgenic crops, biodiversity, and protected areas are all exposed to the increasingly skilled eye of all who wish to dabble in the historical study of environmental changes. At the same time, the questions posed in this essay some ten years ago remain surprisingly pertinent. Not only does the current scholarship continue to find the terms of analysis presented here of abiding relevance, but the question of forest conflicts itself is resurgent—both in the reserves and outside. The proliferation of laws and agencies, originating in the colonial enterprise, seems to have magnified the conflicts and perhaps multiplied them. As renewed controversy in the Silent Valley of Kerala indicates, plantations, forced occupations, and industrial conversions have diminished Kerala forests right through the last fifty years. This has compelled tired activists of the Kerala Shastra Sahitya Parishad to relaunch a campaign that they started thirty years ago.[6] So, it remains true that forests in India are at the center of highly charged conflicts.

Introduction

Use of the past by the different historical subjects engaged in contests over forest lands in India results in several threads intertwined across a shared frame. I shall try to unravel only one strand in this chapter, namely, the official ideologies implicated in colonial forestry and the technologies of power that it spawned. I will show how the colonial state, drawing on several pasts, constructed the question of forests in India.

The discussion of alternate constructions of forests that emerge from resistance to forest control issues, I believe, is integral to my project, which suggests that there is a dialectical relationship between discourses of rule and discourses of protest and that we can advance the study of this relationship by treating resistance as a diagnostic of power.[7] There are several advantages to doing this. First, we can avoid wrongly attributing particular forms of consciousness and politics to acts of resistance. Second, we can detect historical shifts in configurations of power (Abu-Lughod 1990, 48). This is important because, as Foucault (1980, 119) says, "power . . . produces things . . . [—]forms of knowledge and discourse. It needs to be considered as a productive network that runs through the social body." At the same time, the agency manifest in resistance cannot be displaced completely onto extant power structures. A theory of practice must be used. But, as Cohn and Dirks (1988) have pointed out, this theory has to be applied to the state-making process by inserting culture into a larger historical program of interpretation and analysis.[8] Hegemony is not self-securing. It is constructed, maintained, and modified by human agents and state agencies through contest and cooperation on sites like India's forest lands. It is important, in studying the refracted technologies of control and self-constitution that the modern state employs, to analyze the political moments of culture embedded in colonialism's history.

Colonial State Discourse and Forestry

How do we historicize debates over forest use and management in India today? We could start with the insight offered by Said (1979), who argues that all knowledge is a historically contingent construction that cannot be adequately understood without referring to contemporary politics and power. At the same time, the politics of representation, originating in the modernizing project of colonialism, continue to dominate the postcolonial scene. For instance, postcolonial custodial forest policy in India remained captive to the self-inflicted whittling process set in motion by the ambiguous treatment of customary rights and privileges in the second half of the nineteenth century. In this regard the debates between colonial administrators and Indian parliamentarians, separated by a century, frequently resonate.[9] When they reproduced the terms of the argument between Brandis and Baden-Powell, different branches of the Ministry of Environment and Forests in the Government of India disagreed over the definition of national forest policy. The conflict was consummated in the practical irony of Parliament approving contrary proposals on the same day in December 1988. An amendment to the Forest Conservation Act of 1980 categorizing medicinal plants and fruit trees as nonforest species, approved in the forenoon, placed greater onus on the local forest bureaucracy to seek central approval for working plans. Later in the day the National Forest Policy Resolution was passed. It said a basic objective was to "creat[e] a massive peoples' movement" to achieve goals primarily related to protecting the environment and meeting subsistence needs of rural populations (Government of India 1988, 1–2).

Therefore, the study of colonial discourse is important, especially the contradictory nature of colonial intervention and the institutional bases of colonial impact (Dirks 1989). Key continuities in the hegemonic discourses about forest management in the aftermath of decolonization may be noticed, and these can help assemble the pieces that went into realizing colonial discourses and their manifestation in state authority structures. Many Orientalist ideas about primordial Indian ways of living informed the approach to forestry in the nineteenth century.[10] On the one hand there was the idea of the epiphenomenal, ancient monarchic state presiding nominally over self-governing, durable village communities that appears in the writing of Henry Maine, Marx, Weber, and

Louis Dumont (1970). This could in turn feed the notion of forest communities engaging in precapitalist forms of forest use that were ecologically sustainable.

Alternatively, the assertion of sweeping and overriding state power over forest resources (most dramatically instanced by the Forest Act of 1878) drew on divine kingship's dictatorial hubris to link the concept of royal trees to the ultimate justification for forest preservation. In fashioning strategies of power, colonial administrators delved selectively into the precolonial pasts of subject peoples. The lengthy legislative debates preceding the Forest Act of 1878 were punctuated by references to the practice adopted by Tipu Sultan and some other Indian rulers in which certain trees such as teak were declared to be royal, thereby reserving the right to harvest them for the state.[11] In manipulating such flimsy evidence of precolonial state regulation of forest use to buttress sweeping usurpation of local rights in forests, colonial foresters acted in the same spirit as their distinguished colleagues did a few years later when they compiled ethnographies of Indian castes and tribes.[12] Here the silvicultural experts, naturalist foresters, and some civil servants joined in imagining a village community that was inherently hostile to the natural environment and its preservation.[13]

What was happening in the forestry sector was to some extent a manifestation of the larger Orientalist colonial project of constructing India as knowable by representation. The enormous growth, change, and increasing complexity of such knowledge were of crucial importance to technologies of rule. For example, when the ethnographic surveys and census operations commenced, society was fragmented into groups, households, and individuals and became available for reassembly as statistical units (Prakash 1990). With its inclusive classificatory enterprise, the state was incorporating the classic episteme of modernity, which, according to Foucault (1973, 74–75), was an "articulated system of mathesis, a taxonomia and genetic analysis. The sciences project . . . was an exhaustive ordering of the world." While forest dwellers were being sorted into types by tribe and caste, the forests themselves were arranged in categories by dominant genera and species. Such description and the laying down of taxonomic structures to represent biotic communities presaged colonial development projects in which human and natural resources were harnessed for imperial purposes.

In India's forests, these massive developmental projects materialized in railway expansion and in the construction of more roads and tracks into hitherto inaccessible hill regions, resulting in extensive deforestation (Guha 1989; Whitcombe 1972). The government's role in transforming the affected areas, often in tribal belts, included restricting swidden cultivation and forest reservation. The nineteenth and early twentieth centuries marked similar developments in different parts of the colonized world. In Tanganyika, German colonial administrators established a number of forest reserves in the decade preceding World War I. This was an attempt to control the use of forest resources in an area and culture where such use—certainly in terms of scientific forestry—had been traditionally unregulated (Schabel 1990). In Java, Dutch colonialists had started by negotiating with Javanese kings and other nobles for access to particular species, notably teak, and for forest labor. However, a bureaucracy within the colonial state managed forests there, too, by the middle of the nineteenth century (Peluso 1991).

In India the jungle that had been the refuge of beleaguered peasants became the object of keen commercial interest, thus reproducing the pattern emerging in different colonies. Forest officers sent to assess the jungle's value wrote dramatic reports predicting the imminent destruction of forests, soil erosion, landslides, and the dessication of springs if conservation was absent. Dr. Gibson, the first conservator of forests in the Bombay Presidency, compiled, around 1850, a list of rivers and creeks that had silted up along the Malabar coast. He did this by ethnographic interviews, drawing on the memory of villagers. As Stebbing (1922) reveals, the question of real importance for scientific forestry was to determine how far the destruction of forests in the catchment areas and on the sides of hills in the drier parts of the country affected the level of water in big rivers, decreased local water supply and rainfall, and caused erosion and avalanches. Thus, the rhetoric of conservation, environmental protection, and sustainable development, commonplace in current debates on forestry internationally, was being generated in the colonial project and laying the foundation for state forest management.[14] The observations made by surgeon naturalists like Alexander Gibson in Poona, Hugh Cleghom in Mysore, and Edward Balfour in Madras had created a body of reports and influential opinions that linked deforestation to the disturbance of hydrological regimes, dessication, and aridification. The direct effect of such work on Lord Dalhousie, who initiated colonial forest management in India, is noted by

Grove (1988, 38–39). The discursive device consisted of blaming the eco-logical misfortunes of local populations, including occasional events like drought, on the villagers' practices and ignorance of conservation strate-gies.[15]

As was true of other British colonies, deforestation in India was the logical outcome of the principal economic and ecological changes dur-ing colonial times (Tucker 1983; Adas 1983; Gadgil and Guha 1992).[16] The history of ecological imperialism would be manifest in the pattern of tree species exploited, planted, and regulated by law and silvicultural science.[17] To enable systematic extraction of desired economic products from the forests, the first step was to classify and take inventory of stock.[18] In addressing the demand for more intimate knowledge of Indian forest resources, British policymakers evolved an elaborate administrative structure, a stringent legal code, and a body of scientific practice. Forest policy also rested on ideological formulations arising from culturally delineated pasts of colonists and indigenous societies. This suggests several questions relating to perceptions of nature among the different interacting cultures, issues, and idioms of protest and the structuring effect of such matters on policy. The following examination of instruments of state forestry, peasant protest, and the interplay of cul-tural constructions that may be discerned is part of an approach to understand the dynamics of power relations in the forests of India. It is also an attempt to formulate ways of looking at the canopy of hege-monic discourse that at once constrained and was penetrated by the emerging undergrowth of practice and resistance in the management and use of these forests. This approach seeks to make cultural forms and historical events contingent on power relations.[19]

Instruments of Power: Administrative Structures and Laws

The determination, codification, control, and representation of the past have been central to the establishment of the nation-state and directly implicated in colonialism. Not only did the empire provide the ground for European domination, but it reproduced itself after its demise through the documentation projects initiated in previous centuries (Cohn and Dirks 1988).[20] A consideration of the forestry subproject, so to speak, is then vital from this angle. The circumstances under which the Indian Forest Department was created and the debates preceding the formal legislation of the Indian Forest Act are significant as the historical context of and as one set of structuring forces on modern forest management practice.[21] These conditions included the objective economic compulsion of railway development and the financial crisis faced by India's government after the revolt of 1857 (Metcalf 1964).[22] These conditions were also shaped by the intellectual predilections of the administrators imposing the imperial will and securing national revenues.[23] A combination of revenue needs, expansion of commercial crops, and development of the mining industry accentuated the powerful impact that building railways had on Indian forestry in the nineteenth century (Richards and McAlpin 1983; Tucker 1983; Guha 1989).[24] By 1921, Indian railways, the greatest in any colonial country, covered over thirty-seven thousand miles. They linked ports to agricultural hinterlands and urban centers to support the export of primary goods and import of finished products (Hurd 1975). Wood from the forests, in the form of sleepers for railway tracks and fuel for steam engines, provided vital inputs into this system. Forests were integrated into the market economy by forest administration initially demarcating areas with promulgated regulations for their management and directives to generate budget surpluses in forest operation. The appointment of Brandis as the first inspector general (IG) gave the central government an agency for formal intervention in provincial forest management. His image as the "hero of Pegu" who had rescued the teak forests of Burma from timber traders and made them available to British shipbuilding had much to do with his appointment (Troup 1940).[25]

Brandis toured the presidencies and centrally administered provinces, laying down more specific duties for the Indian Forest Service. In his nineteen years as IG of forests, Brandis produced several reports, based on relentless traveling through the jungles, that became the basis for a forest administration with specific responsibilities in the provinces.[26] These included forest settlement, demarcation, surveying, and formally constituting state forests; preparation of working plans; and construction of roads, bridges, buildings, drainage channels, and anicuts.[27] Protection work was directed against fire, cattle, and natural calamities. A few years later, German foresters in Tanganyika regulated burning, cutting, and grazing, reproducing discourses and technologies of state forestry rehearsed in India (Schabel 1990). Exploitation and artificial regeneration were mainly for major produce (timber) and minor produce (lac, bamboo, leaves, nuts, and fruits) of commercial value (Ribbentrop 1900; Troup 1940; Reports 1900–1930).

By 1920 the Forest Service consisted of three branches: the Imperial Forest Service (399 officers), recruited in Britain and trained at Oxford, Cambridge, and Edinburgh; the Provincial Forest Service (293 officers), recruited in India and trained at Dehradoon; and the Subordinate Forest Service, comprising over 15,000 rangers, deputy rangers, and guards recruited and trained in the provinces (Parker 1923).

In most provinces the Forest Service was placed administratively under the Revenue Department, a good indication of the primary role assigned to forestry.[28] As Stebbing (1926, 345) points out, the Forest Service came to be regarded "as a purely commercial concern—its chief raison d'être the production of revenue." He makes this assertion based on an extensive survey of government documents in the last quarter of the nineteenth century. By 1920 net revenues from state forests had increased fourfold to 21 million rupees, from the 5.5 million rupees of the 1880s.[29] Even as the administrative machine was being created, legal sanction for taking over sporadically explored territory was being cobbled together, first in the Act of 1865 and later, after much debate within the government, in the Indian Forest Act of 1878. To some scholars this represents a feature of British administration that blended and blurred executive and judicial functions even as British jurisprudence was transplanted into exotic settings with scant modification (Tinker 1966). A comparison of the forestry case with parallel developments in the legislation for control of nomadic groups all over India is illuminating in this respect.

In a discussion of the genealogy of the Indian Criminal Tribes Act of 1871 and its application in North India, Nigam (1990a) mentions considerable conflict between the judiciary and the district administration over interpreting the causes of the criminality of Sansis, Bawarias, and other nomadic tribes in Uttar Pradesh. The executive used the argument of intrinsic criminality to further the case for special powers acts and for enhanced magisterial powers that tilted the scale in favor of the subjective satisfaction of the magistrate, as opposed to the due process of law, which ultimately was the jural domain of courts. This was a struggle among different branches of the government for control over the criminal justice system. We can see regulatory systems in colonial India developing out of the tension between abstract libertarian legal principles and

the more pragmatic jurisprudence of suspicion, which favored surveillance, deterrence, and draconian measures for social control. The intellectual history of British colonial lawmaking in nineteenth-century India
can be written as an extended conversation with utilitarian philosophy
and classical economics. The influence of John Stuart Mill, Lord
Macaulay, and the evangelical movement was deep and lasting on the
colonial administrators (Stokes 1959). "The belief that certain collective
or corporate forms of social organization and property relations stifled
initiative and/or encouraged lackadaisical and careless use of resources
was generally held by colonial officers, missionaries and traders. It was
embedded in an ideology that regarded private ownership as the superior opposite of communal forms and whose premises were based on a
long tradition of western thought" (Peters 1987, 179).[30] Land settlements
made throughout this period, such as those for subsistence agriculture
and areas producing cash crops, reflect an abiding faith in the ability of
well-delineated private property rights to engender a productive climate
that would enhance revenue generation. The emphasis was on economic
productivity and the underlying belief that "a productive society without any form of ownership is an impossibility" (Grunebaum 1987, 128).
Thus, Bengal had a landlord settlement, while in the Central and Northwestern Provinces village communities were made responsible for land
revenue through their chieftains and headmen and in Madras and Bombay Presidencies the revenue demand was fixed with the peasant cultivator (*ryot*) in most cases (Baden-Powell 1892).

Land administration policy was definitely formulated to accomplish
specific imperial objectives, and the cultural background of those who
performed this task influenced their choice of ways and means. However, it does not therefore follow that the consciousness of agents of
colonial domination is a simple reflex of political and economic processes or the expression of a solidary hegemonic intellectual tradition
(Comaroff and Comaroff 1991). Several cultural constructs came into
play. These cultural constructs also colored the perception of colonial
administrators when they sought to comprehend local systems of rights,
privileges, and land management. Often the local community defined
the networks of rights, responsibilities, and privileges through cultural
symbolism and the social organization of economic activity. They were
not explicated or recorded on parchment. There was often no evidence
of secular sanctification for such arrangements, which nevertheless per-

formed functions very similar to property rights.[31] The validity of unwritten arrangements of common property management was not recognized by the dominant elements in the British administrative hierarchy.[32] This had as much to do with administrative expediency as with an intellectual persuasion that state institutions identified as rational and progressive would better serve public interest. The British entered a medieval landscape in which absolute possession appeared not to exist. By contrast, their cultural legacy exalted the basic value of unqualified possession. This combined with the Roman notion of *res dominium* to inform British settlement policies in India.[33] This paternalistic approach, a powerful mix of conviction and coercion, undermined traditional structures of authority. At the same time, the legal and political environment that the Raj was creating for the operation of market forces and the penetration of capital remained contradictory and left social groups room to maneuver (Washbrook 1981).[34]

For such reasons, it may be simplistic to conclude that a single dominant ideology informed the process through which the legal framework for forest control and management evolved. In the land settlements that had preceded these efforts, there had been a sharp divergence between regions. Although the Bengal *zamindar* (landlord) settlement tried to recreate the British yeoman farmer, Thomas Munro in Madras made a *raiyatwar* (peasant cultivator) settlement, arguing its efficacy on the basis of a legitimacy conferred by the regional history of agrarian relations, as he read it. Munro's position was both moral and pragmatic in seeking a place for Indian institutions in land and judicial administration (Stein 1983, 1990). His view of an enduring British empire built on a reconstruction of Indian national character also emanated from the same reformist zeal that in other contexts was proselytizing nonliterate communities and was characterized by a spirit of responsibility to oneself. This gave the British administrator greater freedom than the system appeared to allow (Cohn 1966).

Such a distinctive interpretation of a shared past (cultural tradition and training) and present assignment among the British policymakers was also evident in the debate about forest law. Several approaches to forest management were put forth. One extreme recommended the complete extinction of customary usage, while the other, especially in the Madras government, speaking in the Munro tradition, advocated the preservation of rights and local institutions. The rest can be placed on a continuum between these extremes. European experiences in dealing with communal forest rights were cited by all parties in the debate to support their respective proposals, but each had a different interpretation to bolster disparate cases (Guha 1990). For Brandis (1875, 13), "the proposal was to give expression to that limitation of forest rights which follows as a necessary consequence from their origin and development." The most annexationist view prevailed and, relying heavily on the draft by Baden-Powell, resulted in the passage of the Forest Act of 1878.

The bedrock of the law was the assertion that all uncultivated land was the state's property. In a narrow sense this was consonant with Vedic law and historical precedent, but Indian monarchs had rarely interfered with local usage (Singh 1986). Timber-cutting restrictions, creation of hunting preserves, and grazing regulation by regional chiefs were occasional exceptions that are described by Brandis (1897) and Rangarajan (1994). The restrictions found in certain parts of eighteenth-century India that applied to cutting certain species of trees by calling them royal were used by India's rulers to justify a monopoly on exploiting teak *(Tectona grandis)* and sandal *(Santalum album)* when a lucrative trade developed in these species (Stebbing 1922). The Marathas in western India found it expedient to acquire control over large tracts of coastal forests to set up plantations both for shipbuilding and revenue (Grove 1988, 27). To legitimize its attempts at forest reservation, the colonial state nonetheless made use of such slender evidence of indigenous efforts in state forest control by successor states to the Mughals. The intellectual strategy was to invest state monopoly with antiquity.[35] In another instance, the constitution of sacred groves and game preserves in native polity was cited as evidence that supported forest reservation. Brandis (1875, 13) argued that "the state had not exercised its full rights over the forests, which were left open to anyone who might choose to use them; but the right of the state was unimpaired and was asserted when a Native Ruler chose to close whole areas of forests to preserve the game, as in the well-known instances of the Belas of Sindh enclosed by the Amirs."

The state established total ownership of forested lands by using the principle of eminent domain, in which the state, drawing on European jurisprudence, claimed to be acting in the public interest (Singh 1986). But even this classical notion of state supremacy provided for due compensation, a notion built into the 1894 law for the acquisition of agricultural land (Ghosh 1973). But in the case of forests, procedural artifice was used to evade juridical obligation to provide compensation for rights abrogated in the process of declaring them exclusive state property. As has already been noted, Baden-Powell was influential in drafting the Forest Act of 1878. A crucial contribution was his distinction between rights that could not be abrogated without compensation but must be engraved in the settlement record and privileges that were always regulated, could be terminated, and, where allowed, were not alienable. He averred that villagers, who from time immemorial were accustomed to cut and graze in the nearest jungle lands, did not acquire a right by prescription because they used the forest without any distinct grant or license. All customary usages were therefore merely privilege.[36]

A simple gazette notification stating that forest land was reserved nullified all customary usage and rights if those lands were not claimed and ownership was not proven by legal methods and standards common to Western literate society (Legislative Department 1890). For the non-literate communities affected, this amounted to nothing less than unilateral forfeiture.[37] Shifting cultivation was one major, traditional subsistence activity that got banned from the reserved forests.[38] Other rights were curtailed and regulated.[39] Protected forests were constituted with slightly less stringent restrictions, but in either case the question of compensation was left to a subjective definition of "substantial infraction," which in the case of prescriptive rights exercised *ab antiquo* and unqualified in village record was pretty much a matter of government whim. Across the board this resulted in considerable hardship to local communities as their sustenance from the forests was sharply reduced (Singh 1986; Anderson and Huber 1988; Guha 1989; Nadkami 1989).[40] Even in open forests, variously referred to as protected, unreserved, and district forests, the restrictions on cutting, girdling, and any manner of harvesting certain species by villagers were total. When the manner of exploitation of some of these tree species is examined further, specific clues about the imperatives of commerce and industry behind the process emerge. More important, such unified reservation policies covering a range of species undermined the very basis of life and work among many communities, especially those not yet sedentarized and incorporated in commercial agriculture.[41]

Instruments of Power: Scientific Forestry

In their pursuit of a self-professed brand of forest preservation, the British broke with the traditional pattern of authority, which was normative, flexible, and bound by a cultural and personalized idiom of reciprocity (Guha 1989).[42] This adversely affected the self-provisioning ability of the village and precapitalist agriculture (Blaikie and Brookfield 1987). As Marx ([1852] 1990, 123–24) wrote about precapitalist peasantries in eighteenth-century France, "each individual peasant family . . . directly produced the greater part of its means of life more through exchange with nature, than through intercourse with society." Policies like forest reservation and scientific forestry impinged in several ways on the "exchange with nature," exercising control over it both by confining peasantries and by altering nature. In this respect the British colonial administrators seem to have replicated the social upheavals that accompanied the transformation of the open-field agriculture of England through enclosure (Dahlmann 1980). Studying these changes, scholars have characterized this movement from community to household as the organizing principle of agricultural production (Roseberry 1991). The virtue of such change was proclaimed in the language of the same rational ideology. Thus, the lexicon of colonial forest management is crowded with words like "conservancy" and "scientific forestry" that need to be understood in their political economic and ideological context.

Conservancy came to denote the restriction of local rights and customary usage of the forest (Reports 1900–1930). The forest settlement was, therefore, the most unpleasant task of conservancy, as it made the forester unpopular. However, any sense of moral disquiet within the Forest Service was quelled by the prevailing hegemonic idea that the villagers' greed for grass made them heedless of destroying timber (Parker 1923). Grass was important too to the early conservationists, for they were interested in preserving wildlife habitat as a sporting ground.[43] The first reported attempts at forest conservancy were made in western and South India by sportsmen naturalists—mostly civil servants and army officers who had a romantic fascination with the forest and enjoyed a good *shikar* (hunt). Lieutenant Michael of the Madras Infantry, working in the Annamalai teak forests in the early 1840s, is credited with making the first attempt to protect Indian forests from fire.[44]

To these early advocates of conservancy, the indigenous people, being "ignorant," "careless," and undiscerning of the ecological functions of the forest, were destructive of forests. Thus, a report of the British Association to the East India Company in 1852 recommended forest regulation, arguing that it was necessary to maintain hydrologic regimes, water quality, and catchment protection. The association claimed that native populations had recklessly ruined forests to meet insatiable consumption needs due to growth in their own and livestock populations (BAAS 1852). The report was heavily influenced by the ideas of Hugh Cleghom, the surgeon naturalist from Madras Presidency and ardent early advocate of conservancy. The appropriation of this report to the emerging agenda of unambiguous state control, not entirely endorsed by Cleghom and his ilk, was made possible by the interventionist and managerial notions that it fed by suggesting that the government should assume responsibility for halting environmental degradation.[45] This view crystallized over the next decade as the Government of India wrote to the Home Government categorically stating that "personal interest cannot be made compatible with public in working of forests due to the lack of moral and social restraints on forest exploitation in India" (Stebbing 1922, 526).[46]

In these famous dispatches the idea of formally segregating forest land so that it could be efficiently administered was mooted to secure the largest quantity of produce from forests consistent with their permanent usefulness. Thus were the concepts of maximum sustained yield (MSY) and scientific forestry introduced to India.[47] To accomplish rational forest management, the working plan was devised as a management tool. "A working plan sets forth the purpose with which a forest should be managed *so as to meet the interests and wishes of the owner,* and indicates the means by which this purpose may be achieved" (D'Arcy 1898, 1; emphasis added). Generally these plans laid out long-term treatment, prescribed felling cycles and schemes for trees in different forest coupes, and detailed short-term silvicultural practices. Estimation of the growing stock of valuable species was crucial to the plan. Curiously, the Forest Department in India seems to have neglected the work of another German silviculturist, Faustmann, who, around 1850, had developed a different model of steady state forest harvesting that maximized revenue more efficiently. In this model the rotation age was fixed at the year the growth rate of stock equaled the real interest rate (Davis and Johnson 1986).

The silvicultural agenda of the Forest Service was chiefly the transformation of mixed forests into homogeneous stands of commercially valuable species. First sal, teak, and deodar were classified as the superior species, since they were most important to railways, shipbuilding, and military needs (Parker 1923).[48] Then silvicultural research over the first sixty years of scientific forestry was directed to moving from selection and improvement felling systems to regeneration block systems, in which these desired species were raised and harvested in blocks (Trevor 1923). This necessitated the restrictions of grazing and burning practices, thus disrupting traditional agrarian systems (Guha 1989). There was not only a resultant increase in forest law violations but also spectacular gains in revenue (Reports 1900–1930).[49] The spread of commercial agriculture converted a limited and inelastic demand for biomass products into a limitless and elastic export demand that led to overexploitation of land and forest (Repetto and Holmes 1983). Thus, the British struggled to set aside the deciduous monsoon forests of the Burmese highlands as protection reserves to conserve valuable teak and ironwood (*xylia dolabriformis*) building material but promoted wet rice agriculture by ravaging the Kanazo evergreen forests in the Irrawady deltaic lowlands. In this case the pursuit of scientific forestry in one region starkly contrasts with unmitigated deforestation in another, at the expense of vast pools of genetic material destroyed in the process (Adas 1983). The role of political economy in determining the sites of purported scientific practice can hardly be ignored here.

Another important aspect of scientific forestry was the diversification of research to broaden the band of species being exploited commercially. World War I gave considerable impetus to this process (Stebbing 1926). By 1920, the properties of lesser known species were being investigated. Softwoods other than Himalayan conifers came into use for tea boxes, matches, and pulp (Parker 1923). Even earlier, Brandis had spearheaded research on creosoting (a chemical treatment) chir pine (*Pinus longifolia/roxburghii*) for railway sleepers when teak and sal became scarce in the 1880s (Brandis 1897).[50] Research on medicinal plants and pesticides for timber species was frequently reported in special technical bulletins designed and published by provincial governments.[51]

The commencement of systematic forest research in India can be dated to 1906, when, at the instance of Sir Eardley Wilmot, IG of forests in India, the Imperial Forest Research Institute was established at

Dehradoon in North India. The main branches were silviculture, zoology, botany, economics, and chemistry. Even though a chronicler of this process felt that research facilities developed in the face of opposition from the government (Hart 1922, 247–48), they were soon harnessed to priorities fixed by the state. The main lines on which research was organized can be classified as wood technology, timber testing, timber seasoning, and woodworking (Rodger 1925). A lasting irony of the silvicultural research carried out in India was the continuous struggle to come up with systems that could be used to generate pure stands of valuable species in a situation where most of the important timber species (notably teak and sal) did not grow in large pure stands (Joshi [1921] 1980).[52]

The Imperial Forest Research Institute at Dehradoon carried out elaborate tests on hitherto useless jungle woods to evaluate their performance as structural timbers for use in bridges, buildings, and so on. Indian *Terminalia tomentosa,* after creosoting, was found superior to American *Quercus alba* (white oak) as sleeper wood. *Parrotia jacquemontiana,* previously known as a forest weed, was developed for various manufacturing applications, especially serving the department of military stores (Stebbing 1926). Yet another area of research was in growing seeds on different sites as a precursor to introducing what were considered valuable species into new territories. From these nurseries were launched massive exotic breeding programs that led to the export to Africa of teak, sal, mahogany, and sandalwood, among other lumber species (Schabel 1990). A more detailed review of forest research in India over the past one hundred years is likely to reveal strong continuities in priorities, suggesting that the comprehensive extraction of commercial value from the reserved and protected forests was a greater cause of deforestation than population growth per se. In fact, studies of demographic trends and forest dependance have argued this point both for the Himalayan region and for South India (Saxena 1987; Nadkami 1989).

Thus, the edifice of state forestry was erected on the foundations of law, bureaucratic structures, and scientific knowledge that excluded contiguous village communities from forests in two ways. First, physical access was restricted. Second, the use value of the forest for subsistence was minimized by altering species composition and reducing biological diversity. This two-pronged strategy moved forests from the margins of subsistence agriculture to the center of commercial biomass production. At the larger level, discourses of protest mirrored these fundamental transformations of forest use and management. A consideration of the idioms and rhetoric of social protest is therefore necessary. However, when we proceed to the particulars of practice, policy and protest do not fit neatly into an impact-response model. Resistance, power, and cultural constructions of nature all interact to modulate state practice and reorganize peasant lives around forests in diverse ways that need to be situated in their specific histories of development and change.

Issues and Idioms of Protest

Speaking on the degradation of the environment and its effect on the subsistence economies of the rural poor, Chandi Prasad Bhatt, a noted leader of the Chipko forest protection movement in the western Himalayas, lambasted the abrogation of natural and legal rights of forest communities by a culture of state forestry that sought to optimize the yield in timber and generate revenue (Bhatt 1987). He was voicing the logic of a narrative in which the men and women of Uttarakhand, in the Indian Himalaya, have literally wrapped themselves as human shields around trees marked for felling, creating a discourse variously labeled as conservation, subversion, and a struggle for survival. The marginality experienced by forest dwellers, while perceiving the interconnections with other discourses of resistance and official ideologies, merits examination on its own terms. Limited work has been done in this direction. Ramachandra Guha (1989) and Gadgil and Guha (1988) are fine examples of recent historical-sociological analyses of forest movements as autonomous discourse, somewhat in the subaltern tradition. The weakness of this approach, as more generally of much of the compilation called Subaltern Studies (Guha 1982–89), is the neglect of the dialectic between discourses of rule and discourses of protest arising from the search for essential subaltern ideologies. The manner in which indigenous groups as communities of resistance are imagined has much to do with this. At the risk of oversimplification, it can be said that Gadgil (1985), Agarwal (1986), Shiva (1988), and Gadgil and Guha (1989) provide an environmental variant of what has become a major theme of nationalist rhetoric against colonial rule, namely, its penetration and destruction of self-sufficient village communities. For instance, Gadgil and Guha (1992, 114) say that "despite the grave inequalities of caste and class . . . pre-colonial Indian society had a considerable degree of coherence and stability. This permitted a rapid turnover of ruling dynasties without major upheavals at the level of the village. . . . cultural traditions of prudence ensured the long-term viability of the system of production." All of these writers forcefully argue that precolonial tribal and caste Hindu peasant communities understood their intimate dependence on nature and had developed systems of husbandry attuned to nature's regenerative cycles. Such respect for nature translated into a conservation ethic, which for Shiva (1988) especially could be retrieved from Sanskrit texts. In another more recent work, Shiva (1991, 15) restates this claim of indigenous conservation practice based on the knowledge that recognized the same ecological processes that scientific forestry sought to safeguard, a practice embedded in social norms rather than laws or elite expertise.

Having constructed a precolonial society untouched by baneful commerce and competition for resources, colonial impact is then described as entirely external, completely new in ideologies of resource control, and, given the power balance, disruptive of ancient equilibria. Tribal people (the ultimate subalterns) are presented not as people who were pushed to margins but as groups found on the advancing frontier of colonial expansion. The cumulative impact of commercial forestry is seen to result in the increasing exposure of autochthonous primitive isolates to processes of degradation (Gadgil and Guha 1989, 148–50). The danger of such an approach is to place hunting and gathering and sedentary agriculture on opposite ends of an evolutionary scale that has come in for criticism even within human ecology (Orlove 1980; Wilmsen 1989). For our purpose, the outcome is the analysis of domination and resistance within the framework of an impact-response model in which subaltern protest emerges from an autonomous subaltern identity and collides with monolithically conceived imperial states.

However, this is not to deny insights provided by the systematic analysis of ecological factors and their meshing with peasant practice or colonial definitions of silvicultural science. Eric Stokes did some of the earliest work on the relationship of ecology to peasant movements in India. In his analysis of peasant disturbances in central and North India, the roots of revolt were found not in the frustrations of degraded proprietary classes but in pockets of poverty caused by ecological differences and British land settlement policies. For instance, he found greater unrest among graziers and seminomadic communities of central India like the Gujars, Bhattis, and Rangars who were forced to accommodate sedentary agriculture in their pastoral economy (Stokes 1986). He enriched the focus of his material by allowing such imponderables as the loss of honor, withdrawal of richer groups from traditional patterns of marital alliance, and the desecration of traditional rank by colonial state power to creep into his framework; but ecology became the fundamental explanatory variable, while caste, mentalities, and culture seemed to refer ultimately back to the fickle environment for food production.[53]

Along with the work of Metcalf (1979), this ecological approach also led to a geographic distinction of rebellious and loyal areas, on the basis of the degree to which tenurial arrangements and commercial agriculture favored the emergence of cooperative elites who used their prosperity to dilute potential protest. The poverty of the argument is the way ecology remains tied to economics, leaving undescribed the conditions of marginality as they came into sharp relief in generating protest. If market incorporation was the magic touch that removed disaffection, the following question remains: How did forest movements develop around resistance and hostility to commercial forestry? It can be argued, remaining within economistic terms of debate, that the nature of commercialization was substantially different. Subalternists recommend the insertion of religion and the fashioning of a distinctive consciousness thereby into the framework of analysis.[54]

Describing the wave of fish pond looting and the violation of restrictions on forest rights that broke out in Midnapore district of Bengal, Sarkar (1984) points out that the movement was rooted in the resentment engendered by the Midnapore Zamindari Company and the construction of railways that impinged on Santhal (tribal villagers) use of the forest but that the movement was activated by a memory of times in the recent Santhal past when jungles were open and ponds freely available for fishing. This collective mentality favors subaltern militancy when reality is constructed in subaltern consciousness as a period of breakdown in the patterns of hegemony and coercion. Such construction uses as its raw material rumors, contingent events, and norms of resistance inculcated by the Gandhian movement. However, in Sarkar's version, the actual subaltern outburst is mediated by the "magico-religious character of peasant society . . . untouched by creeds of secular progress" (1984, 308–9).[55] While Sarkar seems to argue a distinctive ontology for peasant consciousness based on the Santal tribal case, Hardiman (1987) shows that *adivasis* (tribals) have cultivated land in diverse ways, engaged in extensive economic interchange with other ethnic groups, and shared religious belief and practices with caste peasantries.

Nevertheless, the way Subaltern Studies treat collective traditions and cultures of subordinate groups is unsatisfactory. An ahistorical, consensual, and undifferentiated notion of primordial loyalties permeates much of the work.[56] Guha, who includes in his book *The Unquiet Woods* (1989) an earlier essay from *Subaltern Studies* IV on forest movements in British Kumaon, frequently resorts to such treatment of the ecological consciousness of the Chipko agitators, even though the book is full of rich ethnographic material showing the separate construction of the ideology of protest by women, men, villagers, and leaders.[57] The deleterious consequence of this portrayal is that "it restores within a redrawn and smaller notion of the collective exactly that notion of unity . . . of the absence of the relations of power, which is the subject of attack" (O'Hanlon 1988, 212). The point is that a shared moral economy is itself a contingent historical creation, which is modulated and contested and used both for internal solidarity and repression.[58]

Seen from this perspective we can identify the historical creation of a tribal world that came to be treated as autochthonous primitivity by the sympathetic ethnography of the 1930s and 1940s.[59] By implementing a forest policy that denied property rights in woodland to tribals and other rural poor, the state generated a discourse of exclusion that made subaltern marginality a historically emergent condition. To take but one example, Baker (1991, 356) notes that "while the administration sought to confine tribals to *malguzari* villages, it also excluded them from forests. Settlement officers simply forbade Baigas from cultivating in the forest and sought to confine them, to certain localities." This sedentarization project of the late nineteenth century divested the affected populace of material claims to the forest, leaving them no recourse other than to assent a religious affinity to the forest. Albeit in a different context, but still pertinent to our discussion, Foucault tells us that the establishment of territorial, administrative, and colonial states frequently was accompanied by the efflorescence of moral and religious issues relating to governance and its legitimacy. "There is a double movement . . . of state centralization on the one hand and of dispersion and religious dissidence on the other: it is, I believe, at the intersection of these two tendencies that the problem comes to pose itself with peculiar intensity" (Foucault [1978] 1991, 88).

From Resistance to Power

For these reasons, ultimately, resistance becomes a limiting construct for the analysis of disputes over forests in India and the more general consideration of the creation, sustenance, and alteration of discourse and the technology of power. A tendency develops to romanticize resistance and read all forms of resistance as signs that the systems of power are ineffective, thus inferring that the human spirit is resilient and creative in its refusal to be dominated. Guha (1989) defines the problem in the context of forest movements in India by demonstrating that structural organizational histories and cultural-symbolic anthropologies, in explaining peasant protest in Uttarakhand, have been artificially segregated to the detriment of the analytical product. What he leaves undone is the cohesive treatment of instrumental and expressive aspects of protest to develop a single, integrative explicatory model. We need to explore further the idea of multiple resolutions to tussles among peasants, landlords, and the state, as Brenner (1976) has evocatively argued, by examining institutions of power and ideology that intervene in political structures. These structures have specific histories encompassing movements of population, conquest, and subjugation; the stabilization of complex relations of obligation and reciprocity within local society; and incorporation into larger structures. This would require understanding not only local but also multifaceted elite cultures. In the case of forestry, these cultures were manifested in the interpretation of imperial imperatives and the structure of scientific forestry. We cannot confine ourselves, then, to considering the voices of discord and the agenda of protest. A complete inquiry into human agency would entail uncovering cooperation, as well as conflict and complicity, interleaved in resistance. An account would be incomplete if it did not analyze the manner in which the local communities interacted with the edifice of forest administration to influence its shape and design as it was being erected. Much of the reconstruction of human agency can emerge from the skillful interpretation of historical record, even when it has been generated by state authority (Sabean 1984).

We are told that conventional social science in India ignored many resistive events merely because they went down in the official record as outlawry, dacoity, or some other form of statutory crime (Dhanagare 1983). Ranajit Guha (1987) has demonstrated how the judicial record can be utilized in the manner that Sabean suggests to recover protest and its special cultural forms in the case of the subaltern. This requires making the minuscule grain of history visible in order to expose the exchange between familiar and remarkable, the quotidian and the historic. The exchange develops into a struggle between state and community, appropriating the story of the crime as a discursive site. Thus, the details of clashes between villagers and forest officials may be gleaned from statistics of crime in the forest reported annually by the Revenue and Forest Departments.

For example, the introduction of "early burning" as a silvicultural practice in certain Himalayan provinces of India was motivated ostensibly by efforts to propagate chir pine monoculture for commercial uses; but it also served to preempt such conflict (Guha 1989). In this context, reports of increased violation of grazing regulations lend themselves to a variety of explanations, depending on the analytical perspective. Very often they were symptomatic of fundamental disagreement in the exercise of property rights.[60] The government reports merely note the correlation between commodity price fluctuations and the incidence of forest offenses (Reports 1900–1930). The same trends have been noticed in contemporary conflicts, indicating a basic competition over natural resources between rural subsistence and urban commercial economies in times of intensified demand on a shared, shrinking base (Agarwal 1984; Sivaramakrishnan 1987). In all periods the influence of these dialectical exchanges on redefinition of state attitudes and priorities is understated.

The case of *dhya* cultivation in the Central Provinces presents a more complex case and a paradigm for appreciating the interaction of colonialism with swidden agriculture,[61] which was the most widespread form of shifting cultivation by the Gonds, who ploughed the ashes of burnt trees into the soil to grow light millets for subsistence. The forests, according to Stebbing (1922, 398), had "been devastated by the cutting and burning of the best timber to form ashes and manure fields of coarse

rice and pulses." The dhya cultivator would select teak stands for slash
and burn because teak ash was the best fertilizer for the broadcast crop.
As the chief commissioner of the Central Provinces, Sir Richard
Temple, put it, "the best ground for this peculiar cultivation is precisely
that where the finest timber trees like to grow" (Dyer 1925, 349). Because
teak and sal were the most valuable hardwoods for the Forest Department, the conflict was direct.[62] Not surprisingly, the Forest Act of 1878
emphatically ruled that "the practice of shifting cultivation shall in all
cases be deemed a privilege subject to control, restriction and abolition"
(Legislative Department 1890, 13).[63]

   In carrying out this explicit legal mandate, provincial governments
were frequently placed in difficulty. In some areas, tribal resistance to
curbing *jhum* was violent and confrontational.[64] Tribal resentment dis-
played a range of other responses as well. Forsyth, the most extensive
surveyor of the forests of the Central Provinces, found noncooperation
in the building of a forest rest house in Pachmarhi. He wrote, "I saw the
chief himself and his advisors hated our intrusion. . . . they feared we
[had] come to break up . . . their untrammeled barbarism" (Forsyth
1889, 100–101). Others like the Baiga slipped away when they spied
approaching officials. Religion was sometimes invoked to stall attempts
to take over the forests.[65] All manifestations of protest were regarded as
"rejection of development and progress" (Baker 1991, 347).[66] The consequences of resistance to jhum control were diverse. In some areas, small
demarcated zones were given up to this "intractable tribal practice." The
state's most innovative response was the introduction of modified
taungya systems.[67] According to Leach (1977), this traditional technique
of highland Burma for shifting cultivation had clearly distinguishable
subsystems, depending on climate and physiography. The British developed an agrosilvicultural system based on Burmese taungya in which
tribal villagers were allowed to grow rice, millets, tobacco, and poppy
among rows of teak seedlings (Blanford 1925, 1958). Once again the
ubiquitous Brandis was in the forefront, taking direct credit for the
introduction of taungya forestry in Burma. He records that "as soon as
I had seen the first Karen taungya in 1856, I determined to devise some
method, by which this mode of cultivation might be utilized for planting
teak on a large scale in the forest" (Brandis 1897, 37).

   Traditional agriculture was melded in this way with commercial
forestry, the former proving a source of cheap labor for the latter. As a

method of co-opting the intransigent jhumia this mode of cultivation obviously met with considerable success and spread to different parts of India. In 1868, the first large-scale taungya teak plantations were made; by 1895, they covered fifteen thousand hectares in Burma alone and annual yields of teak had doubled. In that region, teak came up in bamboo forests (mainly *Dendrocalamus strictus* and *Bambusa polymorph*), which were periodically burnt to push back the canopy and to provide light for teak seedlings.[68] By the last decades of the nineteenth century, taungya had been introduced in Java. In this variant, peasants moved every two years, giving up all usufruct rights in the taungya field and leaving behind a young stand of teak saplings (Peluso 1991). The more lasting and powerful response to shifting cultivation, as to all forms of nomadism, was the sedentarization of mobile groups.[69] Drawing on European and Indian pasts, a complex discourse of representation and rule was created as the colonial state grappled with what were called criminal tribes throughout the nineteenth century. Radhakrishna (1989) has argued, regarding the notification of criminal tribes in Madras, that forest policy restrictions on grazing and the collection of forest produce traditionally bartered for salt, railway expansion, government takeover of the salt industry, and famine were all instrumental in destroying the livelihood of many wandering tribes like Korava, Koracha, and Yerukula, who were later declared criminal, settled, or transported. Settlement schemes tended to coincide with labor requirements for newly established quarries, mines, factories, and tea and coffee plantations. Nigam (1990a and 1990b) presents similar evidence of the transportation of Bawarias from Uttar Pradesh to clear forests in the Dehradoon hills. Forest policy interacted with the creation of a distinctive colonial anthropological discourse as part of the enduring sedentarization project of the nineteenth century that sought to delegitimize the life and culture of banjaras, jhumias, shikaris, Rangars, Bhattis, Mazhabis, Meenas, Mevs, Bhils, and other peoples who were itinerant traders, nomadic pastoralists, shifting cultivators, and so on. According to Bayly (1990), throughout most of the nineteenth century the crucially scarce factor of production in the agricultural sector was labor, not land; and dealing with this shortage drove colonial policy. Tucker (1989) certainly proves this in the conversion of forests to plantations in Assam and Kerala.

However, the strategies of power and the discourses in which they were enmeshed cannot be disentangled from the political economy that provided the discursive background. Mayaram (1991) has shown how the colonial state appropriated narratives of self-constitution among the Mevs of Rajasthan in their reconstitution as a criminal tribe. Such narratives had the potential to represent the negotiation of an internal solidarity that would be inimical to the effective penetration of state power. This might have caused the state to view certain cultural forms with suspicion. Frietag (1985) proceeds on these lines to suggest why the British were more perturbed by collective crime than by individual criminality. Even a sympathetic, Indophile bureaucrat like A. O. Hume believed that criminal tribes lay "like an infernal machine beneath the keel of good government . . . a sudden mischance calling forth to rapine and murder the jungle thousands that haunt the delta of the Jamuna" (Nigam 1990a, 151).

Colonialism defined and thus reproduced an indomitable sense of community inimical to the individualizing state. Contrasting such essential communal solidarity of peasantries against the depredations of the rational state based on contracts has become a powerful metaphor in the hands of popular environmentalism in postcolonial India. This needs to be placed in the context of the cultural constructions of nature that environmental politics draws on and reproduces.

The Cultural Construction of Nature

In the study of colonial and postcolonial complex state agrarian societies, the vision of an equilibrated relationship between man and nature is a pervasive metaphor, in which predation and symbiosis were held in a fine balance until the advent of European expansion. The present constitution of New World biota and society is, according to Crosby (1986), a distinctive product of the European portmanteau and the ecological change it wrought. Intersecting ecology, politics, and culture, the capitalist transformation of world biota then provides elements of a shared past.

This notion of something shared but not entirely is conveyed by Scott (1990, 100) in his statement that "myths, hegemonic ideas, are the product of joint struggle in which the basic terms are shared, but in which interpretations follow widely divergent paths in accordance with vital interests." I would like to proceed with such an approach. For instance, the placement of forests at the margin of agriculture, as an appendage to the food production system, may be shared as a cultural formulation of the relationship between forest and agriculture, both among peasants and colonial administrators in British India; but interpretation varied to the extent of fueling violent conflict between the state's powerful impulse to preserve the forest and that of the peasant communities to use the forest. This had much to do with the communities dependent on forests being on the margin of caste and the periphery of power structures that summed up caste and class.

The use of religion and other large mythic structures was often innovative when a resistive discourse was fashioned from the kind of ambivalence mentioned previously. The Chipko agitation reached out to overarching Hindu belief when the Gita was read in the forest to protest the trees being cut down. This was crucial when successfully appealing to nonlocal labor used by timber contractors. Equally, the act of hugging trees by women, the traditional controllers of the hearth, was aimed to strike a chord in an ethic of shared subsistence that transcended differences of territory, gender, and caste. Religion was important precisely because it developed syncretic forms using adivasi rites and Hinduism. Fifty years earlier, the incorporation of adivasi religious sites into Koya and Bagata pantheon became important to the rebellious hillmen Arnold (1982) writes about. This incorporation demonstrated autochthonous origins for the hillmen's faith among the hills and streams where they lived.

As Lévi-Strauss (1972) shows, tribesmen do not use religion and myth as devices to repudiate reality. Rather, religion and myth provide structures for comprehending the immediate reality and responding to them. In the Gudem-Rampa case, religion was used to express dissatisfaction with subjugation and to frame the terms of deliverance in a known model that provided symbolic capital to counter the superior control of economic capital exercised by oppressors. Traveling clerics (*sivasaris*) moved through the region, with the prophecy of one Bodadu (in 1886) that God had ordained a successful *fituri* (rebellion). This was rendered authentic by the encounter of Bodadu with the five *pandavas* (the redemptive brotherhood of the Mahabharata epic in the Hindu tradition) in the jungle, a symbolic mediation of local and national culture that was politically expedient for integrating hillmen with supporters in the plain (Arnold 1982). At a later stage, RamaRaju, a *telugu kshatriya* leader of the agitation against forest reservation, gained local control through his knowledge of astrology and medicine, giving him magical powers in the eyes of the hillmen. However, by advocating temperance and *khadi* (homespun cloth), he also strategically allied with Gandhian politics (Arnold 1982).

Thus, we can see that the cultural construction of nature is grounded in practice and that a holistic view of such a practice must be taken to relate systematically disjunctive moments to conjunctive ones by going from resistance to power and from the religious idiom of confrontational protest to the religious idiom of complicit modulation of social processes. To communities dwelling in the forest, the forest was a source of sustenance, so their religion led them to make special sacrifices to forest gods. It is striking to see in how many myths and legends a deep sense of identity with the forest is sharply etched. Law and policing could not take away from the forest villages their heartfelt ownership of the forest (Anderson and Huber 1988). The clash between state forestry and village management was not only an economic one. The contending management styles rested on radically different systems of meanings. The social idiom of protest reflected the threat to traditional cultural and communal values that commercial forestry has represented. Therefore, that idiom invoked both an alternate system of use and an alternate structure of meanings.

To comprehend the finely interwoven language and substance of debate, it is necessary to examine these constructions of nature implicit in the philosophical ways that different societies used to deal with forests. In their review of sacred groves, Gadgil and Vartak (1976) have pointed out that these systems of indigenous conservancy arose in hunting and gathering communities. In a later work, Gadgil and Malhotra (1983) argued that prudent and sustainable use of natural resources was instrumental in the stability of the caste Hindu society and its resistance to transformation. All this points to the existence of traditional forms of forest conservation contradicting colonial forest histories that describe local communities as "careless and ignorant" in dealing with forests.

These need some elaboration. In precolonial India, a variety of social groups exercised claims on forest resources in different regions—hunters and gatherers, shifting cultivators, plough agriculturists, pastoralists, and artisans. This led to a diversity of arrangements for communal management of the forest, consisting of religious proscription, communal sanction, and active tree planting. Sacred groves were one such mechanism and are still in existence in the Himalayas and in coastal South India. Their connection with religious practice, as revealed by their proximity to temples, is often explicit. Even colonial foresters recognized the biological diversity of tropical forests, preserved in little patches where these groves existed (Brandis 1897; Edwardes 1922).

Stretching from the Khasi Hills of northeast India to the Devara Kadti of the Coorg in the southwest, Brandis notes the occurrence of sacred groves in different parts. "These sacred forests as a rule are never touched by the axe, except when wood is wanted for the repair of religious buildings" (Brandis 1897, 12). One problem with this view is that it makes precolonial practices frictionless and devoid of conflict. Indigenous conservation ethics seem to be embedded in the structural-functional perceptions of the societies espousing them. The environmental movement has sought to naturalize sacred groves as an icon of indigenous conservation, placing them outside politics precisely to make them a more potent political symbol in the struggle between peasants and the state on issues of forest use and management.[70] As Sahlins (1981) has suggested, the ritual power of taboo encompasses the protection of property, and this could become transformed in pragmatic structures of trade. The manner in which such ritual conservation is remembered and reconstituted in contemporary power relations would be influenced by the history of taboo and its implication in historical power structures. Alongside the designated sacred groves, village communities practiced a system of managing woodland by rotation and also regulated the supply of fuel, fodder, and small timber from the forest to individual households. Sanctions in the form of fines and social boycott were imposed by the community on those who violated these regulations (Guha 1989). In Kumaon (Uttar Pradesh, North India), unofficial *lath panchayats* composed of village elders protected village forests (Somanathan 1991). The modern system of *van panchayats* both continues and appropriates this practice.

Sometimes resources were conserved by partitioning land among different social groups on a seasonal basis. Examples are the seasonal sharing of the forest and grazing lands between nomads and sedentary agriculturalists, in which the nomads repaid access to land by providing manure and other services, and the allocation of different wildlife species among different hunting castes (Gadgil and Malhotra 1983).

There is also evidence of tree planting in which the choice of species and crop management reveals the care bestowed by the forest communities on their habitat. For instance, the Apatani peasants of Kumaon planted trees that had a span of maturity far exceeding a human lifetime (Pant 1922). In addition to notions of enduring potential of enhanced resources, apparently selfless and genuinely cooperative use of natural resources has emanated from ecological histories of uncertainty and the need for minimizing risk (Fernandez 1987; Wade 1988).

In contrast, the dominant European view of nature, as it emerged with the spread of capitalism, was qualitatively different. Landscapes were seen as commodities, and members of an ecosystem were treated as isolated, extractable units (Polanyi 1957; Cronon 1983; Merchant 1990). This perception was dominated by ideas of exploitation and appropriation that viewed nature as a machine given by God to man to be managed for maximal productivity (White 1967). At the same time that Dr. Gibson, the first conservator of forests in Bombay, was preparing his reports on the consequences of forest destruction for water supplies, soil erosion, and siltation of rivers, ardent naturalists were making similar associations of human influence and resource degradation in the New World (Cox et al. 1985; Glacken 1967). The vital difference was that, in the colonies, the critique was of "unreclaimed backwardness," while in the free world it was more introspective. In both situations, however, the idea that the state should control forests was evolved as a modified utilitarian vision of conservation and of the spirit of free enterprise to promote MSY and multiple-use forestry (Hays 1959; Pinchot 1947).[71]

We must, however, be wary of the incipient dichotomization emerging out of the preceding discussion. Recent environmentalist and polemical literature has seized selectively upon the complex history of forest conservation and degradation in India to sharpen the edge of this idealized antinomy.[72] Many historians have worked with the assumption that the environmentally destructive aspect of the colonial experience had to do with imperialist attitudes to the environment. The problem with this has been the concomitant tendency to characterize attitudes to nature "by a simple dualism of Arcadian attitudes on the one hand and imperialist attitudes on the other" (Grove 1988, 20). Even Gadgil and Guha (1989, 177) conclude their fine study of forest conflicts in the colonial period by referring to "two opposed notions of property and resource use: communal control over forests being paired with subsistence . . .

state control with commercial exploitation." The social construction of forests that underlies this formulation is clearly intended to provide the contemporary environmental movement with history and antiquity, a discursive strategy deriving from the era of freedom struggles in the colonized world (Anderson 1991). The problem that remains is how to incorporate into this model the most recent struggles in Uttarakhand—the home of the chipko movement—where traditional roles have been reversed. Those who inherited the chipko legacy are conducting a violent agitation against the Forest Conservation Act of 1980, seeking development, self-determination, and forest clearance in a way that fundamentally breaks with much of their past and yet remains encapsulated in the modern debates of nation-states.

Conclusion

Ways of imagining the past simultaneously construct and are shaped by the historical circumstances in which human agents are placed. Unpacking this dialectical process in the case of colonial forestry and of relations between peasants and the state in India has involved the discussion of administrative structures, legal frameworks, scientific programs organizing knowledge, and the discursive formations in which they were located. The attempt of this study has been to integrate such a discussion into one of resistance and indigenous knowledge systems, which are often treated as reactive or autonomous discourses.

Another facet of the several fusions undertaken in this study is the belief that culture and political economy combine in complex ways as the past is imagined and that they are then used in contesting and negotiating relations of power, which lead to the creation and perpetuation of certain ideologies. These ideologies are inflated into discourse formations and hegemonic structures as the politics of representation unfolds. Instrumental to this process is the propagation of a theory of knowledge. This theory of knowledge is "a dimension of political theory because the specifically symbolic power to impose the principles of the construction of reality . . . is a major dimension of political power" (Bourdieu 1977, 165). Such a combination of power and knowledge also elevates ideology to wider representative authority by generalization and naturalization—"to claim for specific interests a natural universality" (Kelly 1991, 423). As was demonstrated, both the ideologies of rule and the rhetoric of resistance made selective use of the past, precisely to attain these effects, by developing their naturalized accounts of forests and their use in India.

The central concern of this chapter has been to describe the practical world in which the articulation of hegemonic and counterhegemonic discourses occurs. Equally, the point stressed is that we need to shift our focus from the dichotomous polarities of these discourse formations to their construction inside fields of power and within ongoing processes of contention and struggle. As O'Brien and Roseberry (1991, 18) have reminded us, "metaphorical oppositions give us imagined pasts . . . that . . . are bound together in a unified set of social, political and cultural processes."

NOTES

1. This aspect of Greenough's commentary has stood the test of time and remains relevant, as several authors, in several disciplines, have commented as well on the particular decline and fall narrative that informs the historical sense and context present in a wide range of scholarly and policy analyses.

2. Arguably, the increasing scholarly and policy attention paid to parks and wildlife conservation since the 1990s has rectified this lacuna, and there is now a rich body of work on wild animals and their fate in India in colonial times and beyond.

3. See, for instance, Bhattacharya 1999 and Agrawal and Sivaramakrishnan 2000.

4. For more on this, see Grove 1995; Sivaramakrishnan 1999; and, most recently, Arnold 2006.

5. See, among others, Edney 1997; Arnold 2000; Kumar 1995; and Grove 1997.

6. See Prabhakaran 2004. The success of the first Silent Valley movement was an inspiration to Indian environmental movements in the 1970s.

7. I use the term "discourse" in combination with the term "practice" as originally utilized by Bourdieu (1977). Such melding of the concepts was suggested by Feierman in February 1992, while speaking at the weekly colloquium of the Program in Agrarian Studies at Yale. He defined "discourse" as an underlying set of practices—a combination of speech, writing, and action. He makes admirable use of this formulation in his historical anthropology of agrarian change in Tanzania (Feierman 1990).

8. By theory of practice I refer not merely to the analysis of structured interaction presented by Bourdieu (1977) in his study of Kabyle gift exchange. More recently, Ortner (1984, 1989) has elaborated the concept for examining social discourse and institutions. Isaacman (1990) provides another dimension to theories of

practice by suggesting a focus on peasant labor processes, including their development and change. All these refinements are relevant here.

9. Guha (1990) gives a flavor of the earlier exchanges. Their reenactment, in
emancipated India's highest legislative forum several years ago while debating the
New Forest Policy, was something I witnessed from official galleries of the lower
house of Parliament.

10. I refer to what Said (1979) has called the containment and representation of
the Other within dominating frameworks. "A priori Orientalist assumptions . . .
produced definitions that could be redeployed to prove the original belief. This was
typical of colonial knowledge" (Nigam 1990a, 136).

11. Similar instances are cited in other colonial encounters. In the Sandwich
Islands, the history of sandalwood trade shows chiefs quick to regulate items valued and demanded heavily by Europeans (Sahlins 1981). Again, in Java, some
foresters argued that forests were considered the property of Javanese kings and
sultans and, hence, were state property. "Yet the property rights of early Javanese
kings, enjoyed only along local systems of use rights, were vastly different from the
notion of exclusive state property . . . inherent in the system imposed by the Dutch"
(Peluso 1991, 69).

12. See the excellent discussion of similar processes in the colonial constitution
of caste in Dirks 1989 and 1990. It seems to reflect a more widespread approach to
the appropriation of Indian pasts and their utilization in framing colonial policy.

13. See Stebbing 1922 and Troup 1940, which represent both the scientists and
the administrators directly involved. For similar processes in Tanganyika under
German colonial rule, see Schabel 1990.

14. Even in the nineteenth century, the intercontinental similarity of rhetoric is
striking. See Schabel 1990 for the way the justification for forest regulation was
couched in environmental rather than fiscal terms in Tanganyika.

15. For a discussion of nineteenth-century conservationism and its construction around an image of destructive, senseless natives in Africa, see Grove 1989.
There are several resonances with the Indian case.

16. For a description of the transformation of virgin forests into plantations of
tea, rubber, and spices in the northeastern and southwestern parts of India, see
Tucker 1989.

17. For example, in the Himalayan region, sal (*Shorea robusta*) and deodar
(*Cedrus deodara*) were first exploited for railway sleepers and construction in the
infrastructure development phase. Later chir pine (*Pinus longifolia*) was merci-
lessly tapped for chemical industries in the manufacturing phase.

18. This process began in Brandis 1873 and was built upon in Watt [1889–96]
1972; Ribbentrop 1900; Brandis [1906] 1971; Troup [1921] 1980; and Pearson and
Brown 1932 [1981]; it was most recently exemplified in Champion and Seth 1968.
The classification schemes kept changing in terms of number of zones and types
(by rainfall intensity and climate), but the species considered important remained

the same. This of course is not to deny the foundation laid by botanical researches of the surgeon naturalists, an outstanding example being Cleghorn 1860 and the creation of facilities like the Calcutta Botanical Gardens established in 1788 (Grove 1988).

19. As an emergent tradition, the pedigree for such analyses may be found in the works of Thapar (1978) and Cohn (1987), who, writing on ancient and modern India respectively, have stressed the historicization of cultural forms essentialized during colonial rule. For, as Anderson (1991, 6) says, "all communities . . . are imagined. Communities are to be distinguished . . . by the style in which they are imagined." While the imagined community may be the nation-state, the discourse of nationalism has been a derivative discourse, the overweening concern of nationalist elites being the purchase of used ideas from the West (Chatterjee 1986). National forestry is implicated at several levels in colonial forestry, in a scientific and institutional culture that can be neither removed from history nor separated from power, even as it is being produced, constructed, and deployed.

20. One needs only to think of the massive amounts of documentation that the nineteenth- and twentieth-century British state produced in India, in the form of investigations, commissions, and the compilation, storage, and publication of statistical data on finance, trade, health, demography, crime, education, transportation, agriculture, and industry. Forestry was molded in the same documentation project that was at once totalizing and individualizing. See, for instance, the copious official forest histories generated continuously from the 1870s, when Brandis did his seminal work, until the National Commission on Agriculture in 1976.

21. The Indian Forest Department originated in 1864 with Dietrich Brandis, a German botanist turned forester, as the first IG of forests. A hurriedly drafted Forest Act was passed in 1865 to facilitate the acquisition of forest areas earmarked for railway supplies. However, the Indian Forest Act that is still largely in force came about only in 1878 after vigorous debate over the suggested provisions. In its final form it bore the distinctive stamp of B. H. Baden-Powell, the civil servant best known for his voluminous work on the land systems of British India.

22. There are government reports contemporary to the debate on forest legislation in which certain states, such as the Madras Presidency, are chastised for trying to obstruct the process of rapid revenue augmentation by achieving complete control over forest lands, when they expressed dismay over the effacement of customary rights enjoyed by indigenous people (Guha 1990).

23. It is important to comprehend the scientific content of silvicultural and watershed management programs designed and undertaken in the name of "scientific forestry" in their own terms, in addition to placing these specifics of praxis in their cultural, political, economic, and historical context. Though minimally addressed in this chapter, my research has also focused on this aspect.

24. This is abundantly evident from the official literature as well, which puts

the process in terms of "forest conservancy" for the larger public good (Stebbing 1922).

25. More biographical information on Brandis may be found in Guha 1991, which discusses the various stages through which the botanist from Bonn became the conservator of Burma and then the first IG of Indian forests. In this case the turn to forestry from botany seemed to follow a divine signal. His successor reminisced, "on arrival in Rangoon Brandis was informed that the vessel which brought his botanical library to India had gone down in the Rangoon river. He looked upon this as being almost a sign from heaven that he should put botany aside and devote himself to forestry" (Schlich 1925, 293).

26. Though his recommendations pertained specifically to the Central Provinces (Brandis 1876), Northwestern Provinces and Oudh (Brandis 1881), and Madras (Brandis 1883), their impact was more widespread and generalizing.

27. Around the same period, the Dutch state in Java took over all teak forest lands and provided detailed guidelines for staffing, logging, planting, and maintaining forests (Peluso 1991).

28. According to one revenue secretary of Central Provinces, railways not only stimulated the demand for hardwoods but also reduced the cost of transport and increased profit margins on forest operations, thus contributing doubly to the boom in revenues (Reports 1900–1930).

29. These figures are not adjusted for inflation or fluctuations in currency values.

30. Though written on the basis of African experience, these words admirably underscore the dominant view in South Asia as well.

31. Human ecologists, such as Madhav Gadgil (Jain 1981), have documented the role played in this respect by sacred groves in particular, though the symbiotic relationship of indigenous cultures to forest resources is richly treated in the various classic ethnographies of Verrier Elwin. Rustomji (1990) is a good place to sample them.

32. This is best exemplified by the elaborate provisions for assessing commercial value and compensation in proportion to rights for agricultural land acquired under the Land Acquisition Act (VII of 1894). Contemporaneous forest legislation did not share this interpretation of domain and chose to rely upon different principles of jurisprudence, whereby divine and monarchic ownership of land not in tillage was held to be complete.

33. Sir William Blackstone's views most closely reflect this position. While Blackstone accepted the general proposition that the institution of property is a natural right, he argued that it was, at the same time, a product of civil government and its laws (Embree 1969).

34. Making a similar assertion for forestry and conservation, Grove (1988, 20–21) says that "the colonial state in its pioneer conservationist role provided a forum for controls on the unhindered operation of capital for short-term gain

which, it might be argued, constituted a contradiction of what is normally supposed to have made up the normal currency of imperial expansion and profit maximization."

35. Thus, Brandis wrote of the manner by which teak forests were taken over in Burma: "at annexation the teak forests had by proclamation been declared the property of the state, and this was in accordance with old established custom, for under the Kings of Burma teak had been a royalty, all teak trees were the property of the King and teak timber was a monopoly" (Brandis 1897, 30).

36. The extent to which Baden-Powell managed to prevail can be seen from the draft of the forest bill he prepared, which incorporated the comments and statement of object and reasons by Brandis (1875) in his final memorandum to the government on the nature of the proposed forest legislation. Also see Baden-Powell and Gamble 1875.

37. Marx's comment ([1852] 1990, 31) on the French republican constitution of June 1848 that the document espoused "liberty in the general phrase, while abrogating liberty in the marginal note," would be apposite here.

38. The authority to stop shifting cultivation was the work of Baden-Powell (1893), who argued that it was temporary and destructive, hence incapable of leading to any right of prescription or easement. For definitions of such legal terms as "easement," "subservience," "prescription," and "protected and reserved forests," see Troup 1940.

39. The rights enumerated included grazing and pasture, grass cutting, lopping boughs and gathering leaves, wood rights, rights to dead and decayed leaves for litter and manure, rights to other forest produce, and hunting and fishing (IFC 1906; Troup 1940). For similar, though more summary, action in Java, see Peluso 1991.

40. In his study of South India, Nadkami (1989) has estimated the forest dependence of poor peasants at 25 percent of family income. He traced the local population's decline in the period from 1850 to 1900 to the abrogation of forest rights.

41. This compilation of the reserved species reflects the outcome of early forest rules and regulations promulgated between 1865 and 1875 in the cited provinces. Teak, sal, unjun, and babul were reserved in several of the regions mentioned.

42. The classic examination of the salience of violating the reciprocities between peasantries and the state is, of course, Scott 1976. I have gone into this question elsewhere in discussing the transformation of Bengal agriculture under colonialism (Sivaramakrishnan 1992).

43. Insights into the motivations behind nineteenth-century conservancy ideas are often to be gained from biographical accounts of the Forest Service officers. For example, in one account, an officer of the Indian Forest Service is described as choosing the career out of his fondness for hunting and fishing, epitomizing the sportsmen-naturalists who initially dominated the service and were drawn from certain classes of Victorian genteel society (Burke 1955). See also Baker 1991, 54, which describes the first conservator of Central Provinces, G. F. Pearson, as "a romantic who loved the wild woodland and ever varying scenery."

44. This was reported by Lieutenant Colonel Bailey, director of forest surveys, in the *Scottish Geographical Magazine* (1897) and quoted by Birdwood (1910). Birdwood also noted the widening of the conservation lobby by the surgeon naturalists, something that finds detailed discussion in Grove 1993. The strong cultural influence of this phase of conservancy on later scientific silviculture is well conveyed by the approving tones in which Stebbing (1922) writes about the personalities involved and his own association with them. Even though he was a professional, trained forester, Stebbing called his autobiography "Diary of a Sportsman Naturalist in India." I believe *shikari* is still noted on the masthead of the *Pakistan Journal of Forestry* (Michael Dove, personal communication).

45. As Grove (1988) points out, the surgeon naturalists were influenced by the French Physiocrats and the radical-humanitarian ideas of Rousseau (also a botanist). So while he helped lay the groundwork for forest reservation, Cleghom later became a critic of plantation crops in the Nilgiris, decried railway development, and "consistently claimed that activities of European planters were far more destructive than long established shifting kumri cultivators" (Grove 1988, 40). There is an interesting parallel to the preservationist ideas of George Perkins Marsh and the conflict with progressive conservation that developed in nineteenth-century environmental politics in the United States.

46. The text of these dispatches and the replies of the secretary of state for India in London supporting the introduction of sweeping regulations may be seen in Stebbing 1922.

47. An MSY forest has been defined by a professor of forest management at the Imperial Forestry Institute in Oxford as "a forest furnishing regular annual outturns in perpetuity, and producing the maximum outturn which the soil and climate are capable of producing" (Troup 1940). MSY forestry originated in eighteenth-century Germany and had been adopted in France by 1820 before reaching India (Lowood 1990). This fixes the rotation age of the forest at the year when biological growth of stock is maximized but growth rate is zero.

48. The continued interest in teak spanned more than a century, starting with the orders of the Bengal-Bombay Joint Commission in 1800 to ban felling of Malabar teak less than twenty-one inches in girth.

49. Forest revenues went up from about 10.5 million in current rupees in 1900 to 60 million in current rupees in 1930, although the area of forests remained constant at 16,941 square miles in the Central Provinces, which had the largest forest area in any Indian administrative unit.

50. Creosoting refers to the chemical treatment of wood to impregnate it with creosote oils. This is a dark-colored, heavy oil that consists chiefly of liquid and solid aromatic hydrocarbons, tar acids, and bases obtained by the distillation of coal tar. Creosote acts as a preservative for wood, serving as an insecticide.

51. See, for example, the work on white ants (Ribbentrop 1902) and pepsin substitutes (Umney 1896) published by the Central Provinces administration.

52. The case of sal (*Shorea robusta*) is particularly revealing in this respect and has been examined in detail in Sivaramakrishnan 1999.

53. For the Marxist/nationalist critique of Stokes and the relative underestimation of colonialism in his and similar explanations of economic change in the British period, see Habib 1985.

54. The subaltern school critique of Stokes is best read from Guha 1982 and Pandey 1980.

55. The value of the historical contingency argument is evident from Sarkar's description of the way widespread violation of forest laws restricting collection of building materials in Chittagong erupted into the burning of forest offices in the aftermath of the noncooperation movement in 1921–22; but by the same token, similar evidence seems to erode the plausibility of his structuralist formulations as determining forms of protest.

56. See the article by Chatterjee (1982) on communalism in Bengal and by Chakrabarty (1983) on jute millworkers, as well as Sumit Sarkar's ideas about shared structures of religiosity previously discussed.

57. The environmental movement's appeal to a precapitalist notion of community as an essentializing stereotype is discussed in the context of progressive politics in the industrialized states by Paehlke (1989), in a manner that provides interesting parallels to our more localized case.

58. See, for instance, the excellent discussion in Thapar 1989 of the modern construction of Hinduism that draws on precolonial and Orientalist texts in the historical processes of colonialism and nationalism.

59. See Elwin 1936, 1938, 1942, 1950, [1964] 1989, and the Hyderabad phase work of Cristoph Von Furer-Haimendorf (1943, 1945b, 1948). For the retention of this powerful trope and hence the treatment of Indian tribes continuously isolated from surrounding high civilizations of Hindus and Muslims, unaltered therefore in their backwardness (thereby lacking in history), until the extension of state power in the nineteenth century to hills and forests by the British, see Von Furer-Haimendorf (1982). A fuller critique of Subaltern Studies and their use of anthropological discourse may be found in Sivaramakrishnan 1995.

60. See, for instance, the discussion of firewood thefts from commons as an assertion of endangered rights by tenant farmers in eighteenth-century England (Thompson 1978). The manner in which the assertion occurs has to do with a pragmatism that in turn had to connect with a popular complicity of groups engaged in poaching, firewood collection, and so forth by the blurring of certain proprietary boundaries, even as others were asserted. For a similar discussion of wood theft from teak forests in Java, see Peluso 1992.

61. Shifting cultivation is known by various names, such as *dhya* in central India, *kumeri* and *podu* in South India, *jhum* in Bengal and eastern India, *taungya* in Burma, and *ladang* and *tegal* in Indonesia.

62. Pejorative description of shifting cultivation in the context of forest conser-

vation remains prevalent in the hegemonic discourses of World Bank reports. See, for example, Binswanger 1989 on the deforestation in Amazonia. This challenges recent research, especially in the neotropics, that has shown that basic traditional practices for swidden fallow agroforestry are adaptable to varying ecological and economic situations (Boom 1987; Gholz 1987; Henley 1982). Shifting cultivators in Asia, Africa, and the Americas have been reported to plant tree species in their fields.

63. This legacy of the Brandis era remains with us in the form of the conviction that shifting cultivation is ecologically unsound and exhibits cultural primitivity. Even the otherwise democratically worded National Forest Policy of 1988 says, "shifting cultivation is affecting the environment and productivity of land adversely. Alternative avenues of income, suitably harmonized with the *right land-use practises* should be devised to discourage shifting cultivation" (Government of India 1988, 4; emphasis added).

64. See the vivid accounts of Saora protest in the Central Provinces and Guden-Rampa uprisings in Madras (Elwin 1945; Arnold 1982; and Von Furer-Haimendorf 1945a).

65. On the religious idiom of peasant protest, see Guha 1983. Also see the detailed discussion of precise forms taken by the idiom and the lexicon of religious discourse as protest in Hardiman 1987 and Arnold 1982. The latter work remarks on the later *fituris* becoming overtly religious when the issue of customary forest rights came to the fore.

66. For an excellent detailed discussion of forest policy toward shifting cultivation in the Central Provinces and resistance, see Rangarajan 1992.

67. On earlier forms of taungya in Asia, see Menzies 1988. It was clearly a very old and indigenous system of agriculture.

68. A curious sidelight is that Brandis (1897, 40), otherwise more concerned about local rights in forests than his contemporaries making forest policy, also could not countenance shifting cultivation, as the following words clearly bring out. "This destructive mode of cultivation is now confined within definite limits. . . . the Karens are gradually abandoning their nomadic habits, they establish permanent paddy fields in the valleys and by terracing the hills they plant gardens and groves of fruit trees. The money they have earned by timber work and by planting teak enables them to purchase cattle, and they thus gradually rise in the scale of civilization."

69. Treating nomadic pastoralists as robbers and socially disruptive elements to be converted to settled agriculture is a discourse that runs through Mughal politics and colonial state making in India (Zaidi 1989; Nigam 1990a). In Africa, similar state intervention has been observed to precipitate a gradual dismantling of common property resources in favor of privatization by sedentary groups at the expense of pastoral nomads like the Orma in Kenya (Ensminger and Rutten 1991). Another example would be the gradual decline of the Kalahari San as the water

holes crucial to their lifestyle came under the control of Tswana herdsmen (Wilmsen 1989).

70. The sacralization of resource management institutions has its own political history—a narrative of contest and accommodation that has to be uncovered. Examining the history of the processes whereby sacred groves and such institutions of nature conservancy came to be established in India is a methodological and theoretical challenge still to be taken up by scholars.

71. For a detailed discussion of the intellectual approaches to conservation introduced to the West by the work of colonial surgeon naturalists in India, see Grove 1988.

72. See, especially, Bandhopadhyay and Shiva 1989 and Shiva 1991.

IV Revolutionary Mosquitoes of the Atlantic World

Malaria and Independence in the United States of America

J. R. McNeill

Every war and every seismic political shift is a complicated affair. The events are confusing to those involved and no less so to historians who afterward struggle to make sense of what evidence of events remains. The most difficult part of the historians' task is to take into account considerations of which the participants were unaware. These normally leave no trace in the surviving written record. They are like the dark matter of the universe: invisible and undetectable yet (as astrophysicists currently see matters) undoubtedly present and important. Dark matter has to be out there in the universe, because it exerts observable effects on observable phenomena, such as light itself or the rotational speed of galaxies. Military and political history is full of the equivalent of dark matter: things that must have been there, even though they left no direct trace.

This chapter concerns an example of historical dark matter: an instance in which mosquitoes and infections shaped political struggles. The mosquitoes left no memoirs or manifestos nor any archeological trace. But they played powerful roles in determining the outcomes of quests for independence in the United States (1775–83), the case examined here; in Haiti (1791–1804); and in Spanish America (1808–26). It is comforting to our species to suppose that the bravery, skill, and determination of George Washington, Toussaint L'Ouverture, Simon Bolivar, and the men under their commands were responsible for the military successes that led to independence. Comforting and true. Less comforting, but no less true, is that these campaigns ended as they did in large measure because Washington, Toussaint, and Bolivar had airborne allies of whom they were unaware: the mosquitoes that communicate malaria and yellow fever. The airborne allies left no trace in the historical record, so historians have frequently tried to explain these revolutions without them. Focusing on the American case, I offer a different portrait, a fuller one, that sketches ecological and epidemiological contexts and circumstances—the dark matter—that framed human events.

The argument, in brief, proceeds as follows. In the American Revolution, the British southern strategy ultimately led to defeat at Yorktown in part because British forces were much more susceptible to malaria than were the Americans. Malaria was ubiquitous in the Carolina low country in part because of changes in the agroecology of the Carolinas since 1690. Americans were more resistant to it, on average, than British and German troops because of repeated prior exposure. Differential susceptibility to malaria constrained British strategy and presented a dilemma from which there was no escape. Either the British could keep their forces within reach of the Royal Navy, in which case they could easily be resupplied and reinforced but could not be kept healthy, or they could leave the coasts, in which case they could expect better health but could not be resupplied or reinforced.

Mosquito Determinism and Its Limits

At this point, many readers will be tempted to accuse me of mosquito determinism. Environmental determinism in any form is now unfashionable among historians and geographers, let alone mosquito determinism.[1] What we call human history is often, not always, the interplay between social and natural processes. Just how important each of these may be is a variable that changes from instance to instance. In matters of intellectual history, let's say the influence of Hegel upon Herzen, one can safely ignore environment and geography. In the economic history of New Zealand, a country that has undergone dramatic environmental change in the past five hundred years, one ought not do so.

My case falls toward the opposite end of the spectrum from Hegel and Herzen. Infections killed far more combatants in the American Revolution than did violence, and two of the most deadly, malaria and smallpox, were systematically partisan because of differential immunities. American forces were more vulnerable to smallpox than were the British (and German) troops arrayed against them, because most of them had grown up in regions where smallpox was not endemic and they had not encountered and survived it. The British and Germans, on the other hand, were almost all survivors of smallpox and immune to it. A smallpox epidemic, probably originating in Mexico, raged throughout North America during the American Revolution, and its partisanship posed one of George Washington's most vexing problems, one he solved through compulsory inoculation of the Continental Army.[2] Similarly, many of the Americans, especially those from the South, had survived many bouts of malaria and had developed some resistance to it, whereas their enemies, for the most part, had never encountered the disease. Malaria by the eighteenth century had become rare in Britain and Germany and in any case had never been widespread. The argument, clearly, cannot apply to Loyalists; those Americans who sided with King George III had different ideas and interests from the revolutionary patriots but roughly the same portfolio of immunities.

In centuries past, differential immunity, where it existed, routinely had sovereign effects over warfare, migration, and settlement patterns. This is hard to appreciate today, as we live in a golden age of health and longevity—more golden for some than others, of course, but even Sierra Leoneans, who have the shortest life expecxtancy of any national population today, are longer lived on average than any large population 250 years ago.

In times before antibiotics, widespread vaccination, and other modern health practices, armies and navies were especially unhealthy populations.[3] Although composed mainly of men in the prime of life, military routines subjected those men to various hardships, often including malnutrition and stress. Moreover, as large agglomerations of men from different regions, armies and navies brought infections together with inexperienced immune systems as a matter of course. Infectious diseases probably killed more military men than did combat in every war in history until the Russo-Japanese War of 1904–5. In the British Army during the Seven Years' War (1756–63), diseases killed roughly eight times as many men as did combat.[4]

In cases where war brought rival armies together from regions that had been in long-standing communication with one another, say armies from Britain and France fighting in Flanders, the disease experience of both forces would, over time, be roughly the same. Many more men would die from typhus, dysentery, and other diseases than from combat, but generally neither side enjoyed a great advantage on account of differential immunity. And certainly neither side enjoyed an ongoing systemic advantage. On European battlefields, when Europeans fought one another, disease was an important killer, but not consistently partisan. Epidemics might randomly strike one army rather than another, but they did not systematically favor one over another. The same was true on Chinese battlefields when Chinese fought Chinese or on Indian battlefields when Indians fought Indians.

However, the significance of disease in warfare changed when armies fought far from home in unfamiliar disease environments or fought against people with sharply different immunities and susceptibilities to disease. For example, when Chinese fought on the inner Asian steppe against Dzungar Mongols in the eighteenth century, the Chinese enjoyed a systematic advantage, because their troops carried immunity to smallpox and the Dzungars did not.[5] The Dzungars had been too isolated from the large populations of Eurasia through which smallpox circulated to encounter it in childhood (when it is usually a mild disease) and thereby acquire immunity. But almost every Chinese who reached adulthood was immune. Similarly, when Spanish conquistadors fought Amerindians in sixteenth-century Mexico or Peru, their immunities to smallpox, measles, mumps, whooping cough, and influenza gave them a potent advantage over their enemies (and their Amerindian allies). These were situations in which populations carrying fuller arrays of immunities to the so-called crowd diseases enjoyed persistent systematic advantages over more isolated populations who had none. Such situations were routine in world history before the twentieth century and go some ways toward explaining the successful spread of civilization.[6] The key to this phenomenon is that the crowd diseases were maintained by circulating among millions of people. They prevailed where populations were dense and interactive; they did not depend on specific environmental conditions.

Less routine, but common enough, were situations in which armies and navies operated far from home in hostile disease environments for which their backgrounds did not and could not prepare them. The most conspicuous cases took place when invasion forces entered regions with local diseases that could not spread around the world because they depended on specific environmental circumstances. Malaria and yellow fever fall into this category because their spread requires mosquitoes and the mosquitoes require certain conditions (particularly of temperature). Where those conditions existed, malaria and yellow fever might reign, and populations who lived in such zones paid a considerable price, mainly in the form of childhood mortality. But in the bargain they acquired resistance to lethal diseases that would help them against invaders. Most African societies between the Sahara and the Cape of Good Hope, for example, enjoyed a systematic edge over invading foreigners because of their resistance to malaria and (in some cases) to yellow fever—an edge that modern military medicine reduced from the 1890s, thereby making European colonialism in Africa much more affordable, tempting, and likely.[7]

It is the dependence of malaria and yellow fever upon mosquitoes for their transmission that made them diseases of specific environments, mainly warm and humid ones. This made it impossible for troops from elsewhere to have acquired resistance through childhood exposure. And so, in contests between troops recruited primarily in warm and humid regions and others recruited elsewhere, malaria and yellow fever worked in systematically partisan ways, not at random, and affected the outcome of campaigns.

The fact that malaria and yellow fever are vector-borne diseases may help account for their virulence. Via evolutionary pressures, pathogens normally evolve so as to flourish in their hosts without killing them; that is, they normally evolve toward benignity. But parasites that divide their time between more than one home cannot easily evolve toward benignity on multiple fronts. In effect, it seems the malaria parasite and yellow fever virus evolved so as to do no harm to the mosquitoes that bear them. From the point of view of these microbes, human bodies are disposable conduits by which they get from one mosquito to the next.[8]

Even in cases of virulent infections, where mosquitoes and diseases exerted a strong effect upon political events, they could do so only because of circumstances both natural and social. Nature makes its own history, one might say, but not just as it pleases.

Atlantic Geopolitical Contexts

The Revolutionary War in America was the first successful rebellion by local populations against European colonial power. From the fifteenth century onward, the Atlantic European kingdoms (and eventually the Dutch Republic too) used their growing seaborne capacities and their increasingly effective military organization to assert themselves throughout the Atlantic world and beyond.[9] Most of Africa remained too difficult for them to overcome, partly for reasons of the disease environment and partly because many African societies fielded formidable armies. But in the Americas all the Atlantic European powers met with success in conquering territory and establishing colonies in the sixteenth and seventeenth centuries—in large part because their soldiers, sailors, conquistadors, buccaneers, and *bandeirantes* enjoyed disease immunities that Amerindians did not have.[10] By the early eighteenth century, the political configuration on the Atlantic seaboard of the Americas was a stable one. The Dutch had been ejected from Brazil by 1653, and the Spanish from Jamaica in 1655. From that time until 1763 no large territories changed imperial hands except temporarily until 1763; what modest conquests were made were almost always restored by treaties in 1697, 1713, and 1748.[11] Each Atlantic empire except the Dutch continued to grow, however, at the expense of Amerindian states and societies.

Spain held (rather loosely) territories extending from Argentina to California, a sprawling, lucrative expanse that through its silver production financed the Spanish state. Portugal ruled Brazil, the world's leading sugar producer and a major source of gold after the 1690s. France claimed Canada, valuable mainly for its offshore fish and inland furs; the Mississippi valley region; and a scattering of islands in the Caribbean, including the western third of Hispaniola, then called St.-Domingue and now called Haiti.[12] The Dutch, expelled from Brazil and New York (1664–74), held only small islands in the Caribbean, useful for their sugar and salt (crucial to the Dutch Atlantic herring fishery), and the plantation colony of Surinam. The English (after 1707, the British) controlled a collection of Caribbean islands, the largest of which was Jamaica, and the settlement colonies from the Carolinas to Newfoundland (acquired by treaty in 1713). Each time war broke out among these Atlantic powers, campaigns were fought on the North American continent and in American waters, as well as in Europe and on occasions elsewhere, often India, too. Religious quarrels, dynastic interests, and power politics inspired major wars in 1689–97, 1702–13, 1739–48, and 1754–63. In addition, freelancers, freebooters, and buccaneers engaged in their own operations during times of both war and peace. By and large, in the Americas Britain proved the strongest, on account of firmer finances and a steadfast commitment to naval power.

However, despite the Royal Navy and a strong interest in acquiring Spanish territory, British forces routinely failed to conquer and control Spanish strongholds. Lightly defended outposts were easy to take and destroy. But fortified positions stymied the British time and again. A principal reason for this, and indeed for the durability of the Spanish empire in the Americas, was differential immunity to yellow fever and malaria. British forces were recruited from Britain and the mainland colonies of North America, whereas the Spanish relied heavily on militias recruited in and around their Caribbean ports—and upon Spanish troops stationed in the Caribbean and therefore often immune veterans of bouts of malaria and yellow fever. Indeed Spanish troops in many cases would have acquired some resistance to malaria by growing up in Spain, whose river valleys generally hosted endemic malaria in the eighteenth century. By building fortifications, the Spanish in America could oblige attackers to lay siege, something that normally took weeks or months, and thereby to risk the rigors of the Caribbean disease environment. There is some evidence that both the Spanish and the British understood that local forces and good fortifications gave the Spanish an advantage over forces from far away and conducted their wars accordingly. They did not have to understand epidemiology and disease ecology to notice who died and who did not in a yellow fever epidemic and to shape their strategies with this in mind. In short, whether contemporaries recognized it or not, arthropod-borne disease helped defend the Spanish empire in the Americas through the eighteenth century.[13]

The interimperial wars in the Atlantic continued until 1815, and to some degree both the American and Haitian Revolutions were chapters in this ongoing saga. But these revolutionary wars were also fundamentally different from their predecessors. Whereas prior to the 1770s the populations of the Americas had fought on behalf of one or another imperial power, henceforth they sometimes fought for themselves and in particular for independence from any and all imperial powers. This political shift altered the significance of infectious tropical diseases. No longer did they underpin the geopolitical status quo by making expeditionary warfare so difficult. Now they systematically abetted revolutions launched by American- or African-born populations whose bloodstreams carried protective antibodies.

Slave revolts in some respects prefigured this shift. Although they failed in almost every case, in Palmares (Brazil) runaway and rebellious slaves managed to defend a *quilombo* (maroon community) for several decades until 1694, despite repeated attacks. The *palmarinos* may have enjoyed a strong advantage in terms of disease immunity: they were born either in west-central Africa (Angola mainly) or in northeast Brazil and were presumably all or almost all veterans of malaria. Many of those sent out against them were Dutch (the Dutch controlled Pernambuco in 1624–53) or Portuguese and were likely highly susceptible to it. But the surviving records have little to say on this front, and it is possible, although unlikely, that Palmares and environs were free of malaria and other tropical diseases.[14]

A slave rising in Surinam in the 1770s shows the power of disease resistance more clearly. Dutch planters had organized a sugar economy along the coastal rivers based on African slave labor, but slaves gradually founded maroon communities in the abundant forestlands of the interior. Beginning in 1772, the maroons embarked on large raids against the plantations, prompting the dispatch from the Netherlands of some 1,650 soldiers. The Dutch forces succeeded in pushing the maroons deeper into the forests and relieved the threat upon the plantations, but only about 200 of them survived to return to Europe. John Steadman, a Scottish soldier of fortune who served with the Dutch, noted in April 1777 at the end of the campaign:

> In Short out of a number of near twelve hundred Able bodied men, now not one hundred did return to theyr Friends at home Amongst whom Perhaps not 20 were to be found in perfect health, all the others (a verry few of the Remaining Relief Excepted) being Repatriated, sick; discharged, past all remedy; Lost; killed; & murdered by the Climate.[15]

Steadman went on to remark upon the importance of differential immunity by observing:

> Amongst the Officers and Private men who had *formerly* been in the West Indies, none died at all, while amongst the whole number of

1200 together I Can only Recollect one Single marine who Escaped from Sickness.[16]

The sickness in question might well be many things or a combination of things. Judging from the swampy terrain of Surinam the chief suspect would be malaria. However, the sharp distinction between veterans of the West Indies, among whom none apparently fell ill, and the others, among whom almost all did, suggests yellow fever, which more completely immunizes its survivors than does malaria. That is, one can get malaria repeatedly, and a spell or even a lifetime in the West Indies would not guarantee immunity to it; but surviving yellow fever confers a strong lifetime immunity. Whatever the case, Steadman's account shows how powerful prior disease experience could be in shaping vulnerability and resistance to disease.

The maroons of Surinam avoided defeat, but they were too few and too poorly armed to convert the destruction of the Dutch regiments into a political triumph over the Dutch plantation colony. Mosquitoes and diseases alone might destroy an army, but they could not make a revolution.

The Southern Colonies and the American Revolution, 1780–81

While the maroons waged their war in the swamps of Surinam, a larger-scale revolt brewed in North America and resulted in war by 1775. The rebellious Americans organized the Continental Army, led by George Washington, to counter British forces. After a few years of inconclusive ebb and flow, by 1779 the British were firmly ensconced in several port cities, chiefly New York, and the Americans were unable to dislodge them. But the Americans controlled most of the countryside, and the British were unable to lure them into decisive battles. It was a considerable achievement that Washington was able to maintain an army, despite precarious finances, uncertain loyalties among his troops, quarrels in the fledgling Congress, and the toll exacted by smallpox and other diseases. It was an expensive engagement for the British to maintain a large force (they sent sixty thousand men to America in all) so far from home for so long. After the Battle of Saratoga (1777) had showed them that the Americans would not lose quickly, the French joined the war (1778) and Spain followed (1779). Britain and Holland went to war in late 1780.

Britain thus faced an international war of the utmost seriousness, with multiple enemies and no allies. The British Army, which had numbered only forty-eight thousand at the outbreak of the war, was thinly stretched from Bengal to Barbados and beyond. Since the British Army in America could not be supplied locally (commandeering food and supplies was a good way to turn Loyalists into patriots), the Royal Navy had to safeguard each British enclave in the Americas. Now, with the expansion of the war, the Royal Navy would be thinly stretched, too, by threats in the English Channel and North Sea, the West Indies, the Mediterranean, and the Indian Ocean.

But until late 1781 the main theater remained America. Campaigns in the northern colonies had frustrated the British. They hoped that if Washington's army could be shattered, colonists loyal to the king would easily restore British authority. But although Washington had been defeated in battle (Long Island) the rebellion could not be extinguished. Washington prudently would not allow a showdown. With the internationalization of the war, the standoff of late 1778 and most of 1779 could not last, and time seemed to favor the Americans. Britain needed a new strategy, one that would bring matters to a head quickly.

Britain's warlords in London and the commander of the army in America, Sir Henry Clinton, settled on a southern strategy. They hoped the Loyalists, who in the North had proved too few or too timid, existed in sufficient number in the Carolinas. They also hoped to ruin the lucrative export trades of tobacco and rice in the southern colonies and so starve the rebels of funds with which to pay the Continental Army. Accordingly, early in 1780 the British invested Charleston and after a successful siege took it in May. The Carolinas certainly had Loyalists, but as it turned out they had anopheles mosquitoes too.

The Carolinas and Mosquitoes

The coastal Carolinas had been colonized by English and Barbados planters, and by the 1690s was a fast-growing slave plantation society.[17] Rice was the principal crop, well suited to the swampy lowlands from Cape Fear to Savanna. Raising rice in these environments required endless labor, such as diking and draining swamps, and careful management of irrigation. (Indigo, the second most important plantation crop, also involved irrigation and was also first undertaken on the inland swamps.) Many slaves from West African rice-growing regions had the necessary technical knowledge for rice cultivation in tidal estuaries and inland swamps, and by 1760 their knowledge, skill, and labor had created a thriving plantation regime that exported tens of thousands of tons of rice each year. Slave owners specifically sought slaves from Senegambia and Guinea who had the requisite rice-growing skills.[18]

The landscape they created was ideal habitat for the anopheles mosquito, the carrier of malaria.[19] There are about four hundred species of the genus anopheles in the world, of which perhaps thirty to forty can transmit malaria. Some anopheles existed in the Americas before Columbus, although malaria apparently did not. Like all mosquitoes, their lives pass through four stages: egg, larva, pupa, and adult. The first three stages take place in water. Some species prefer fresh water, some like salt water, but to flourish all need unpolluted water full of algae, bacteria, and other organic material on which they feed. The first three stages last about five to fourteen days, depending in part upon temperature: the warmer it is the faster the maturation. Once adult, male anopheles typically last only about one week, feeding on nectar and sucrose and devoting all available energy to finding females of their species. Females survive about one to three weeks on average. They too can feed on sweet substances, but to deposit eggs and reproduce, they must find a blood meal. They feed chiefly at dawn and dusk. Some anopheline species strongly prefer human blood and thus are highly efficient vectors of malaria, such as *Anopheles gambiae,* the world's most deadly insect; some prefer other mammals and only rarely bite humans; most will take what they can get, since there can be no reproduction without a blood feast. In the Carolina low country, the climate was warm enough for more than six months of the year, allowing upward of twelve generations of anopheles each year—if other conditions were favorable.

The dominant anopheline mosquito in the eastern United States in the twentieth century was the *Anopheles quadrimaculatus.*[20] It presumably reigned in the eighteenth century as well, an inference supported by its very widespread distribution today, from Florida to Quebec and from Mexico to the Dakotas.[21] It breeds on the edges of big bodies of fresh water, such as ponds, swamps, ditches, and irrigated fields. Rice fields meet its every specification. But its larvae can also survive in brackish water and salt marshes. It needs temperatures between ten and forty degrees Celsius, with its ideal around thirty degrees Celsius, that is, midsummer weather in the Carolinas and Virginia. The female feeds on large mammals, including deer, pigs, cattle, horses, and humans. It is not as efficient a malaria vector as *An. gambiae,* because of its eclectic feeding habits. A blood meal usually amounts to two to four milligrams, which allows oviposition (laying of eggs) within three days. In her lifetime, a female *An. quadrimaculatus* might lay nine to twelve batches, or maybe two thousand eggs in all. Females hibernate, often in close proximity to humans and domesticated animals, and in spring when temperatures reach twenty degrees Celsius they become active again, usually only long enough to lay one more batch of eggs.

To sustain thick populations of *An. quadrimaculatus,* the Carolina low country had to provide good breeding habitat and abundant blood meals. The landscape was suitable to anopheles habits even before the installation of the rice economy, but the extensive irrigation of fields with shallow water laden with organic matter made conditions even better. It may also be that the widespread presence of maize, or corn, helped anopheles to flourish in the Carolinas. Recent research in Ethiopia shows that maize pollen serves as an ideal food for anopheles larvae, which are much more likely to survive to the pupal stage if located close enough to maize fields so that the wind carries pollen to their aquatic cradles. In Ethiopia the relevant anopheles species is *arabiensis,* and it is uncertain (to me at least) whether other anopheles, specifically *quadrimaculatus,* react so favorably to the presence of maize pollen. Perhaps any pollen would do, and in the Ethiopian case it just happened to be maize. But it remains a possibility that there is a general maize-anopheles link, and, if there is, then the low country plantations would have been especially hospitable to anopheles.[22]

However helpful rice, indigo, and maize may have been for the anopheles, the mosquitoes still needed blood meals. Once again, the plantation economy provided generously. The Carolina coastlands had been thinly populated in the seventeenth century. Only with the rise of rice and the importation of Africans did human population grow quickly. By 1708 there were about 9,000 people (about evenly divided between whites and blacks) in the areas surrounding Charleston, and by the first U.S. census (1790), there were about a hundred thousand in the low country. In addition to the rapidly growing human population, the Carolinas also offered cattle blood for the thirsty anopheles. Low country plantations sometimes maintained pastures and cattle for their own purposes, and the Carolina back country had more. Back country cattle were routinely driven to the coast for slaughter. Every plantation had a few horses too. So between rice and maize and between people and cattle, conditions for the anopheles mosquito in the Carolina low country improved markedly throughout the eighteenth century. Indeed contemporary observers often noted how thick the mosquitoes were in summer and early fall.[23] Dense populations of vectors and of hosts improved conditions for the transmission of malaria.

Malaria and Resistance to Malaria in the Southern Colonies

Malaria is among the most ancient of human diseases and the most deadly. Today it kills upward of two million people a year, mainly children, mainly in Africa. It is caused by a parasite, a plasmodium, that comes in four varieties, the two most important of which are *Plasmodium vivax,* which causes a milder form of malaria, and *Plasmodium falciparum,* the more deadly. The parasite has a complex life cycle, divided between time spent in humans and in female anopheles. The time spent in mosquitoes is called the extrinsic cycle, which lasts for nine to twenty-one days. In warmer temperatures, the parasite reproduces faster within mosquitoes. The extrinsic cycle requires temperatures of fifteen degrees Celsius in the case of *P. vivax* and twenty degrees for *P. falciparum.* The parasite does mosquitoes no harm.

When anopheles mosquitoes bite people, they inject the parasite into the bloodstream (beginning the intrinsic cycle). The parasite then migrates to the liver, where it reproduces exuberantly, and thence to red blood cells. It spends seven to thirty days incubating in human bodies before symptoms appear. If not checked by a vigorous immune system, the parasite can reproduce abundantly within the red blood cells, so that an initial sortie of a few dozen parasites becomes a few trillion invaders. The symptoms include shivering chills, high fever, sweats, bodily pains, and malaise—not easy to distinguish from a variety of other infections. Falciparum malaria often brings an elevated heart rate, a mild jaundice, and an enlarged spleen or liver. In severe cases of falciparum malaria the parasite turns one's red blood cells into a sticky plaque that clogs the circulatory system, bringing on organ failure, seizures, coma, severe anemia, and cardiovascular collapse, among other grave symptoms.

Malaria often kills people who are already weakened by other conditions, such as malnutrition, another disease, or a compromised immune system.

Immunity to malaria is hard won. Most people in tropical Africa are immune to vivax malaria on account of genetic characteristics (the absence of Duffy antigen in red blood cells), as are many people of African descent. Moreover, long exposure to the deadly *P. falciparum* strain has favored the evolution and survival of genetic resistance among West Africans, even at the cost of higher risk of anemia. This comes in the form of the so-called sickle cell trait, common but not universal among people of West African origin and descent. The sickle cell makes one's hemoglobin indigestible to *P. falciparum*. People from other parts of the world in which malaria has long been present have also evolved genetic shields in other forms.

Anyone can acquire conferred resistance by surviving repeated bouts of malaria. Acquired resistance is a complicated matter, not fully understood today, because the parasite passes through different stages in its life cycle and different antibodies provide protection against it in its different phases. But in short the more often one has hosted the parasite, the more resistant one is likely to be, although rarely if ever fully immune.

Hence people born and raised in endemic malaria regions who hosted the parasite frequently (and survived) by adulthood enjoyed strong resistance to infection. People born and raised elsewhere, unless their ancestors came from malarial regions, carried no immunity and if infected with *P. falciparum* stood a fine chance of getting severely ill and a good one of dying.

Whether malaria kills a lot of people or just a few depends not only on immunity but on the efficiency of transmission from mosquito to human to mosquito. As with all vector-borne diseases, this depends chiefly on three things: (1) the population densities of people and vectors; (2) the feeding focus of the vector, that is, whether it bites only people or bites people among other mammals; and (3) the longevity of the vector. Of these factors, it is the longevity of the anopheles mosquito that matters most. Old mosquitoes are the most dangerous, because they are more likely to have bitten an infectious person and to harbor malarial parasites. As it happens, under suitable conditions—such as prevailed on the Carolina coasts—one infected person can easily spread malaria to another one hundred.[24]

Thus in the years after 1690 the Carolina coastlands increasingly became a perilous landscape, but more perilous for some than for others. People of West African birth or descent had less to fear from malaria than anyone else. People born and raised locally, if they survived childhood, would normally have carried strong resistance and had little cause for concern, although they might experience recurrent vivax malaria (which stays with one forever and can flare up from time to time). People who came to the Carolinas from malaria-free zones—in practice from high latitudes—ran great risks.

Contemporaries recognized a connection between swamps in general—and rice plantations in particular—and fevers. Lord Adam Gordon, a British officer traveling through the Carolinas in 1764–65 unknowingly identified the link: "In general what part of South Carolina is planted, is counted unhealthy, owing to the Rice-dams and Swamps, which as they occasion a great quantity of Stagnated water in Summer, never fails to increase the Number of Insects, and to produce fall fevers and Agues."[25] Slaves, despite their relative safety from malaria, considered rice work the most dangerous to their health. Thomas Jefferson regretted that rice cultivation "requir[es] the whole country to be laid under water during a season of the year, [and] sweeps off numbers of the inhabitants annually with pestilential fevers."[26] Whites tried to spend the summers away from the rice plantations, preferably inland, where malaria (and yellow fever) was less prevalent. In the years before the American Revolution, the most prosperous families summered in Rhode Island to avoid the fever season. Gradually, people learned not to build their homes next to swamps or rice fields.[27]

This knowledge, however, did not prevent what contemporaries often called "country fever" from ravaging the low country population in the eighteenth century. Every summer and fall, especially in wetter years, it carried off hundreds or thousands. Newcomers from Britain, lacking all immunities, were the most likely to suffer and die.

Malaria and the British Army in the Southern Colonies, 1780–81

This was the environment into which the British Army stepped in early 1780. Sir Henry Clinton had brought a combined force of British and German troops from England at the end of 1779 and after a month's voyage had reached the Georgia coast and soon lay siege to Charleston at the healthiest season of the year. Clinton commanded the siege, but soon after its end he returned to New York, leaving the infantry in the hands of Lord Edward Cornwallis. Cornwallis commanded about nine thousand regulars. He looked forward to the support of Loyalists, especially in the back country. He also had allies in the slave population, of whom perhaps twenty thousand escaped to join British forces, mainly as laborers. Finally, the Cherokee, Choctaw, and other Indians of the back country made common cause with Cornwallis, as they had long-standing grievances against the colonials. But the heart of the British strategy lay with the Loyalists, whom Cornwallis, Clinton, and their superiors in London assumed existed in quantity throughout the South. They hoped that if the British Army could temporarily secure a given region, Loyalists would then declare for the king and could be relied upon to hold and administer territory. Thus the regular army would be free to move on and repeat the exercise elsewhere. With only a modest commitment of men and resources—all that was available given the entanglements elsewhere—the South could be won through this policy of Americanization.[28]

The British had one further ally in smallpox. Most of their regular troops (not the Loyalists) had been exposed to smallpox in Britain or Germany and were immune. Comparatively few of the Carolinians were. The North American smallpox epidemic so threatened Washington's army early in the war that he had written he had more to fear from it than from the sword of the enemy, a situation that inoculation remedied.[29] However, the irregular forces and militia, upon which the Americans depended heavily in the southern campaigns, remained for the most part susceptible to smallpox. So did Cornwallis's allies, the Amerindians and most of the slaves. (Thomas Jefferson claimed that, of the thirty thousand Virginia slaves who joined the British cause, twenty-seven thousand died from smallpox and "camp fever.")[30] Through inoculation, which killed a few but saved the rest, the Continental Army acquired an effective shield against smallpox. Without it, the epidemic might have sapped the American forces faster than other diseases drained the British.

Cornwallis and his men faced enemies both human and microbial. After the British capture of five thousand rebel Americans at Charleston, Washington dispatched an army commanded by the victor of Saratoga, General Gates, to counter the British southern strategy. Cornwallis also had to worry about irregular forces throughout the Carolinas and Virginia, the patriot militias skilled in guerilla tactics. And, deadliest of all, he had to worry about malaria. In pursuing the southern strategy, the British put an army in the awkward position noted at the outset of this chapter. Cornwallis needed to find a place where the Royal Navy could reach his troops but the anopheles mosquito could not—but there was no such place in the South.

British forces coming to America in the 1770s and 1780s arrived in a vulnerable state. The men first had to withstand the hazards of their ports of embarkation, which offered all the unhealthy temptations known to man. They then faced a cruise of four weeks or more, in crowded conditions with sometimes spoiling food. Regiments shipping out to the West Indies during the war lost 10–25 percent of their men while crossing the ocean.[31] Sailing to North America was usually a little healthier, because the journey was shorter. But, nonetheless, many died en route and more fell sick. Arriving in the Americas brought men into an alien disease environment, with new diseases (such as malaria) and unfamiliar strains of old diseases, which could also circumvent their immune systems.[32] Conditions in camps, barracks, and garrisons anywhere were often crowded and unsanitary, although the British Army in the eighteenth century was developing sanitary regulations that helped check some infectious diseases somewhat.[33] To exacerbate matters, British soldiers in America were often underfed, because of the difficulties of supplying an army from across the sea, making the men more vulnerable to infection.

Doctors were normally of no help. The British Army maintained a medical establishment, although it probably had difficulty recruiting the best doctors of the day. Even the best probably killed more patients than they cured. Medical procedures had not changed much since 1685, when the best doctors in England treated King Charles II, whom they diagnosed with malaria, by drawing a pint of blood from the royal arm, purging impurities from the king with emetics made from antinomy, and feeding him the powdered skull of a man who had never been buried.[34] The king soon died. Ordinary soldiers could expect to be bled and purged if they fell into the hands of doctors, as these remedies, it was conventionally held, would allow evil humors to escape the body. A healthy distrust of doctors was commonplace in the British military.[35]

The greatest exception to the lethal incompetence of eighteenth-century doctors involved malaria and "the bark." Powder derived from the bark of the chinchona tree, native to Peru, offered some protection against malaria. By the middle of the seventeenth century the bark was known in England and was part of doctors' common knowledge by the 1680s. But the bark was expensive, and the British Army rarely had enough. And what it had was needed more urgently in India and the West Indies than in the Carolinas. So an army based in Charleston and expected to operate in the southern colonies faced acute dangers to its health with little to no medical help. A garrison in Georgia, for example, found that in any given week two-thirds of its strength was "disabled by malaria."[36] The British Army in the southern colonies needed to find the equivalent of the inoculation shield Washington had mandated for the Continental Army.

Cornwallis was fully aware of the problem. Soon after taking over from Clinton in South Carolina, he wrote that he needed to keep his troops away from the coastal lowlands between late June and mid-October to avoid "a certainty of their being rendered useless for some time for military service, if not entirely lost."[37] Cornwallis had to abandon his position at Cheraw Hill in South Carolina in the summer of 1780, because two-thirds of the regiment stationed there fell ill, enfeebling the British presence, which encouraged the locals to side with the rebellion.[38] The British director of the war, Lord Germain, also understood the hazards of the summer and early autumn. He instructed Cornwallis in June 1781 to employ his (modest) reinforcements as "a co-operating army until southern provinces are reduced, or the season becomes too advanced for active service."[39]

In August 1780, before malaria had taken firm hold of his forces, Cornwallis managed to deliver a smashing blow to Gates's army at Camden. It was the last time the British would administer a convincing defeat to the rebels. Then, in October 1780 a Loyalist militia (not Cornwallis's army) suffered a defeat at King's Mountain. By now the vulnerability of the British Army to malaria had begun to tell. Cornwallis (six months later) said his forces were "nearly ruined" by disease in the autumn of 1780.[40] His surgeon, John Hayes, considered that "health once more begins to smile on us" by mid-November, when he counted only 198 sick in the hospital of the Charleston garrison and only 5 dead in the previous week. In anticipation of further encounters with malaria, Hayes reported that he had ordered "two hundred weight of best powdered bark."[41]

In the healthier conditions of the winter months, Cornwallis's forces lost a battle at the Cowpens (January 1781) and held the field after the bloody encounter of Guilford Courthouse (March). For almost a year his army had been engaged in an exhausting game of cat and mouse with American forces led first by Gates and then by Nathaniel Greene. The Americans, after Camden, took care not to risk all on a single battle, and Greene excelled in drawing Cornwallis deeper and deeper into the country, farther and farther from his bases. The British Army, although normally the superior force in any set-piece battle, did not have nearly enough men to hold the country it won, and the Loyalists, on whom the British counted to administer and police secured regions, were unable to perform their assigned role. So Cornwallis chased the Americans the length and breadth of the Carolinas, hoping for a decisive encounter that would change the political balance. Greene prudently did not give it to him. At one point, in a desperate attempt to catch Greene's forces as they retreated, Cornwallis ordered all his supply train burned, except for salt, ammunition, and—revealingly—medicine.

Although Greene's forces suffered from diseases as well, and many more died from them than from battle, on the whole his men enjoyed better health than did the British. At most points roughly two-thirds of his force was made up of locally recruited militia men, veterans of the Carolinas disease environment and in particular survivors of repeated bouts of malaria. The component of his army that had come with him from the northern colonies suffered more severely, especially New Englanders, most of whom would never have encountered malaria before. The regulars of the Continental Army under Greene's command were almost as susceptible to the disease as were Cornwallis's soldiers.

After Guilford Courthouse, in April 1781, Cornwallis moved his force back to the coast, to Wilmington, North Carolina, in hope of rest and resupply. But as he contemplated the onset of the summer months, he concluded he would have to go inland again, "to the upper parts of the Country, where alone I can hope to preserve the troops from the fatal sickness, which so nearly ruined the Army last autumn."[42] Despite occasional reinforcements, Cornwallis's army grew weaker with each passing month, and another malaria season would, he recognized, cause a considerable proportion of what he had remaining to melt away.

Cornwallis had had enough of the Carolinas. He did not have enough men to hold the upcountry, and the Loyalists could not do it for him. He could not keep his army healthy in the low country, and fever deaths depleted his strength so that even maintaining his garrisons was becoming difficult. So, bowing to these unpleasant realities, on April 25 Cornwallis gave up on the Carolinas, leaving a garrison to hold Charleston, and moved the bulk of his force northward toward Virginia and the Chesapeake. He did this on his own initiative, without orders from his superiors, who were distressed to learn of his flight. Neither they nor Cornwallis knew it, but he was fleeing from *An. quadrimaculatus.*

After a long march and a few raids in Virginia, Cornwallis received orders to move to the tidewater coast. His commander, Clinton, fearful that a French fleet and Washington's army might attack New York, had instructed Cornwallis to find some "healthy" anchorage along the coast from which it would be possible, with suitable transports, to move the army to New York within days if necessary. Cornwallis obeyed but objected, wanting to avoid the perils of the coast, aware that his army would be much healthier in the months to come if it stayed on higher ground. On June 30, from Williamsburg, he wrote: "I submit to your Excellency's consideration whether it is worth while to hold a sickly defensive post in this Bay."[43] Eight days later he continued, writing that his position "only gives us some acres of an unhealthy swamp."[44] On July 17 he reported he had "many sick."[45] Cornwallis wanted reinforcements from Clinton, and Clinton wanted reinforcements from Cornwallis. But Clinton was in charge, so Cornwallis grudgingly kept to the tidewater estuaries of the James and York rivers, and on August 1 he chose to install himself at Yorktown, a derelict tobacco port along the marshy banks of the estuary of the York River. He built his earthworks on a low bluff overlooking the town and the estuary. It was good mosquito country.

Meanwhile, to Clinton's surprise, the French fleet sailed not for New York but for the Chesapeake. When in September, at the Battles of the Capes, it defeated a British squadron, the mouth of the Chesapeake was effectively sealed and Cornwallis trapped. Cornwallis had the worst of both worlds: he was on the coast, malaria and other diseases were sapping his army, and the Royal Navy now could not get through to relieve him. Soon after he learned of the destination of the French fleet, Washington had begun to march his army south from the vicinity of New York to join forces with a small army of French and American soldiers and Virginia militia, under the command of the young Marquis de

Lafayette. Together they laid siege to Yorktown, beginning in mid-September, with siege guns provided by the French navy.

They did it competently, and on October 19 Cornwallis surrendered. In his account of the siege and surrender, Cornwallis gave credit to the siegecraft of Lafayette and Washington but stressed the importance of sickness in hampering his ability to resist. The day after the surrender he wrote to Clinton:[46]

> I have the mortification to inform your Excellency that I have been forced to give up the post of York and Gloucester [a small encampment across the York River estuary] and surrender the troops under my command. . . . The troops being much weakened by sickness, as well as by the fire of the besiegers; and observing that the enemy had not only secured their flanks but proceeded in every respect with the utmost regularity and caution I could not venture so large sorties as to hope from them any considerable effect. . . . Our numbers had been diminished by the Enemy's fire, but particularly by Sickness, and the strength and spirits of those in the works were much exhausted by the fatigue of constant watching and unremitting duty. . . . Our force diminished daily by Sickness and other losses, I was reduced, when we offered to capitulate on this side to little more than 3,200 rank & file fit for duty including officers, servants, artificiers, and at Gloucester about 600 including cavalry.

When it first arrived in Charleston in 1780, the British Army had over 9,000 men. After thousands of losses and reinforcements in the next seventeen months, Cornwallis had commanded some 8,300 at the outset of the siege of Yorktown. Some 7,250 remained at the surrender. If he was honest in his account and he truly had only 3,200 fit for duty by October 19—something he could expect to be investigated—then Cornwallis's army must have suffered grievously indeed from "sickness," with some 3,500 too ill to perform their duties. Only 500 of his men were killed or wounded in action.[47]

When news of Yorktown reached London, the government of Lord North soon fell and was succeeded by one determined to make peace. That took another twenty-two months, during which small battles took place in America (and larger ones at sea between the French and British fleets). But Yorktown decided the war.

Conclusions and Comparisons

Mosquitoes and malaria helped Cornwallis decide to give up on the Carolinas and then sickened his army at Yorktown. American resistance to the British Army had been made more effective by American resistance to malaria. Mosquitoes and malaria did not win the American Revolution on their own. Washington and Greene had to fight (and avoid fighting) as prudently as they did; the French had to intervene; the British had to gamble on their southern strategy; and no doubt much else had to happen as well for things to come out as they did. My point is simply that differential vulnerability to malaria put Cornwallis's forces at a systematic disadvantage compared to the local militias arrayed against them. The regulars of the Continental Army, once inoculated against smallpox, also enjoyed an immunity edge compared to British and German troops, although northerners certainly suffered from malaria when serving in the southern colonies (hence Greene took his army to the hills of the Santee district in the summer of 1781).[48] Since "fevers" killed British soldiers at roughly eight times the rate that battles did in the American war,[49] a small edge in disease resistance translated into a significant advantage.

Cornwallis had been fortunate to avoid yellow fever in his army. Charleston hosted many epidemics in the eighteenth century and would suffer more in the nineteenth. But in 1780–81, yellow fever did not strike. It was a much deadlier disease than malaria, even falciparum malaria, as the British and French armies learned from bitter experience in the West Indies during the Napoleonic Wars.

Mosquitoes and fevers played a strong role in deciding the Haitian Revolution (1791–1804). In that struggle, both these Atlantic powers took turns trying to suppress a giant slave rising and between them lost one hundred thousand men, almost all to disease. The rebels, people born and raised in yellow fever zones in Africa or in the Caribbean, were overwhelmingly immune to the virus. Their commanders seem to have recognized that foreign whites easily fell sick in Haiti—this was clear to everyone—and conducted their war strategy so as to take advantage of the fact. According to C. L. R. James, one of the Haitian generals, Jean-Jacques Dessalines, told his followers to take heart because "the French will not be able to stay long in San Domingo [Haiti]. They will do well at first, but soon they will fall ill and die like flies."[50] Which they did.

Yellow fever and malaria also helped win the Spanish American revolutions (1808–26). Throughout the Spanish empire, locals took advantage of the French occupation of Spain during the Napoleonic Wars to declare independence. But when the French were driven back north over the Pyrenees, and the Spanish monarchy returned to power, it sent an army to reconquer the American empire. The largest contingent, some ten thousand men under the command of General Pablo Morillo, went in 1815 to feverish coasts in what is now Venezuela and Colombia. By 1817 a third of Morillo's men had died from disease, and before the war was over, some 90–96 percent of the Spanish forces sent to Venezuela and Colombia were dead, almost none of them from combat.[51] While the revolutionaries suffered ailments as well—just as had the Americans in the Carolinas—they proved more resistant, especially to malaria and yellow fever, because they had encountered these diseases before and had developed at least partial immunities. In his memoirs, Bolivar noted with grim satisfaction that his Spanish enemies were more vulnerable to disease than were his own troops.

In all these cases, the American, Haitian, and Spanish American revolutions, the differential resistance to arthropod-borne disease gave a systematic advantage to the revolutionaries. That advantage was strongest in the Haitian case, where yellow fever was involved and the discrepancy between the opposing forces' relative immunities was greatest. It was weakest in the American case, where only malaria was involved and where locally born forces, Loyalist and patriot militias, did much of the fighting. Yet even in the American case the lowly mosquito helped advance the lofty goals of human freedom, which could well be the only helpful thing mosquitoes have ever done for Homo sapiens.

NOTES

1. See, however, recent works that can be construed as environmental determinism: Felipe Fernandez-Armesto, *Civilizations: Culture, Ambition, and the Transformation of Nature* (New York: Free Press, 2002); and Jared Diamond, *Guns, Germs, and Steel* (New York: W. W. Norton, 1997).

2. See the fascinating account in Elizabeth Fenn, *Pox Americana: The Great Smallpox Epidemic of 1775–1782* (New York: Hill and Wang, 2001), 92–103.

3. A useful general treatise is M. R. Smallman-Raynor and A. D. Cliff, *War Epidemics* (Oxford: Oxford University Press, 2004).

4. Sylvia Frey, *The British Soldier in America* (Austin: University of Texas Press, 1981), 28.

5. Peter Perdue, *China Marches West: The Qing Conquest of Central Eurasia* (Cambridge: Belknap Press of Harvard University Press, 2005), 47–48, 91–92.

6. Diamond, *Guns, Germs, and Steel;* William H. McNeill, *Plagues and Peoples* (New York: Doubleday, 1976).

7. Philip Curtin, *Disease and Empire: The Health of European Troops in the Conquest of Africa* (New York: Cambridge University Press, 1998). Even as late as World War II, malaria proved an important factor in campaigns in Southeast Asia and the South Pacific, despite the best efforts of military doctors in the Japanese, British, and American armies. But in this case it was not systematically partisan, as all of these armies suffered severely from it since their manpower was mainly recruited from zones that did not provide soldiers with experience of and resistance to malaria.

8. See Paul Ewald, *The Evolution of Infectious Disease* (New York: Oxford University Press, 1994).

9. For the British experience, see Jeremy Black, *The British Seaborne Empire* (New Haven: Yale University Press, 2004).

10. The most recent entry in an enormous literature on this subject is Suzanne A. Alchon, *A Pest in the Land: New World Epidemics in a Global Perspective* (Albuquerque: University of New Mexico Press, 2003).

11. The small territories that did change hands were mainly islands of the Lesser Antilles but also Newfoundland, then a collection of fishing ports.

12. A recent survey is James Pritchard, *In Search of Empire: The French in the Americas, 1670—-1730* (Cambridge: Cambridge University Press, 2004). The French also held Cayenne in South America.

13. J. R. McNeill, "Yellow Jack and Geopolitics: Environment, Empire, and the Struggles for Empire in the American Tropics, 1640–1830," *Review of the Fernand Braudel Center* 27, no. 4 (2004): 343–64.

14. Décio Freitas, *Palmares, a guerra dos escravos* (Rio de Janeiro: Graal, 1982).

15. John Gabriel Steadman, *Narrative of a Five Years Expedition against the Revolted Negroes of Surinam,* ed. Richard Price and Sally Price (Baltimore: Johns Hopkins University Press, [1790] 1988), 607. Dutch documents put the strength of Dutch forces at 1,650, not 1,200. See Wim Hoogbergen, *The Boni Maroon Wars in Suriname* (Leiden: E. J. Brill, 1990), 104.

16. Steadman, *Narrative,* 607. The italics are in the original.

17. Judith Carney, *Black Rice: The African Origins of Rice Cultivation in the Americas* (Cambridge: Harvard University Press, 2001); Robert Olwell, *Masters, Slaves, and Subjects: The Culture of Power in the South Carolina Low Country, 1740–1790* (Ithaca: Cornell University Press, 1998); Peter Wood, *Black Majority: Negroes in Colonial South Carolina from 1670 through the Stono Rebellion* (New

York: Knopf, 1974). On the adjacent Georgia coast, see Mart A. Stewart, *"What Nature Suffers to Groe": Life, Labor, and Landscape on the Georgia Coast, 1680–1920* (Athens: University of Georgia Press, 1996), esp. chap. 3.

18. Daniel Littlefield, *Rice and Slaves* (Baton Rouge: Louisiana State University Press, 1981).

19. On the habits of the anopheles, see A. N. Clements, *The Biology of Mosquitoes,* 2 vols. (Dordrecht: Kluwer Academic, 2004); for laymen, see Andrew Spielman and Michael D'Antonio, *Mosquito* (New York: Hyperion, 2001). Also useful is the Center for Disease Control and Prevention Web site, http://www.cdc.gov/malaria/biology/mosquito/#generalinformation.

20. P. Kaiser, "The 'Quads,' Anopheles quadrimaculatus Say," *Wing Beats* 5, no. 3 (1994): 8–9; Claudia M. O'Malley, "The Biology of Anopheles Quadrimaculatus Say," *Proceedings of the Seventy-ninth Annual Meeting of the New Jersey Mosquito Control Association,* 1992, 136–44, available at http://www.rci.rutgers.edu/~insects/mal5.htm.

21. Wood, *Black Majority,* 86, says *An. quadrimaculatus* was present in the Carolina wetlands when settlers first arrived, citing M. D. Young et al., "The Infectivity of Native Malarias in South Carolina to Anopheles Quadrimaculatus," *American Journal of Tropical Medicine* 28 (1948): 302–11.

22. The Ethiopian research is presented in James McCann, *Maize and Grace: Africa's Encounter with a New World Crop, 1500–2000* (Cambridge: Harvard University Press, 2005), chap. 8.

23. Wood, *Black Majority,* 75–76, has quotations from original sources.

24. On average, an AIDS victim is likely to infect only slightly more than one other person; a measles sufferer will infect about twelve to fourteen people. The vector makes diseases like malaria (and yellow fever) much easier to communicate and thus much more likely to take epidemic form—if enough nonimmune people are available. Spielman and D'Antonio, *Mosquito,* 96–97.

25. Quoted in John Duffy, *Epidemics in Colonial America* (Baton Rouge: Louisiana State University Press, 1953), 213.

26. Quoted in Carney, *Black Rice,* 147.

27. Wood, *Black Majority,* 74. Walter J. Fraser, *Charleston! Charleston! The History of a Southern City* (Columbia: University of South Carolina Press, 1989), includes mentions of several yellow fever epidemics, notably in the mid-1740s. Yellow fever seems to have made its first appearance in the 1690s, about the same time as falciparum malaria.

28. See John Shy, *A People Numerous and Armed: Reflections on the Military Struggle for American Independence* (Ann Arbor: University of Michigan Press, 1990), rev. ed., 193–212.

29. George Washington to William Shippen, January 6, 1777, quoted in Fenn, *Pox Americana,* 92.

30. Cited in Fenn, *Pox Americana,* 131.

31. British Library, Additional Mss. 38, 345, "An Account of the Number of Troops Sent to the West Indies for the Years 1775–1782."

32. Malaria did still exist in England in the eighteenth century, in the Fens in particular, but it was disappearing rapidly. The great majority of British soldiers had never experienced it unless they had served in India. I do not know what proportion of troops fighting in the southern campaigns had formerly been to India, but the likelihood is that the number was very small. The Germans in the British Army, of whom twenty-nine thousand or so fought in the American war, were recruited mainly in the northern parts of the country and probably had minimal exposure to malaria.

33. Neil Cantlie, *A History of The Army Medical Department,* 2 vols. (Edinburgh: Churchill Livingstone, 1974). See also Frey, *British Soldier,* chap. 2.

34. Benjamin Woolley, *Heal Thyself: Nicholas Culpeper and the Seventeenth-Century Struggle to Bring Medicine to the People* (New York: HarperCollins, 2005).

35. On eighteenth-century medical ideas, see Roy Porter, *The Greatest Benefit to Mankind: A Medical History of Humanity from Antiquity to the Present* (New York: HarperCollins 1997), chaps. 9–10. A fine example of a sailor's distrust of the medical profession appears in the novel by Tobias Smollett, *The Adventures of Roderick Random* (Oxford: Blackwell, 1925), 1:267–68. Smollett's hero was sick in a Caribbean campaign of 1741 (in which Smollett himself had served).

36. Frey, *British Soldier,* 42.

37. Cornwallis to Germain, August 20, 1780, Germain Papers, Clements Library, University of Michigan, cited in Frey, *British Soldier,* 38.

38. Ibid., 43.

39. Germain to Cornwallis, June 4, 1781, Public Record Office (henceforward PRO) 30/11/6, ff. 215–16.

40. Cornwallis to Clinton, April 10, 1781, Clinton Papers, University of Michigan (cited in Frey, *British Soldier,* 43).

41. Hayes to Cornwallis, November 15, 1780, PRO 30/11/4; "Return of Sick and Wounded in H.M. Hospital at Charleston," November 1780, PRO 30/11/4.

42. Cornwallis to Clinton, April 10, 1781, Clinton Papers, University of Michigan (cited in Frey, *British Soldier,* 43).

43. Cornwallis to Clinton, June 30, 1781, PRO 30/11/74, f. 26.

44. Cornwallis to Clinton, July 8, 1781, PRO 30/11/71, f. 33.

45. Cornwallis to Clinton, July 17, 1781, PRO 30/11/74, f. 44. In early September, however, he reported the army was not very sickly—a situation soon to change. See Burke Davis, *The Campaign That Won America* (New York: Dial, 1970), 138.

46. Cornwallis to Clinton, October 20, 1781, PRO 30/11/74, ff. 106–10.

47. William H. Hallahan, *The Day the Revolution Ended: 19 October 1781* (Hoboken, N.J.: John Wiley & Sons, 2004), 206, 209.

48. And in 1782 his troops suffered heavily from malaria while encircling the remnant British forces at Charleston. Mary C. Gillett, *The Army Medical Department, 1775–1818* (Washington, D.C.: Center of Military History, U.S. Army, 1981), 121–22, cited in John Duffy, "The Impact of Malaria on the South," in Todd L. Savitt and James Harvey Young, eds., *Disease and Distinctiveness in the American South* (Knoxville: University of Tennessee Press), 37.

49. Frey, *British Soldier,* 41, citing a British army doctor.

50. James, *Black Jacobins* (New York: Vintage Books, 1989), 314. James also quotes the principal architect of the Haitian Revolution, Toussaint L'Ouverture, as saying, "the rainy season will rid us of our foes" (299). James does not give citations for his quotations. The most recent general account of the Haitian Revolution is Laurent Dubois, *Avengers of the New World: The Story of the Haitian Revolution* (Cambridge: Belknap Press of Harvard University Press, 2004). But see also David Geggus, *Haitian Revolutionary Studies* (Bloomington: Indiana University Press, 2002), and, with somewhat greater emphasis on yellow fever, Michel Martin and Alain Yacou, eds., *Mourir pour les Antilles* (Paris: Editions Caribéennes, 1991).

51. Julio Albi, *Banderas olvidadas: el ejército realista en América* (Madrid: Ediciones de Cultura Hispánica, 1990), 403–5.

V Sustainable Development on China's Frontiers

Peter C. Perdue

Historical Roots of Sustainable Development in China

"SUSTAINABLE DEVELOPMENT" has become a prominent buzzword among United Nations agencies, environmentalists, and economic planners throughout the world. The following simple tables illustrate the explosive rise of writing on this topic (table 5.1). Widespread use of the term began in the 1980s, and it spread like wildfire during the 1990s.

The People's Republic of China (PRC), after some delay, has also joined the chorus of support for this concept (table 5.2). In the first decade of the reform period (1978–80s), environmental impact was of little concern to either government planners or ordinary people. They focused primarily on developing a market economy, attracting foreign investment, and raising agricultural and industrial output. Foreign observers saw obvious signs of damage, citing high levels of water and air pollution, deforestation, and diseases as threats to public health. Many predicted that these environmental effects would soon slow down China's economic boom or even lead to a major political crisis.[1] The Chinese themselves, at first, paid little attention.

State policy began to stress environmental protection somewhat more with the establishment of the State Bureau of Environmental Protection in 1984, coordinating the activities of twenty agencies, and the publication of its official newspaper, *Chinese Environmental Protection* (*Zhongguo Huanjingbao*). Vice premier Li Peng's speech in December 1983 stressed that environmental protection and economic reconstruction must develop together. The inaugural issue recognized that China had started environmental protection activities late, that environmental degradation was severe, and that it was not under control.[2]

By the mid-1990s, government authorities and the general public had begun to recognize environmental degradation as a serious threat. Urban people knew that air quality had seriously declined with industrialization and the great rise in the use of automobiles, and rural people suffered from poor water supplies and declining standards of health. Newspapers began to publish data on air quality standards. The government realized that it could attract international funding for projects that appealed to world interest in conservation, including preservation of the panda's habitat, ecotourism, and investment in water conservancy.

Responding to the Rio Declaration of 1992, the State Planning Commission and State Science and Technology Commission formulated China's Agenda 21 program, designed to develop a "set of projects that respond to the country's pressing developmental needs within the framework of sustainable development principles." By 1996, the government claimed to have secured international support for 36 percent of these 128

TABLE 5.1. Books Including "Sustainable Development" in Title in HOLLIS Catalog

Years	Number	SD and China or Chinese
1970–79	2	0
1980–89	46	0
1990–99	809	6
2000–2003	212	9

TABLE 5.2. Chinese Books with "ke chi xu" (sustainable) in Title

Years	Number
1995	1
1996	2
1997	11
1998	6
1999	19
2000–2003	16

projects, with 33 percent more under negotiation. The government had "promulgated 5 laws on environmental protection, 9 laws on the conservation of natural resources, more than 30 administrative regulations on environmental protection and 364 environmental standards."[3]

The term "sustainable" (*kechixu*) in Chinese translation began to appear in book titles after 1995. Scholars at Beijing University founded the Research Center for Sustainable Development and held their first conference in 1994.[4] Putting the academics alongside the state planners, we can find nearly the entire range of Western environmental discourse expressed in China. For example, engineers and planners talk about the near future in terms of projects, costs, and new technologies, while cultural analysts project the evolution of humankind over the long term toward new forms of civilization: primitive, agricultural, industrial, and sustainable.

At the same time, China has undertaken some of the largest development projects in the world, projects that will radically alter the ecology of the country and even the planet. The Three Gorges Dam is the most famous of these huge undertakings, pursued by the national government in defiance of the World Bank and considerable opposition within China. With the completion of the dam, the PRC government has announced an even more grandiose plan to divert river waters from southern China to supply the drought-stricken north. It has also diverted water from Central Asian rivers, depriving neighboring Kazakhstan of this resource, and begun large-scale development on the Mekong.[5] Intensive exploitation of grasslands has turned many of them into deserts, while industrial development has polluted air and water supplies. The new "Develop the West" program aims to raise the economic level of interior China with a massive program of road and railroad building, energy exploitation, dam construction, and Han immigration.[6] Now, many Chinese analysts argue that the environmental costs of China's headlong rush into industrialization will soon slow down its economic growth, and some even predict imminent political collapse because of environmental crisis. Others minimize the cost of environmental impacts and dismiss efforts at environmental protection as little more than lip service.

Most current Chinese discussion of sustainable development, however, neglects the political conflicts and historical legacies that lie behind debates over the environmental impact of economic growth. Authors at the academic conference on sustainable development in 1994 focused either on technical issues or on sweeping cultural interpretation. Since the Communist party has quickly suppressed autonomous political movements, it is not surprising that no mass environmental movement has emerged in China. On the other hand, many Chinese have protested official corruption, low wages, poor health, and religious restrictions, so environmental issues may join the agenda soon.

China today is torn between the passionate drive for profit unleashed by the reform program and the growing anxiety that the successes of the last two decades cannot continue without attention to their environmental impact. The slow rise of sustainability as a theme in Chinese discussions indicates that many are trying to balance the gains of economic growth against negative impacts on the quality of people's lives.

As with any such widely used term, the exact meaning of "sustainable development" is elusive. Many varied political interests hide behind the apparent global consensus on the desirability of sustainable development. Agreement on particular policies requires new methods of measuring economic growth. William Nordhaus, for example, has argued that conventional measures of national income need to be extended to incorporate nonmarket activities like the environment. He proposes measuring "the maximum amount that a nation can consume while ensuring that members of all current and future generations can have expected lifetime consumption or utility that is at least as high as current consumption or utility." He calls this "the maximum sustainable level of consumption."[7] These new measures, which incorporate depletion of natural resources into calculations of GDP, have only just begun to be introduced into U.S. economic accounting, and they have not been applied to China. Without reliable measures, the debate over which economic policies are sustainable will not have a clear resolution.

Supporters of sustainable development agree on the need to control economic development so that it can continue, but the measures actually taken and the conception of the problem differ widely. Even in strictly economic terms, it is hard to judge any specific development policy by these criteria. Under such broad definitions, one could just as easily argue, for example, that oil drilling in wilderness regions is "sustainable development" (because it ensures the continuation of current industrial growth) or unsustainable (because it delays the move to non-fossil-fuel–based development).

In addition, current discussions of environmental policy tend to ignore the historical experiences of the societies engaged in these debates. They focus on the future, trying to come up with common understandings of goals on which all nations can agree. They tend to assume that the recent idea of sustainable development requires global education in universal norms. Since different political goals and societal experiences lie beneath the apparent consensus, however, the historical legacy of each society strongly influences how it interprets the term.

China's interpretation of sustainable development clearly reflects its past. In part, it is a reaction against the heedless rush into rapid development schemes of the Maoist era. Judith Shapiro has shown how so many of the great Maoist mobilization projects invoked the conquest of nature by sheer human will, disregarding limits set by physical constraints. Many of them turned out to be gigantic wastes of human time and effort.[8] The reform leaders have insisted on more efficient use of resources, directed by market incentives. They have also, however, retained the basic goals of the Maoist era: rapid industrialization and technological modernization. Only the means have changed, and the measures of results. Sustainable development really means for China the ability to continue a long-standing developmental goal indefinitely: making China into a powerful economy and state equivalent to the leading industrial nations of the world.

This goal, however, has even deeper historical roots. From the late nineteenth century, Chinese elites advocated rapid industrialization to catch up with the West. In the early twentieth century, the Nationalist government planned large projects to transform natural resources into economic and political power: the first outlines of the Three Gorges Dam were conceived by Sun Yat-sen in 1919. The Nationalist government's industrial planners carried out many of their projects under the PRC in the 1950s and 1960s.[9] Even though Communist leaders attacked the Nationalists as capitalist exploiters, they shared many economic goals with them. Despite sharp political opposition, they used much of the same developmental language.

We can push this logic even further back. Officials of the Qing dynasty (1644–1911 CE) also invoked the language of development, stressing the need for the government to improve the welfare of its people. Until recently, both Nationalists and Communists regarded the Qing period as a backward legacy that needed to be entirely rejected.

The May Fourth movement of 1919 had attacked all aspects of the imperial period as nothing but obstacles to revolutionary transformation, and most Nationalists and Communists endorsed the program of all-out Westernization that it implied. They refused to give the Qing credit for making any steps forward to help China meet the global competitive world of the twentieth century.

Now, however, new studies of Qing economic policy have offered a much more positive interpretation. We know that eighteenth-century China had very active, large-scale market networks, significant numbers of wealthy merchants, and aggressive farmers who raised crops to feed and clothe urban consumers.[10] Qing officials also actively debated the role of the government in market activity. They did not try to repress commerce but only to direct it toward improving the people's welfare. Even though they did not promote industrialization, they still thought in terms of increasing the overall production of society. Like Communist party cadres today, they expected that economic growth would not threaten the political structure. Many of their terms and the style of their thinking about "development" would be recognizable to today's economic planners.

In this chapter, I shall focus on several eighteenth-century writers who discussed the impact of economic growth on the environment of frontier regions. (Frontiers here include both the territorial borderlands of the empire in Central Eurasia and the internal frontiers on the shores of lakes and rivers.) In a number of ways, their analyses resonate with those of Chinese discussing sustainable development today; in some respects, in fact, they were more honest than are contemporary Chinese about the difficulties of enforcing sustainable policies in a vast bureaucratic apparatus and peasant population. At a distance of two hundred years, we can gain some perspective on the challenges that sustainable development presents to the PRC today (fig. 5.1).

A number of important Qing officials actively promoted development, in the form of increased agricultural development and settled frontier regions. In their view, "wastelands," which produced little of value, should be replaced with high-yielding crops cultivated by Han Chinese migrants. What they called wasteland was usually not empty land: it was forestland or grasslands used by swidden agriculturalists, hunter-gatherers, or nomadic pastoralists. Just like their contemporaries in eighteenth-century America, however, the land developers

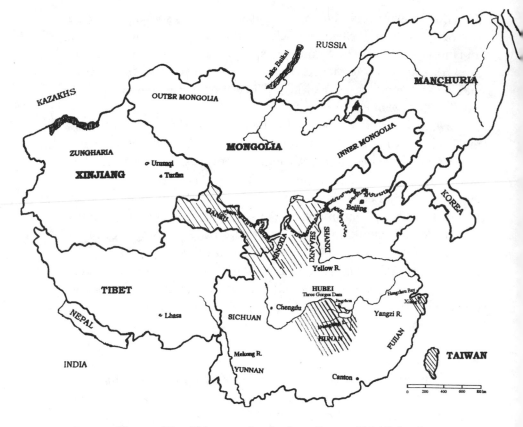

Fig. 5.1. Qing China, ca. 1800 (regions discussed highlighted).

regarded these forms of agrarian production as inefficient and the indigenous populations as "lazy." By replacing them with hard-working, productive Han settlers, they thought they could benefit popular welfare, raise agrarian output, and create greater social harmony.

Other Qing writers also had concerns about what we now call sustainability. They knew that population growth, the development of commerce, and the growth of cash-cropping agriculture were threatening the environment, and they worried that popular welfare could not continue to improve. Excessive building of dikes to clear land around Dongting Lake in Hunan province in central China, for example, reduced the area available to act as an overflow basin for high water of the Yangzi River to the north. Late eighteenth- and early nineteenth-century officials observing the increase in flooding in Hunan astutely connected it with this excessive dike building and land clearance. They tried to stop it, but they could not. Similarly, they knew that peasants migrating to forested uplands of the Yangzi River watershed had deforested the hillsides, increasing soil erosion, which brought heavy loads of silt into Dongting Lake, further reducing its volume. They linked these widely separated processes into a single ecological system. The eighteenth century was a time of increasing awareness of the interconnectedness of human and natural change over large scales of space and time. Its insightful writers anticipated the concern with survivability and sustainability today.

The concern with sustainability was especially prominent on imperial China's frontiers. As China's population doubled during the eighteenth century, peasants moved out from densely settled core regions to clear new land. They moved in all directions, into the uplands of river basins, up the Yangzi River into Sichuan, across the sea to Taiwan, northwest across deserts into Mongolia and Xinjiang, and southwest into the jungles and forests of Yunnan. Qing writers debated extensively the impact of this great settlement movement. On the one hand, peasant emigration relieved pressure on the rice paddies of the south and the dry fields of the north, offering families new chances to make a living. On the other hand, the migrants were unreliable elements, difficult to supervise and liable to cause unrest if their dreams of an independent life were unfulfilled. Only a limited amount of land was available on the hillsides and in the oases, and its yields were often too low or unreliable to support a family for long. Having stripped a hillside of vegetation, causing heavy erosion, the migrants then moved on to find new fields, leaving denuded lands in their wake. Many of them abandoned farming and turned to more rewarding pursuits: burning charcoal or collecting indigo in forests or becoming raiders who preyed on merchants and new settlers.[11] Official policies on frontier migration tried to balance improvement of welfare with social stability, but both welfare and stability depended on how humans transformed the environment. If erosion of newly cleared hillsides caused unrest in the uplands, officials could provide peasants with capital to allow them to create terraces to hold back the soil. This meant encouraging merchants and landlords to invest in the region, tying it more closely to the lowland core. On the other hand, they might restrict migration so as to slow down the rate of clearance, in the hope of reducing the damage. Just as now, these writers shared an interest in long-lasting growth without irreversible ecological damage, but they had different understandings of the means to that end.

Some Qing Writings on Agrarian Development and Sustainability

I shall examine here the writings of four scholar-officials: Lan Dingyuan (1680–1733), an active proponent of the colonization of Taiwan; Chen Hongmou (1696–1771), governor of many provinces of the empire; Yang Xifu, governor of Hunan province in the 1740s; and the scholar Mao Qiling (1623–1716), who attempted to rescue a beautiful lake from destruction. These highly educated and influential eighteenth-century literati perceived drastic transformations of the Chinese landscape around them. They all wanted to improve the livelihood of the people of their region while ensuring that nature's resources continued to support future generations. They were, in a word, advocates of sustainable development before their time. On the other hand, each responded to a different kind of ecological change, and each had his own way of addressing it. They span the range from aggressively developmentalist to preservationist views. Their spectrum of opinion reflects the same kinds of paradoxes that afflict environmentalists today.

Lan Dingyuan: The Civilizing Mission on Taiwan

The island of Taiwan was added to the empire in 1683, when Qing forces drove out the last ruler of the Chinese merchant-pirate regime established by Zheng Chenggong (fig. 5.2).[12] Before Zheng, Taiwan had been under Dutch rule, from 1614 to 1661. The Dutch and the Zhengs had begun to transform Taiwan from a land of aboriginal deer hunters and swidden cultivators into one with a few settled villages, but this development had not progressed very far.

Taiwan's peoples and landscape, unknown before the seventeenth century, inspired wonder, bafflement, and criticism.[13] Chinese writers viewed the native inhabitants as a primitive people, innocent of history, writing, or civilization. Some writers treated them as remnants of an unspoiled paradise, the blessed isles placed by mythology off the eastern coast; others saw them as threats to core Chinese values, because their sexual and familial practices violated orthodox codes.

Qing officials at first discouraged immigration from the mainland,

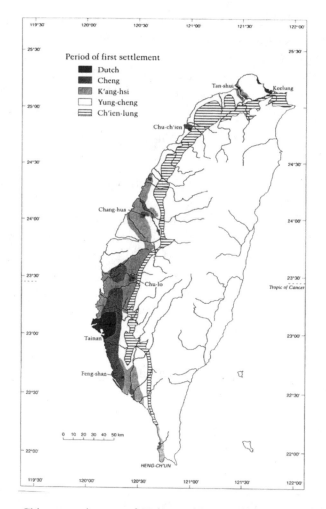

Fig. 5.2. Chinese settlement of Taiwan. (From John Robert Shepherd, *Statecraft and Political Economy on the Taiwan Frontier, 1600–1800.* Copyright © 1993 by the Board of Trustees of the Leland Stanford Jr. University.)

because they feared disruption, but peasants from the overcrowded southeastern coast of Fujian flocked to the sparsely populated lands despite official prohibition. These single young men looking for a chance to clear their own land fought back against official efforts to tax and register them. After a major rebellion in 1721–22, Qing officials debated vigorously how to ensure peace on the island. Most argued for tightening up immigration restrictions, but Lan Dingyuan advocated faster settlement and land clearance. In his view, restricting immigration only created a violent, lawless young male population. The best way to ensure a stable, settled peasant class was to allow family immigration and to promote land reclamation by Han settlers.[14] In addition, economic development of the island, making it into a significant exporter of grain and sugar cane to the mainland, would provide higher tax revenues that could support the costs of administration. Migration and development would turn the island from a remote backwater under military rule into an integral part of the civilian bureaucracy, tied to the mainland by extensive commerce.

Lan Dingyuan was the most extreme proponent of a "civilizing mission" that included aggressive promotion of settlement by Han peasants from the mainland, education, and compulsory assimilation to orthodox values. Other officials tried to protect the aboriginal inhabitants from Han encroachment, both to preserve social order and to minimize the costs of administration, but Lan argued that aborigines had no rights to their land, unless they turned their hunting grounds into fields (fig. 5.3):

> If we talk of aborigine land, then all Taiwan is aborigine land; the aborigines may want it restored, but it is beyond restoring. The government should decree that each aborigine can reclaim land; all that thereby becomes paddy and garden within the year should be considered theirs; what is left unreclaimed, [Han] settlers should be allowed to open.[15]

In other words, the only type of land that supported private property rights was settled agriculture; hunting grounds and swidden cultivation deserved no protection.

The Yongzheng emperor (r. 1723–35) found Lan's argument for increased tax revenue attractive, but many other local officials warned against the disturbing effects of dispossession of aborigines and rapid immigration. His successor, the Qianlong emperor (r. 1736–95), reversed the most extreme colonization policies, trying to balance the rights of new Han settlers and the native population. From an environmental point of view, it is clear that Lan Dingyuan saw no value in alternative production systems, even though deer hunting had been a profitable commercial activity before the Qing conquest. In the long run, he viewed

Fig. 5.3. Aboriginal peoples of Taiwan: hunting and settled (from Fusinian Library, Academia Sinica, Taibei, Taiwan).

sustainability as providing an ever increasing agrarian output to meet the needs of growing immigrant populations. He also promoted export trade with the mainland and Southeast Asia to further enrich the new settlers of Taiwan.

His opponents tried to defend the rights of the aborigines by restricting immigration, but they too regarded only settled agriculture as entitled to protection. If lowland aborigines rented their lands to Han settlers, the state would protect their claims, but the "wild" peoples who fled to the mountains received no state support. Both sides of the debate over Taiwan settlement accepted the goal of intensifying production on settled lands; their only difference was over who would receive the gains.

Turning forests into fields did raise the productivity of Taiwan enormously, without straining its agrarian system. It was not as vulnerable as the small tropical islands described by Richard Grove, where European settlers soon noticed signs of severe environmental strain.[16] Taiwan could support substantial immigration and intensified export agriculture along its western coastal strip. The new migrants certainly improved their living standards by leaving the overcrowded lands of Fujian. As Lan Dingyuan predicted, Taiwan did gradually evolve from a rude military borderland to a "civilized" part of the empire. Rebellions did break out during the eighteenth century, but these were complex battles between different groups of Han Chinese, not a simple opposition of natives versus migrants. Until Japan took the island in 1895, Taiwan grew increasingly integrated with the mainland, and its agricultural and industrial development looked dynamic and sustainable. In the long run, Lan Dingyuan had been vindicated.

Chen Hongmou: The Versatile Frontier Official

Chen Hongmou served in eleven of China's eighteen provinces during his long and illustrious career. He is the subject of a brilliant new study by William T. Rowe.[17] He spent most of his official life as governor or governor-general of frontier provinces, where he mobilized the provincial bureaucracy to carry out ambitious plans of economic development. Chen shared with Lan Dingyuan and others the belief that it was the responsibility of officials to lead the people in projects that improved their economic welfare, and these projects required extracting maximum possible benefits from the land, "exhausting the earth's bounty" (*jin dili*). Yet he also believed that the state should "store wealth among the people" and not extract their hard-won gains in the form of excessive taxation or labor service. Ideally, when local people diligently improved their own productive capacities under the benevolent guidance of local officials, society and nature worked together in harmony. This was his version of sustainable development.

Chen put his economic ideas into practice when he served as governor of Shaanxi and Gansu provinces in the 1740s and 1750s. In a memorial written in 1755, he surveyed the productive potential of Gansu, China's poorest province, in the far northwest, and proposed to raise its output with extensive irrigation works:

> I hear Gansu is remote and the people are poor, yet there are broad expanses of cultivable land. Places with irrigation works like Ningxia use Yellow River water to open canals and build dikes to irrigate land. The officials supervise and the people take care of the canals; they divide up labor and do yearly repairs. Recently irrigation has gradually expanded, increasing private land. Local landowners have made great profits.
>
> In Hexi, Ganzhou, Liangzhou, Suzhou and beyond the passes [of

the Great Wall], in each military garrison little rain falls in summer and autumn, but they all rely on snow piled up in the Nanshan mountains [to the south] which melts in summer and flows down the mountain. The water is divided into canals and drawn from south to north, from higher to lower. This is heaven's creation used for earthly construction (*tianzao dishe*). The annual snowfall eternally provides irrigation water to support the livelihood of myriads of people. It is all indescribably beautiful!

I went out beyond the passes to the borderlands and saw thick groves of trees along the canals and villages connected together; the climate was humid, there was little wasteland without canals, and the people were happy. So improving nature through channeling helps peasant welfare. But inspecting more carefully I find that some canals are not completed, and many dikes have collapsed, so that canal water overflows on the roads. Regrettably, these flooded places everywhere make transportation difficult. This is because people's efforts vary from diligent to lazy. Their will and effort is sporadic; it is not systematic. Also, since up to now people repaired canals without supervision by local officials, in times of water shortage they fight with each other, and in times of flood they individually dig and waste water with abandon.

Chen argued that the people needed supervision to coordinate their efforts:

I've now told officials to find out the large and small canals' names, record them in registers, and in the slack season lead those who are next to canals and profit from them to divide them into sections and work together on repairs for public good [*gongxiu*]. Build dikes, dredge canals, open side canals; build wood and stone embankments, build reservoirs to store water, build bridges to facilitate crossings: put effort into making the water-return to canals flow smoothly. In years of scarce water it can be allotted to fields and in flood years it will pass through downstream so all benefit from it and there is no flooding. Set up *shuilao* [water elders] and *juzhang* [channel heads] to be solely in charge of this work. And order local officials each year when the snow melts to personally investigate and report on how to do repairs and dredging. Also evaluate the merits of officials for promotion in terms of their diligence in repairs.

As for the region beyond the passes [of the Great Wall] . . . it was originally sandy unproductive land, but our dynasty opened up canals, calling in households to clear it. Villages now contact each other just as in interior. I've looked into these old achievements and I see that there are still places that can be dredged. . . . If we can build a foot or an inch of canals and irrigate many acres of land we will nourish many peasant households; if we repair canals everywhere and put real effort into it the welfare of the local people [*minsheng*] will truly benefit.[18]

Chen unequivocally supported agricultural development through infrastructural investment. He had no concerns about exhausting water supplies or soil fertility. In his eyes, if the desert could be made to bloom, the people would only benefit. The initiative should come from local people under the supervision and coordinated planning of officials. Rationalizing the water system would eliminate waste, remove conflicts over water supplies, and support an increased population. Notably, he also praised the military settlements beyond the Great Wall that brought wasteland into cultivation.

Other frontier officials who promoted land clearance in Mongolia and Xinjiang also saw these desert borderlands as a great land of opportunity. In their view, converting pasture lands into agriculture increased the productivity of land and gave new livelihoods to peasants emigrating westward from the overpopulated northern China fields. Unlike Taiwan, they had few qualms about ejecting the native Mongolian nomadic population. For centuries these nomads had been warriors who threatened the borderlands. Now under Qing rule, the tamed nomads were confined to strictly patrolled pastures, while Han merchants and peasants tied their homelands to the interior. Like the Taiwan officials, however, they saw peasant settlers as more reliable than mobile nomads, and they promoted the transformation of the region from military to civilian rule.[19]

Any problems with cultivation in the arid region could be resolved by intensive searches for water sources. Chen and his supporters were fascinated by the underground canals that directed melting snow from the mountains to the fields. These were a Middle Eastern technology brought to China by Turkic oasis cultivators. Chen and other frontier officials tried to promote it further by transplanting Turkic peoples from other oases to the newly developing lands they had conquered.

Some Chinese visitors found the developing frontier exhilarating. Ji Yun (1724–1805), a prestigious scholar, spent two years in exile from 1769 to 1770 in Urumqi, Xinjiang, because of his involvement in a bribery case. He wrote 160 poems about his time on the frontier, later published as *Miscellaneous Poems of Urumqi* (*Wulumuqi Zashi*).[20] He did not lament the exile's life. He enjoyed the bustling life of the city, with its tightly packed shops, its crowds of shoppers, its brothels, and flute music in the evenings. He also boasted about the natural wonders of Xinjiang, describing the marvelous mountain torrents that burst out so fast they flowed over dams and the powerful winds that "blew men and horses around like whirling leaves."[21] Ji Yun fully embraced the developmental ethic of Qing officials and tried to make himself useful by constructing a reservoir. Local people put him off with objections until he had to go home.[22] In Ji Yun's poetry, as in Chen Hongmou's projects, we sense the exhilaration of mastery represented by the new conquests of the northwest. He even claimed that the weather had changed since the Qing conquest of Xinjiang in the eighteenth century: Urumqi used to be cold and barren, but now with the home fires burning from thousands of new settlers, the entire region had become warmer.[23] He showed no nostalgia for the lost primitive cultures of the Mongols or Hui, and he praised the abundant yields from the military colonies.

Ji Yun's writings expressed an emotional commitment to the official policies of integration and development of the northwest and broadcast exotic information and enthusiasm for the new possessions of the empire to the audience of literati back home. The long tradition of "border poetry" usually depicted this frontier as a place of forlorn exile, but Ji Yun, at least temporarily, had made it his home. The domesticated frontier now became another resource to be added to the Qing literary tradition.

Yang Xifu: Water and Collective Goods in Hunan

In the core of China proper, in the southern Chinese province of Hunan, Governor Yang Xifu also tried to promote increased agricultural production to accommodate a growing population (fig. 5.4).[24] He found, however, that relations between humans and nature on this internal frontier were not so harmonious. Like Chen Hongmou, he believed that officials must lead the people to recognize their own best interests, but he found that local pressures to clear land threatened to undermine the survivability of settlements over the wider region. Since the late seventeenth century, migrants to Hunan had cleared polder lands around Dongting Lake, the large body of water in the north of the province, just south of the Yangzi River. Hunanese had prospered by increasing their rice yields on these rich soils and sending their crops downriver to feed the urban populations of the lower Yangzi. By the mid-eighteenth century, these polders had reduced the volume of Dongting Lake significantly. Dongting Lake, however, collected the waters of four major rivers in Hunan and also served as an overflow basin for Yangzi River waters in flood time. As the polders encroached inexorably on the lake, the danger of major flooding by the bottled-up river waters increased. In addition, the dikes built by peasant landowners with very little capital investment were alarmingly weak and poorly maintained. In the 1740s, Yang Xifu pursued two policies to save the local people from the threat of major floods: he tried to increase official supervision over dike repairs while also prohibiting any further clearance of land around the lake. Both policies ran up against fierce resistance. Local landowners vigorously defended their rights to conduct repairs autonomously (because they profited from using tenant and hired labor to protect their own fields), and peasant settlers, desperate for new fields, continued to build polders in defiance of official regulations.

Chen Hongmou arrived in Hunan in 1755, fresh from his development projects in the northwest. Chen, a very quick study, soon realized that the south was not like the north. He wrote, "In the last several decades there is no high land that has not had dikes built on it. Dikes on the lake border fill the view endlessly like fish scales, and there are cases of fighting with the water for land."[25] Chen knew that disaster threatened because of short-sighted local interests:

> Now, since the population has begun to grow daily, all the wasteland has been cleared. The foolish people are blind about long-range plans and often abandon waterworks and plot to create more land. Not only the borders of the rivers and the great lake (Dongting), but other lakes several acres in area gradually have dikes constructed along them to clear land, and in the end all trace of them disappears. . . . People think that the reservoirs are useless, not realizing that if a drought or flood happens to come, what they have gained will not compensate for their loss.[26]

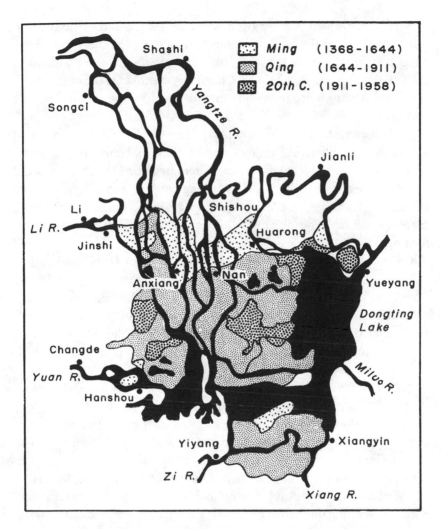

Fig. 5.4. Clearance of land around Dongting Lake, Hunan. (From Peter C. Perdue, "Official Goals and Local Interests: Water Control in the Dangting Lake Region during the Ming and Qing Periods," *Journal of Asian Studies* 41, no. 4 [1982]: 747–65. Reproduced by permission of the *Journal of Asian Studies*.)

Now, Chen was much less optimistic that people and officials could work together for the common good. He and Yang Xifu even recognized, to their dismay, that local officials often conspired with local landowners to build illegal dikes. Chen left the province the next year to continue his activist programs on other frontiers, but he returned in 1763 and ordered wholesale destruction of illegal dikes. His hard-line program, however, ruined many peasant households' livelihood, stimulated more lawsuits, and drove landowners to collude and conceal their activities even more. The local gazetteer writer concluded that "Laws could not be carried out justly, people's feelings and customs became daily crueler. . . . Even a good official like Chen Hongmou" suffered from the corruption of his subordinates, who were "controlled by wicked people for profit."[27]

Chen's successors in Hunan and to the north in Hubei still had to wrestle with conflicts over dike building and land clearance. In 1788, the illegal clearance of sandbars in the middle of the Yangzi River threatened to flood the major city of Jingzhou because of official corruption.[28] As predicted, major floods struck the province in the nineteenth and twentieth centuries, and Hunan continues to suffer from major floods today.

The conflicts in Hunan showed the limits of the Qing's developmentalist policies, based on the ideal of harmonious cooperation between paternalist officials and grateful peasant cultivators. When the lure of cash cropping grew too strong, landowners defied the officials or bribed them to ignore well-meant policies. Large-scale planning of water conservancy was undermined from below by the individual drive for profit. The limits to polder development in Hunan were both natural and social. Sustaining this drive to increase production required both careful engineering of water flows and a state structure strong enough to enforce its regulations and legitimate enough to gain public support. By the nineteenth century, the Qing bureaucracy had lost much of its ability to enact regional policies, while its subjects increasingly pursued their own private interests.

Mao Qiling: Public and Private in Hangzhou

Officials described the conflicts over dike building in Hunan in terms of opposition between the "public good" (*gong*) and "private interest" (*si*).[29] These moral terms have a long legacy in Chinese political thought. They intersected, but did not necessarily coincide with, the institutional practices described as "official" (*guan*) and "popular" (*min*). According to orthodox ideology, officials with the proper training and moral codes would lead the people to carry out their duties in a public-spirited manner. But writers on administrative practice realized that officials did not always act in the public interest and that the people were not necessarily selfish. Corrupt officials could oppress the people by exacting bribes and taxes for their own private interest; they needed to be restrained by superior officials and by consulting with local elite opinion *(yulun)*. Likewise, although the official should lead the people, he should not force them into sacrificing their self-interest for others; orthodox teaching supported the Chinese philosopher Mencius's conviction that human nature was essentially good and fundamentally oriented to care about the welfare of others. Just as anyone would rush to save a child who had fallen into a well, anyone should be willing to contribute to public works projects that benefited the larger community. *Gong* and *si, guan* and *min,* should be mutually supportive.

In practice, as we have seen, local interests frequently clashed with the benefits of larger communities when it came to deciding policies on water control and land clearance. Over the long term, from the eighteenth through twentieth centuries, the gap between particularist local interests and state perspectives widened. Local elites and landowners increasingly focused on their immediate goals, while officials were unwilling, or incapable of directing, larger efforts. The experience of the dike builders around Hangzhou Bay illustrates how this gap widened. Ultimately, this divergence of public and private interests made agriculture unsustainable in many regions (fig. 5.5).

In the twelfth century, a local magistrate near Hangzhou Bay persuaded public-spirited elite landowners to donate some of their land to form a new reservoir, called Xiang Lake.[30] Its water, supervised by the local people, would help to relieve local droughts and regulate the water supply. Over the centuries, officials had to struggle to protect the lake against encroachment from those who wanted to turn it back into rich cultivated land or dig up the bottom to make clay bricks. Violent conflicts broke out over the lake's use, and little by little local elites whittled away at the lake's surface.

In the eighteenth century, Mao Qiling, a local writer and proto-envi-

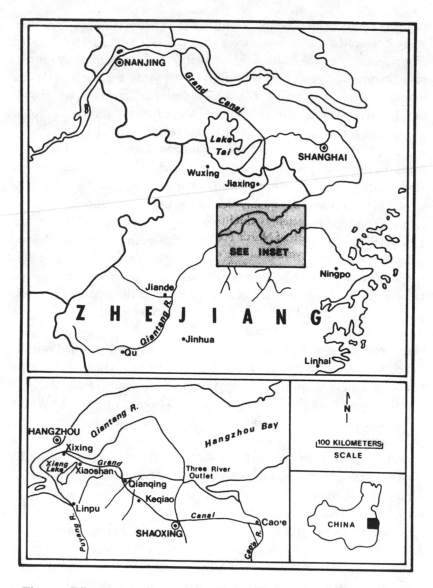

Fig. 5.5. Dike construction on Xiang Lake, Zhejiang. (From K. Schappa, *Xiang Lake: Nine Centuries of Chinese Life* [New Haven: Yale University Press, 1989]. Copyright © Yale University Press.)

ronmentalist, wrote a detailed history of the lake, celebrating its beautiful views and defending its value against its enemies.[31] He showed, with
support from official documents, that the purpose of the lake was to
provide irrigation water for the entire local population, but two powerful local families, the Suns and the Wus, had repeatedly exploited the
lake for their own profit. They built dikes to carve out pieces of land,
and they dug out the lake bottom to make tiles. Under the Ming
dynasty, officials had repeatedly issued proclamations forbidding further reclamation of land, but the two lineages ignored them. The Sun
lineage took a drastic step in 1689, when, after a drought exposed the
lake bottom, they recruited their lineage kinsmen to dig a dike completely across the lake, cutting it in two. The real value of the dike was to
give the Suns a direct route to the market town: it was a private road for
their own profit that benefited no one else. As Mao Qiling noted, "Xiang
lake was created to store water, certainly not to benefit personal travel.
If one dike is built then we lose water capacity; if this continues in the
future Xiang lake will entirely turn into cultivated fields."[32]

Efforts by the local magistrate, the prefect, and Mao Qiling to prevent
this encroachment met fierce resistance from the Suns and their local
allies.[33] These powerful local families successfully prevented the local
people from raising their voices: they did not dare speak up to Mao or the
local officials. Still, Mao investigated the lake and reported the "four
damages and five impermissibles" of dike building to the local government. The dike, in sum, by blocking the flow of water, destroyed lower
Xiang Lake, allowing the Suns to dig out its clay for tile production.
Even though he and the prefect demanded floggings and exposure in the
cangue for the violators, the Suns bribed the local police to avoid their
sentence. Finally the dike was destroyed and one of the Suns punished.

Mao Qiling had won a temporary victory, but he lost in the long run.
On one side, entrepreneurial peasants, merchants, and officials kept
exploiting the lake for quarries, fishing weirs, and private dikes, but
local elites formed a dike society in the early nineteenth century to raise
funds for water conservancy projects. During the turmoil of the nineteenth and twentieth centuries, almost no one spoke up for the public
interest in water, and by the 1920s the lake had nearly disappeared. In
1955 the new People's revolutionary government finished it off. The
struggle over this lake raised familiar issues of public versus private
interest and the balancing of economic development against aesthetic

appreciation. The lake endured for nearly nine hundred years, while many others disappeared, because of its literary fame and the beauty of its scenery. But the lake could not hold out against the relentless pressure of private interests looking for economic gain. This lake may serve as a metaphor for the fate of classical Chinese civilization: a balanced, long-lasting system of values and institutions destroyed by the violent pressures of the modern world. Mao Qiling and other local scholars fought a rear-guard battle on behalf of harmony between man and nature and the use of natural resources for the benefit of all. Instead, private interests undermined the public good, and valuable water resources disappeared.

Conclusion

The four men discussed in this chapter addressed issues of environmental change on Chinese frontiers, where the pressure of population and profit inexorably drove the exploitation of water and land. They shared concerns about sustainability, but they took different stances. Lan Dingyuan had the most openly developmental approach. For him, Taiwan was only a barren, remote wasteland until Han settlers turned its jungles into fields. He had few regrets about the loss of forests and deer populations and actively promoted the settlement and civilization of the aboriginal population. Chen Hongmou also threw himself with gusto into the development of water resources in the arid northwest. He saw more severe environmental dangers in this hostile environment than Lan did in Taiwan, but he believed they could be overcome by active official engagement in digging and channeling water. When Chen moved to Hunan, however, he, like Yang Xifu, saw disturbing signs of the individual search for profit undermining the social order. The private dikes in Hunan, unlike the canals of the northwest, did not increase agricultural yields in an unsettled region; instead they threatened to cause floods that would inundate the local population. Mao Qiling in Hangzhou likewise exposed a severe gap between public interest in a stable irrigation supply and the local lineages who used the lake for their own profit. Open frontiers in Taiwan and the northwest seemed to promise abundant resources for all, but in the long settled regions of southern China, elites, local peasants, and officials fought with each other for diminishing gains. All these writers perceptively analyzed the natural and human processes under their gaze, but they also knew that the state had only limited powers to direct environmental change. Human political and social interests inevitably challenged the most far-sighted policies.

Returning to the contemporary world, what do these eighteenth-century writers have to tell us about the prospects for sustainable development in China? They clearly recognized the need to balance commitments to economic growth with respect for the forces of nature. They often deferred to market forces and popular initiatives driven by private interests, but they asserted the duty of the state to intervene in order to guide the people and protect the public good when environmental damage approached. In some ways, they had an easier job than modern cadres, since their guiding principles derived from a well-defined set of classical texts and they all had passed examinations that enforced agreement on these principles. On the other hand, the Qing state and its officials had nowhere near the resources and personnel of the modern Chinese state, and many official efforts to direct private activities were ineffective. During the Maoist period, the Chinese state built up its apparatus of party officials and administrative cadres so as to penetrate all levels of society down to the village, but it conducted an all-out war on nature for the sake of rapid industrial development. The catastrophes of that period are well known. Recently, some Chinese have realized that sustainability depends on providing incentives that direct individuals' activities in ways that will not damage the prospects for future growth. Their discussions have begun to echo what Qing officials said. Now that the state has withdrawn from many spheres of Chinese society, many features of the imperial regime have, remarkably, returned. These include the revival of popular religion, local marketing networks, local and ethnic identities, patriarchal family values, and a new consciousness of the need to integrate human activity with the environment. Hence, Communist party officials and academic writers, without knowing it, repeat the style of analysis of their imperial ancestors. If this is true, then, as Confucius remarked, "reheating the past will help us to understand the present."

NOTES

1. Jack A. Goldstone, "Imminent Political Conflicts Arising from China's Environmental Crises," *AAAS Occasional Papers* (December 1992): 41–59; Vaclav

Smil, "Environmental Change as a Source of Conflict and Economic Loss in China," *AAAS Occasional Papers* (1992); Vaclav Smil, *China's Environmental Crisis: An Inquiry into the Limits of National Development* (Armonk, N.Y., 1993).

2. Lester Ross, *Environmental Policy in China* (Bloomington: University of Indiana Press, 1988); "Fakansi" (inaugural issue), *Zhongguo Huanjingbao,* January 1, 1984.

3. Administrative Center for China's Agenda 21, *Priority Programme for China's Agenda 21* (Beijing, 1996), Introduction, 1.

4. Beijing Daxue Zhongguo Chixu Fazhan Yanjiu Zhongxin, *Kechixu fazhan zhilu: Beijing daxue shouci kechixu fazhan kexue taolunhui wenji,* Di 1 ban (Beijing, 1995).

5. Gavan McCormack, "Water Margins: Competing Paradigms in China," *Critical Asian Studies* 33, no. 1 (2001): 5–30.

6. David S. G. Goodman, "Qinghai and the Emergence of the West," *China Quarterly* 178 (2004): 379–99; David S. G. Goodman, "The Politics of the West: Equality, Nation-Building, and Colonisation," in François Godement, ed., *La Chine et son Occident: China and Its Western Frontier* (Paris, 2002).

7. William D. Nordhaus, "New Directions in National Economic Accounting," *American Economic Review* 90, no. 2 (2000): 259–63.

8. Judith Shapiro, *Mao's War against Nature: Politics and the Environment in Revolutionary China* (Cambridge, 2001).

9. William C. Kirby, "Continuity and Change in Modern China: Economic Planning on the Mainland and Taiwan, 1934–58," *Australian Journal of Chinese Affairs* 24 (July 1990): 121–41.

10. See, for example, Robert B. Marks, *Tigers, Rice, Silk, and Silt: Environment and Economy in Late Imperial South China* (Cambridge, 1998); Sucheta Mazumdar, *Sugar and Society in China: Peasants, Technology, and the World Market* (Cambridge, Mass., 1998); Kenneth Pomeranz, *The Great Divergence: China, Europe, and the Making of the Modern World Economy* (Princeton, 2000); Evelyn S. Rawski, *Agricultural Change and the Peasant Economy of South China* (Cambridge, Mass., 1972).

11. Anne Osborne, "The Local Politics of Land Reclamation in the Lower Yangzi Highlands," *Late Imperial China* 15, no. 1 (1994): 1–46; "Highlands and Lowlands: Economic and Ecological Interactions in the Lower Yangzi Region under the Qing," in Mark Elvin and Liu Ts'ui-jung, eds., *Sediments of Time: Environment and Society in Chinese History* (Cambridge, 1995), 203–34.

12. John Robert Shepherd, *Statecraft and Political Economy on the Taiwan Frontier, 1600–1800* (Stanford, 1993); see my review in *Harvard Journal of Asiatic Studies* 55, no. 1 (June 1995): 261–69.

13. Emma J. Teng, *Taiwan's Imagined Geography: Chinese Colonial Travel Writing and Pictures, 1683–1895* (Cambridge, Mass., 2004).

14. Lan Dingyuan, *Pingtai Jilue* (Taibei, 1958).

15. Lan Dingyuan, quoted in Shepherd, *Statecraft and Political Economy*, 17.

16. Richard Grove, *Green Imperialism: Colonial Expansion, Tropical Island Edens, and the Origins of Environmentalism, 1600–1860* (Cambridge, 1995).

17. William T. Rowe, *Saving the World: Chen Hongmou and Elite Consciousness in Eighteenth-Century China* (Stanford, 2001).

18. Guoli Gugong Bowuyuan, ed., *Gongzhongdang Qianlongchao Zouzhe* (Taibei, 1982–88), 12:8–9.

19. For more details, see Peter C. Perdue, *China Marches West: The Qing Conquest of Central Eurasia* (Cambridge, Mass., 2005), chap. 14.

20. See further discussion in ibid., chap. 11.

21. Ji Yun, *Wulumuqi Zashi* (1937), nos. 6 and 19.

22. Ibid., no. 20.

23. Ibid., no. 3.

24. Peter C. Perdue, *Exhausting the Earth: State and Peasant in Hunan, 1500–1850* (Cambridge, Mass., 1987).

25. Cited in ibid., 221–22.

26. Ibid.

27. Ibid., 228.

28. Peter C. Perdue, "Official Goals and Local Interests: Water Control in the Dongting Lake Region during the Ming and Qing Periods," *Journal of Asian Studies* 41, no. 4 (August 1982): 747–65.

29. Mizoguchi Yûzô, "Chûgoku ni okeru kô, shi gainen no tenkai," *Shisô* 669 (1980): 19–38.

30. Peter C. Perdue, "Lakes of Empire: Man and Water in Chinese History," *Modern China* 16, no. 1 (January 1990): 119–29; Keith Schoppa, *Xiang Lake: Nine Centuries of Chinese Life* (New Haven, 1989).

31. Mao Qiling, *Xianghu Shuilizhi,* (ca. 1700) 3 vols. (Jinan, 1997).

32. Ibid., 2:11a.

33. Schoppa, *Xiang Lake,* 105–9.

VI Naming the Stranger

Maize's Journey to Africa

James C. McCann

Maize's Arrival in Africa

AFTER THE OPENING OF the Atlantic basin to trade, cultural exchange, and violent exploitation, the Old World was for maize a tabula rasa. A New World plant, maize arrived in Africa after 1500 as part of the massive global ecological and demographic transformation that historian Alfred Crosby called the "Columbian Exchange."[1] The great irony, of course, is that the same Atlantic economy that wrenched captive labor from Africa to the preindustrial economies in the New World also provided Africa with new cultigens (cassava, beans, cocoa, potatoes, and maize) that reinvented Africa's food supply over the next half millennium. By the middle of the twentieth century maize had become the primary staple of eastern and southern Africa; by the first decade of the twenty-first century this crop's dominance had spread and deepened across the entire continent. Strangely, however, there is little documentary evidence of what must have been a conscious process of Europeans or Africans introducing the maize plant to Africa. The importation of the maize seeds to various parts of Africa went unremarked, though it certainly was not unremarkable.

The goal of this chapter is to understand the meaning of and response to maize's arrival in Africa through the lens of African culture and linguistic expression. In naming the stranger, African farmers, traders, and consumers defined its meaning in their lives and histories.

The first documentary reference to maize's introduction to Africa may be that of an anonymous Portuguese pilot in 1540 who described already well-established cultivation on the Cape Verde Islands:

At the beginning of August they begin to sow grain, which they call Subaru [*zaburro*], or in the West Indies mehiz [*sic*]. It is like chick pea, and grows all over these islands and along the West African coast, and is the chief food of the people.[2]

On the island of Sao Tomé another Portuguese pilot in the mid-sixteenth century reported that the island's slave traders fed their captives on "zaburro, which we call maize in the western islands and which is like chickpeas."[3] The reference to chickpeas is enlightening. While we have no direct evidence of how West African farmers received maize (except that they planted it forthwith) the first Portuguese to see it cultivated in Africa thought of it as a legume. Docs that suggest that the African farmers had treated the maize on their farms more as a vegetable or legume than as a grain?

By the middle of the 1600s European references to maize in West African settings became more commonplace. The Dutch traveler and writer Olfert Dapper in 1668 remarked that maize had been carried from the West Indies to Sao Tomé and thence to the Gold Coast (where he saw it):

First of all there grows there Turkish wheat, which the Indians call mays and which was first brought from the West Indies where it is plentiful by the Portuguese to the Island of Saint Thomas [Sao Tomé] and which was distributed thence along the Goldcoast for cosumtion [*sic*] by the blacks.[4]

Here Dapper's use of the term "Turkish wheat" imposes the European idea of maize as grain. Whatever the early perceptions of West African farmers may have been, the French scholar Dominique Juhé-Beaulaton has cited in great detail historical *recits de voyage* that describe the appearance of maize on West Africa's Gold Coast beginning in the early seventeenth century. She notes that by the late 1600s both millet and sorghum had declined dramatically against maize. Presumably West African farmers had already been exploring the new plant's possibilities as food and as a farm crop that filled a distinctive agronomic niche and found that they preferred the new crop to the indigenous millets and sorghums. By the eighteenth century maize was the principal *céréale cultivée* in the region. In 1795 the traveler Mungo Park found that the people around the Gambia River cultivated it in considerable quantities.

Only in two areas, the Volta River delta and at coastal Axim, did rice remain the dominant cereal.[5]

While most twentieth-century writers take these early accounts as evidence that the Portuguese had been the agents of introduction, the Portuguese claim no such thing, or at least they remain mute on the subject.[6] Without mentioning the Portuguese, some Africans implicitly recognized maize's external provenance by the names they gave to the new crop or food. In other cases African testimony clings to the idea of maize as primordially African. The veteran ethnographer of the Yoruba William Bascom was "exasperated" by his Ife informants' insistence that maize had always been with the Yoruba, and the linguist gadfly M. W. D. Jeffreys took early Portuguese references to *milho zaburro* (which could easily be translated to mean any grain) to signify that maize in Africa was pre-Columbian.[7]

The Nigerian evidence of multiple points of entry, including some Portuguese role, is much more illuminating, even if more complex. A team of British historical linguists, including the indefatigable Roger Blench, has offered more precise evidence from language. They have pointed out that they have no direct evidence of a Portuguese role in introducing maize to what is now Nigeria. The linguistic patterns they cite, in fact, seem to suggest maize's primary arrival with long-distance trade from the north, via Bornu, and lesser routes from the west and northwest. In only one linguistic case (Isekiri, in southern Nigeria) is there evidence of a possible Portuguese role.

In southern Africa, however, the story began much later. Maize still may not have arrived at the Cape by 1652; Jan Van Riebeeck of the Dutch East Indies Company did not report seeing it there in that year, despite his hope to identify new local food sources for the company's fledgling settlement. In fact, as part of his plan to provision Dutch East India Company shipping in 1658 he asked for maize seed to be sent from home, planning to test its value at the supply station he hoped to erect at the foot of the Cape's Table Mountain.[8]

The shell game of searching for maize's first introduction makes for an amusing story but is perhaps a distraction; the central point here ought to be how we understand early African reactions to it as food and as crop. In Africa as a whole, maize took its place within smallholder farms finely tuned to the vagaries of Africa's capricious climate and old soils. It succeeded in part because the new crop was potentially very nutritious, enough, in fact, to underpin population growth and concentration, once it had become established. Traditional grain yields in Africa were less than half those of Asia and Latin America, reflecting the obstacles of aridity and poor fertility that attain in many parts of the continent. Maize and other New World crops (such as cassava, coco-yams, and potatoes) helped redress that imbalance in key parts of the continent. Unlike New World farms that depended heavily on maize as a primary starchy staple, most African farmers adopted maize initially as a vegetable niche crop tucked within a complex cropping system that relied on intercropping, rotation, and swidden management of fertility. It is interesting to note, however, that while European observers first compared maize to chickpeas (as did the anonymous Portuguese pilot mentioned previously), Africans who named it tended to compare it to sorghum, thereby choosing to stress the appearance of the plant itself and the use of the grain rather than the shape of the kernel. In these polycultures, shaped by Africa's sharply defined wet/dry seasonality, averting risk demanded diversity of cropping strategies rather than rewarding efficiencies of scale. It was the late (i.e., 1900s) transformation of maize into a monocropped grain staple that historically changed its effects on diet and recalibrated modern African farming systems.

Genetic Expressions

For most African societies and agrarian systems there is no direct testimony to a historical "moment" that marks maize's arrival in local diets and in farmers' fields. Yet, the hidden genetic and phenotypic evidence (in other words, what it looked like) within the maize ear itself offers intriguing glimpses into the crop's historical geography. Though all maize types can cross-pollinate, each of the many cultivars has distinctive characteristics in its starch content, number of seed rows, color, insect or disease resistance, maturation rates, and so forth. These traits are the smorgasbord from which farmers and consumers from year to year chose taste, appearance, and growth characteristics to breed the next year's seed. Each of the five major maize types (pop, floury, flint, dent, and pod) moved into Old World settings already having evolved within distinctive New World ecologies, consumer choices, and farming techniques.

The political geography of Europeans' New World conquests and trans-Atlantic trade determined the patterns of maize's genetic emigration to Africa. Spanish ships, for example, began their New World contacts with the Caribbean and necessarily first encountered distinctive Caribbean flint maizes, identifiable by their hard starch, early maturation, and variegated bright colored grains, especially red.

Spanish flint maize, particular for its strikingly and uniformly scarlet kernels, first came to the Old World at Seville, thence to Venice, and thence to Africa via Egypt and the Nile Valley, where many observers remarked on the kernels' striking red color, also reflected in local names.[9] Roland Portères argues that such Caribbean flint maize then moved south and west across to West Africa following the routes of the Islamic pilgrimage. Certainly, the core names of *makka* and *masa(r)* (Egypt) in Fula, Hausa, and other West African languages imply this route (see later discussion). At an early date, the Portuguese may have also introduced *cateto,* a flint maize ranging in color from yellow to orange from the uplands of Brazil and Argentina (called *Maiz Argentino* in Cuba), a variety also found in the nineteenth century among Xhosa and Zulu maize farmers at the Cape and Natal, respectively, but also among Bantu speakers who settled in southern Somalia and even in China. All of these regions were, of course, along lines of trade within the early Portuguese commonwealth, though the evidence of their involvement is only circumstantial at best.[10]

Hardy and early maturing, flint maize adapted well within many of the same niches in which Africa's indigenous sorghums and millets had thrived, such as the drier areas of Senegambia. Maize never fully replaced sorghum and millets, but it complemented them. In many other less arid areas maize quickly dominated and replaced local crops. The new crop was quick to ripen and thus also offered a low-labor food source in the preharvest "hungry season," that is, well before long-maturing sorghum was edible. In more humid areas of West Africa, especially the Upper Guinea Coast, where rice was the dominant cereal, maize remained a vegetable niche crop consumed fresh and not stored or hand milled.[11] Whereas rice dominated moist bottomlands of that zone, maize could occupy uplands and serve as a pioneer crop for new forest clearings, a role it also played in its spread into China and Southeast Asia.

In other nonrice areas of West Africa, farmers apparently disdained the hard starch and lower yield of flints and chose floury maize as their dominant staple, replacing or avoiding the flint types that complemented the agronomic cycle of rice.[12] Floury maize may have come later to Africa, since its origins in the Andes and dry areas of northern Mexico made it less accessible to early European settlers and merchants than the maize types available from the New World's coastal regions and islands. Once it arrived, however, the soft floury maize made dramatic inroads into West African areas as part of massive forest clearance and state building in the era of the slave trade and the new Atlantic economy. The floury maize that dominated much of West Africa until the late twentieth century served not as a vegetable but as a grain paired with New World root crops such as cassava and yams. Indeed, floury maize provided the carbohydrates essential to support large concentrations of population and state power.

Floury maize, like its flint cousin, offered new options to West African farmers who needed an annual crop that could adjust to a forest-savanna mosaic; that thrived in newly cleared forest soils; and that was transportable, divisible for taxation, and resistant to the preharvest bird damage that plagued sorghum, millet, and rice. In West Africa, as in northern China, maize proved to be an excellent "relay" crop with cowpeas (or wheat in China), which were planted between rows and matured in succession, and it was also successful in intercropping with other food crops, especially nitrogen-fixing legumes like beans and peas. Most important, maize proved a pioneer crop par excellence in establishing forest fallow cultivation systems in new frontier forest settlements.[13]

Outside of West Africa, maize had a different history of movement and adoption. Maize appeared in most areas of Africa within a century, and sometimes just a generation, of the birth of the Atlantic system but often unobtrusively as a novelty or niche crop. Farmers on the Ethiopian highlands obviously kept it within their repertoire as a garden vegetable crop but disdained its use as a field crop until well into the 1900s.[14]

In eastern Africa the geography of maize followed closely on the penetration of mercantile imperialism and then formal colonialism, though lexical information (see later discussion) intriguingly suggests patterns of adoption much earlier. Along the Swahili coast Portuguese settlers of the 1500s may have begun cultivating maize to provision their garrison at Mombasa, and it certainly became one of their dietary staples. Alternatively, maize may have arrived via the Arab and Banyan Indian Ocean trade that probably also brought it to the Horn of Africa. East African naming patterns imply the latter, as we shall see. In any case, by the mid-1800s it is clear that the Swahili caravan towns that helped coastal traders penetrate the Great Lakes region used maize as a food, once entrepreneurial farmers along the caravan routes adopted maize as a saleable commodity. Maize appeared as part of African farm repertoires described in early European accounts of local farming systems generally dominated by starchy bananas (*matooke*), New World root crops (including cassava and sweet potatoes), and African cereals (sorghums, eleusine, and bulrush millet). In Uganda by 1860 maize appeared in the garden agriculture of most of the major state systems—Buganda, Bunyoro, Toro, Ankole, and Acholi—where maize as a low-labor annual crop complemented perennial banana cultivation and local horticultural traditions. By 1876 on the shores of Lake George, Henry Stanley's "first footsteps" found that local cultivation had "an abundance of Indian corn, millet, sweet potatoes, bananas, and sugar cane."[15] By 1880 Emin Pasha, a European entrepreneur turned East African mercantile potentate, reported that maize was widely cultivated in the Acholi region of Uganda, where he had undertaken to introduce a "horse-tooth" maize variety, probably an American dent, that "thrives well."[16] He may have been referring to what Angolans called *dente de cavalho,* an early flat white dent found earlier in southern Africa. Other Europeans dutifully recorded maize and consumed it, often gratefully, in their travels, though it was African farmers who found ways to build it into their rhythms of labor, diet, and daily life.

Cultural Expressions

More enigmatic evidence of maize's arrival in Africa is represented by the threads of cultural, aesthetic, and popular responses by African peoples who appropriated the New World crop into their diets and economies. West African societies also incorporated maize imagery into elements of ritual, popular oral tradition, sumptuary law, and material culture in ways that suggest the plant's profound influence on their life. In Akan oral tradition, one *ntoro* (exogamous patrilineal division), Bosommuru, has maize as its totem. On Tuesdays, the ntoro's day of veneration, there is a ban on consuming maize. Ivor Wilks's reconstruction of Asante aetiology through oral traditions reaches back to around 1500, proposed as the time when Asante cultural identity originated; perhaps not coincidentally, it is also the approximate time of maize's first arrival in West Africa.[17] By the 1700s, maize became strongly associated with the Asante army and perhaps with state power in general. One Akan proverb notes: *Aduane panin ne aburoo* ("The chief/elder among foods is maize").[18]

Elsewhere in West Africa, maize again appears as an anthropomorphic figure. In a nineteenth-century Yoruba folktale maize is a mysterious, ghostlike stranger:

I do not know at all, but I wish I knew
What clothes the maize plant wore
When he first came
To this Origbo from Olufe town
But this I know surely
That he was disguised upon his journey here.[19]

In Yoruba the symbolism of maize (*àgbàdo*) also plays a role within Ifá divination's oral verse, or ÉsÉ Ifá. Here the oral text recounted to me and published by Awishe Wande Abimbola celebrates the plant's almost human fecundity:

Maize went nakedly to the farm
She brought back two hundred clothes
Two hundred clothes
Maize went to the farm alone
Two hundred clothes
She brought back two hundred clothes
Maize went to the farm alone
She brought back two hundred children
Two hundred children.[20]

This expression of wonder at maize's productivity is reminiscent of sixteenth-century European amazement related in Du Bartas's *Divine Weekes and Workes* from 1544–90:

Heer of one grain of maiz, a reed doth spring
That thrice a year five hundred grains doth bring.[21]

Maize also established itself within West African aesthetic traditions of material culture. In ceramic ware artisans among the Yoruba and several other groups used discarded maize cobs as a tool to imprint "maize-cob roulette," a distinctive rolled design on pottery. At Ife, the ritual center of Yorubaland, potsherds with this design formed the paving materials for elite household walkways. Common traditions of the Fon, Aja, and Nago peoples who made up the historical state of Dahomey assert that their kings reserved millet for royal consumption in an effort to save the traditional crop from maize's rapid expansion.[22] These examples are simply illustrative: the range of these rich and creative expressions is vast and still awaits collection by scholars of local traditions across Africa.

Naming the Stranger

A fascinating, if often perplexing, measure of local historical perceptions of the new crop, and the timing of its arrival locally, is the panoply of names that African languages attach to maize. Comparing words for maize in Africa's languages produces a unique source, but one whose analysis must depend on intuitive and sometimes idiosyncratic methods. Yet the rewards of such analysis are considerable, since collecting and studying the names given to something new, such as maize, reveal aspects of local imagination not evident in other sources. Despite the seemingly kaleidoscopic variety of maize terms in African languages, there are a number of patterns that repeat themselves across linguistic groups, ecologies, and economic categories. The comparative study of African words for maize also reveals several kinds of encounters, universes of the material life of food, farming systems, and networks of cultural exchange—as with trade networks and ecology—that cut against the grain of formal language categories.

For each society that encountered maize, naming the stranger was a process of trying to make the exotic more familiar. Thus the most common Old World theme in naming the new arrival was the use of a name for an already known grain combined with popular ideas about its provenance. In highland Ethiopia Semitic speakers called it *yabaher mashela* (Amharic) or *mashela baheri* (Tigrinya), both terms meaning "the sorghum [from] the sea." Among East African languages (Chagga, Akamba, Samburu, Pokomo, Taita), spoken by people who must also have received maize first from the coast, the common name for maize is *pemba* (including cognates *bemba* in Kikuyu and *hemba* in Chagga). A. C. A. Wright argues that the word *pemba* derived from the name of the island on which Portuguese planters in the sixteenth century began to raise foodstuffs, including maize, to supply their coastal garrison. The historian Steven Feierman, however, has told me that the Shambai term *pemba* refers to sorghum, and Christopher Ehret, master of evidence from historical linguistics, confirms *pemba* as a reference to sorghum.[23] This gloss is made more plausible by the older version in Kiswahili, *pemba muhindi,* or Indian sorghum.

Another pattern related to use of the word for the more familiar sorghum has already been hinted at in the Ethiopian cases—this is reference to a distant place or to the notion of provenance "from the sea." In Malawi the Chichewa language called it *chimanga* ("from the coast"), indicating a perception of its origin similar to the Semitic speakers in Ethiopia; on the East African coast the Kiswahili short-hand term is *muhindi* ("from India"). It is worth noting that the only African localities to use *burro* or *aburro,* borrowed terms derived from the Portuguese *milho zaburro,* were two early sites of Portuguese trade: the earliest Portuguese permanent trading station on the coast of West Africa at El Mina (established in 1482) on the Gold Coast and in Mozambique. In Akan *aburo* is maize, but Akan speakers also describe overseas countries as *aburokyire* ("countries where maize comes from"). The Akan call the English (their colonizers) *abrofo*—another form of the term that denoted maize.[24] The Dutch Gold Coast historian James LaFleur argues effectively that *aburro* in the old Dutch transliterations is a direct reference to sorghum.

At the mouth of the Congo River in the mid-sixteenth century local Kikongo speakers called maize *maza mamputo* ("grain of the whiteman"); Mande speakers in Senegambia offered *tuba-nyo* ("white man's grain"), a similar gloss. From Egypt south and along the trade route south to Lake Chad local lexical terms for maize, especially Hausa and dialects of Fulfulde, derived from the root *masa* or *masar* (Egypt), describing maize's likely direction of introduction to the region. Among other groups, the Bambara use *maka,* a word that suggests maize's introduction by pilgrims returning from the *hajj* (referring to the goal of the Islamic pilgrimage), or *kaba,* a word that also designates sorghum but seems related to the shrine around which Muslims process when they reach Makkah.[25]

Nigeria provides an example of the rich collection of local terms for maize, reflecting a variety of cultural and linguistic responses to the new crop over time. The names for maize fall into distinctive clusters around the major languages, but the list of terms also includes local variations, indicating that the crop had probably initially arrived from several different directions and in several different types.

Maize in southern Africa followed a somewhat different chronology of contact, though, like other regions, the crop percolated onto southern African farms through international trade and population movements. Portuguese trade seems to have provided the earliest introduction, as suggested by the use of names such as *zaburro* (in Mozambique from the Portuguese *milho zaburro*), *masa mamputo* (in Angola and Congo, "grain of the white man"), and *mealie* (in Afrikaans from the Portuguese *milho*), a term now widely used generally by many linguistic communities in South Africa and Zimbabwe.[26] Other names have more enigmatic referents or seem borrowed from neighbors where the crop had had a longer history. Swazi traditions, for example, associate maize's arrival with the origins of their Dlamini royal clan, but the siSwati language also borrows the Zulu term *m'lungu* ("white man") or *u'hlanza-gazaan.*[27] Among the Tswana and Sotho maize arrived with missionaries who established agricultural stations as part of mission churches, and they called it *sefele* or *mdidi.* Up to the first third of the twentieth century, however, southern African diets still consisted of sorghum and millet, reflecting landscapes where maize was sometimes known but never dominant.

Still other patterns of naming suggest local farmers' sometimes whimsical response to the appearance of the plant itself. In some Tigrinya-speaking areas of northern Ethiopia, maize's name comes from what must have been to farmers the unusual feature of the husked ears; they called it *ifun* ("covered") or *ilbo* ("uncircumcised"). As noted previously, other societies like the Akan and the Yoruba consigned images of sexual potency to the phallic ears that bore maize's grain kernels.

These patterns emerge most coherently when we look at particular language families and language regions. Sir Harry Johnston's impressive 1922 compendium of Bantu vocabulary contains a full list of words meaning maize. Patterns of maize naming in these languages refer to wider types of cultural and linguistic change. In some of his early work Christropher Ehret argued that Bantu languages emerged from a root crop "planting" culture, did so over the span of about one thousand years of interactions with central Sudanic groups, and gradually borrowed and adapted the concepts of grain cultivation and processing.[28] The process by which Bantu speakers named the fairly recently arrived new crop of maize seems to have been part of a longer-term adjustment to grain agriculture as a whole. Maize terms adopted as borrowings for grain and grain processing in eastern Bantu languages include -*bele* ("grain"), -*caka* ("sorghum"), and -*papa* ("porridge"), among others. Maize's arrival on the African scene after 1500 thus formed a new layer on these older patterns.

Bantu languages' words for maize include virtually the full range of naming patterns seen in African languages as a whole. The term *(pa) manga* ("of the sea") or *mapira manga* ("sorghum of the sea") names maize in Yao, Nyanja-Chewa, and Karanja languages. The term *pemba muhindi* ("Indian sorghum") for maize appears in Kiswahili, Pokomo, Pare, Chaga, Thaiicu, Saghala, Seuta, Zalamo, and Kami. In several of these cases the languages have adopted the shorthand expression of either *pemba* or *muhindi,* similar to American English's shortening of the original term "Indian corn" to simply "corn" to mean maize. In many other African languages, words for maize were simple adoptions of older terms for sorghum, such as *saka* (Sabi, Fipa, Mambwe, Lungu, Nyiha, and Bambusangu), *bila* or *pila* (Northern and Southern Nguni, Southern Sotho, Holengwe), *tama* (Gogo, Kagula, Sagala, and Ngazija), or *kusa* (Konjo, Amba, Littuku, Vamba, Bira). In some cases languages chose to adopt their maize name from the term for bulrush (or pearl) millet, an African crop generally confined to the driest areas, where maize could not survive. Thus for Hehe, Bena, Kinga, Lenje, and Nsanga the word *cebele* (or *kebele*) meant maize, while in other languages spoken by groups in more arid zones *cebele* or *kebele* continued to refer to the indigenous bulrush millet more familiar to them.

Another common pattern of maize naming appears in a number of Bantu languages: the identification of the maize plant not by reference to other grains but by the appearance of its stalk. So, in Nyamwezi the word *dege* means maize, but in the Southern Cushitic language family from which it was borrowed, the cognate term (*dig*) designates "stalk." The widespread Bantu term *konde,* meaning "thick stalk," is the word for maize in a cluster of East African regional languages. The word *gombe,* which means maize in Nkoya, means more precisely "thick stem" or "stick" in a scattered number of other Bantu languages. In a wide range of Savanna Bantu languages in southern Africa (Ovimbundu, Bemisa, Yao, Zulu, etc.), *ngoma* denotes a "heavy stick," whereas in Bisa, Lala, and Nsenga it means maize.[29] In a number of cases in the Bantu maize word list farmers named the maize plant "stick" or "stalk." Perhaps this was especially the case in language groups from historically root-cropping, or "planting," agricultural systems.

Finally, exactly who was it that named the new plant and its distinctive food products? Christopher Ehret argues that in historical and prehistorical eras that predate the arrival of maize many nongrain cultures simply borrowed words from central Sudanic languages, where a tradition of cereal cultivation had created a rich vocabulary for grains and boiled grains (porridges).[30]

It may also have been that women either borrowed or coined words to apply to the new crop from the New World. Certainly in the modern era women comprise the majority of Africa's farmers, but in the 1900s, as maize shifted from a household garden crop to a valuable cash crop, it often was a male domain. We know from more recent evidence that farmers apply names of their own invention to new maize varieties, following much the same pattern as did the original namers of the new plant centuries ago. In recent times there is ample evidence that women were the namers. For example, Jean Hay tells us that in western Kenya it was women who lost male labor to early urban migrations and who named crop varieties. In 1917 a new white dent maize (probably what Americans had called "Hickory King") was novel enough that Luo women called the new type of maize *orobi* (or Nairobi, the city founded in 1901), perhaps a sign that it marked a new era in their lives, an era when urban economies mattered more.[31]

Just as African maize in the twentieth century has evolved into a standardized white form, losing the rich color and texture variations of the original New World imports, so too have the names lost their brilliance and evocativeness. In the modern parlance of hybrid and improved maize types produced by national seed centers and private corporations, maize types merely take numbers and initials of scientific trials or the location of the research station (such as BH660 or Kitale 522). This new custom removes the initiative from farmers, increasingly deprived of the ability to imagine their maize's characteristics, and favors instead the

bland and homogenous and scientific over local aesthetic expression.
Maize is no longer the stranger.

NOTES

1. See Alfred Crosby, *The Columbian Exchange: Biological and Cultural Consequences of 1492* (Westport, 1972). A few scholars have claimed that maize in the Old World predated 1492, citing early Portuguese references to *milho zaburro* on the West African coast.

2. M. D. W. Jeffreys, "How Ancient Is West African Maize?" *Africa* 33, no. 2 (1963): 198. In this quotation the common mistranslation of the Portuguese *milho zaburro* as maize (as opposed to sorghum, an indigenous African grain) is not a factor. The reference to *mehiz* and the grain's resemblance to chickpeas suggests maize was the cereal in question.

3. Jeffreys, "How Ancient," 121. Jeffreys cites a translation by Lains e Silva. See also Willett, "The Introduction of Maize to West Africa," *Africa* 1 (1982): 1–13 at 11. Robert Harms (personal communication) tells me that the French slaving ship *Diligent* called in at Sao Tomé in December–January 1731–32, where it took on cassava flour and "unc Demy gamelle De mil" (a half barrel of maize/sorghum) as food for the middle passage. The latter may be maize rather than millet since maize is elsewhere described as a major provision for such vessels calling at Sao Tomé. It is not clear why the *Diligent* did not take on a larger consignment of maize, though perhaps the harvest was delayed and supplies were low.

4. O. Dapper, *Nankeurige Beschrijvinge der Afrikaensche Gewestern* (Amsterdam, 1668), 463, quoted in Helma Pasch, "Zur Geschichte der Verbreitung des Maizes in Afrika," *Sprache und Geschichte in Afrika* 5 (1983): 189.

5. Dominique Juhé-Beaulaton, "La diffusion du maïs sur les côtes de l'or et des esclaves aux XVII et XVIII siècles," *Revue française d'histoire d'outre-mer* 77 (1990): 188–90. See Mungo Park, *The Life and Travels of Mungo Park, with a Supplementary Chapter Detailing the Results of Recent Discovery in Africa with Illustrations* (Edinburgh, 1870), quoted in Joseph Burtt-Davy, *Maize: Its History, Cultivation, Handling, and Uses. With Special Reference to South Africa* (London, 1914), 56.

6. Roger Blench, Kay Williamson, and Bruce Connell, "The Diffusion of Maize in Nigeria: A Historical and Linguistic Investigation," *Sprache und Geschichte in Afrika* 15 (1994): 109–14. For assertions about the Portuguese role, see, for example, Marvin Miracle, *Maize in Tropical Africa,* (Madison, 1966), who cites no evidence but seems to be the source cited by most writers.

7. See M. D. W. Jeffreys, "The History of Maize in Africa," *South African Journal of Science* (March 1954): 197–200, and Jeffreys, "The Origin of the Portuguese Word Zaburro as the Name for Maize," *Bulletin de l'Institut Français de l'Afrique Noire, Serie B, Sciences Humaines* 19, no. 1–2 (January–April 1957):

III–36. For Bascom's complaint and the full body of evidence from Nigeria, see Blench, Williamson, and Connell, "The Diffusion of Maize," 9–46.

8. A. J. H. Goodwin, "The Origin of Maize," *South African Archaeological Bulletin* 8 (1953): 13.

9. The primary maize cultivated for polenta in the Veneto region of Italy until 1952 was a red flint called Marano. I am grateful to Ms. Emma Meggliolaro and Dr. Armando DeGuio for this information. As a young girl Meggliolaro cultivated maize near Vicenza. Colloquial Venetan for maize is *sorgo rosso* ("red sorghum").

10. Burtt-Davy, *Maize*, 316. There was a white-grain version of this flint found on black South African farms. For further description of Brazilian cateto flint maize, see also Christopher Dowswell, R. L Paliwal, and Ronald Cantrell, *Maize in the Third World* (Boulder, 1996), 17, 106–7; and E. J. Wellhausen, "Recent Developments in Maize Breeding in the Tropics," in David B. Walden, ed., *Maize Breeding and Genetics* (New York, 1978), 61.

11. Juhé-Beaulaton, "La diffusion," 187, states that the seventeenth-century inhabitants of Aquapim consumed maize exclusively fresh or roasted on the cob.

12. See Roland Portères, "L'Introduction du Mais en Afrique," *Journal d'Agriculture Tropicale et de Botanique Appliquée* 2, no. 5–6 (May–June 1955): 224–26; and Marvin P. Miracle, "Interpretation of Evidence on the Introduction of Maize into West Africa," *Africa* 33, no. 2 (1963): 133. Portères argues that floury maize types came via the West African coast and flint types via the Nile Valley. Miracle suggests that flints may also have come from the coast but found less favor among farmers, especially women, who preferred the soft starches more suitable to hand milling. Most current evidence indicates that women prefer flinty types for hand milling and storage. Current local maize varieties in Ghana are semident floury types: interview with S. Twumasi-Afriyie, Kumasi, July 1997. Burtt-Davy, *Maize*, 322–23, mentions a Brazilian flour corn that resembles a Zulu bread maize known as *u'hlanza-gazaan* ("white man's grain").

13. Dowswell, Paliwal, and Cantrell, *Maize in the Third World*, 48–49. Relay cropping involves the quick sowing of a crop on the same plot occupied by another crop within the same growing season.

14. See James C. McCann, *People of the Plow: An Agricultural History of Ethiopia* (Madison, 1995), 56. For an earlier (but dubious) date for pod maize, see Burtt-Davy, *Maize*, 13.

15. Henry Stanley, *Through the Dark Continent* (New York, 1878), 1:439.

16. G. Schweinfurth, ed., *Emin Pasha in Central Africa* (London, 1888), 418.

17. R. S. Rattray, *Ashanti* (Oxford, 1923), 47. Also see Ivor Wilks, *Forests of Gold: Essays on the Akan and the Kingdom of Asante* (Athens, Ohio, 1993), 66–72.

18. J. J. Christaller, ed., *A Collection of Three Thousand and Six Hundred Tshi Proverbs* (New York, 1990), 150. I am grateful to the work of James D. LaFleur and to the advice of Maxwell Amoh and Edward Kissi for this citation.

19. A. Babalola, "Folk Tales from Yoruba Land," *West African Review* 23, no.

292 (1952): 14. Willett, "The Introduction of Maize," 9, ascribes this tradition to the early nineteenth century.

20. Wande Abimbola, *Ifá: An Exposition of Ifá Literary Corpus* (New York, 1997), 221–22.

21. Quoted in Burtt-Davy, *Maize*, 1.

22. R. Soper, "Roulette Decoration on African Pottery: Technical Considerations, Dating, and Distributions," *African Archaeological Review* 3 (1985): 31–44, at 31, 44.

23. A. C. A. Wright, "Maize Names as Indicators of Economic Contacts," *Uganda Journal* 13, no. 1 (1949): 64. Wright mentions a Portuguese manuscript of 1634 that refers to maize production on Pemba Island. Steven Feierman and Christopher Ehret, personal communication. Also see Helma Pasch, "Zur Geschichte der Verbreitung des Maizes in Afrika," *Sprache und Geschichte in Afrika* 5 (1983): 196–97.

24. My thanks to Dr. Edward Kissi for this information.

25. For many other West African languages the evidence is not at all clear. For a comprehensive list of West African maize terms compiled in 1854, see Sigismund Koelle, *Polyglotta Africana*, ed. P. E. H. Hair and David Dalby (Graz, Austria, 1963), 104–5, 112–13. Also see Christine Chiang, "Determining the Origins of Maize in West Africa Using Ethnolinguistic Evidence," unpublished paper, UCLA, 1997, 4. These names suggest possible patterns of adoption, though any conclusions can only be speculative and await a more detailed, systematic linguistic survey. In India the word in Hindi, *makka* or *makka jouar,* implies an introduction from Arabia and the Eastern Mediterranean. In each of these cases it seems likely that maize returned with *hajji,* whose pilgrimages provided both intellectual and agronomic cross-fertilization. I am grateful to Professor Christopher Ehret for his linguistic insights and willingness to share them.

26. Burtt-Davy, *Maize,* 13–14, 18–24.

27. Burtt-Davy, *Maize,* 13. I am grateful to Sandra Sanneh of the Department of African Languages at Yale University for help on South African languages.

28. Christopher Ehret, "Agricultural History in Central and Southern Africa, ca. 1000 B.C. to A.D. 500," *Transafrican Journal of History* 4 (1974): 5.

29. This section on Bantu glosses relies heavily on Christopher Ehret, who generously commented on my Bantu maize word list. His insights derive from long experience with that language family, as well as with Cushitic and Semitic languages in eastern and southern Africa.

30. Ehret, "Agricultural History," 5–7.

31. John Gerhart cites the pioneering work of Margaret Jean Hay. See John Gerhart, *The Diffusion of Hybrid Maize in Western Kenya* (Mexico City, 1975), 35. Hay has pointed out that Luo farmers readily accepted maize but initially rejected cotton cultivation, pushed by the expanding colonial state.

VII Two Landscapes, Two Stories

Anglo-Saxon England and the United States

Nicholas Howe

> We need the past, in any case, to cope with present
> landscapes.
>
> —David Lowenthal[1]

IF THE MAKING OF landscapes by human beings begins with such physical acts as terracing slopes, diverting water flows, and building structures for shelter and worship, it also extends to the shaping of landscapes into myths and narratives that inform the lives of these same human beings.[2] Any reconstruction of "natures past" thus must consider what kinds of ideas and beliefs animated those who did that terracing, diverting, and building. Indeed, this volume's title with its various resonances conveys this concern: the natures of the past are not limited simply to the ecological environments we conventionally call the natural world but also include the complex of attitudes, beliefs, and dispositions we designate as human nature. That the same word can be used, at least by English speakers, to designate two seemingly disparate spheres suggests there is reason to explore the relations between landscapes and stories.

Landscapes fill human lives by serving as natural environment, productive terrain, habitation, decorative scenery, aesthetic inspiration, and mnemonic territory for recording history—to name only a few that come to mind as I look out my window at the wall of my neighbor's house twelve feet away and think about the books on the shelves next to me. None of these categories or functions should be taken as necessarily excluding any of the others; difficulties arise, in fact, when one tries to distinguish between them too sharply instead of letting landscape serve some or all of these purposes at the same time. As Alan R. H. Baker puts it, landscape is "the visible manifestation of the relationship between people and the space/land they occupy."[3] For the human beings who live within them, landscapes also matter because of the stories that gather in them. Many of these stories are local. They ask questions that pertain to those who live in that landscape: "Do you see that the hills over there look like a reclining human figure? Might that be in some visible form our ancestor? If it is, what shall we call that ridge and how shall we treat it as sacred?" And then, "Do the people on the other side of the ridgeline look at the hills as we do?"[4] Some of the stories written on a landscape can endure for a long time because they hold the history of those who live there, as Keith Basso has shown of the Western Apache or, in very different ways, as Bruce Chatwin explored for Australian Aborigines in *The Songlines.*[5] These stories about landscapes are attempts to interpret the visible surrounding scene that was there before the stories took form and that will exist after generations transform these stories themselves.[6] Yet landscapes have, it needs to be remembered in this connection, their own stubborn, physical reality. They preexist the stories told about them and are likely to outlast them.

This human fascination with interpreting landscapes through their stories has a long and wide lineage, especially if one includes the work of visual artists and imaginative writers. Nor has this fascination gone unnoticed by the academic discipline of geography. Recent scholarly collections with titles such as *Understanding Ordinary Landscapes* and *The Iconography of Landscape* display the cultural turn that marks geographers' thinking about landscape.[7] More specifically, the possibility that natural landscapes may contribute to the shaping of national identities has become a pressing topic, as in Oliver Zimmer's argument in this volume that the iconographic celebration of the Alps was a determining condition of nineteenth-century Swiss identity. One might posit similar claims about the iconographic centrality of the Rhine Valley to Germany or the Lake District to Great Britain or Monument Valley and the Grand Canyon to the United States. These sites all possess, by their own cultures' standards, a memorable or sublime beauty. They are not the landscapes that most citizens of a nation live within but rather are those featured in paintings, school books, postage stamps, and the like. The aestheticization of landscape as national myth lies beyond the bounds of the current study, but it does suggest that landscape can captivate a national imaginary and become a conveyance for a sense of history and identity.

The cultural geographer D. W. Meinig has gone so far as to claim that the relation between natural landscape and national identity is a widespread if not universal phenomenon: "Every nation has its symbolic landscapes. They are part of the iconography of nationhood, part of the shared set of ideas and memories and feelings which bind a people together."[8] The key adjective here is "symbolic" because it suggests that certain landscapes are marked by some figurative meaning that extends beyond the literal topography and allows them to represent the beliefs of people who live and work within them. Put another way, landscape can become a repository of stories.[9] Meinig's claim about the power that symbolic landscapes exert on the formation of national identities bears a striking resemblance to Benedict Anderson's widely influential thesis in *Imagined Communities* that stories, especially as they circulate among citizens of a nation who will never meet each other face to face, provide symbolic forms necessary to create political communities.[10] Following Meinig, Anderson might well have noted that landscapes participate in this creation of community, especially because they contain stories that can be read without the formal skills of textual literacy. That landscapes are topographies to be terraced, diverted, or built upon as well as theaters of memory or sites of ideological definition makes them as valuable as texts for anyone struggling to understand natures past as well as cultures present.[11]

Yet Meinig's commonsensical claim may not fully register the contradictory, unverifiable, even irrational ways in which myths based on symbolic places function within their community of believers. Put another way, various members of a community will assign more discordant and even contradictory meaning to a particular symbolic landscape than would seem possible at first. The symbolic meanings that gather around a place can often be elusive and can frustrate attempts at verification or quantification. Beliefs and myths are harder to measure than hectares planted in grain or cubic meters of earth moved to raise ramparts. The contemporary British writer Iain Sinclair puts the case for the elusiveness of place in a usefully hyperbolic way: "Myth is what place says. And it does lie. It spreads a seductive field of pits and snares. You go mad if you try to pursue place through myth: your path will disappear over the nearest cliff."[12] Sinclair is a relentless walker of places, an expert in their irrational properties. He styles himself a "psychogeographer," fully aware that his prefix has meanings that range from the technical to the colloquial. Without disappearing over cliffs, those who study myths of place should heed Sinclair: they must resist succumbing to their seductive charms or at the very least should maintain a lover's quarrel with them.

By evoking the imaginative resonances of landscape, Meinig and Sinclair prepare this discussion of two historically and geographically distinct landscapes seen as human constructs: that of Anglo-Saxon England (ca. 600–1100 CE) and that of the United States.[13] The questions that appear throughout this study about these two landscapes concern their interpretation as—and also through—stories and myths. As careful scholars, we recognize that national landscapes do not in themselves create stories and myths ex nihilo or give voice to them spontaneously but rather that their inhabitants impose such narratives on landscapes or at least locate them there. Yet this same scholarly care also requires us to recognize that at certain moments a people may come to believe that its landscape has indeed produced the narratives that it lives by. The relations of cause and effect that one might deduce about landscape and its narratives retrospectively are not necessarily those of the people who live in a place and tell stories about it.

The differences between the landscapes of early medieval England and the modern United States are dramatically apparent, so much so that they may seem to foreclose any possibility of useful comparison. The Anglo-Saxon landscape was quite limited in geographical scale and extent. It often, if not always, showed highly visible signs of human labor by its current occupants as well as those who preceded them, such as prehistoric makers of earthen ramparts, hillforts, and burial tumuli, as well as Roman builders of walls, roads, and cemeteries.[14] To complicate matters for us, the Anglo-Saxon landscape has long since been overlain with countless accretions, from Norman churches through modern highways and airports, so that it can seem at times obscured or invisible. Studied from our moment, it appears less as an identifiable place to be walked or viewed than as a reconstructed body of knowledge based on archival and archaeological evidence. The landscape of contemporary America is immediately present to the eye, yet often on so vast a scale as to be overwhelming and potentially beyond representation. That it is there for the walking (or, more usually, the driving) does not necessarily make it more accessible to interpretation. That work is complicated by a long-lasting and by no means past tradition of defining landscape as that which remains unspoiled or innocent of any human intervention. The American scene has typically been described through evocations of Eden, and the use of that originary narrative for the human entry into place and time has sometimes made it difficult to separate the landscape from its stories.

If these and other differences between the two landscapes can easily be noted, the likeness between them is more elusive because it draws less on visual or experiential senses of landscape than on stories of human migration. To think about these landscapes invites one to ask what it might have been like to come into them as emigrants from another place with memories of some other landscape fixed in mind. The profound differences of topography and use in the landscapes of Anglo-Saxon England and the United States are all the more intriguing, I want to suggest, precisely because the dominant culture of each located a common core of memory in its story of migration or exodus. Not surprisingly, the displaced Celts of Britain and the native peoples of North America had other stories to tell about their contact with these unwelcome newcomers. Nonetheless, the historical similarity between these two landscapes can be traced to the dominant group's practice of reading migration as the search for a spiritual homeland and, more specifically, as embodying the narrative of belief taken from the book of Exodus in the Hebrew Bible.[15] To translate this similarity into specific questions: "What did Canaan look like to those who had fled Egypt?" Or, more radically: "What did the new Eden look like to those who had fled the corruption and decay of Europe?" Somewhere along the way, it seemed, the vision of landscape had to acknowledge the necessary fictions of history. The point of this study is not to reduce landscape to the status of cultural construct but rather to suggest that there have been at times certain interpretive paradigms that have proved necessary for making sense of a people's experience of—and within—the landscape. Put baldly, my subject is less the landscape in itself as it is ways of talking about landscape. To inhabit a landscape is not simply to live in a topography; it is also to find a source of self-identification. In that sense the topic of this study might be described as the ways in which landscape becomes imbricated within the culture of a people, how it becomes home ground. As stories imbue a landscape with more than economic value, landscapes can become a form of cultural capital.

Tracing the stories that a people might tell about its landscape means looking at the primary texts or artifacts of that culture as well as the scholarly conventions that have shaped the reading of those primary texts and artifacts. We do not come innocently, as it were, to the evidence itself, nor can we blithely assume that it speaks for itself. The dominant tradition for studying the Anglo-Saxon landscape derives from W. G. Hoskins's classic *The Making of the English Landscape* (1955), which lays down as its chief axiom: "Everything is older than we think." Hoskins glosses this statement further:

> Not much of England, even in its more withdrawn, inhuman places, has escaped being altered by man in some subtle way or other, however untouched we may fancy it is at first sight. Sherwood Forest and Wicken Fen are not quite what they seem.[16]

Landscape for Hoskins is not in any sense unspoiled and thus ageless but is historical record, a position that runs directly contrary to the idealizing American story that sees landscape as that which survives distinct from human occupation and use. The presence of history in Hoskins's book sometimes manifests itself as nostalgia for a past landscape—but tellingly it is never one innocent of human intervention. If Hoskins believes that everything that has happened on the English landscape since 1914 "has either uglified it or destroyed its meaning, or both," he can still celebrate the view from his study window as "an epitome of the gentle unravished English landscape. Circumscribed as it is, with tall trees closing it in barely half a mile away, it contains in its detail something of every age from the Saxon to the nineteenth century."[17] "Unravished" is a polemical adjective in this context because, as it raises the specter of sexual violation, it also celebrates a landscape that is agricultural and preindustrial, rural and pastoral, rather than urban and mechanical. It is, on its own preferred terms of virginal innocence, as much a landscape of desire as is the one evoked by Ansel Adams as he removed human history from his landscape photographs of the American West.

Yet Hoskins's axiom that "Everything is older than we think" is a powerful interpretive tool for studying the landscape of Anglo-Saxon England.[18] In ways that may seem very surprising to readers shaped by the American tradition, the Anglo-Saxons did not cultivate a moralizing binary between the innocence of the natural landscape and the corruption of human civilization. They tended instead to contrast the ephemeral life on earth with the enduring joys of heaven, a binary that may help to explain why there is so little explicit description of the earthly landscape in Anglo-Saxon texts, whether in the vernacular or in Latin.[19] They looked more at the eternal heavens above than at the transient earth below. That acknowledged, perhaps the closest we have to a deliberate description of the Anglo-Saxon landscape appears in the opening chapters of the Venerable Bede's *Ecclesiastical History of the English Church and People* (*EH*), completed in 731 CE.

Bede writes as the historian—or the canonizer—of the Anglo-Saxon migration myth.[20] By tracing the Germanic migrations from the northwest of the European continent to the island of Britain, his *History* provided a master narrative that was frequently used by later writers. Having identified the homeland and then the places of settlement for the Saxons, Angles, and Jutes (*EH* I.15), he also designates them as newcomers to England in the mid-fifth century CE. He specifies that among the attractions that drew these Germanic tribes to Britain was "the fertility of the island" (*insulae fertilitas, EH* I.15).[21] Bede's monastic life was so thoroughly circumscribed that he rarely if ever traveled outside of his native Northumbria. Most of his facts about the British landscape come from Roman writers, especially Pliny the Elder, and yet he describes the land that the Angles, Saxons, and Jutes found across the North Sea in terms meant to evoke an earthly—that is, a cultivated and worked—paradise:

> The island is rich in crops and in trees, and has good pasturage for cattle and beasts of burden. It also produces vines in certain districts, and has plenty of both land- and waterfowl of various kinds. It is remarkable too for its rivers, which abound in fish, particularly salmon and eels, and for copious springs. . . . The land possesses salt springs and warm springs and from them flow rivers which supply hot baths, suitable for all ages and both sexes, in separate places and adapted to the needs of each. (*EH* I.1)[22]

This paradisal description of the island with its abundance and fertility, so similar to the tropes used for America by various writers (as I shall soon suggest), evokes and also underlies the common belief during the Anglo-Saxon period that England was home to a chosen people that had arrived there in an exodus or, to use the Old English word, an *utgang.* And yet, the careful reader of this passage cannot fail to notice that this landscape is postlapsarian: men and women take their baths in separate places because of the shame that was brought on them by the Fall.

That the landscape of Britain was already historical when the migration occurred is made manifest throughout the early chapters of Bede's *History.* He notes, in the midst of enumerating the island's mineral riches and explaining its long nights in winter and long days in summer, that it "was once famous for its twenty-eight noble cities as well as innumerable fortified places equally well guarded by the strongest of walls and towers, gates and locks" (*EH* I.1).[23] The references to cities and fortifications visible on the terrain are knowing allusions to the occupation of the island by the Romans, for they were the great urban dwellers and builders of stone fortifications in the history of the island. This Anglo-Saxon vision of the Romans is borne out by the archeological record that shows over and over again that the English reused Roman stonework as spolia for their own buildings, that they made regular use of Roman roads, and that they buried their dead in Roman cemeteries. The Anglo-Saxons reshaped the Romanized landscape that they had inherited, for, as Hoskins had predicted, everything was older than it seemed at first glance.

Later in this same chapter of his *History,* Bede will complicate the record of the landscape by noting that the island was then home to five languages and thus five peoples: British (i.e., Welsh), Irish, Pictish (another Celtic language), Latin, and English. Of these, four were present in Britain when the Germanic emigrants arrived: English is the language of the newcomers, one derived from the Germanic dialects they spoke on the continent. These migrating tribes from Germania did not find an unpopulated paradise on the island, as some Europeans believed they had in America. The Anglo-Saxon biblical model for the chosen land drew less explicitly on the original site of Eden than on the figurative—that is, historically analogous—site of Canaan. As a people within human time, as a people whose ancestors had been expelled from paradise, the Anglo-Saxons could not envision themselves in a landscape untouched by other tribes and peoples.

This Anglo-Saxon awareness of the deep pastness of the landscape can manifest itself in unexpected documents. Among the most widely surviving texts from the period are land charters that memorialize the ceremony by which property is transferred from a donor, usually a king or other aristocrat, to an individual or, more often, to a monastic foundation. These charters are, as one would expect of legal texts, quite formulaic in their structure. They fall into four sections: a statement of the authority by which the donor makes the grant of land; a description of the property in question that lists its important landmarks on a circumambulation; a warning of the dire consequences that will befall anyone who tampers with the grant; and the signatures of those involved in the transaction as well as the appropriate witnesses. Some of these charters are written throughout in Latin, while others are bilingual, with the boundary clause appearing in vernacular Old English and the remaining sections in often quite ornate Latin.

One of these charters records a grant from King Athelstan to his follower Ealdred in 929 CE. The boundary clause of the charter runs as follows:

> These are the boundaries of the aforesaid land: Where the dyke runs into Watling Street, along Watling Street to the ford, then along the brook to the other ford, then from that ford up to the spring, and thence into the valley, thence from the valley . . . [through other diverse topographical features] then straight up to the highway, along the highway to the dyke, along the dyke to Watling Street.[24]

The historically notable feature here is the old Roman road running northwest from London known in Old English as "wæxlingga strate" or Watling Street. The reference would have carried another resonance for the Anglo-Saxon reader of this charter: Watling Street was also the dividing line between the southern part of the island dominated by the Anglo-Saxons and the northern regions known as the Danelaw because it was under the political control of rulers descended from Viking raiders. This bifurcation followed from agreements made between King Alfred and the Viking king Guthrum in the late 870s.

"Wæxlingga strate" is thus a multiply inscribed trace along the landscape, one that records the coming to the island of two outsider peoples at two distinct moments in time: the Romans starting in 43 CE with the arrival of Claudius and his legions and the Danes in the late eighth century beginning with their raids on Lindisfarne and other sites in Northumbria. Between these two waves of invasion occurred the migration of the Germanic tribes in the mid-fifth century and following. Looking at this boundary clause carefully, the reader can detect the island's history on the record of its landscape: the arrival of the Romans as signaled by the building of Watling Street; the arrival of the ancestral tribes of the Anglo-Saxons as embedded in the Germanic vernacular of the passage itself; and the arrival of the Scandinavians as marked by the reuse of Watling Street to demarcate a political frontier. While it would be foolish to argue that every vernacular boundary clause in an Anglo-Saxon land charter offered a landscape as historically stratified as does this one of Athelstan's, it certainly may be observed that the textual record has just begun to be sifted for this sort of historicizing evidence about the Anglo-Saxon landscape.[25]

The description of landscape in Athelstan's charter is absolutely neutral; it offers no emotive or evocative response on the part of the official who drafted it. Other Anglo-Saxon texts, however, do contain historical traces that seem to have aroused wonder and curiosity on the part of their authors. One of the most haunting descriptions of landscape we have from Old English poetry appears in *Maxims II,* a poem made up of short normative statements about the proper workings of human life, that is, of pithy maxims meant to be read as embodying accepted cultural wisdom. The poet, using a phrase found elsewhere in such other Old English poems as *The Ruin,* opens by alluding to a city of stone buildings as "the skillful work of giants" that could be seen from a distance:

> A king should hold the kingdom. Cities may be seen
> from afar,
> those that are on the earth, the skillful work of giants,
> the artfully crafted work of wall stones.
>
> (ll. 1–3a)[26]

Such descriptions of the inhabited landscape are all too rare in texts from Anglo-Saxon England, especially in suggesting the presence of structures built in an earlier period. One wishes that the poet of *Maxims II* had said more about the site. From what distance is the site visible? What do its structures look like? Who, if anyone, was living in it at the time he saw it? What sense of historical knowledge did he derive from it?

From what angle or perspective did they actually see the city in its landscape and history? Such additional commentary would have been especially welcome in a poem distilling traditional wisdom.

Yet even without such explicit commentary we can take something valuable from this passage. The work of giants is labeled as such because it was made with dressed stone, as the Romans typically used and the Anglo-Saxons rarely did. It is thus starkly visible against an agrarian landscape, all the more so for being built on a much larger scale than were the wooden halls and outbuildings characteristic of the Anglo-Saxons. This sense of distant perspective is also, I would suggest, meant to include a sense of the temporal: these stone cities are visible from a distance because they have lasted the centuries. The poet is looking across a visible landscape and also back across the generations to a time of Roman habitation, as is made clear by his use of the Old English *ceastra,* from the Latin *castra,* in the opening line of the poem. However they are read, these few lines about the landscape speak of prior occupants that were displaced by time and the arrival of the Anglo-Saxons.

This passage from *Maxims II* raises questions that go beyond its own moment of composition. If landscapes are seen through the stories they can tell and also through the stories told about them, then looking at landscapes from afar, across long historical and cultural divides, adds another element to this story of desire. For it makes us wonder what one will ignore on a richly stratified historical landscape in order to discover the place of one's imagining. What accretions or intrusions or excrescences must one overlook to see the landscape of the desired moment? It is the impulse to ignore that needs to be considered here, because it can lead one to reduce the visible complexity of a scene to suit the image of one's desire. Looking at a landscape of Anglo-Saxon England today, I can still see the gentle rise at Athelney where King Alfred took refuge in 878 as he fled across the Somerset Levels to escape Danish invaders.[27] As I gaze, I choose to ignore the lay-by on the bordering highway A361, complete with its mobile canteen truck and parked trucks. Or, looking at the Anglo-Saxon church in Escomb in County Durham, perhaps the finest extant stone structure from pre-Conquest England, I try to mask out the post–World War II council estates surrounding it. With patience and the right lens, I can photograph each site to elide these intrusions on the scene. At such moments, these contemporary features appear as a disturbance in the visual field, because I want to see the human-made and human-used landscape of early medieval England untouched by intervening history. These attempts can never finally be successful. The intervening centuries, the traces of the present on the landscape, cannot be excised. Nor should they, because the landscape was never purely of that period we conventionally designate as Anglo-Saxon, from circa 600 to circa 1100. There was never anything "pure" or "indigenous" about the Anglo-Saxon scene, always already touched by human hands, by the builders of such substantial constructions as earthen mounds, hillforts, ridge paths, burial tumuli, stone-paved roads for Roman legionnaires, as well as the still enigmatic stone circles of Stonehenge and Avebury.

For an American raised amid 1960s environmentalism, with its wistful echoes of Thoreau (that our salvation lies in wildness) and overglamorized photographs of Yosemite by Ansel Adams (that the beautiful must exist apart from people), the inescapable presence of the human past on the English landscape can come as a profound relief. To stand, for example, amid the stone circle at Avebury and see within the near distance such sights as a Norman church with reused Anglo-Saxon stonework incorporated into its fabric, an Elizabethan half-timbered manor house, a large truck on its way to deliver groceries to Safeway, and dozens of those pilgrims we now call tourists—all this is a way to enter the medieval landscape, to learn that it had always offered a version of the historical record. That recognition in turn reminds one that so much of the mythic American sense of landscape was also an act of forgetting because it brutally excised from the story those who lived on the landscape before the arrival of Europeans or else sentimentally reduced them to another species living peacefully at one with nature like the deer and buffalo.

The implicit genealogy for this study begins, as the previous paragraph hints, with my lived experience of the American landscape. The interpretive myths for coping with the vast newness of America that circulated among Americans of European descent took different forms. But they were often alike in setting a pristine landscape without recognizable signs of human use against a heavily manipulated landscape littered with evidence of human conflict and evil. That is, they derived their power by setting innocence against decadence, the New World against the Old World. The terms of this myth had at least as much to do with the landscape of human desire as with the landscape of topography. Yet, as Richard Hofstader observes at the start of his *America at*

1750, this American myth of newness had some genuine basis in the immigrants' sensory perception of landscape:

> It is hard now to imagine, but it is a matter of record that a mid-eighteenth-century mariner approaching the American strand could detect the fragrance of the pine trees about 60 leagues, or 180 nautical miles, from land. Before nightfall he might thus be reminded, even after more than a century of white settlement, of the essential newness of the New World.[28]

The fertility of the soil as well as the abundance of wild game and fish were as much signs of the landscape's newness as were the "conspicuous absences" of public buildings and paved roads. Not to be found on the landscape were features an English emigrant would have remembered from his home country in the form "of Roman survivals, of ruined castles, and of tumbled monasteries and smashed faces of church idols." This binary of the American landscape as the work of nature and the European as the accumulation of history is, Hofstadter reminds us, a matter of actual fact as much as it is of desire: that was the way newcomers to America, especially those who sought to leave behind them the orthodoxies and religious struggles of the old country, wished to think of the landscape.[29]

Among the many versions of this Edenic myth one might cite from American literary and historical sources, a brief passage from Herman Melville's novel *Redburn* (1849) is especially evocative. Its interpretive value lies partly in allowing for a suggestive disparity between the rhapsodic thoughts of the young narrator, Redburn, and the more distanced skepticism of the mature novelist. Following the life story of his creator, Redburn is a young American who has gone to sea as a common sailor after his family experienced financial reverses. Dispossessed of his genteel inheritance, he finds himself in Liverpool, where he looks at German emigrants preparing to journey to America. This location of transmigratory or cross-continental meeting yields a reverie about the exceptional nature of Americans:

> We are the heirs of all time, and with all nations we divide our inheritance. On this Western Hemisphere all tribes and peoples are forming into one federated whole; and there is a future which shall see the estranged children of Adam restored as to the old hearthstone in Eden.

The other world beyond this, which was longed for by the devout before Columbus' time, was found in the New; and the deep-sea-lead, that first struck these soundings, brought up the soil of Earth's Paradise. Not a Paradise then, or now; but to be made so, at God's good pleasure, and in the fullness and mellowness of time.[30]

The authorial Melville was less taken than the callow Redburn by the possibilities of Eden; he knew that seascape and landscape were likely to become the province of figures like Captain Ahab and the Confidence Man who made their own twisted uses of the Edenic myth. Yet he also knew that to give voice to this claim of God's election through the mouth of Redburn was to acknowledge a common sentiment among his compatriots: America was the future landscape of paradise, the setting that would annul all of the historical sufferings of exile that began with the expulsion from Eden, that would allow Americans to circumvent the historical dead end that was Europe. That hope of unfulfilled promise has been registered in our own time as a sense of loss: that there are fewer and fewer of the last good places left on this continent and those that still exist must be saved at all costs. We have let paradise slip through our hands yet one more time, it would seem.

That wish to envision the landscape as virgin soil or as a new Eden (to use just a few of the enabling clichés) remains to the current moment an enduring element of American self-definition. For all that the landscape has been dammed over, strip-mined, turned into suburban sprawl, Americans still find comfort and identity in such words and phrases as "unspoiled," "virgin land," "untouched by human hand," "wilderness preservation," "national park," and "wildlife refuge." This vision of the newness of the landscape, of its condition before human beings were visible on it, has survived in the United States as an enabling myth or necessary fiction long after it was contradicted by all of the visible evidence. Its continuing power can be registered not simply in such obvious forms as activist organizations dedicated to conservation and green politics as well as a national park system visited far beyond its capacity, but more immediately in the common belief that landscape is not really landscape if it includes structures and roads built by human beings. To deserve the honorific term "landscape," the scene must be free of any trace or taint of history.[31] There is in this definition of landscape more than a little confusion, more than a little denial of history—but that response has of course so deeply shaped the history of the United States that it might almost be said to have become the history of the United States.[32]

The idealization of the western American landscape as topography untainted by history, first by explorers and travel writers and then by painters like Albert Bierstadt and Thomas Moran in the mid-nineteenth century, found its apotheosis in the photographs of Ansel Adams—especially as they were reproduced on modestly priced posters.[33] His photographic representations of California landscapes, in such classic images as "Clearing Winter Storm, Yosemite National Park, California" (1944) and "Mount Williamson, the Sierra Nevada, from Manzanor, California" (1944), as well as other sites taken in the 1940s, bear a curious and troubling resemblance to the airbrushed female forms of then contemporary art pornography.[34] Both styles revel in the cold allure of perfection, both present the image of desire as flawless and beyond the corruptions of time. As the dream of an Edenic America slips further and further away, Adams's photographs continue to appeal because they fulfill the desire to find solace in images of a landscape impossibly distant and unattainable, forever young in a future beyond reach.

The presence of that Edenic landscape was, it should be remembered, one of the great attractions for those who contemplated migration to America.[35] The tracks of migration, both literal and figurative, that they left on the landscape made it increasingly more a site of human occupation than a place of natural innocence. The historical traces of movement and settlement on the landscape explain why it should be that the most telling photographic images of the American West have been made not by an idealizer like Ansel Adams but by an understated recorder of the inhabited landscape like Robert Adams.[36] (There is no relation between these two photographers, to the best of my knowledge.) His photographs bear documentary captions that record the human presence, such as "Newly Occupied Tract Houses, Colorado Springs, 1974."[37] This image shows in the middle ground seven or eight unlandscaped tract houses being built or just completed, while in the foreground a two-toned mid-1950s Ford is parked in a circular cul-de-sac, and the high plains sweep off to a distant mountain range in the background. Robert Adams's photograph alludes to the great nineteenth-century pictorial photographers of the American landscape, such as Timothy O'Sullivan, who often featured their mules and wagons in the scene and then framed the image against the horizon line of hills or mountains. But his photograph also reads very much of its own time and place by focusing on the archetypal houses of postwar American suburbia set in raw, bulldozed terrain. The image of landscape in this photograph is yet more complicated, for the fact remains that it repeats in its own time the defining experience of nineteenth-century America, that of settling the West and making its harsh terrain habitable. It does so by placing the necessary means of transport—an automobile—in the center foreground. America remains, in this image, a landscape of movement and new settlement. Migration remains a matter for myth.

Robert Adams is a gifted and canny photographer, as well as a former English professor, so he knows well the myths that inhabit his images. Looking at "Newly Occupied Tract Houses, Colorado Springs, 1974," one sees the influence of O'Sullivan's work as well as, in a necessarily distancing way, that of Ansel Adams. As Mike Davis observes of Robert Adams and other photographers engaged in reimaging the American West, "They have rejected [Ansel] Adams's Manichean division between 'sacred' and 'profane' landscape."[38] The landscape in Robert Adams's work is far from unravished; it is a place of habitation, of another migration made not in Conestoga wagons leading to sod houses on the high plains but in Fords to split-level houses. Robert Adams is also a fine essayist who writes in a quiet, chastened style much like that of his photographs. At the close of his important book *Why People Photograph,* he offers a brief essay called "Two Landscapes." The first is the familiar territory he has worked for years on "a plateau northwest of Denver" that has been heavily overbuilt and contains the Rocky Flats Nuclear Weapons Plant. His photographs of this human-built landscape are unsparing and often frightening. The other is an ideal landscape, though one found in many places in the American West: "a country crossroads on the high plains. There are thousands from which to choose. Often there doesn't seem to be anything there at all—just two roads, four fields, and sky."[39] In this landscape he finds a certain perfection and thus some solace of hope, though he worries that he is sentimental for doing so. And yet its stark geometry—of four roads at ninety-degree angles to each other within the grid pattern of the American West—is an austere reminder of the federal government's plan by which the Edenic landscape was cut up for human use. No one who knows that landscape can stop at such a crossroads and not be struck by the knowledge that it is a postmigratory place of settlement.

Using the work of a contemporary photographer such as Robert Adams to think about depictions of landscape reminds us that our visual take on landscape today is more photographic or cinematographic than painterly. The remark Kenneth Clark made years ago about the painter Giovanni Bellini holds yet more literally for photographers: "He was born with the landscape painter's greatest gift: an emotional response to light."[40] Robert Adams's quiet but resonant claim in "Two Landscapes" to the effect "that we live in several landscapes at once" reminds us that human responses to the historical landscape and topography that surround us are necessarily complex and multivalent. That we know several landscapes at once is a caution against offering a quick and clever claim about the benefits that come with studying the Anglo-Saxon and the American landscapes together: namely, that doing so allows us to think about the fact of newness in the former and the presence of history in the latter. This claim would be symmetrical but also reductive. For the historical remains on the American landscape as we see them today do not easily evoke images of giants and their works (though I might make an exception for the grain elevators that punctuate the American West), nor did the newness of the landscape that greeted the Anglo-Saxons in the mid-fifth century bear much resemblance to wilderness (though I might make an exception for some of the remote regions of Britain where early monks ventured).

In writing about these two landscapes, there is the immediate and inescapable problem of perspective, taken in the literal sense of that term. The American landscapes I have alluded to through the work of Ansel Adams and Robert Adams are by and large visible to anyone who seeks them out. Research means walking across the terrain, looking intently, trying to find an elevation to gain a different view. To find an Anglo-Saxon landscape in today's England requires all of this and more: it requires an act of informed reimagination and re-creation. This act does not mean wiping away all that is of a later date (especially post-1914 violations), but it does mean always asking what would have been there at some fixed moment, such as 878 when King Alfred took refuge in Athelney. It means as well not looking simply for that which was Anglo-Saxon in origin but instead embedding the landscape in its history. The American landscape seems transparently available to the observing eye, as Emerson used that modifier when he spoke of the visionary desire to become a "transparent eyeball," a being that saw all and was itself nothing.[41] The Anglo-Saxon landscape requires the historical eye to identify all that might have been visible a thousand years ago.

These are, of course, our interpretive constructs or, if one prefers, fictions. Emerson's transparent eyeball could never be as innocent of history as it wished to be; the scholar's historical view of the Anglo-Saxon landscape depends heavily on written texts because that is where one may find the telling evidence. Contemporary British scholars such as Oliver Rackham and Della Hooke have emphasized legal texts like land charters, repositories of clues about how the Anglo-Saxons demarcated and worked the landscape.[42] Their approach partly reflects the immediate access they have to the landscape and partly the empiricist's distrust for interpretive narratives or myths. Yet I would suggest that a given landscape and the cultural uses made of that same landscape are not neatly separable. Using land charters and their boundary clauses to learn about the Anglo-Saxon landscape is not simply a matter of collating their references to woodlots, ditches, embankments, hedgerows, and the like as if they are self-explanatory features. It requires—not instead but as well—that those boundary clauses be set in their legal and linguistic contexts so that we can understand why so many of them are in the vernacular while the remainder of the charters in question are in Latin.[43] Why are matters concerning the eternal duration of the land grant written in Latin when the demarcation of the parcel being granted is so often stated in Old English? Even when Anglo-Saxon texts get local and stay close to the ground, that is, when they trace the boundaries of a grant across the landscape by noting trees, hedges, fords, paths, and the like, even then they exist within larger interpretive constructs.[44] If one uses textual evidence to study the landscape of a historically distant culture, especially one that rarely offers explicit commentary on the subject of landscape, then one must struggle with the larger interpretive frameworks and cultural questions of language, audience, genre, intention, and the like. Documents do not speak for themselves, especially when read for purposes never anticipated by their drafters.

Moreover, as we read these documents, we have to remain alert for the ways in which ideas about landscape change over the centuries. Among such changes, as I have just hinted, is the notion that landscape can itself be a subject for explicit study and theorizing. Nothing survives from Anglo-Saxon England to suggest that landscape was conceived of in such terms. Not least there is no word in the vernacular to mean "landscape" in any of our large senses for the term. The Old English word "landscipe" has sometimes been mistakenly read as the direct etymological source for the Modern English "landscape," but such is not the case; it simply means "region." "Land" means "land," and "-scipe" is an abstract suffix denoting the quality of the noun to which it is attached, as in Old English "freondscip" and Modern English "friendship."[45] The word is, in any case, a very rare compound, appearing only once in the poetry. This use is, or at least should be for us, cautionary; the narrator of the Old English poetic *Genesis* says of hell: "I have never seen a more hateful region [landscipe]."[46] The absence of a term in Old English for "landscape" does not in itself prove the absence of interest in landscape, but it does suggest that it may not have taken explicit or consciously self-referential forms. For that reason, I have approached Anglo-Saxon attitudes toward, and representations of, landscape through the larger cultural memory of migration, of human movement across the visible earth. These traces of migration—even if inscribed in memory and narrative rather than on the physical landscape—may be likened to roads that demarcate a landscape by showing how human beings use it.

John Brinckerhoff Jackson concludes the preface to his *A Sense of Place, A Sense of Time* by positing an epochal change in the landscape through which architecture or the human-built environment of stasis has given way to roads and highways or the human-made network of mobility: "The road generates its own patterns of movement and settlement and work without so far producing its own kind of landscape beauty or its own sense of place." These conditions explain why "a landscape tradition a thousand years old in our Western world is yielding to a fluid organization of space that we as yet do not entirely understand."[47] Jackson's work is an engaged, if preliminary, mapping of that new American landscape of roads and cars and mobile homes. Driving the twenty-four hundred miles from Ohio to California during June 2003 in four and a half days, I continually felt the truth of Jackson's claim that a decisive shift in our understanding of landscape was occurring, that it was everywhere visible along the vast, underpopulated length of I-80 from Omaha to Reno. At the least, I know that my vision of these places was deeply mediated through Jackson's claim for an epochal shift in our paradigm for defining landscape. But the Anglo-Saxonist in me kept wondering if Jackson's claim was not in fact more relevant to the United States than to other parts of the world. Was he not invoking in a different way that old, recurring myth of American exceptionalism?

An experiential reading of this argument about roads, one that follows from moving through the landscape, from observing and photographing it from the highway shoulder, throws some doubt on Jackson's concluding historical echo:

> In time, we will find our way and rediscover the role of architecture and man-made forms in creating a new civilized landscape. It is essentially a question of rediscovering symbols and believing in them once again. Many centuries ago, when Britain was no longer Roman and not yet Christian, a nameless poet was one of those who glimpsed the symbolism of the surrounding scattered remains:

> Wonderful is this wall of stone,
> wrecked by fate.
> The city buildings crumble,
> the bold works of the giants decay.
> Roofs have caved in, towers collapsed,
> Barred gates have gone, gateways have gaping mouths,
> Hoarfrost clings to the mortar.
> Out of a ruin a new symbol emerges, and a landscape finds form and comes alive.[48]

The prose here is beautiful, as it should be for writing about landscape; the quotation of the Anglo-Saxon poem *The Ruin* is movingly apposite; the acknowledgment of the symbolic or mythic in our sense of landscape is stirring. And the history is wrong. The Romans were long gone when *The Ruin* was composed in England, but its poet was Christian, as was its audience. Without that religious belief, the poet would not have been able to write about the ruined city and its baths as the old work of giants, as evidence of a race that built in stone on a monumental scale. He belonged to a people that built almost entirely in timber and on a relatively modest domestic scale. Beneath the poet's reading of the built landscape lies the master trope of Christian historiography: that the world is, generation by generation, slipping into decline. Jackson's offering of *The Ruin* to speak of a time at once post-Roman and pre-Christian has the effect of removing the poem from the actuality of history. In this reading, it exists in a space shaped by his desire rather than in a documentable moment of the past. Jackson's reading of the poem, one is tempted to say, is deeply American.

I have interwoven quotations from Hoskins, Jackson, and Hofstadter with passages from Melville, Bede, and an anonymous Old English poet to establish a tentative genealogy for thinking about landscape and practice. These writers are especially important because they suggest that there are certain historiographic traditions for writing about landscape.[49] Or perhaps, one wonders at times, certain national assumptions? Hoskins is not alone in his distaste for the England of iron and coal; Jackson is not alone in his conviction that America is the product of its roads and highways. Hofstadter is, in this regard, more distanced from the story of landscape that he evokes to capture the experience of coming into the country. His concern lies with the stories that these immigrants attached to the landscape and then bequeathed to those who followed them.

The connection between these two landscapes lies in stories, that is, in the ways that landscapes were interpreted by those who knew that they were at once new and historical. They are landscapes that belong in the experience and imagination of those who have made, or have cultivated a memory of, migration. Writing between them today, as a methodological exercise, means recognizing that the stories of a past landscape can reveal striking affinities with those of a present landscape, while each can also maintain its own historical specificity. The comparative study of a past and present landscape is a means to historicize the act of interpretation, to disrupt scholarly assumptions, and to recognize the inescapable human presence on the scene. Most rewardingly, it means that one can live in several landscapes at once and call it scholarly work.

NOTES

1. David Lowenthal, "Past Time, Present Place: Landscape and Memory," *Geographical Review* 65 (1975): 1–36, at 5.

2. As a starting point, I follow Edward Relph's definition of the term, though I will complicate it as this chapter develops: "I generally use the word 'landscape' to refer to everything I see and sense when I am out of doors." In this he includes natural phenomena and human-made constructions. See Relph, *Rational Landscapes and Humanistic Geography* (London: Croom Helm, 1981), 22. For the French terminology related to landscape—*paysage, territoire, pays,* and others—

see the thoughtful book by Jean Marc Besse, *Voir la Terre: Six Essais sur le Paysage et la Géographie* (Arles: Actes Sud, 2000), 95–101.

3. Alan R. H. Baker, *Geography and History: Bridging the Divide* (Cambridge: Cambridge University Press, 2003), 78.

4. On landscape as a part of folklore, see David Lowenthal, "European Landscape Transformations: The Rural Residue," in Paul Groth and Todd W. Bressi, eds., *Understanding Ordinary Landscapes* (New Haven: Yale University Press, 1997), 180–88, at 184.

5. Keith Basso, "'Speaking with Names': Language and Landscape among the Western Apache," in George E. Marcus, ed., *Rereading Cultural Anthropology* (Durham: Duke University Press, 1992), 220–51; and Bruce Chatwin, *The Songlines* (London: Jonathan Cape, 1987).

6. The literature on landscape and story is rich and takes many different forms. A few sources that have influenced my thinking include Ann Whiston Spirn, *The Language of Landscape* (New Haven: Yale University Press, 1998); James Corner, ed., *Recovering Landscapes: Essays in Contemporary Landscape Architecture* (New York: Princeton Architectural Press, 1999); Richard Muir, *Approaches to Landscape* (London: Barnes and Noble, 1999); and Malcolm Andrews, *Landscape and Western Art* (Oxford: Oxford University Press, 1999).

7. Groth and Bressi, *Understanding Ordinary Landscapes;* and Denis Cosgrove and Stephen Daniels, eds., *The Iconography of Landscape* (Cambridge: Cambridge University Press, 1988).

8. D. W. Meinig, "Symbolic Landscapes: Some Idealizations of American Communities," in Meinig, ed., *The Interpretation of Ordinary Landscapes: Geographical Essays* (New York: Oxford University Press, 1979), 164.

9. For two very different but complementary treatments of this topic, see John K. Wright, "Terrae Incognitae: The Place of the Imagination in Geography," *Annals of the Association of American Geographers* 37 (1947): 1–15, esp. 11; and William Cronon, "A Place for Stories: Nature, History, and Narrative," *Journal of American History* 79 (1992): 1347–76.

10. Benedict Anderson, *Imagined Communities: Reflections on the Origin and Spread of Nationalism,* rev. ed. (London: Verso, 1991), esp. 5–7.

11. Lowenthal, "European Landscape Transformations," 180.

12. Iain Sinclair, *White Chappell Scarlet Tracings* (London: Granta, 1998), 153.

13. This study is part of an ongoing project on landscape, geographical and national identity, and narrative. See also my *Across an Inland Sea: Writing in Place from Buffalo to Berlin* (Princeton: Princeton University Press, 2003); and the forthcoming *Writing the Map of Anglo-Saxon England* (New Haven: Yale University Press), sections of which have appeared as "An Angle on This Earth: Sense of Place in Anglo-Saxon England," *Bulletin of the John Rylands University Library of Manchester* 82 (2000): 1–25 (Toller Memorial Lecture, 1999); and "The Landscape of Anglo-Saxon England: Inherited, Invented, Imagined," in John Howe and

Michael Wolfe, eds., *Inventing Medieval Landscapes: Senses of Place in Western Europe* (Gainesville: University Press of Florida, 2002), 91–112; as well as the forthcoming "Anglo-Saxon England and the Post-Colonial Void," in A. Kabir and D. Williams, eds., *Post-Colonial Middle Ages* (Oxford: Oxford University Press).

14. To cite only a few possibilities from a large range of studies, see David Pelteret, "The Roads of Anglo-Saxon England," *Wiltshire Archaeological and Natural History Magazine* 79 (1985): 155–63; Howard Williams, "Ancient Landscapes and the Dead: The Reuse of Prehistoric and Roman Monuments as Early Anglo-Saxon Burial Sites," *Medieval Archaeology* 41 (1997): 1–32; and Paolo Squatriti, "Digging Ditches in Early Medieval Europe," *Past and Present* 176 (2002): 11–65, esp. 58–61, and "Offa's Dyke between Nature and Culture," *Environmental History* 9 (2004): 37–56.

15. Nicholas Howe, *Migration and Mythmaking in Anglo-Saxon England* (1989; repr., Notre Dame: University of Notre Dame Press, 2001), esp. chap. 3.

16. W. G. Hoskins, *The Making of the English Landscape* (New York: Penguin, 1985), 11 and 19, respectively. See the fine study by D. W. Meinig, "Reading the Landscape: An Appreciation of W. G. Hoskins and J. B. Jackson," in Meinig, ed., *The Interpretation of Ordinary Landscapes,* 197–244.

17. Hoskins, *The Making of the English Landscape,* 298, 299–300.

18. For a very useful background study, see Petra Dark, *The Environment of Britain in the First Millennium AD* (London: Duckworth, 2000).

19. Through an allegorical, Augustinian reading of the texts, Alfred K. Siewers, "Landscapes of Conversion: Guthlac's Mound and Grendel's Mere as Expressions of Anglo-Saxon Nation Building," *Viator* 34 (2003): 1–39, argues, somewhat melodramatically, that "The thematic motif of the battle for the haunted barrow in the Guthlac narratives and *Beowulf* can be taken as a metaphor of the Anglo-Saxon literary construction of the landscape of Britain" (21).

20. Howe, *Migration and Mythmaking,* esp. chap. 2.

21. B. Colgrave and R. A. B. Mynors, eds., *Bede's Ecclesiastical History of the English People* (Oxford: Clarendon Press, 1969), 50, hereafter cited parenthetically in the text by book and chapter. See further the early study by H. Darby, "The Geographical Ideas of the Venerable Bede," *Scottish Geographical Magazine* 51 (1935): 84–89.

22. Colgrave and Mynors, *Bede's Ecclesiastical History,* 15, for translation; 14 for Latin text: "Opima frugibus atque arboribus insula, et alendis apta pecoribus ac iumentis, uineas etiam quibusdam in locis germinans, sed et auim ferax terra marique generis diuersi, fluuiis quoque multom piscosis ac fontibus praeclara copiosis; et quidem praecipue issicio abundat et anguilla. . . . Habet fontes salinarum, habet et fontes calidos, et ex eis fluuios balnearum calidarum omni aetati et sexui per distincta loca iuxta suum cuique modum accommodos."

23. Colgrave and Mynors, *Bede's Ecclesiastical History,* 17, for translation; 16 for Latin text: "Erat et ciuitatibus quondam XX et VIII nobilissimis insignita,

praeter castella immumera quae et ipsa muris, turribus, portis ac seris erant instructa firmissimis."

24. Dorothy Whitelock, ed., *English Historical Documents, Vol. I: c.500–1042,* 2d ed. (London: Eyre Methuen, 1979), 546–47. The Old English text reads: "Dær se dic sceot in þæclinga stræte anlanges þæxlinga stræte ðæt in ðane ford þæt anlang broces in þanne oðerne ford þonne of ðæm forde up on þane pelle y banan in ðæt dele banan . . . þæt up rihte in ðiod þeg æftær ðiod þege in þone dic æft dice in þæxlingga strate"; see Walter de Gray Birch, *Cartularium Saxonicum: A Collection of Charters Relating to Anglo-Saxon History* (London: Whiting and Co., 1887), II:334–36.

25. In this regard, the charter may be read as a kind of archive for understanding landscape; see Deryck W. Holdsworth, "Landscape and Archives as Texts," in Groth and Bressi, *Understanding Ordinary Landscapes,* 49–55.

26. Translation by author; Old English text in E. V. K. Dobbie, ed., *The Anglo-Saxon Minor Poems Book* (New York: Columbia University Press, 1942), Anglo-Saxon Poetic Records, 6:55: "Cyning sceal rice healdan. Ceastra beoð feorran gesyne, / orþanc enta geweorc, þa þe on þysse eorðan syndon, / wrætlic weallstana geweorc." For a very useful inventory of Roman stonework that was incorporated as spolia in Anglo-Saxon buildings, see Tim Eaton, *Plundering the Past: Roman Stonework in Medieval Britain* (Stroud, Glous.: Tempus, 2000).

27. For the story as told by Asser in his "Life of King Alfred," see *Alfred the Great,* trans. Simon Keynes and Michael Lapidge (New York: Penguin, 1983), 83.

28. Richard Hofstadter, *America at 1750: A Social Portrait* (New York: Vintage, 1973), xi.

29. For a European response to the American landscape as seemingly without human traces, one might quote Theodore Adorno from 1951: "The shortcoming of the American landscape is not so much, as romantic illusion would have it, the absence of historical memories, as that it bears no traces of the human hand." See his *Minima Moralia: Reflections from a Damaged Life,* trans. E. F. N. Jephcott (London: Verso, 1974), 48.

30. Herman Melville, *Redburn: His First Voyage* (Garden City, N.Y.: Doubleday, 1957), 163, chap. 33.

31. Quoting the dictionary to make a point is a favorite stratagem in undergraduate papers, but since I have found this idea of landscape in student essays in places as diverse as New Jersey, Ohio, Oklahoma, and California, it seems right to note the absence of any reference to human beings in the primary definition of landscape by the paperback *American Heritage Dictionary:* "A view or vista of scenery on land."

32. The denial of history thus becomes a form of history. See Peirce F. Lewis, "Axioms for Reading the Landscape: Some Guides to the American Scene," in Meinig, ed., *The Interpretation of Ordinary Landscapes.*

33. As the earlier landscape painters of the nineteenth century, especially those associated with the Hudson River School, painted a more populated and occupied

view of the scene, Bierstadt's and Moran's monumental paintings of the American landscape were a post–Civil War development, one that barely preceded or coincided with the opening of the American West to railroads and then extensive settlement by European Americans.

34. These photographs are conveniently reproduced, and set in a fascinating larger context, in the valuable book by Estelle Jussim and Elizabeth Lindquist-Cock, *Landscape as Photograph* (New Haven: Yale University Press, 1985), 23, 136. For Ansel Adams's practice of removing evidence of human use from the scenes of his photographs, see Mike Davis, *Dead Cities and Other Tales* (New York: New Press, 2002), 39, where he speaks of Ansel Adams as "the dead pope of the 'Sierra Club school' of Nature-as-God photography." Davis's essay in the same volume, "Ecocide in Marlboro Country," is a tour de force on the human degradation of the American West.

35. See further G. Malcolm Lewis, "Rhetoric of the Western Interior: Modes of Environmental Description in American Promotional Literature of the Nineteenth Century," in Cosgrove and Daniels, eds., *The Iconography of Landscape,* 179–93.

36. As Baker observes, landscape photographs "must be understood in terms of their production and the uses to which they were put in the past both by their producers and by their consumers"; see his *Geography and History,* 127.

37. Reproduced in Jussim and Linquist-Cock, *Landscape as Photograph,* 44.

38. Davis, *Dead Cities,* 39. For a current project directed by Rebecca Solnit to rephotograph Yosemite against images by Eadweard Muybridge, Ansel Adams, and Edward Weston, see James Gorman, "Yosemite and the Invention of Wilderness," *New York Times,* February 9, 2003, D1.

39. Robert Adams, *Why People Photograph* (New York: Aperture, 1994), 179–82.

40. Kenneth Clark, *Landscape into Art* (London: John Murray, 1976), 49. On landscape and light, see further Denis Cosgrove, "The Geometry of Landscape: Practical and Speculative Arts in Sixteenth Century Venetian Land Territories," in Cosgrove and Daniels, eds., *The Iconography of Landscape,* 254–76, esp. 261.

41. Ralph Waldo Emerson, "Nature," in *Selections from Ralph Waldo Emerson,* ed. Stephen E. Whicher (Boston: Houghton Mifflin, 1960), 24.

42. Oliver Rackham, "The Forest: Woodland and Wood-Pasture in Medieval England," in Kathleen Biddick, ed., *Archaeological Approaches to Medieval Europe* (Kalamazoo, Mich.: Medieval Institute Publications, 1984), 69–105; *Trees and Woodland in the British Landscape: The Complete History of Britain's Trees, Woods, and Hedgerows* (London: Phoenix, 1996); and *The History of the Countryside* (London: Phoenix, 1997); and Della Hooke, *The Landscape of Anglo-Saxon England* (Leicester: Leicester University Press, 1998). See also the studies by Richard Morris, *Churches in the Landscape* (London: Phoenix, 1997); and Michael Reed, *The Landscape of Britain, from the Beginnings to 1914* (London: Routledge, 2002).

43. See Howe, "An Angle on This Earth," 15–19; and "The Landscape of Anglo-Saxon England," 98–101.

44. The shaping of land boundaries by planting trees remains a cultural practice in the Mananara-Nord district of Madagascar. As Genese Sodikoff notes (personal communication, March 9, 2004): "These boundary markers do not encircle the entire plot if and where other natural markers, such as rivers, streams, or embankments, serve the purpose of delimitation. To the untrained eye, the rows of living trees, each planted several feet from the next, are indistinguishable from the surrounding vegetative growth of garden spaces and regenerating fallow land." I suspect that "the untrained eye" would have struggled with Anglo-Saxon boundary demarcations too.

45. For the Old English, see Bosworth-Toller, *An Anglo-Saxon Dictionary,* s.v. "landscipe"; for the modern English, see the *Oxford English Dictionary,* s.v. "landscape." For the (erroneous) claim that "landscape" came as a word with the Anglo-Saxons on their migrations, see John Brinckerhoff Jackson, *Discovering the Vernacular Landscape* (New Haven: Yale University Press, 1984), 5.

46. Translation by author; Old English text in G. P. Krapp, ed., *The Junius Manuscript* (New York: Columbia University Press, 1931), Anglo-Saxon Poetic Records, 1:14: "Ic a ne geseah / laran landscipe" (ll. 375b–76a).

47. John Brinckerhoff Jackson, *A Sense of Place, A Sense of Time* (New Haven: Yale University Press, 1994), viii. The idea that roads shape the human understanding of landscapes may be older than Jackson argues. As Clarence J. Glacken, *Traces on the Rhodian Shore: Nature and Culture in Western Thought from Ancient Times to the End of the Eighteenth Century* (Berkeley: University of California Press, 1967), 283, observes of Roger Bacon, "Corporeal roads signify spiritual roads, and corporeal places, the ends of spiritual roads."

48. Jackson, *A Sense of Place,* viii–ix. The translation of *The Ruin* quoted here is by Kevin Crossley-Holland and appears in *The Battle of Maldon and Other Old English Poems,* trans. Crossley-Holland and ed. Bruce Mitchell (London: St. Martin's, 1966), 69. Jackson slightly misquotes the last line of this translation; it should read "hoar frost clings to mortar."

49. See also Michael Aston, *Interpreting the Landscape: Landscape Archaeology and Local History* (London: Routledge, 1997); Alain Corbin, *L'homme dans le paysage* (Paris: Les éditions textuel, 2001); Lowenthal, "European Landscape Transformations"; and Adorno, *Minima Moralia.*

VIII In Search of
Natural Identity

Alpine Landscape and the
Reconstruction of the Swiss Nation

Oliver Zimmer

ELIAS CANETTI, IN A BRIEF PASSAGE of his *Crowds and Power* (first published in German in 1960), argued that neither language nor territory nor history is at the heart of what today we would call national identity. What nations cannot do without, however, and what has contributed most to turning different individuals into conscious members of a particular nation is a national "crowd symbol." Canetti went on to show that most European nations possessed one such symbol around which a popular feeling of national belonging could be generated and sustained. In the case of England, he maintained, it was the sea that took this function, while for the Germans it was the forest. In France, on the other hand, it was the revolution that came to play this very role. And in Switzerland—the case Canetti probably knew best from his own experience—it was the mountains (see Canetti [1960] 1971, 191–203).

While it would be difficult for me to judge the accuracy of Canetti's comments on national mass symbolism in the English, German, and French cases, I broadly agree with his statement about the important role of Alpine symbolism in Swiss national identity. But why the mountains? Here his admittedly thumbnail explorations need some qualifying. First, there was nothing inevitable about the Alps becoming Switzerland's most salient national symbol—an impression that one could easily get from reading Canetti's text. On the contrary, it was under particular circumstances and as a result of context-bound ideo-

240

logical activities that the Alps evolved into a national mass symbol of the Swiss. Second, as a national mass symbol, the Alps did not replace but, rather, complemented history: The national past or, to be more precise, the popular memory of that past was closely intertwined symbolically with the Alpine landscape.[1]

Starting from these premises, this chapter explores the role of Alpine landscape in the formation and reconstruction of Swiss national identity from the late eighteenth century to the end of World War II. It proceeds, first, by tracing the history of thinking about geography and cultural characteristics and by developing a framework for the analysis of the relationship between landscape and national identity. It then distinguishes, in the substantive part of the analysis, between the two historical phases that each gave rise to a distinct conceptualization of the relationship between Alpine landscape and the Swiss nation. The first one (common from the late eighteenth century to roughly the 1870s)—what I will call the nationalization of nature—is metaphorical: The Alps reflect what is held to be authentically Swiss. The second conceptualization (prevalent from the 1870s until the end of World War II) —what I will call the naturalization of the nation—is deterministic: Alpine landscape is portrayed as determining national character. The last section looks at the popular bases of the Alpine myth and discusses the reasons for its widespread appeal.

Landscape and National Identity

Thinking about Geography and National Character in History

Attempts to establish meaningful links between nature and culture communities are not confined to the modern era. Since antiquity, various groups or "peoples" have turned to their natural environment as a source of inspiration and collective identification. It was probably in the Hellenistic world that some of these themes were first developed in a more systematic manner. They have remained at the heart of natural discourse ever since. The juxtaposition of rural and urban, the idea that to cultivate nature is the civilized man's mission, or the notion that certain physical environments might be more favorable to the emergence of high civilizations than others provide examples of such themes. Some Greek dramatists, such as Aeschylus and Aristophanes, and the historian Herodotus referred in their writings to climatic factors to account for the emergence of different culture communities. These Greek precedents, in their turn, exerted considerable influence on Roman writers. This became apparent, for example, when Tacitus, in the first century AD, described the Germanic tribes as rude and primitive and mentioned how closely tied they were to the Teutonic woods to support this claim.[2]

Yet it is particularly in the sixteenth century, that is, during a period marked not only by the discovery of non-European cultures but also by territorial consolidation and the rise of national consciousness in some European countries, that we witness a fairly widespread change in perception from nature as a more general idea to the more specific notion of a landscape.[3] A statement of Stefano Guazzo, dating from 1574, in which the author tries to explain alleged national differences by referring to a mixture of climatic and environmental factors marks this transitional stage: "There is no help for it, but you must . . . think that every nation, land and country, by the nature of the place, the climate of the heaven, and the influence of the stars has certain virtues and certain vices which are proper, natural, and perpetual."[4]

On the whole, however, neither geographic determinism nor cultural voluntarism prevailed in the works of early modern thinkers. Rather, the two conceptualizations of the relationship between nature and cultural activity made for a dualistic, and sometimes even conflicting, dialogue. That is to say, alongside the argument that nature in general, and geography in particular, delimited the scope open for voluntary human action,[5] there existed at the same time the belief that human beings should interfere in nature for the sake of culture. In fact, this latter notion figured prominently in the theories of many outstanding thinkers of the sixteenth and seventeenth centuries (such as Machiavelli, Botero, Charron, and Milton). In its broad form, this belief asserted that a people's degree of civilization found its clearest expression in its ability to cultivate nature. Perhaps Giovanni Botero best encapsulated this classical ideal in his *Reason of State* (1589): "Nature gives a form to the raw materials and human industry imposes upon this natural composition an infinite variety of artificial forms; thus, nature is to the craftsman what raw material is to the natural agent."[6]

More systematic efforts to illuminate the link between particular natural environments and alleged national characteristics were to follow in the eighteenth century, especially in the works of Montesquieu (1689–1755), Rousseau (1717–28), and Herder (1744–1803). As was the case with their precursors in the sixteenth and seventeenth centuries, the works of many of these authors reveal, although to varying degree, a tension between the notions of geographical determinism and human voluntarism. For Herder, for instance, as he cogently expressed in his *Ideen zur Philosophie der Geschichte der Menschheit* (1784–91), geography was merely one among several factors affecting the course of cultural development and must take its place alongside "the circumstances and occasions of the times, and the native or generated character of the people."[7] And even in the work of Montesquieu, known as the most influential proponent of geographical determinism of the eighteenth century, things are less clear-cut upon closer inspection. At one point in his *L'Esprit des Lois,* for instance, he clearly adheres to the argument of multiple causes without conceiving of climatic factors as determinative in the last instance: "Mankind are influenced by various causes: by the climate, by the religion, by the laws, by the maxims of government, by precedents, morals, and customs; whence is formed the general spirit of nations."[8]

As the foregoing discussion indicates, the philosophical and moral interest in the natural environment was not constant over time. It commonly gained in intensity during periods of profound change in the social, demographic, and cognitive structure of a given society. Such periods of transition provided fertile ground for the emergence of new conceptualizations of the relationship between nature and culture. This is true of the Hellenistic era, whose metropolitan authors created the notion of an idyllic place while they were exposed to the phenomenon of urbanization (Wozniakowski 1987, 17). It also applies to the Renaissance period, when a more critical view of religious affairs and the emergence of new modes of scientific and moral thinking provoked a rethinking of humanity's position vis-à-vis the natural environment. And it surely holds true for the latter half of the eighteenth century. In a world in which traditional terms of religious attachment and solidarity were declining at a disquieting speed, geography and the natural environment at least seemed to offer some degree of stability, calm, and purity. It was in this context that landscape became critical as a source of moral reflection and social orientation. Commenting on the rise of landscape art at the end of the eighteenth century, the German painter Philip Otto Runge exhorted: "We stand at the brink of all the religions which sprang up out of the Catholic one, the abstractions perish, everything is lighter and more insubstantial than before, everything presses toward land-scape art, looks for something certain in this uncertainty and does not know how to begin."[9] Furthermore, as politicized nature, particular landscapes evolved into integral parts of historicism's search for national pedigrees, that other powerful movement that in the latter half of the eighteenth century came to form the centerpiece of most European nationalisms and national identities.[10]

Landscape Symbolism and the Study of National Identity

Given that the rise of nationalism in the late eighteenth century conspic-uously reinforced the interest in geographical symbolism, it is somewhat surprising that, so far, little attention has been paid in the field of nations and nationalism to the conditions under which specific natural environments acquire significance in definitions of nationhood.[11] On the other hand, scholars working in fields such as human geography, art his-tory, or environmental history have recently made use of existing theo-retical approaches to nationalism and national identification.[12] Yet these theories have served these researchers as signposts to be passed rather than as springboards for the construction of new theories that deal with the question of how landscapes are valued in different histori-cal and political contexts. Lowenthal (1994, 283) expresses this marked and apparently widespread reluctance to formulate general statements when he accuses those predisposed toward particular explanations of landscape attachments of misreading ambiguous material.

Despite the absence of appropriate theoretical tools for landscape analysis, however, three broad positions are discernible. Adherents of a "primordialist" perspective view people's attachments to their natural surroundings as a manifestation of basic sociopsychological needs and as a phenomenon that is both universal and historically persistent.[13] Basing their analysis upon a psychological reductionism, however, those taking this position are at a loss to explain why people's interest in land-scape can vary significantly over time. Applying an explicitly descriptive approach, a second group of researchers are concerned mainly with the way depictions of landscape are regarded as reflective of "national virtues," such as freedom, liberty, or independence.[14] In contrast to the first two approaches, a third group of scholars emphasizes the situational aspect by identifying the way in which the public role of landscape symbolism is contingent on particular cultural and political contexts.[15]

Landscape and National Identity: A Framework for Analysis

Even though each of the three positions outlined previously has something to recommend them, I believe that none is satisfactory when it comes to analyzing the possible causes of the changing currency enjoyed by geographical symbolism in definitions of nationhood. In what follows I shall put forward an analytical position that places equal weight upon received patterns of thinking about nature and society on the one hand and on factors of a more contingent, context-bound nature on the other.

To move from description to explanation, I shall begin by defining the nation as a cultural order (composed of certain idioms, values, symbols, and myths).[16] Nations, thus understood, are not static entities. It is first and foremost to a recurrent project of national reconstruction—to the process whereby nations are being fostered and redefined in the course of history—that I am referring when I make use of the term "national identity." The key concept with regard to national identity is *authenticity:* reconstructing nations over time inevitably means reconstructing them as distinctive, original, and historically embedded orders. Once they cease to be perceived as authentic in this sense, nations lose much of their former legitimacy and meaning. Thus although authenticity, as a concept, refers to an organic order that needs to be recovered rather than created, the authentic national community is the product of recurrent ideological activity. Rousseau put forward this point succinctly by declaring that "the first rule which we have to follow is that of national character; every people has, or must have, a character: if it lacks one, we must start by endowing it with one."[17]

From a formal point of view, the authentication of a national culture entails two processes: the construction of continuity with a nation's alleged ethnohistorical past (historicism) on the one hand and the creation of a sense of naturalness (naturalization) on the other. The two processes, while analytically separate, are mutually intertwined and reinforce each other in the reality of nation formation: Whereas references to significant features of the natural environment serve to buttress a cultural community's claims of continuity, the historicist curiosity for the collective past inevitably directs attention to significant features of a designated "homeland." Broadly speaking, the fundamental role of both historicism and naturalization has to do, in large part, with their preventing the historical and cultural contingency of modern nations from entering into the picture.[18]

In addition, what is assumed here is that modern nations go through "settled" and "unsettled" periods. During settled periods the values, symbols, and myths that make up the nation as a cultural order are more or less taken for granted, so that they form, as it were, a cultural tradition or common sense. During unsettled historical phases, on the other hand, national authenticity is put into question, prompting endeavors at redefining national identity. Such efforts to reconstruct nationhood are both path dependent and contingent. They are contingent insofar as they present symbolic "responses" to specific conditions and events that can be both domestic and international in nature. Yet at the same time, such projects of national reconstruction are path dependent. That is to say, their mostly intellectual protagonists are bound to draw, to some degree at least, upon existing cultural resources (consisting of certain cultural idioms, symbols, values, and myths) that are salient in a given society. The impact of such cultural resources on the process of national reconstruction is conditional rather than determining. By furnishing the cognitive and expressive frameworks for those involved in the project of national reconstruction, these resources reduce the likelihood of pure invention. And yet, it needs stressing that the situational aspect is key for any explanation of the respective outcome of such national projects: While certain intellectuals and social movements may regard it as sufficient, at one point in time, to define a particular nation by emphasizing its voluntaristic character, this alone may be viewed as inappropriate under altered circumstances.[19] This leads me to the Swiss example.

From the Nationalization of Nature to the Naturalization of the Nation: The Swiss Scenario in a Comparative Context

We can envisage various ways of establishing a symbolic link between a national community and a particular landscape. As we shall see, the conceptualization of the relationship between the Alps and the Swiss nation thereby could take either of two forms. The first form could be termed the "nationalization of nature." What is characteristic here is that popular historical myths, memories, and supposed national virtues are projected into a significant landscape in an attempt to lend more continuity and distinctiveness to Swiss national identity. In this way, not only is the Alpine landscape put to use in such a way as to reflect alleged national characteristics, but an image of national authenticity is developed in which the Alps appear, as it were, as the physical dimension of the national past. As a way of conjoining landscape and nation, this first form of discourse (the nationalization of nature) came into use in the second half of the eighteenth century. It can be regarded as a delicate synthesis between the neoclassical approach to nature (which is anthropocentric in orientation and sees culture as prevailing over nature) and its early Romantic counterpart (which depicts human beings as organically linked to the natural environment). I shall argue that, as a way of incorporating landscape imagery into the fabric of national identity, the nationalization of nature was to remain predominant in Switzerland until roughly the 1870s.[20]

The nationalization of nature, though crucial as a mechanism for rendering Swiss national identity authentic, was not confined to the Swiss case. We encounter it in the English discourse on landscape, which ever since the late nineteenth century—at least in its prevailing current of rural paternalism—showed a preference for tamed over savage lands, equating the former with stability, permanence, and harmony, while associating the latter with what was seen as the anarchism epitomized in American and French republicanism.[21] In France, too, where Vidal de la Blache invented "human geography" as a scientific discipline at the end of the nineteenth century, landscape, for a time at least, was crucial as a means of defining national identity. As in England, geographers and historians in France depicted humans as having the upper hand over nature rather than being determined by it, a theme most cogently expressed by Michelet: "Society, freedom have mastered nature, history has rubbed out geography. In this marvellous transformation, spirit has won over matter, the general over the particular, and idea over contingencies."[22] Germany, to cite another instructive example, presents us with a different picture. Here, where since the late eighteenth century the belief in ethnic homogeneity had not been seriously questioned, the concern, at least among geographers of the late nineteenth century, was primarily with the determination of boundaries rather than with specific landscapes. After 1890, geography as a discipline became the vehicle of an attempt to elevate the "relatively low awareness of the 'colonial question' by the public," with *Kolonialkunde* and *Meereskunde* becoming elements of the curriculum of national education (Sandner 1994, 77). At the same time, however, there had been a long-standing preoccupation in the German case with the influence of the natural environment and of the "soil," especially the Teutonic woods, on what contemporaries commonly called the Germanic character; and this notion became a centerpiece of the organicism of the Romantics and later of *völkisch* nationalism (Schama 1995, chap. 2).

This leads me to the second formal possibility of establishing a symbolic connection between nations and their natural environment, which I designate the "naturalization of the nation." This point of view, resting as it does upon a notion of geographical determinism, regards the natural environment as more than the physical expression of certain presumed national virtues and characteristics. Here, nature—or in the Swiss case, the Alps—is depicted as an active force capable of determining national identity and giving it a compact, homogeneous, unified form. Measured against the continuum ranging from the classical to the Romantic approach to nature, the naturalization of the nation, with its stress on organic growth and natural determination in opposition to deliberate human interference with nature, doubtless is located closer to the Romantic pole.[23]

To be sure, ideas of how certain geographical features might be connected symbolically with the Swiss nationhood existed well before 1870, constituting as they did a vocabulary and a symbolism familiar to a substantial proportion of the public (Marchal 1992b; Walter 1990). However, two elements give the Swiss discourse on landscape between 1870 and 1945 its specificity: First, in response to certain sociopolitical conditions, this mechanism of establishing a symbolic fusion of landscape and nation came to prevail.[24] Second, the Alpine myth spread from its ideological producers and most vocal proponents to ever wider sections of the population, culminating in the 1930s in an almost obsessive preoccupation with the alleged national significance of the Alps that crossed both linguistic and political boundaries.

On the substantive level, three different portrayals of the Alps—as a unifying agent, a defensive castle, and a purifying force—obtained particular prominence. This is not to say that the analogy between Alpine landscape and national community was the only element that entered into the fabric of Swiss national identity during this time. It can plausibly be argued that the most basic process at work was a historicist interpretation of the national present. But landscape was crucial as an intervening variable that contributed to the refocusing of public attention to, and the rendering natural of, a rich and complex heritage of existing national myths, symbols, and values. In short, landscape came to serve as a vehicle of ideological ethnogenesis.

In Search of National Authenticity: Nationalizing Nature

The Swiss Alps had been of interest long before they became a symbol of the sublime and of virtue in the eighteenth century. As early as the sixteenth century, painters like Albrecht Dürer drew on their imagination, rather than actual topographical experience, to use mountains as an expression both of frightening power and of the dualism between the divine and the profane (Schama 1995, 427–28). Furthermore, the interest in Alpine nature was intensified by a humanist concern or natural history. It comes as no surprise, therefore, that many Swiss humanists were among the first to create a more positive picture of the Alps, which hitherto had been seen as "horrid, misshapen locales to be shunned" (Lowenthal 1978, 382). In 1555, the naturalist Conrad Gessner climbed Mount Pilatus and summed up his experience in emotive tones, singling out, among other things, "the clarity of the mountain water, the fragrance of the wild flowers . . . the purity of the air, the richness of the milk" (Schama 1995, 436). Some twenty years later, in 1578, the Bern physician and geographer Johannes Stumpf produced the first detailed map of the High Alps (Schama 1995, 436). Learned men like Gessner and Stumpf, along with a tiny number of mountain enthusiasts from all over Europe, no doubt set the tone for future Alpine discourse (Boerlin-Brodbeck 1998).

Notwithstanding these precedents, the breakthrough toward the nationalization of Alpine nature came only in the course of the eighteenth century, when the mountains "had ceased to be the monstrosities and had become an integral part of varied and diversified Nature" (Hope Nicolson 1959, 345) and when, toward the end of the century, a cultlike enthusiasm was focused on the Swiss Alps in particular. Various Enlightenment scientists and poets, foreign and Swiss alike, contributed to this development. The English scientist Thomas Robinson, in his *Natural History,* described the Alps as an "integral and necessary part of nature's harmony."[25] The Swiss Johann Jakob Scheuchzer (1672–1733), after two decades of traveling the Alps, published in the 1720s a topographical description of the Alpine landscape entitled *Itinera Alpina.* Of considerable influence was the poem "Die Alpen" by the Bern mathematician and medical scientist Albrecht von Haller (1708–77). His poem, first published in 1732 and subsequently translated into most European languages, became an eighteenth-century bestseller and an inspiration for successive generations of Alpine travelers (Bernard 1978, 9–13).[26] From the middle of the eighteenth century onward, moreover, the classical view, which had conceived of nature primarily in utilitarian and anthropocentric terms, gave way slowly but surely to a more romanticized conception in which nature was elevated to a source of inspiration of almost religious importance.[27] In an age of enlightened criticism of aristocratic politics and opulence, a large section of the educated public, many of them influenced by Rousseau's *La Nouvelle Héloïse* (first published in 1761), began to see in the Swiss Alps and their inhabitants an embodiment of simplicity, purity, honesty, and liberty, the republican virtues par excellence.

Thanks in no small part to the works of Johann Jakob Scheuchzer, Albrecht von Haller, and an ever increasing body of foreign travel literature, the Alps increasingly became an important concern of Swiss patriotic circles in the last third of the eighteenth century (Walter 1990, 57). The intellectual focal point of this rapidly progressing movement, the Helvetic Society (founded in 1761), presented the Alps as the seat of the country's national virtues. One of its founding fathers, Franz Urs Balthasar, expressed the significance of this connection in 1763 by saying that the character of the Swiss nation found its complete expression in its untamed Alpine landscape. Besides, the Alps were conceived of as the genuine scene where the Swiss Confederation had been founded and had experienced its golden age of the thirteenth and fourteenth centuries. The mountains of central Switzerland, especially the Gotthard, where the then territorial authority, the Habsburgs, had been defeated in 1315 and 1386 respectively, were portrayed as the ultimate birthplace of liberty and independence (Marchal 1992b, 45).

A decisive step in the popularization of the symbolic link between landscape and the core myths in Switzerland's history was taken with the publication of Friedrich Schiller's *Wilhelm Tell* in 1804 (Weishaupt 1992, 23). Not only was Schiller's play to form the picture most German-speaking Europeans had of Switzerland, but it also was read and performed throughout the nineteenth century and became part of the literary canon of Swiss primary schools (Bernard 1978, 24). Although it by no means accomplished this single-handedly, Schiller's drama contributed much to the spread of the late medieval myths of Swiss foundation and liberation (particularly the Oath of the Rütli and the deeds of Wilhelm Tell against Gessler), hitherto largely confined to the educated elite, to ever wider sections of the public.[28] Like Haller and Rousseau before him, Schiller presented the Alps as a natural habitat that was conducive to the emergence of a notion of a pure, simple, honest, and liberty-loving character.

The establishment of the modern Swiss nation-state in 1848 further reinforced the link between nation and Alpine landscape (Walter 1989, 287). In the latter half of the nineteenth century, the Alps became the most common icon on tourist souvenirs. Furthermore, in 1863, the Swiss Alpine Club was founded. Its declared aim was to gain a better knowledge of the Alpine landscape, especially with regard to its topography, natural history, and social implications.[29] Finally, Alpine scenery became a prominent feature in the work of some of the most renowned Swiss artists in the second part of the nineteenth century. The Swiss novelist Gottfried Keller, for example, in his *Der Grüne Heinrich* (first published in 1854), declared that "with the thoughtlessness of youth and childish age, I believed that the natural beauty of Switzerland was a reflection of historical and political merit and of the patriotism of the Swiss people: an equivalent of freedom itself."[30]

In Search of the Determining Principle: Naturalizing the Nation

The Rise of Ethnolinguistic Nationalism

A decisive shift in the public debate about the relationship between nationhood and the natural environment took place in the last third of the nineteenth century. This shift would not have occurred without the rise of a new brand of nationalism in Europe. It has long been acknowledged by scholars of nationalism that the progression of national identities is causally related to international factors, such as geopolitics, ideological competition, warfare, and subsequent invasions.[31] Nationalism established itself as the dominant political force in nineteenth-century Europe, stirring competition among different conceptions of nationality and serving as a major catalyst of national self-assertion. In the Swiss case, what posed a serious challenge to their conception of nationality was the fact that ethnolinguistic nationalism came to dominate from the last third of the nineteenth century until the end of World War II. Particularly in Italy and Germany, this form of nationalism rapidly gained force around 1870, when it came to be seen as somewhat of a normative prerequisite of national legitimacy and served as a fertile ground for the emergence of irredentist movements in both countries.[32] When Nazism rose to power in 1933, its *völkisch* nationalism, with its markedly racial overtones, was tantamount to a denial of the legitimacy of Switzerland's conception of nationality.

It was against this historical background that the second pattern of linking nature and nation—the naturalization of the nation—came to prevail. Already in 1884, the eminent Swiss historian Karl Dändliker warned of the challenge posed by ethnic nationalism when he declared that "the Swiss people did not enjoy the advantage of their neighbors: Being a nation in the true and literal sense of the word, that is to say, being an entity uniform in terms of linguistic and ethnic composition."[33] Dändliker's statement does not represent a marginal view but forms part of a concern apparently widespread at the time, at least among liberal intellectuals and the political establishment, the two groups that had been traditionally in charge of the definition and legitimation of Swiss nationhood. When, in December 1914, German- and French-speaking Swiss had clashed over conflicting sympathies toward the parties involved in World War I, the writer Carl Spitteler, in an emphatic call for national unity, argued that in the current European political climate Switzerland's lack of both ethnocultural homogeneity and a strong centralist state presented a "political weakness."[34]

The Alps as a Homogenizing Force

Faced with the challenge of ethnic nationalism, liberal intellectuals and portions of the political elite endeavored to create a distinct national identity for Switzerland; and it was in this context that the Alpine landscape once more came to play a crucial part. Given that ethnic and *völkisch* conceptions of nationhood emphasized homogeneity in terms of its ethnic or racial composition, the nationalization of nature (the pattern that portrays the natural environment as an expression of an alleged national character) would have been, however, somewhat deficient as an ideological antidote against ethnic nationalism. In view of the challenge at hand, the naturalization of the nation, which represents a form of ideological ethnogenesis, seemed to be the more appropriate response. But to arrive at a better understanding of why that particular Alpine response came to predominate, let me reconstruct the overall ideological reaction in Switzerland to ethnic nationalism in its successive stages.

At first glance, the forging of a civic nationalism (the brand of nationalism that, by and large, had been dominant in Switzerland ever since the late eighteenth century) seemed to provide an appropriate antidote against the threat of ethnic nationalism. The most outspoken supporter of this ideological response in the 1870s was the Bern professor of law Carl Hilty. In 1875, he maintained that Switzerland was the perfect nation and that its destiny and its secular mission were to uphold a truly republican, voluntarist conception of nationality in a Europe in which the ethnic ideal was on the ascendant (Hilty 1875, 29):

> Not race or ethnic community, nor common language and customs, nor nature and history have founded the state of the Swiss Confederation. . . . What holds Switzerland together vis-à-vis [its linguistically more homogenous] neighbors is an ideal, namely the consciousness of being part of a state that in many ways represents a more civilized community; to constitute a nationality which stands head and shoulder above mere affiliations of blood or language.

But Hilty's definition of Swiss nationality (which was undoubtedly influenced by the critical school of Swiss historiography gaining ground at the time),[35] though widespread among liberal-minded intellectuals, did not reflect the dominant current of thought.[36] Instead, a more popular version of civic nationalism traced Switzerland's civic present back to its premodern past. This was based both on the medieval myths of liberation and foundation (in particular the legends of Wilhelm Tell and the Oath of the Rütli), as well as on the memories of allegedly glorious events (especially the victorious battles against the Habsburgs in 1315 and 1386 respectively). On the other hand, it had as its pillars the values and institutions of the modern Swiss nation-state founded in 1848. These two ideological dimensions—one inspired by legalist rationality and liberal-democratic ethics, the other by the emotive power of an ideo-logical myth of descent—were at the heart of Swiss national identity in its most widespread form.[37] And on the whole, this synthesis proved to be highly effective. From the era of the Helvetic Republic (1798–1803) to at least the end of World War II, this was the officially propagated version of national identity and one that was popular in all parts of the country.[38]

Nevertheless, to some contemporaries, both the purely civic concep-tion of national identity and its more popular historicist counterpart seemed insufficient as the sole basis of nationality. Johann Kaspar Bluntschli (1808–81), for instance, a prominent Swiss legal scholar with a chair at Heidelberg University, maintained around 1870 that, in view of current debates on nationality in Europe and the recent severe contesta-tion of "the belief in the existence of a particular [Swiss] nation vis-à-vis the German, French and Italian nationalities," it had become necessary to draw the boundaries of Switzerland's national identity more firmly. To achieve this, Bluntschli argued, a notion of nationality grounded on voluntarism and the institutions of the modern state, as Hilty had pro-posed, would not suffice (Bluntschli [1875] 1915, 4). But neither, he main-tained, would the reference back to the mythical past per se, even if it fostered the reproduction of historical memories of wars fought for independence and liberty in the fourteenth and fifteenth centuries. Instead, to buttress the claim for a distinct national identity that could stand up to the force of ethnic nationalism, a further element was needed. It is here that Bluntschli brings the Alpine landscape into play ([1875] 1915, 11):

I am surprised that Hilty did not, besides referring to the influence of the political idea, seek assistance from the country's nature to make the notion of Swiss nationality acceptable. For Switzerland's land-scape is indeed of peculiar character. If the Swiss possess a particular nationality, then this feeling derives above all from the existence of their beautiful homeland. There may well be Alps, mountains, seas and rivers outside Switzerland; and yet, the Swiss homeland consti-tutes such a coherent and richly structured natural whole, one that enables to evolve on its soil a peculiar feeling of a common homeland which unites its inhabitants as sons of the same fatherland, even though they live in different valleys and speak different languages.

There is evidence that Bluntschli's view cut across Switzerland's linguistic boundaries. The French-speaking intellectual Ernest Bovet, for
example, wrote an article in which he rejected the intellectual and moral
validity of racial theories and ethnic conceptions of nationhood. Not
ethnic homogeneity, he maintained, but the Alps were responsible for
the creation of a Swiss character. In an article with the noteworthy title
"Refléxions d'un Homo Alpinus," he maintained that "our independence was born in the mountains, and the mountains still determine our
whole life, give it its particularity and unity" (1909a, 289). And only a
few months later, in an essay entitled "Nationalité," Bovet resumed the
same theme, linking the Alpine narrative with the two other corner-
stones of Swiss national identity—its marked historicism and its emphasis on liberty and independence (1909b, 441):

> A mysterious force has kept us together for 600 years and has given to
> us our democratic institutions. A good spirit watches our liberty. A
> spirit fills our souls, directs our actions and creates a hymn on the one
> ideal out of our different languages. It is the spirit that blows from the
> summits, the genius of the Alps and glaciers.

Some thirty years later, the geographer Charles Burky, in a brochure
that was on display at the National Exhibition of 1939, an immense popular success, put forward the notion of geographical determinism in its
purest mode: "The physical milieu, the natural environment determines
a people. This is an axiom, and apparently Switzerland cannot escape
from it. . . . This savage and haughty nature remained untamed. Only
the mountain dweller can cope with it."[39] Perhaps unsurprisingly, we
find the most extreme forms of this geographical determinism in the
1930s. Its champions were authors who, while explicitly dealing with
social Darwinist and racial ideas, stopped short of accepting their
premises in the face of Swiss polyethnic reality. In his essay entitled "The
Ethnic Structure of Switzerland," the Zurich geographer Emil Egli put
forward a Swiss version of ideological ethnogenesis: "For the racial
scholar, Switzerland is a difficult field of study because, for logical reasons, the racially pure must step aside in favor of the mixture." In
another paragraph of the same text, he describes how immigrants can be
naturalized and thus become a part of what he conceives of as the
organic fabric of the Swiss nation: Becoming a Swiss national, Egli tells
us, is something that the natural environment (he uses the term

"Alpinization" to describe the process at work) ultimately determines and is thus beyond human will to merely assimilate to certain civic values and cultural codes.[40]

The Alps as a Defensive Castle

But the threat posed by German and Italian nationalism was not confined to the sphere of ideology embodied in different conceptions of nationality. It was real and posed a problem of national security. Memories of Italian irredentism were still fresh in the 1880s and 1890s. When in July 1862 members of the Italian Parliament publicly considered the possibility of incorporating into Italy Switzerland's Italian-speaking southern part, a wave of protests erupted throughout the country (Ramseyer 1987). The external threat, of course, became much more imminent in 1933. Hitler's *Heim ins Reich* not only referred to Austria, the German population of Bohemia, as well as Alsace and Lorraine, but was actually meant to include Switzerland too. The predicament deriving from this external threat was further heightened by the fact that, at least until 1935, Italian and German authoritarianism found adherents in Switzerland, even if only a small minority was sympathetic to the *völkisch* conception of nationality (Beck 1978, 284; Mattioli 1996; Zimmer 2004).

It was against this background that the Alps, as a symbol of protection against external threats, steadily gained in currency toward the end of the nineteenth century; for it was during this time that public interest in the national past (and particularly in the late medieval myths) was increasingly reduced to a military dimension (Marchal 1990, 372).[41] Even though the opening of the Gotthard Pass in 1883 also favored interpretations that depicted the Alps as a source of cultural mediation, the picture that prevailed until 1945 was that in which they appeared as a defensive castle. In 1909, Ernest Bovet singled out the protective function and character-building impact of the Swiss mountains (1909b, 441): "Not accidentally was the mountain herdsman's protective wall to keep out the knights. It was itself their place of birth; the mountain's blank soil, its rough sky have shaped their character, and ever since has the mountain determined our inner life."

When the threat became more imminent in the latter half of the 1930s, the Swiss councillor Philipp Etter, in a similar fashion, alluded to the Alpine myth in an address to a crowd gathered in 1939. He reiterated an important theme of the cultural nationalism of the era of the *geistige Landesverteidigung* when he maintained that the providential character of the Alps was most clearly epitomized in their historical role as protector of the Swiss people: "The divine Creator himself has produced the unity of this country, and he has provided her with a robust rampart made of granite and hard chalk. But while He made his country a fortress as huge and strong as only he could build it, he has at the same time not made her bigger than necessary for her to defend from her rampart a great spiritual mission."[42]

Perhaps the symbolic value of the Alps found its clearest expression in the attitude of the Swiss population toward its army's defense strategy. When General Guisan, on July 25, 1940, gathered the highest Swiss military officers and declared that the army's strategy consisted of building a defensive ring around the Gotthard, the reactions among the Swiss public (with few exceptions) were enthusiastic, and the Alpine myth reached its peak (Im Hof 1991, 247). This is striking, given the rather bleak situation in which the country found itself at the time and the actual implications of the general's statement. Not only had Guisan made his statement shortly after France had been defeated, so Switzerland was therefore encircled by the powers of the Axis, but his defensive strategy, in the event of a foreign invasion, would have left defenseless the great majority of the Swiss population who lived in the industrial and economic centers. Well aware of the symbolic value of the Alps, Guisan had made very deliberate use of them at a time of great public concern, even gathering his officers on the Rütli Meadow, where according to historical legend the Swiss Confederation had been founded and where the struggle for liberty and independence had its roots (Marchal 1990, 396–97).

The Alps as a Purifying Force

The idea that mountains have a purifying effect on human beings, expressed so vividly by some thinkers of the eighteenth century, was to be adopted actively and widely in the process of national self-assertion between 1870 and the outbreak of World War II. Those who depicted the Alps in terms of their homogenizing and protective capacities either were established intellectuals or belonged to the political establishment. Their social status, by and large, was relatively secure. By contrast, the champions of the myth of purity commonly represented those social strata who felt most threatened by the effects of rapid industrialization and increasing state authority.[43] Conservative ideologues, mostly from rural Catholic regions, constituted the driving force behind this movement for purity. One of its protagonists, the Fribourg intellectual Gonzague de Reynold, regarded the liberal state as the major cause of the "materialist degeneration" of the fin de siècle and openly demanded a return to the value system of the ancien régime. Others, such as the peasant leader Ernst Laur, represented the interests of those groups who felt most threatened by the effects of urbanization and industrialization.[44] This was accompanied by widespread criticism of everything associated with the evils of modern society: the secular state, the materialist ethics of both liberalism and socialism, the vanishing of traditional social hierarchies in the wake of the extension of democratic rights, and—perhaps most telling—cosmopolitanism and foreign immigration. Fears of foreign infiltration induced the Federal Assembly to raise the waiting time for the naturalization of foreign residents from two to six years after World War I.[45] A similar public mood can be observed again during the 1930s, but this time anti-Semitism was a frequent ingredient in the cultural criticism of an emerging right-wing nationalism (Piccard 1994; Altermatt 1999).

In a context of accelerated sociocultural change, the eyes of those who were tired of civilization turned to the Alps and their inhabitants, who seemed to belong to a better, happier world. It did not matter that this was an idealized version of the past or that between the sixteenth and nineteenth centuries the harsh conditions of living had forced a great many of the younger inhabitants of Alpine regions to spend their lives as mercenary soldiers in French, Spanish, Dutch, and Italian armies. Unlike contemporary modern society, the mountain regions had remained untouched by the forces of civilization, or so at least it seemed to those who worshiped them. Georges de Montenach, for instance, together with Gonzague de Reynold, one of the foremost Swiss critics of modernity at the time, argued in 1908 that the Swiss were once again looking to the Alps to purify themselves from the "cosmopolitan virus" of the present (Jost 1992, 101). As the religious socialist Leonhard Ragaz wrote in his influential 1917 pamphlet entitled "The New Switzerland": "It is above all the mountains that belong to us in their power and majesty, their tranquillity and purity. And a certain simplicity or way of life, a certain perfume of nature and primitive force, an air of rustic life belongs to us."[46] The interest of those searching for purer surroundings was not confined to the high Alps but included the foothills and their inhabitants, so patriotic enthusiasm for mountains was linked with an idealized picture of an unspoiled peasant world. In 1901, the peasant leader Ernst Laur described in confident tone the regenerating influence of the peasantry on the Swiss "national character":

> It is not an empty phrase to say that a country's defensive capability rests in the peasantry. Yet it is not merely health and force that the peasant lends to a people. He is also the best bearer of Swiss characteristics. . . . Untiring in his diligence, strict in his economizing, simple and sober in his way of life.[47]

Depending on circumstances, the peasant ideal traditionally also linked with liberty and democracy was associated with organic continuity. In the 1930s and 1940s, the organic dimension tended to be stronger in most depictions of peasants than the republican one. As the academic Karl Schmid expressed it in a 1939 address organized by the Swiss Liberal Party: "It is more important to us that [Wilhelm Tell] climbs down from the mountains to us in hobnailed boots than that he speaks the language of human rights."[48] But even though the ideal type of Swiss peasant at times adopted a markedly antimodernist and antiliberal direction of meaning, it was too firmly rooted in republican traditions to become antidemocratic. Besides, unlike in Germany, for example, where the idealization of a "healthy" peasantry took on strong racial overtones, on the whole the Swiss counterpart, though also depicted in naturalist and purifying terms too, lacked such connotations.[49]

The Alpine Myth: Its Popularization and Plausible Structure

The Spread and the Alpine Myth

The previous analysis has mainly focused on intellectuals, naturally the most vocal segments within any society. However, the idea that the Alps formed the ultimate source of national authenticity and that they were capable of fusing different linguistic groups into a single, homogeneous nation was not confined solely to the realm of scholarly and intellectual discourse. To be sure, until the middle of the nineteenth century, the Alpine ideal had been the special preserve of a relatively small but articulate group of intellectuals and members of the political intelligentsia. By the last quarter of the nineteenth century, however, this doctrine had spread to ever wider sections of the population. Indeed, between 1870 and the end of World War II, the Alps were turned into the popular national symbol of the Swiss.[50]

Yet there is an important difference between the intellectual Alpine discourse and its popular counterpart: Although the former showed a marked concern for logical consistency, this was less so in the case of the latter. The Alpine reflections of the intellectuals rested upon a sharp distinction between the two patterns of linking nature and nation—first with the nationalization of nature until roughly the 1870s and then, and largely as a response to European ethnolinguistic nationalism, with the naturalization of the nation until the end of World War II. Within the broader public discourse on the national significance of the Alps, on the other hand, the two patterns were often fused into a single argument.

Even though it is notoriously difficult to grasp precisely how the Alpine myth spread from its intellectual producers to ever wider sections of the public, there are numerous examples that suggest that it had indeed become part of the national consciousness by the turn of the twentieth century at the latest. This was favored, first and foremost, by national festivals and rituals of various sorts. A great many Swiss men and women directly participated in such public national events, many of which were deliberately staged in an Alpine environment. Crucial among these were historical plays, which experienced a remarkable boom after 1885.[51] Of no less importance was a folk song movement that had witnessed a rapid expansion since the latter half of the nineteenth century, thus helping to embed the Alpine myth in the hearts and minds of many Swiss.[52] Furthermore, Alpine and pre-Alpine areas provided the traditional geographical setting for military training courses, which provided a fertile ground for the forging of popular patriotism. Closely linked to the organization of the Swiss army from 1848 onward was the development of cartographic techniques and the popularization of maps and topographical knowledge. Map reading became part of the curriculum at Swiss elementary schools from the 1870s, inevitably directing attention to the significance of topography and no doubt facilitating the imagination of the nation as a bounded territorial space.[53]

Alpine symbolism also played a crucial role in the cultural nationalism of the 1930s, manifested in the National Exhibition of 1939.[54] In official pamphlets on display at the exhibition, the Gotthard was depicted as the mountain that—by fusing four different linguistic groups into a culturally and spiritually united nation—had enabled Switzerland to exist. The ideologies of the major political movements of the time were also replete with images of the Alps. During the two World Wars, the Liberal and Conservative Parties in particular made frequent use of Alpine symbolism in their definitions of the Swiss nation.[55] So did people with direct influence on the course of national education. The school inspector Jacob Christinger, to name but one example, in a much noticed final speech at the National Conference of Swiss Teachers in Basle in 1884, presented the argument with unmistakable clarity:

> It seems that linguistic and religious differences in particular form a barrier to the national education of the Swiss people, and some go ever so far as to deny that our people possess a unified national character. We do not want to accept this delusion. We all gaze upon the same mountains, look back to the same heroic figures in our history, enjoy the same folk songs and are proud of the same rights and liberties.[56]

Moreover, recent analyses of history books and textbooks used in secondary education in all parts of the country have revealed that the Alps served as one of the major motifs in fostering national identity within the education system.[57] Hence, in 1905, on the occasion of the one hundredth anniversary of Schiller's death, the Verein für die Verbreitung guter Schriften (Association for the Promotion of Good Books) launched a special edition of *Wilhelm Tell,* the drama in which the Alpine landscape around the Lake of Lucerne figures so prominently and that had become part of the Swiss literary canon soon after its first publication in 1804 (Helbling 1994, 173).

In the field of artistic production, painting stood out in terms of the attention it devoted to the Alpine theme. Already during the nineteenth century, with Alexandre Calame and François Diday, mountain painting had "come to represent the very embodiment of national art in Switzerland," very similar in style to the Romantic Norwegian artists J. C. Dahl and Thomas Fearnley (Nasgaard 1984, 134). But the peak of Swiss landscape painting was not reached until the turn of the century, in the form of the work of Ferdinand Hodler. In paintings such as *Dia-*

262 / NATURES PAST

logue with Nature, Communion with the Infinite, and *Eiger, Mönch and Jungfrau above a Sea of Mist,* Hodler revived "the Romantic belief in the spiritual replenishment and uplifting experience to be derived from one-ness with the grandeur of nature" (Nasgaard 1984, 125). Hodler's natu-ralistic paintings, wrote the art critic Hermann Ganz, added "an over-powering force and magnitude to the Swiss landscape, enabling Switzerland to stand out as an independent entity against the countries which surround it."[58]

Finally, in an age of quickly expanding popular travel and mass com-munications, tourist propaganda amid newspapers was an important vehicle for the dissemination of the Alpine myth. In an advertisement launched by the Federal Swiss Railway Company during the interwar period, the beauty of the country's rivers, its countryside, and forests was described at length, principally to underline the predominance of Alpine symbolism. As the text pointed out, the Alps "encircle the coun-try and thus delimit its space, . . . defend and erect it, and . . . elevate it."[59] In newspapers and pamphlets, too, the Alps figured prominently as one of the most frequently evoked symbols of national identity and unity. As described in October 1935 by a Zurich-based newspaper aimed at a lower middle-class readership:

> We understand by Swissness a certain inheritance of spiritual and physical features which we find among the people as a whole between the Alps and the Jura throughout the centuries of our history to the present day. . . . We are the only typically Alpine state in Europe. . . . The Alps are our actual strength, for it is in the Alpine human being that we find our common ground.[60]

The Plausibility Structure of the Alpine Myth

As the Swiss example shows, using geographical symbolism can be a highly effective way of reconstructing the nation as an authentic com-munity. This process of naturalizing the nation, in the course of which group history and nature are fused into one single discourse of national identity, is vital to the task of linking nations firmly in time and space. Nature in general and specific landscapes in particular thus contribute greatly to buttressing the belief in the historical continuity of nations and in their being determined by external and physical rather than social factors. However, as the foregoing analysis equally demonstrates, the role of landscape in the reconstruction of nations varies according to time and circumstance. In the case of Switzerland, the Alpine myth gained considerably in currency between 1870 and 1945, when the country's polyethnic conception of nationality was severely contested by the rise of ethnolinguistic nationalism in Europe. This provoked a crisis of national identity in Switzerland that, in turn, engendered a project of national reconstruction. Unlike in France and England, where human beings were supposed to have the upper hand over their natural environment, in Switzerland, at a time of considerable social uncertainty, people sought guidance from a rugged example of nature, which they found in their Alpine landscape. Intellectuals and portions of the intelligentsia portrayed this landscape as a relentless force capable of determining the character of their nation and of its inhabitants—an ideological pattern that I have termed the "naturalization of the nation."

Does this mean, however, that the Alpine myth became an important part of Swiss national identity during this period simply because of external challenges, which, in turn, provoked a fierce nationalistic response based upon public rituals and ceremonies, the education system, new and more effective means of transport, and influence of the media? Much does indeed support this view. To begin with, it is surely true that, as an eminent student of geographical symbolism has put it, "What men see in Nature is a result of what they have been taught to see" (Hope Nicolson 1959, 3). Like all sustaining national myths, the Alpine myth did not depend for its effectiveness upon its being true. What is more, by the latter half of the nineteenth century, a potent Alpine narrative did emerge that was able to set the tone for the heightened public debate on national identity that set in after 1870 and then again during the 1930s.

This phenomenon becomes obvious if we look at some of the themes that constitute the Alpine myth. It can hardly be argued that the Alps, as the myth would have us believe, actually acted as a defensive castle that protected the Swiss against external military threats throughout the centuries. These mountains did not, at any rate, pose an insurmountable obstacle for the French troops when they invaded Switzerland in 1798 to establish the Helvetic Republic. Nor was the military defense ring built around the Gotthard massif in the late summer of 1940 the only, or indeed the major, reason why Hitler's Wehrmacht did not invade Switzerland—a belief to which a great many Swiss who grew up during the 1940s and 1950s chose to subscribe against a considerable amount of contradicting evidence.

Were the mountains responsible for what contemporaries called the Swiss "national character"? Had the Alps created a people of pure and simple herdsmen, a bit rude perhaps but otherwise proud and certainly not to be ridiculed when their independence and liberty were at stake? Even if one endorsed this (highly questionable) notion and the geographical determinism it implied, this way of reasoning would be hardly plausible: Especially during the period under consideration, Switzerland, a country extremely poor in natural resources, was transformed from a rural to an industrial nation. By 1910, it was the most industrialized European country next to England; and the bulk of its population resided in towns rather than small villages, with only an insignificant number actually dwelling in Alpine regions (Von Greyerz 1980, 1094–95; Mathieu 1998).

But why did the Alpine myth seem plausible all the same? Why, then, did so many Swiss apparently subscribe to the belief that the mountains were a vital source of Swiss national identity, that they had shaped their character and, hence, "their" nation? I believe that an additional argument is necessary to arrive at a fuller explanation for the important role played by the Alps in defining Swiss national identity. The argument asserts that the Alpine myth possessed a "plausibility structure" (Berger and Luckmann 1966) that favored its widespread appeal. It proved plausible to a great many Swiss for two reasons: first, because it was grounded on certain material conditions; and, second, because it could be related to certain historical events, myths, and symbols that had formed part of the narrative of Swiss national identity after the latter part of the eighteenth century.

One such condition is plain physical topography. Topography mattered in that it formed a potentiality, from which human actors selected particular landscapes and endowed them with national significance.[61] The size of the proportion of land covered by mountains—more than 60 percent, with many of the peaks rising above four thousand meters—to Switzerland's overall territory (which is indeed small by European standards) can scarcely be ignored.[62] Furthermore, toward the end of the nineteenth century travel and tourism started to affect the masses (Bernard 1978, chaps. 5 and 6). Armed with relatively cheap and sophisticated maps, many Swiss men and women became acquainted with Alpine landscape through actual experience. For some this was because they took the opportunity to travel through them, while for most this was because they could see them on a clear day, whether they lived in Zurich, Bern, Geneva, Lucerne, or Lugano.[63]

The second condition of importance concerns the economic and political significance of the Alps in the evolution of the Swiss Confederation from the fourteenth century onward. Gaining control over the mountain passes as a means to secure the exchange of goods and capital with the prosperous Italian city-states proved vital to the economic and cultural development of the valley communities and city-states that constituted the emergent Swiss Confederation (Marchal 1986, 152–53). What is more, the mountains of central Switzerland, along with the military success of the Confederate peasant armies in the battles against the Habsburgs at Morgarten (1315) and Sempach (1386), helped prevent feudalism from taking root and let the Swiss Confederation emerge, in the words of Perry Anderson, as a "unique independent republic in Europe" (1979, 301). This exceptional historical development was subsequently exaggerated by the chroniclers of the sixteenth and seventeenth centuries. The powerful mythical repertoire that emanated from their elaborations came to form the kernel of an emerging early modern Swiss identity. In the second half of the eighteenth century and during the nineteenth century, the increasing prominence of a romanticized conception of nature put the crucial finishing touch to the symbolic fusion of the Alps with the national past. To sum it up, a specific sociopolitical context, articulate ideologues, effective means of communication, as well as the country's geographical structure and historical development were together the factors responsible for the fundamental role of Alpine imagery in the reconstruction of Swiss national identity between 1870 and the end of World War II.

NOTES

An earlier version of this chapter was presented at the conference "Collective Identity and Symbolic Representation," held at the Fondation Nationale des Sciences Politiques, Paris, July 3–4, 1996. For comments and criticisms I am indebted to Eric Garcetti, Eric Kaufmann, and Anthony D. Smith. I should also like to acknowledge the financial support I received from the Erziehungsdirektion des Kantons Zurich and the Janggen-Pöhn Stiftung, St. Gallen.

1. Here I follow Pierre Nora's (1996) distinction between "history" (which, in the course of the nineteenth century, came to be dominated by the standards set by professional historiography) and "memory" (for which historical myths and popular narratives about historical events are constitutive).

2. Schama 1995, 83–84, 254–55. For an analysis of ideas about the natural environment in antiquity, see Glacken's illuminating *Traces on the Rhodian Shore* (1967, part I).

3. Schama 1995, 10. Hirsch (1995, 2) maintains that the term "landscape" has its origin in the Dutch word *landschap* and was introduced into the English language not until the late sixteenth century "as a technical term used by painters." Lowenthal (1978, 377) maintains that the notion of a landscape emerged where significant parts of the natural environment began to be perceived in scenic rather than strictly utilitarian terms.

4. Quoted in Hale 1994, 55. On the proliferation of climatic theories in the sixteenth century, see Glacken 1967, 449–561.

5. A way of reasoning so clearly expressed in what may rightly be regarded as the two greatest works on the influence of the natural environment on human beings that appeared in the sixteenth century: Jean Bodin's *Methodus* (1566) and *Republic* (1576).

6. Quoted in Glacken 1967, 371. As Thomas (1983, 257) argues in his recent analysis of attitudes toward nature in early modern England, "For the neo-classical theorists of the later seventeenth century, it was axiomatic that geometrical figures were intrinsically more beautiful than irregular ones."

7. Quoted in Glacken 1967, 542.

8. Quoted in Glacken 1967, 578.

9. Quoted in Rosen and Zerner 1984, 52.

10. On the part played by ethnic historicism in the emergence of nationalism and the fostering of national identities, see, for instance, Smith 1995, chap. 3; Bell 2001, ch. 4; Zimmer 2003, chap. 2.

11. With the partial exception of Smith 1986, 183–90.

12. Good recent examples are the reader *Geography and National Identity* (Hooson 1994) and Daniels 1993. And there is of course Simon Schama's (1995) pathbreaking historical account.

13. See Hooson 1994, introduction. For a primordialist account of the connection between nature and group life that uses the term "territoriality," see Grosby 1995.

14. This approach is characteristic of most contributions in Hooson 1994.

15. See Lowenthal 1978, 401; Schama 1995, 15.

16. This definition presupposes an analytical distinction between "nation" and "state." It presupposes that the nation, as an ethnocultural concept, lends meaning and legitimacy to the state. The latter, in turn, is rooted in a set of civic (legal, political, and economic) institutions. In the public controversies that accompanied the formation of the European nation-state in the nineteenth and twentieth centuries, the nation supplied the central moral frame of reference. General reflections on this problem can be found in Smith 1995, chap. 4; Eley and Suny 1996, introduction. For a concrete historical analysis, see Zimmer 2003.

17. Quoted in Smith 1991, 75. The concept of national authenticity is discussed in Smith 1995, 65–67.

18. The "naturalization of social classifications" as a measure to reduce uncer-

tainty is discussed most illuminatingly in Douglas 1987, 48. Benedict Anderson, in his *Imagined Communities* (1991, 12), has made a related point, arguing that "it is the magic of nationalism to turn chance into destiny."

19. The way I conceptualize the reproduction and change of national identity for the purpose of this analysis draws on Swidler 1986 and Sewell 1996.

20. For differences and similarities between early Romantic and neoclassical conceptions of cultural community, see Smith 1976. On Romantic nationalism's search for poetic spaces and golden ages, see Smith 1986, 179–200.

21. To quote Lowenthal 1994, 22: "The English landscape is not natural but crafted. . . . Englishmen tame and adorn nature." On attitudes toward nature in early modern England, see Thomas 1983. For the symbolic significance of English landscape during the interwar period, see Potts 1989.

22. Quoted in Claval 1994, 44.

23. For an account of Canada and the United States, see Kaufmann 1998.

24. To maintain that this new conceptualization of linking the Alps symbolically with the Swiss nation (the naturalization of the nation) came to prevail around 1870 is of course not to deny that the preceding one (the nationalization of nature) had favored its emergence and spread. Nor is it meant to imply that the break was an absolute one. Nevertheless, as the available evidence clearly suggests, the change of emphasis is marked enough to speak of a transformation.

25. According to Thomas (1983, 261), it was the English who "created the greatest mystique about mountain-climbing." In Switzerland, it was, in the words of the official chronicle of the Alpine Club (founded in 1857), the *Alpine Journal,* notorious that "if you met a man in the Alps, it was ten to one that he was a University man, eight to one (say) that he was a Cambridge man, and about even betting that he was a fellow of his college." Quoted in Thomas 1983, 261.

26. A second edition of Haller's "Alpen" was published as early as 1734. The poem went through twelve editions during the second part of the eighteenth century and was translated into five different languages. What is more, Goethe, in his *Wilhelm Meisters Wanderjahre* (1821), claimed that, along with Kleist's "Frühling" and Gessner's "Idyllen," Haller's "Alpen" had taught the cult of nature to a whole generation of Europeans. See Wozniakowski 1987, 245.

27. The distinction between the classical and Romantic conception of nature is set out in more detail in Wozniakowski 1987 and Short 1991.

28. According to the legend, the Oath of the Rütli (said to be taken in 1307 by the three valley cantons of Uri, Schwyz, and Unterwalden) stands for the beginning of the Old Confederates' struggle for independence against the Habsburg dynasty. Wilhelm Tell is the personification of this struggle for liberation. The Swiss foundation myths are described in Im Hof 1991, chap. 1.

29. Dübi 1900, 440. In 1900, the Swiss Alpine Club counted 5,976 active members who were spread over forty-four different national sections in all linguistic parts of the country. By the turn of the century, thirty-four maps on a scale of 1:50,000 of different parts of the Alps chain had been edited. This is discussed in Dübi 1900, 440–43.

30. Quoted in Jost 1988, 18–19.

31. For recent contributions to the study of national identity that place particular emphasis on this point, see Greenfeld 1992; Colley 1992; Zimmer 2003.

32. The smaller German solution of 1871 was challenged on ethnic grounds from several quarters. While the Pan-German League certainly presented the most radical current within German ethnic nationalism prior to 1900, German "homeland nationalism" enjoyed wide currency and drew support from a fairly developed network of associations and political pressure groups. See Brubaker 1992, chaps. 3 and 6; Eley 1980. On European ethnolinguistic nationalism more broadly, see especially Hobsbawm [1990] 1993, chap. 4; Alter 1985, 112.

33. Quoted in Im Hof 1991, 172.

34. Spitteler 1915, 5. Other prominent personalities of public life argued along similar lines. See Huber 1916, 1934.

35. On the influence of this critical school of historians on the definition of Swiss national identity, see Kreis 1991, chap. 4; Im Hof 1991, 233–35; Zimmer 2003, chap. 6.

36. Frei 1964, 213.

37. The important distinction between ideological and genealogical myths of descent has been introduced by Smith (1984).

38. Im Hof 1991; Marchal 1990. For national identity in the French-speaking part of Switzerland, see Kreis 1987.

39. Quoted in Lasserre 1992, 198.

40. Quoted in Kreis 1992, 176; see also Zimmer 2004.

41. Here too there were ideological precedents. According to Boerlin-Brodbeck (1998, 7), the image of the Alps as a protective castle goes back to the sixteenth and seventeenth centuries.

42. Quoted in Lasserre 1992, 194.

43. On these groups and their leaders in the Swiss context, see Clavien 1993; Jost 1992; and various case studies in Mattioli 1996.

44. In 1798, 62.5 percent of the total population was occupied in the rural sector, 25 percent in the industrial sector, and 12.5 percent in the service sector. In 1900, the respective figures were 31 percent, 44.9 percent, and 24.1 percent. Bergier 1983, 176, 206–7.

45. Marchal 1992a, 45; Zimmer 2004.

46. Quoted in Marchal 1992a, 45.

47. Quoted in Weishaupt 1992, 75–76.

48. Quoted in Mattioli 1996, 9.

49. Ernst 1994, 308. However, it is chiefly in terms of definitions of the Other that the ethnogenesis function of the Alpine myth reveals itself. This kind of naturalized ("alpinized") Swiss nationalism undoubtedly favored an exclusive national self-definition. On the discourse of *Überfremdung* (foreign infiltration) and on anti-Semitism during the interwar period, see Piccard 1994; Zimmer 1993, 2004, 2006.

50. There remains, of course, the question of the place of Alpine symbolism in postwar Swiss identity. While a further study would be needed to satisfactorily tackle this question, a tentative answer may nonetheless be given. First, on the level of everyday life, there are clear indications that the Alps retained much of their traditional importance as a self-evident symbol of Swiss nationhood up to the present day. Nevertheless, where the Alps may have lost considerably of their former symbolic significance is on the level of explicit ideological definitions of national identity. Particularly the belief that landscape in general and the Alps in particular are capable of determining national character may be less sustainable under conditions of "reflexive modernization," to use a term coined by Giddens (1991).

51. A very recent study of newspaper articles in the period from 1891 to 1935 reveals that the Alpine myth occupied a crucial place in liberal and conservative papers all over the country, with the socialist press showing a more critical attitude. See Merki 1995, 67–71. On national festivals more generally, see Santschi 1991. For a discussion of historical plays, see Kreis 1988.

52. Braun 1965, 326–29.

53. See Gugerli and Speich 2002, 90–94.

54. Lasserre 1992, 192; Marchal 1992b, 49–50; Zimmer 2004.

55. This is set out in Widmer 1992, 619–38; Wigger 1997, 86–89.

56. Quoted in Helbling 1994, 160.

57. See, for instance, Helbling 1994; Rutschmann 1994. On the significance of folk songs in Swiss schools, see Im Hof 1991, 158–59.

58. Quoted in Jost 1988, 18.

59. Quoted in Walter 1992, 14.

60. Quoted in Zimmer 1996, 100.

61. The notion that geography shapes cultural evolution in the sense of a "possibilism"—a concept that was first developed by Vidal de la Blache and subsequently became influential in the Annales School of French historiography—is discussed in Braudel 1989, 263–64.

62. This is a considerably higher proportion than that of France, Italy, or Austria, the other three countries possessing major parts of the overall European Alps chain, although Switzerland covers "merely" 12 percent of the Alps of Europe, considerably less than Austria (28 percent), Italy (27 percent), and France (22 percent). The figures are taken from Wachter 1995, 39.

63. Some of Switzerland's most industrialized and densely populated regions—including St. Gall, Appenzell, and the southeastern parts of Zurich—were located in pre-Alpine zones. See Mathieu 1998, 18.

IX Lawn-o-Rama

The Commodification of
Landscape in Postwar America

Ted Steinberg

READERS EXPECTING TO LEARN about crabgrass in Kenneth Jackson's award-winning book on suburbanization in the United States, *Crabgrass Frontier,* will be disappointed. The dreaded weed, it turns out, is not discussed at all; nor does it even rate a mention in the index. To be sure, Jackson briefly discusses the lawn in nineteenth-century America and the emergence of an early front-yard aesthetic. But when it comes to the postwar period—when the lawn rose to dominance across the American landscape and crabgrass became an obsession—he is silent (Jackson 1985, 54–61).

And so are virtually all historians of post–World War II America. This despite the fact that turfgrass occupies, it is estimated, on the order of twenty-seven million acres of land, an area roughly the size of the state of Pennsylvania (Bormann, Balmori, and Geballe 2001, 51). The lawn is one of America's principal crops, in 2001 amounting to twice the acreage planted in cotton (United States Census Bureau 2002, 531). The question for the historian is how this came to be. How did the lawn become the dominant landscape intervention? Why this love affair (or really love-hate affair) with turf?

Thus far, three theories have been advanced. First is the genetic explanation, advanced most famously by the ecologist John H. Falk in the early 1980s. Falk held that, when shown photographs of a variety of different landscapes, subjects drawn from places as diverse as Africa, India, and the United States all showed an affinity for savanna (Balling and Falk 1982).This Falk attributed primarily to genetic factors. "We spent 98% of our evolutionary history in those savanna-like environments," he said. "Our habitat preference for short grass and scattered trees seems to be a vestige of that history" (quoted in Wharton 1986).

Suffice it to say that the evidence in support of Falk's theory is scanty. There are huge cultural differences with respect to turf in the three places from which Falk draws his data—Africa, India, and the United States. Nor does his genetic argument explain why the United States is the turfgrass capital of the world, why the lawn has become a multi-billion-dollar-a-year industry in this country. Moreover, recent evidence on the reconstruction of early habitats in Africa suggests that the savanna hypothesis as applied to early hominid evolution is wrong. In fact, the evidence indicates instead that this phase of human evolution may well have occurred in wooded regions, not grassy ones (Shreeve 1996; Reed 1997).

Theory number two sees the obsession with closely mowed, dark-green expanses of lawn in the United States as primarily the product of industry pressure. This theory has been put forth by a group at Yale consisting of two ecologists and a landscape architect. They are savvy enough to dismiss the idea that the modern "industrial lawn," as they call it, resulted from the machinations of cigar-chomping "CEOs plotting the manipulation of American homeowners." No, the industrial lawn, they argue, had multiple origins stemming from technological advance in agriculture and the long-standing love for grass. But ultimately the authors place most of the weight on industry, writing of the lawn-care industry's "power to determine the structure of our landscapes and to influence our psyches and attitudes toward our environment" (Bormann, Balmori, and Geballe 2001, 49, 54). Because they make this argument without actually citing or consulting industry sources (business records or trade journals, for example), it is difficult to lend it much credence. Moreover, the lack of evidence opens up the authors to the charge that they are arguing for some kind of business conspiracy.

Finally, theory number three comes at the hands of a historian, so far as I can tell the only historian ever to treat the lawn in an extended, detailed way. Virginia Scott Jenkins made the lawn a topic for legitimate historical inquiry, though her argument is rather simplistic. Jenkins maintains that lawns are the result of two things: the ability and the desire to grow lawn grass. She says that historians have long recognized the aesthetics of turf—presumably having in mind people like Kenneth Jackson and others who have looked at the nineteenth-century proponents of the lawn as suburban groundcover. But what historians have missed, she argues, is that the desire for grass is one thing and the ability to grow it is something altogether different (Jenkins 1994, 4).

Over the last century and a half, she explains, a stream of technological advances—power hoses, chemical fertilizers, herbicides, insecticides, improved grass species—has helped make the lawn a reality. "The availability and affordability of the tools and grasses needed to grow a lawn shaped individual choices" (Jenkins 1994, 4). Her book certainly establishes that the lawn is currently an obsession among Americans. What she does not really answer is *why* it has become an obsession. It seems hard to believe that technology alone accounts for it. And, in the end, she backs off that claim, arguing that a long list of factors—the lawn industry (which "nurtured the aesthetic that calls for a smooth, green lawn"), advertising, golf, labor-saving inventions, new grass species, and "shifts in living and working patterns"—contributed in one way or another to the birth of our national lawnscape (183).

None of these three theories—genetics, business conspiracy, or laundry list—seem wholly up to the task of accounting for the American obsession that Jenkins has at least rightly diagnosed. Jenkins is correct when she says that "Americans have moved from regional landscapes based on local vegetation and climate to a national landscape based on an aesthetic that considers grassy front yards necessary to domestic happiness" (Jenkins 1994, 185). What she has uncovered here is nothing less than the commodification of landscape. Can there be any doubt that what Marx called the tendency of capitalist technologies and market mechanisms to drive "beyond every spatial barrier" is applicable to contemporary lawn culture? (Marx 1973, 524). Turfgrass species, most of which originated in the cool, moist European climates and which today can be found everywhere from Massachusetts to California and in between, have literally broken free of space. Landscape, to paraphrase the German social philosopher Max Horkheimer, has deteriorated into landscaping (Horkheimer 1947, 37–38). Indeed, the fact that the word "landscaping" dates from only 1930 seems to confirm this.

Long View of the Lawn

How and when did this great transformation take place? Where did this romance with dark-green grass come from, if not our genetic heritage? Why the lawn's nearly unchallenged dominance over the nation's landscape? Let me begin by providing a brief, capsule history of the rise of the American lawn.

Many of the grass species found in America's yards today are visiting from Europe, where they evolved in conjunction with the moist, cool climates found in such places as Britain and northern France. It is no accident that the word "lawn," which dates from the sixteenth century, derives from the Old English "launde," denoting an open space or glade (Weigert 1994, 89). Even Kentucky bluegrass, the species typical of the proper lawn, first sprouted, it is believed, in the cool, fringe areas of northern Europe's forests, thousands of miles from Churchill Downs.

How did it happen that a set of nonnative plants, not at all adapted to our country's climatic conditions, grew to become the basis for our national landscape? The story begins with the European colonists, who ventured to the shores of North America with an assortment of animals—horses, cattle, and sheep—not originally found here. The native grasses, not adapted to being grazed, quickly died off as the livestock chewed them to death. Into this now empty econiche came imported grass seed—the germplasm of future Levittowns—arriving in fodder and dung, if not by more purposeful means, turning the landscape, in a smattering of places at least, a new kind of green (Cronon 1983, 141–42). This process was advanced by deforestation (the product of colonization, population growth, and economic imperatives), which created a far less congenial habitat for the native grasses. In short, without what Alfred Crosby has described as the "Columbian Exchange," there would be no lawn, no Scotts, Toro, or ChemLawn (Crosby 1972).

The greening of America, however, did not happen overnight. Although there was some interest in lawns among the elite in the eighteenth century, the idea of cultivating grass around the outside of the home did not become popular until after the Civil War. Before that time, most people in the nation's towns and cities either maintained small fenced-in gardens out front or, more likely, simply left the area alone, allowing it to revert to dirt interspersed with whatever vegetation might take root (Jenkins 1994, 14–17). "The well-trimmed lawns and green meadows of home are not there," wrote Charles Dickens on a tour of New England in the early 1840s (Dickens [1842] 1985, 64). And as for the backyard, with its outhouses, no one would dare think of planting turfgrass and holding a family occasion there (Jackson 1985, 56).

Change set in beginning in the 1870s. Dense urban areas gave way to streetcar suburbs filled with detached housing. Setback rules came into being that required homes to be located at least thirty feet from the sidewalk. Suddenly, a new landscape imperative was on the rise, as marked by the appearance in 1870 of Frank J. Scott's *The Art of Beautifying Suburban Home Grounds.* "A smooth, closely-shaven surface of grass," he wrote, "is by far the most essential element of beauty on the grounds of a suburban house" (Scott 1870, 107). Meanwhile, inventors were off refining the lawn mower, with thirty-eight patents secured between 1868 and 1873 alone. Then came the lawn sprinkler—patented in 1871—a device that took on growing importance as the nation's cities brought public water supplies on line (Jenkins 1994, 29, 30).

Despite these developments and the increasing expansion of the lawn, the idea of a *perfect* yard, neatly manicured and devoid of weeds, generated little interest. Time was one problem. Until the passage of legislation in 1938 making the forty-hour workweek the norm, Americans commonly worked half the day on Saturday. With only one full day off, and long hours Monday through Friday, it would have been hard to muster the energy needed to push a mower around outside. To the extent that any mowing at all took place, it was mostly a chore assigned to the boy in the family. "You probably remember, as I do all too well, the boyhood task of mowing the lawn. That's all the attention it ever received," wrote one man reflecting back on the period before World War II (Mills 1961, 5).

Only after World War II did the idea of perfect turf become a national preoccupation. In the 1950s, turfgrass broke free of space, colonizing yards, golf courses, and rights of way from the densely packed suburbs of Long Island to the most distant, parched reaches of the Southwest. It has been observed that like the interstate highway system—itself the product of legislation passed during the Eisenhower years—the lawn has had a unifying impact on the landscape (Pollan 1991, 66). While true enough, such an observation neglects the historical forces that gave rise to both these developments, turning the nation into a sprawling black-and-green canvas. Chief among these forces was the federal government. It subsidized suburban growth by providing billions of dollars for highways, plus low-interest loans and a mortgage interest deduction that allowed all those Americans fleeing the cities in the fifties and sixties to buy homes and plant grass (Steinberg 2002, 213–24). This was not any old grass but improved species that would never have existed in the first place without the work of both the U.S. Department of Agriculture and a host of state-funded university turf programs.

Levittown and Postwar Lawn Culture

While the lawn may have distant roots in America, the invention of a national lawn culture with perfectionist aspirations, I argue, is actually a very recent invention, little more than fifty years old. As late as 1950, an editorial in the *New York Times* advised homeowners to put aside their concerns with crabgrass and condemned the notion that lawns ought to look like billiard tables. "The lawn should remain a lawn, and no lawn can be called just that unless it is somewhat this side of perfection" (*New York Times* 1950). It is almost impossible to imagine an editorial a decade later arguing in favor of the virtues of lawn truancy.

The birth of Levittown, New York, played a key role in the lawn's rise to landscape dominance. The story of Levittown, New York, has been told many times. William Levitt, the hard-charging businessman, is normally the featured protagonist in these tales. What Henry Ford did for cars, William Levitt did for houses, manufacturing them in large numbers and at a low enough price to put them within reach of the thousands of ordinary people searching for a chance at the American dream (Baxandall and Ewen 2000). Less recognized is that Levitt and Sons invented a mass-produced landscape to go along with its ticky-tacky housing. The man chiefly responsible for this development, however, was not William but his father, Abraham Levitt, an avid gardener who used to personally inspect the state of Levittown's lawns and gardens. "A fine lawn makes a frame for a dwelling," Abraham Levitt explained in 1949. "It is the first thing a visitor sees. And first impressions are the lasting ones" (Levitt 1949). Between 1947 and 1951, Abraham and his sons, William and Alfred, built more than seventeen thousand homes on the potato fields that once dominated a large, flat section of Long

Island. And every last one of them had a lawn to mow. "No single feature of a suburban residential community," Abraham wrote, "contributes as much to the charm and beauty of the individual home and the
locality as well-kept lawns" (Levitt n.d.). Not for nothing was Abraham
Levitt dubbed the "vice president of grass seed" (telephone interview
with Peter Costich, September 17, 2003).

Abraham Levitt was born in 1880 in Brooklyn, New York. The son of
a rabbi who came to the United States from Russia and a mother of
Austrian-German descent, Abraham left school at the age of ten to
become a newsboy. A voracious reader, Abraham managed to pass a
high school equivalency test and later studied law at New York University. Upon graduation, Abraham went into real estate law and practiced
in the field for more than twenty-five years. A short time before the stock
market crashed in 1929, Abraham and his sons formed a construction
firm, which started out building high-end homes on the north shore of
Long Island for well-off professionals willing to commute into New
York City.

At the time the Levitts arrived in the northern part of Long Island,
the area rested in the hands of the descendants of America's wealthiest
men, such as J. P. Morgan, Henry Clay Frick, Vincent Astor, and hundreds of other plutocrats who built huge estates in an attempt to imitate
the lifestyle of the British aristocracy, right down to the lawns and golf
courses common among that set. To help engineer the necessary lawn
culture, they brought over gardeners from Scotland (Baxandall and
Ewen 2000, 4–7). Eventually, the Levitts would take this aspect of genteel life and democratize it, giving tens of thousands of Americans a
chance to be lords of their own little manors, even if they had to do the
mowing themselves.

Back before Levittown, when the Levitts first began building on Long
Island, they made a point of landscaping the premises before putting
their homes on the market. "In the Thirties," Abraham's son Alfred
explained, "Father was the one who had the foresight to realize that by
intelligent landscaping the normal depreciation of our houses could be
offset" (*Fortune* 1952, 156). According to William Levitt, his father
called landscaping a form of "neighborhood stabilization" (Levitt 1964,
67).

The housing shortage that marred the postwar years—compelling
millions to double up with relatives—gave the Levitts a golden business

opportunity. Breaking down the work process into a set of twenty-odd steps, the Levitts transformed single-family construction from a craft into an industrial enterprise. "The only difference between Levitt and Sons and General Motors," William Levitt once reflected, "is that we channel labor and materials to a stationary outdoor assembly line instead of bringing them together inside a factory on a mobile line. Just like a factory, we turn out a new house every twenty four minutes at peak production" (Baxandall and Ewen 2000, 125). That house, the Levitts liked to boast, only took up about 12 percent of the lot (Larrabee 1948, 84). With the exception of some concrete paths, the rest would all be landscaped in the spirit of a garden community.

Abraham Levitt saw to it that all the homes in Levittown received some fruit trees and evergreens, but the bulk of the land was covered in grass seed, a quick and dirty means of healing the landscape once the bulldozers and concrete mixers had headed off down the road. "It has been truthfully said," explained Abraham, "that no single feature of the garden contributes as much to beauty and utility as a good lawn" (Levitt 1948a, 13). To underscore the point, in the spring of 1948, Levitt and Sons spruced up, free of charge, all the lawns installed the previous fall, fertilizing them and reseeding where necessary. "This is the first spring in Levittown," Abraham pointed out, "and we want to present to the nation a model community in every respect" (*Levittown Tribune* 1948, 1).

How to take care of a lawn is not something that comes naturally, certainly not to the erstwhile urbanites then taking up residence on Long Island. In a weekly gardening column that appeared in the *Levittown Tribune*—a newspaper owned by the Levitts—Abraham offered advice to the newly arrived immigrants in the land of the lawn. If Levittown was to become the garden community that Abraham hoped, homeowners would need to learn the importance of what is now a weekly suburban ritual: mowing the yard. The ecological logic behind mowing the lawn is fairly simple. By keeping the grass from flowering and going to seed, mowing forecloses on sexual reproduction, with its genetic luck of the draw, and compels the individual plants to reproduce vegetatively by sending out a web of underground and lateral stems. The result is a thick carpet of grass we know as a lawn.

Of course the busy neosuburbanites flooding into Levittown could not be bothered with esoteric ecological principles. What they did understand, many of them being veterans, was the disciplined world of the armed service. Taking note of this fact, Abraham showed them how to apply some spit and polish to the yard:

> In military service, a man must shave and have his hair trimmed regularly for experience has proved that men are worth more if their morale is high, and an unkempt creature thinks little of others and less even of himself. It is so with a dwelling house and so with a lawn. Remember, your lawn is your outdoor living room about 7 months of the year. It is the first approach to your house. Your visiting friends form their opinions of the neatness and cleanliness of your house at their first approach. (Levitt 1948b, 7)

The crew-cut look, popular with both hair and lawns in the forties, so impressed the Levitts that they inserted a covenant in their deeds requiring Levittowners to cut the grass once a week between April and November.

There was more at work here, however, than simply the Levitts' desire to keep up the value of their investment. Without the rise of auto-centered sprawl, for example, American suburbanites would have had no reason to manicure their lawns in the first place. "With increased use of automobiles," Jackson writes, "the life of the sidewalk and the front yard has largely disappeared, and the social intercourse that used to be the main characteristic of urban life has vanished" (1985, 279–80). Without porches or stoops, the front yard in suburban communities like Levittown had no real utility. No longer the locus of community activity, it evolved into something for show, into a reflection of personal identity. A huge sociological experiment was set to begin. As the practical value of the front yard declined, its symbolic value—what it said about the integrity of the homeowner and the neighborhood more generally—skyrocketed. "A fine carpet of green grass," Abraham told readers of his weekly column, "stamps the inhabitants as good neighbors, as desirable citizens" (Levitt 1951, 8).

Although lawns had existed in America since at least the eighteenth century, only in the postwar period did turf take on the attributes of an indoor space. The notion of carpeting the yard fit perfectly with one of the dominant architectural trends of the time. "Perhaps the most noticeable innovation in domestic architecture in the past decade or two has been the increasingly close relationship of indoors and outdoors," wrote the authors of *The American House Today* (Ford and Creighton 1951,

139). Magazines like *Sunset* discussed the virtues of "bringing the out-doors indoors" (Spigel 1992, 101). The patios typically included in ranch homes—an enormously popular form of housing in the postwar years—functioned as an extension of the indoor living space. And the neatly manicured lawn further domesticated the yard, transforming it, in Abraham Levitt's words, into an "outdoor living room."

Scotts and the Perfect Lawn

What began as a simple way of mending a scarred landscape became by the 1950s a national obsession with perfection. While the idea of a business conspiracy seems far-fetched and, in any case, as yet unsupported by any evidence, there is no question that the lawn industry tried in every way it could to convince Americans of the virtues of the perfect lawn. Among the savviest of the postwar green industry marketers were those at the O. M. Scott and Sons Company. The company was founded after the Civil War by Orland M. Scott and pioneered the development of weed-free seed, which it sold to farmers. By the late 1920s, however, it moved increasingly into the lawn-care area. In 1928, the company began publishing its own lawn-care advice magazine titled *Lawn Care.* The company sent the magazine free of charge to any homeowner who requested it. One Wall Street analyst, interviewed in the 1960s, remarked, "*Lawn Care* Magazine is the greatest advertising gimmick in the business. . . . Most direct mailings are read by a tiny fraction of the people they're sent to, but *Lawn Care,* which goes only to people who request it, probably has as high a readership percentage as *Time* or *Life*" (Winter 1967). The company also gave away free seed and fertilizer, which helped to bolster lawn culture in particular areas by shaming neighbors into buying Scotts products. Seed, especially, was a loss leader for Scotts. In the 1950s, the company, employing market segmentation techniques, came out with three different grass-seed mixtures—deluxe, special, and utility. In 1961 the company, in an effort to expand its customer base, moved to uniform pricing among the different blends in an effort to literally seed success by encouraging consumers to choose the right product for their purposes.

While these moves may well have encouraged homeowners to plant turfgrass in their yards, the idea of the perfect lawn was tied up with new ideas about what plant species constituted weeds. Here again, the Scotts company proved a leader. One of the most important developments in the area of chemical herbicides occurred during World War II, when scientists working for the Chemical Warfare Service developed 2,4-D. The driving force behind the discovery was the search for a chemical that could be used to destroy the food resources of an enemy population (Russell 2001, 225). The chemical, as it turned out, proved absolutely central to the revolution in lawn care in postwar America. 2,4-D was a selective herbicide that killed broad-leaved weeds, such as dandelions and chickweed, but left the grass standing. The herbicide, however, did not distinguish between good and bad broad-leaved weeds. Clover, for example, was commonly found in America's lawns until well into the 1950s. Scotts even marketed a special seed product as late as the mid-fifties that could be used to plant a yard full of clover. The popularity of clover rested on one main ecological fact: Clover is a legume that can take nitrogen out of the air and add it to the soil, bolstering soil fertility. But when Scotts (and other companies) began marketing products containing 2,4-D after the war, they needed to convince homeowners that a lawn full of clover was undesirable, which it did through the pages of its *Lawn Care* magazine (Schultz 1999, 54).

Homeowners had, in addition, reasons of their own for eliminating clover. It attracts bees and is a difficult grass species to use for sporting events because it is hard to get much traction on it. By the 1960s, clover was increasingly looked down on as a turfgrass. The 1971 edition of one popular lawn-care guide explained, "Once considered the ultimate in fine turf, a clover lawn is looked upon today by most authorities as not much better than a weed patch" (Carleton 1971, 49). Of course, whatever the reason for the shift away from the clover lawn, there can be no doubt that it redounded to the advantage of those companies such as Scotts that were involved in the fertilizer business. The death of clover meant an increased need for nitrogen-based fertilizer to restore the fertility that planting turfgrass robbed from the soil.

The rise of the perfect lawn was hardly the work of just one powerful company. Americans had their own reasons for embracing a monochromatic lawnscape. Chief among these was that lawn monoculture melded perfectly with the ethos of conformity so central to 1950s suburbia. This was a world where, according to one 1958 survey, a stunning 97 percent of Americans believed in God, a time when nearly everyone was married by their mid-twenties. "The suburb," wrote the sociologist David Riesman, "is like a fraternity house at a small college in which like-mindedness reverberates upon itself" (1958, 386). What better way to show your dedication to getting along than to cultivate grass, a plant that if mowed assiduously would replicate in clonelike fashion, making your front yard look precisely like Mr. Smith's lawn next door.

The obsessive concern with weeds, a hallmark of postwar lawn culture, testified to the power of a landscape aesthetic founded on conformity. And the weed to end all weeds during the cold war years was crabgrass—"public enemy No. 1" (*Chemical Week* 1951). It may be surprising to some to learn that crabgrass, the bane of lawn lovers everywhere today, was introduced in 1849 by the U.S. Patent Office—on purpose. Crabgrass is a forage crop and was imported to feed rising livestock populations. But its virtues were not widely publicized, and it seems to have generated little immediate interest. Then, in the late nineteenth century, immigrants from Poland reintroduced the crop, a form of millet, which they called "manna grits," a biblical reference to the food that appeared, miraculously, as the Israelites wandered through the wilderness on their flight from the land of Egypt (Mitch 1988, 114).

A weed, it has been said, is simply "a plant with a bad reputation" (*New York Times* 1915). Crabgrass's good name initially rested on its ability to grow rapidly and produce bumper yields. It also generated a huge number of seeds; a single plant can produce as many as 150,000 in temperate areas. Once war had been declared on the plant, however, its virtues as a prolific food and forage no longer mattered. Lawn aficionados tear their hair out over crabgrass because it branches out laterally, causing the mower blade to miss it. As a result, large mats of gray-green grass mar the look of the perfect front yard. A 1939 article in the *Washington Post* called crabgrass "the verdant embodiment of original sin" (*Washington Post* 1939).

Yet even as late as 1950, profound ambivalence existed over whether the fight against the alleged weed was worth all the trouble. In a spoof published in the *Saturday Evening Post* titled "I Love Crab Grass," the author tells of his obsessed neighbor, who employs "a fiendish notched steel creese" to yank out the crabgrass plants, gloating "over them as if they were uranium stockpiles." The poor crab "grassophobe" can't even drink a beer in peace, jumping up from his spot on the terrace "to get one more culm with his can opener." Asks the author: "Did you ever stop to think that the countless hours you spend on your lawn you could be spending with your wife and children?" (Knight 1950).

Ecologically speaking, Americans had lost the war on crabgrass before it had even started. Crabgrass is what is known as a warm-season grass. These species evolved out of cool-season grasses—such as Kentucky bluegrass, the dominant turf species in the 1950s because of its ability to stay green throughout most of the year. Forced to adapt across a diverse range of geographic locations, warm-season grasses like crabgrass have much more rugged metabolic systems than their cool-season counterparts. As a result, crabgrass is far better adapted to drought and high temperature than bluegrass and can continue to photosynthesize even in hot weather.

Just such weather blanketed the nation in the summer of 1959. As *Time* magazine wrote, "In Suburbia, where crab grass on a lawn can lower a man's status faster than a garbage can in his foyer, the prolific (up to 50,000 seeds a plant) weed has become a neighborhood problem, like juvenile delinquency." Meanwhile, the people at Scotts could not have been more delighted. "We're almost embarrassed," said one Scotts salesman. "If we ordered the weather, it couldn't be better for our business" (*Time* 1959).

Scotts benefited from more than simply the weather. Mowing practices also contributed to the crabgrass problem. The GI haircut was about the worst thing to happen to the lawn in its brief history on this continent. Keeping grass below three inches, much less the one and a half inches or lower recommended by everyone from Abraham Levitt to the Scotts company itself, traumatizes the grass plants, opening them to disease. Cutting the grass short also interferes with root growth and is like unplugging the plant's refrigerator, where it stores its food. And then there is the effect that mowing low has on evaporation, as the scalped grass fails to protect the soil from the sun's rays, increasing the need for more watering. But when it comes to weeds like crabgrass, repeated close mowings are an invitation to disaster.

The ecology behind the lowering of mowing height and the rise of crabgrass is as follows. In order to germinate, the crabgrass seed must be exposed to sunlight. The shorter the grass, the more likely that is to happen. In other words, keeping the grass at three and a half inches would have made the entire crabgrass problem vanish. Combine this trend toward lower grass heights with developments in weed control and you have a prescription for one huge crabgrass party. Simply put, the rising popularity of 2,4-D eliminated broad-leaved weeds like dandelions and chickweed from the lawn and, because the chemical was useless against crabgrass, made it all the more noticeable. At the very least, crabgrass became the new frontier in weed control after broad-leaved weeds had been conquered.

Instead of holding off on the 2,4-D or, even better, simply going out to the garage and raising up their mowers, Americans plunged headfirst into a giant chemical orgy. By the mid-1950s "preemergent" herbicides entered the market to fend off the crabgrass problem. Scotts, for example, began selling Halts in 1958, a preemergent that used chlordane as the active ingredient. Other companies offered similar products. Suddenly the lawn-care market took one giant step forward.

Preemergent herbicides are the lawn-care equivalent, in military parlance, of a preemptive strike. The philosophy behind preemergents is to treat the problem, as the name suggests, before it happens. Rather than sell consumers postemergent products to clear up a case of bona fide crabgrass, Scotts and others in the green industry simply impressed on Americans the need to add an additional step to their lawn-care regime: another trip around the lawn, early in the spring, to deal with a problem that they might not even have. Preemergents radically expanded the demand for lawn-care products at a time when market saturation, combined with a recession in 1957, led manufacturers forever back to the drawing board to dream up new ways to get Americans to buy things.

In 1961, one brave soul at the U.S. Department of Agriculture revealed preemergents as little more than a clever marketing ploy. "Most homeowners," he explained, "don't need crab grass killers; they simply need to take better care of their lawns. . . . Makers of weed killers are abusing the public with claims about their products, and usually people are simply wasting money by buying them" (*Chemical Week* 1961).

The Cold War Lawn

Notwithstanding the rise of preemergent herbicides, crabgrass continued to dominate public consciousness. "How do you stand on crabgrass?" Senator Kennedy was asked by a reporter in a 1960 televised appearance (Weston 1960). The following year, *Time* again reported on the problem. "Short of atom-bombing one's lawn (or one's neighbor's), the only way to fight this infiltration is to get down and pluck." Some people simply gave up. John Klein, a "labor unionist" from Berkeley, California, in an un-American moment, tore out his grass and planted ivy, much to the horror of his neighbors (*Time* 1961).

In 1962, ten days before the Cuban missile crisis, after a summer of drought and crabgrass infestations galore, *Life* magazine ran an article that made plain how cold war paranoia impinged on the suburban landscape. The article told the story of a fellow whose lawn consisted of Merion bluegrass, a popular species of turfgrass at the time, and his neighbor, Fred Morgew, who was putting the finishing touches on his "Five Year Plan of Landscape Reform." The reform consisted of planting crabgrass.

Despite differing lawn philosophies, the two neighbors together worked hard to put down an invasion of dandelions, an evil, apparently, in the eyes of free people and communists alike. Only when Mr. Bluegrass, as we will call him, lets his peach tree violate Mr. Morgew's airspace does all-out war ensue, as Morgew kills the tree. "All this made the cold war between us grow warmer," writes Mr. Bluegrass. To deal with the heat, both sides go out and buy grass killer ("the ultimate weapon," the man at the garden store assures our protagonist), entering into a state of mutually assured lawn destruction. "Then this last summer," writes Mr. Bluegrass, "long before the expected winter withering, I happened to glance across Morgew's spite fence and saw that great patches of his crab-grass lawn had turned an ugly purplish-brown." Soon thereafter the fence came down. "A little later I was mystified to discover a dozen or so small circular holes in my Merion lawn, as though sample plugs had been taken away" (Snell 1962, 25). Americans had lost China, but in the battle of the backyards, bluegrass could be made to triumph over the gray-green menace. And yet, the spoof is of course poking fun at the obsession with yard conformity, suggesting a level of frustration with the perfect lawn imperative. Perhaps Americans had a little Mr. Morgew in them after all.

Still, the lawn proved central during the cold war years to the American way of life. It tapped into the higher standards of cleanliness—reflected in the sales of everything from room fresheners to garbage disposers—that dominated the home in the postwar period and served as a bulwark against the dirty communist way (Hoy 1995, 170). All the energy postwar Americans spent cultivating their lawns and gardens might also have been their way of taking control over one small aspect of their lives in a world hanging under the threat of nuclear catastrophe. As an article in *Parents* magazine explained: "Youngsters want to grasp what little security they can in a world gone frighteningly insecure. The youngsters feel they will cultivate the one security that's possible—their own gardens" (Gilman 1958).

Men, in particular, may have found in the lawn an antidote to the dilemmas of postwar work and family life. These men—the salaried managers, technicians, and academics, the "organization men" in William Whyte's immortal words—spent their days suppressing whatever competitive and aggressive desires they had for the sake of the larger good of the corporate entity. In their time off they were expected to behave like model consumers—formerly a role almost exclusively reserved for women—buying the very things that in 1959 Vice President Richard Nixon told Soviet premier Nikita Khrushchev made America superior to Russia. Getting along with others, loyalty to one's superiors, taking responsibility for household purchases—these were the values, feminine ones at the time thought to be, that men had to internalize to succeed in the Fordist economy (Corber 1997, 5–6). The beauty of the lawn was that it allowed men, on the one hand, to indulge such feminine impulses, nurturing the grass with every product imaginable while showing that they could not just keep up with the Joneses but could get along with them too, and, on the other hand, to head out into the yard every week and act out their male fantasies for self-assertion, rooted in an earlier tradition of rugged individualism, by firing up the power mower and cutting down the grass.

Throwing oneself into lawn care—a perpetual cycle of nurturance and domestic violence—not only meshed well with the needs of consumerism; it may also have functioned as a form of therapy that allowed men to experience the sense of control missing from their jobs. If life at the office entailed an occasional dressing down from one's superior, at least Dad could come home and wheel out the Lawn Boy, Dandy Boy, or Lazy Boy—brand-name mowers available in the fifties—and show the world who was in charge of the yard (Jenkins 1994, 128). As a 1958 ad exclaimed: "You're the boss when you buy a LAWN-BOY" (*Life* 1958).

A university professor in Chicago named William C. French once tried to come to grips with his father's incredible obsession with lawn care. He wrote:

> Perhaps what drove him in this crusade during those years was fear at the chaos of world events—World War II, Korea, the nuclear arms race, assassinations, Vietnam. Perhaps my father was frustrated in his job as a research engineer working on the first American guided missile system and, later, on hydraulics problems. Perhaps he was angry at his boss. Why else the weekly migraines? At least we could control the crabgrass. (French 1989, 421)

Conclusion

While the concept of the lawn dates to the sixteenth century, the perfect turf ideal is, in the United States at least, a notion that goes back little more than fifty years. The rise of the lawn to dominance across America involved the eclipse of regional and local landscape ideals and their replacement with turfgrass species as part of a standardized approach to yard care. Feagan and Ripmeester, who have studied the sociology of lawns just north of the U.S. border in the Niagara region of Canada, have argued that the lawn became, by the latter part of the twentieth century, an "ideologically naturalized landscape." Lawns moved "from a possible way of organizing space to the way it should or must be organized" (Feagan and Ripmeester 1999, 620). Robbed of any historical contingency, lawns seem utterly logical and natural when, in fact, they are the product of a set of forces unique to post-1945 life.

"Modern environments and experiences," Marshall Berman has written, "cut across all boundaries of geography and ethnicity, of class and nationality, of religion and ideology: in this sense, modernity can be said to unite all mankind" (1982, 15). Perhaps the lawn qualifies as the quintessentially modern landscape, though the existence today of such groups as Citizens Against Lawn Mower Madness and the Wild Ones, organizations that oppose the reigning turf culture, suggests that the lawn inspires as much conflict as it does unification. But, still, it does seem plausible that all the energy postwar Americans have spent domesticating their lawns might well be their way of taking control over one small aspect of their lives in a world where "all that is solid melts into air." In a culture founded on creative destruction, a place where expressways have risen up on the ashes of once vibrant communities, where the legacy of people like Robert Moses weighs so heavily on the landscape, obsessing over the lawn may be one way "to make ourselves at home in a constantly changing world," a means of clinging to control in a society hanging under the threat of nuclear weaponry and dominated by corporations and impersonal bureaucracy (Berman 1982, 6). Organization Man at least could mow his lawn in peace.

X Footprint Metaphor and Metabolic Realities

Environmental Impacts of
Medieval European Cities

Richard C. Hoffmann

T HE FOOTPRINT IS A powerful image for human presence in the land-scape, whether on Robinson Crusoe's desert island or around today's anthropomorphized planet.[1] In current parlance the impression of the human foot has come to symbolize the impact of human activities on their surroundings, for everything that humans—or any other species—do influences other organisms and the nonliving environment. A zone of relatively dense mutual material interactions between living and nonliving things is called an ecosystem. In each of these a flow of energy leads to the exchange of materials between living and nonliving components, so the assemblage tends to act as a unit.[2] Whether human beings know it or not, all participate in ecosystems. Indeed one way to think about environmental history is as an exploration of dynamic relationships over time between human societies and cultures and the natural systems with which those people interacted. How, in a specified historical context, did humans set their footprints on the environment and in turn react to its changes, whether autonomous or in response to human action?

Looking at the European Middle Ages, an environmental historian might then seek to apprehend dynamic relationships between some thousand years of human experience and the natural systems with which those people engaged. Among other major developments during this period, the formation and spread of towns and cities in Europe from around the year 1000 laid the foundation for urban culture and exchange economies still prevalent on the western subcontinent today. Indeed sociocultural life and market development have long been the principal focus of medieval urban history, so scholars are well aware and a good deal is known of power relationships, social stratification, and the multifarious personal and economic networks linking townspeople to their rural surroundings.[3] Among other topics, issues of social and economic exploitation traditionally shaped historical debate over the "parasitic" relation of preindustrial cities to their hinterlands, that is, the extent to which those cities contributed to or merely drained off the productive forces of their societies.[4]

Less commonly acknowledged by urban historians is that this new (for medieval Europe) form of human settlement and economic life had environmental consequences or, at least, poses certain ecological puzzles. Some neglect may derive from the contempt with which humanist medievalists commonly regard things of nature, and some may be explained by the analytical dissolution of the very concept of urbanism. Thomas Glick has reasonably laid just that charge against Peregrine Horden and Nicholas Purcell's important recent blockbuster, *The Corrupting Sea: A Study of Mediterranean History,* and the chosen target of those authors, Fernand Braudel.[5] While Braudel's cities simply performed less as human communities than as nodes of communication,[6] Horden and Purcell argue openly that historic urban centers lack ecological distinction and are to be understood "as 'epiphenomenal' to larger ecological processes."[7]

Scholars more focused on environmental relations have subsumed medieval urban centers under the "overshoot" paradigm. J. Donald Hughes presented Florence as the epitome of medieval Europe's economic expansion beyond ecological limits and subsequent collapse.[8] John Broich advanced a more nuanced microscopic approach to the urban question in "The Wasting of Wolin: Environmental Factors in the Downfall of a Medieval Baltic Town,"[9] arguing that inhabitants of the tenth-century port so depleted their home island's resources of timber, grain, and soil that they could not overcome eleventh-century insecurity in external sources of supply. Broich thus rediscovered for the obscure Baltic entrepôt what Hughes had earlier argued with respect to classical Athens, namely, that cities with an unbalanced relationship to local ecosystems must later affect and become more reliant upon landscapes at greater distance.[10]

Hughes subsequently generalized his analysis in an essay on "the preindustrial city as ecosystem."[11] His chosen nomenclature thus argued that people in an urban community functioned in a distinctively structured relationship with their immediate surroundings, while the urban system itself necessarily maintained further links to other ecosystems, near and far, by cycling energy and materials throughout a region. But, Hughes continued, urban culture typically separated city dwellers from natural systems, obscured their intimate interdependencies, and left people oblivious to unsustainabilities. Regrettably, an ensuing debate between Hughes and Yves Lenoir again dissolved cities into the question of sustainability for medieval European civilization as a whole,[12] leaving the problem of medieval urban environmental impacts unresolved.

By most accounts medieval cities did establish within their limits a new ecological form, a new human environment of their own. Physical landscape, material infrastructures, microclimates, human densities, and even the mix of other fauna and flora distinguished cities from rural agricultural settlements, castles, and monastic communities.[13] But to what extent did medieval urbanism more broadly affect European ecosystems and, to revert to the present-day imagery, did cities set their "footprints" on the medieval landscape?

The issue here confronted, then, is the environmental impact of medieval European urbanism, considered as a historical problem and as a potential benchmark for comparisons with other preindustrial and present-day conditions. The plainly *inter*disciplinary quality of this question doubly affects what is attempted in this chapter. There is a direct, if limited, engagement with theory, with the potential historical usefulness of ways students of contemporary environmental relations conceptualize, measure, and explain relevant phenomena. Just as economic or social theory has helped historians frame questions about the past, ideas from environmental studies invite application and hence testing, to the extent they can be deployed in extant historical evidence. At the same time the subject has relevance for and so must be made accessible to several potential audiences. General historians need to acknowledge the interplay of natural and human forces in the past and elements of both continuity and change between more recent and more distant pasts in the material—dare I say ecological?—conditions of life. Concepts arising from current environmental research should be put to the test against a greater variety of human experience over more than the most recent century or two. Medievalists can usefully recognize that the development of urban communities was not just beneficial or socially important but imposed costs on the human and natural environment. Each specialist's perspective gains understanding from the others.

Hence the following discussion undertakes two successive tasks. First it examines a popular new theoretical approach to human environmental impact, the "ecological footprint" (EF) established during the 1990s by William E. Rees and his followers. As EF methodology appears to offer cross-temporal comparison of urban ecological relations, its application to medieval cities might promise a better grasp of their situation as well as a longer view on modern development and the concepts used to understand it. Closer consideration of EF's purposes and the response of critics reveals, however, important limitations for historical use, while broader application of principles behind EF suggests a "metabolic" approach to resource use, the ensuing flow of materials, and the disturbances to landscapes that arise from that flow. Unlike EF the concept of urban metabolism has operational value for historical research, identifying data worth gathering and relating the findings to larger issues of environmental impact and sustainability. After this chapter so establishes its conceptual direction, its remaining parts investigate first medieval urban consumption demand and then waste disposal in terms of materials documentably moving into and out of certain medieval cities and the evident results of those movements in specific and identifiable extraurban landscapes. Medieval European cities were not without observable effects on much larger ecosystems, though the shape and quality of those "footprints" could differ considerably from industrial and postindustrial experience.

From Metaphor to Method

At least in the published scholarly record, William E. Rees coined the term "ecological footprint" in a 1992 article on urban economics, using it to label the land area required to sustain a population. Cities, he pointed out, typically consume the productive capacity of a space much greater than their buildings or political boundaries cover.[14] As already remarked, the inherent metaphor is simple and intuitive, an image of environmental use by a human community. The academic concept was elaborated and articulated during 1994–96 in the PhD thesis of Mathis Wackernagel, a student of Rees, and in a book and articles that the two published together and separately.[15] The EF is meant to be an indicator of aggregate human consumption levels (the land resources needed to produce mean per capita consumption times population size) compared to biological carrying capacity (measured by the space occupied by the community in question). Engaged and policy-oriented environmentalists promptly seized upon EF methodology as a seemingly concrete and comprehensive tool to assess sustainability and to plan development at national, regional, and urban scales: for instance, at average Canadian consumption levels the 2.5 million people on Toronto's 630 square kilometers require about 181,000 square kilometers, an EF roughly 290 times the space of their city.[16] Meanwhile a wave of scholarly interest gathered, especially in the journal *Ecological Economics*, where a 1997 article by Wackernagel and Rees was followed by one response in 1998, five in 1999, thirteen in 2000 (mostly in a special issue devoted to the subject), five more in 2001, and yet another in 2002.

Critics took exception to the "false concreteness" and misleading comprehensiveness of converting mean national or regional consumption levels into land area now needed to produce those resources plus, in this age of fossil fuels, the biomass necessary for either equivalent energy or absorbing the carbon released by fossil combustion.[17] The concept of carrying capacity is itself contingent, so calculations based on prevailing technologies soon lose historical comparability. Indeed in a time-series calculated for just one country during only the twentieth century, differing assumptions on yields varied results by a factor of two and more.[18] Even if EF calculation becomes conventional, interpretation remains in dispute: sustainability is not the same as self-sufficiency within a given terrain; all cities draw support from a hinterland beyond their physical limits.[19] Continued debate has not deterred social scientists and activists from using EF methodology for comparative measurement of present-day aggregate environmental impact.[20]

Contributions from the periphery of the EF debate may be more willing to adapt the conventional EF analysis to observable complex realities. Writing in *Ecosystems* in 2001, the ecologist Matthew Luck and his colleagues stressed the regional scale of most urban ecological interactions, most notably the supply of resources and assimilation of wastes, and argued from study of the twenty largest U.S. cities for the spatial heterogeneity of the actual footprint.[21] In other words, particular regional ecosystems, not undifferentiated space, absorb the impact of urban resource use. More recently the physicists Richard Wood and Manfred Lenzen declared EF educational but analytically impractical "because it does not reveal where impacts really occur, what the nature and severity of these impacts are and how these impacts compare with the self-repair capability of the respective ecosystem." To assess the real sustainability of institutional consumption they turned to "a hybrid ecological footprint approach," measuring the land actually disturbed by consumption after an input-output analysis backtracked resource use through the production process.[22] Creative responses such as these take the EF concept back to its basic principles, namely, that (1) all activities require resources; (2) resource use must be traced through the supply chain to original acquisition; and (3) resource acquisition disturbs land (ecosystems).[23]

In the same vein, when the environmental historian John McNeill grasped the footprint idea to track even the most recent past, he reverted to its urban application and to its symbolic core: "The Footprints and Metabolisms of Cities" headlines environmental analysis of twentieth-century urbanization, and "The space needed to support a city and to absorb its wastes is, *metaphorically speaking,* its ecological footprint" (emphasis added).[24] McNeill's discussion moves from literal urban space—physical density and sprawl—to urban metabolism, the flow of materials and energy between every city and its hinterlands, drawing on Stephen Boyden's now classic study of Hong Kong and, in particular, its daily import of freshwater and export of human excrement,[25] and recognizing like movements of building materials, food, fuel, and the like. Meanwhile Boyden himself derived a simple model of urban metabolism and linked it successively to the biotic system and to human culture (fig. 10.1).[26] As McNeill demonstrates, the metaphorical footprint is no longer a disembodied index calculated from inferred averages but the observable ecological consequences elsewhere of urban activities.

McNeill argues that twentieth-century urbanization, together with explosive growth in human numbers, broke sharply with the past, driving environmental changes far beyond urban boundaries through two principal mechanisms: pollution and land use change.[27] Effluents from and inputs for urban metabolic processes shaped specific landscapes at ever greater distances. McNeill (and the research he acknowledges) thus

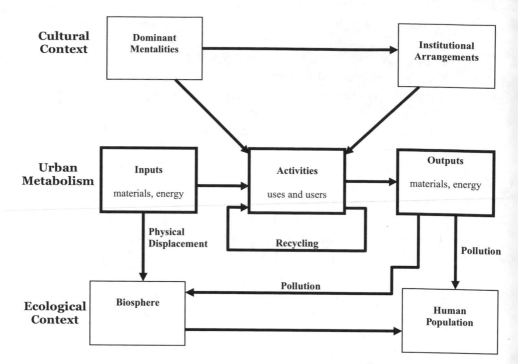

Fig. 10.1. Urban metabolism in cultural and ecological context (adapted from Boyden 2001).

transforms the footprint into a metaphorical label for a set of *ecological* relationships between cities and their surroundings. These relations (and not necessarily other urban activities) are specified in real metabolic processes that, given the requisite sources, historians can trace. His findings restore ecological substance to the city as a focus of inquiry within broader scholarly contexts. The metabolic approach enlarges recognition of the city as ecosystem well beyond the overshoot paradigm, while assessing sustainability within systemic rather than political or spatial limits.

For historians of preindustrial urbanisms the challenge is finding comparable relationships in a deeper past. What earlier experiences with cities in their ecosystems have qualities distinct from those of today, which differ quantitatively, which are effectively parallel?

The present chapter reconnects medieval urban culture to physical and biological realities by tracking historical metabolic links to specific extraurban systems and thus the urban footprints (plural) on them. It demonstrates our ability to map the diffuse, differentiated, and sometimes disparate impact of providing calories and proteins and energy to people in medieval towns and absorbing their wastes. A generation of economic historians and historical geographers studied how and to what extent the medieval European "rural world . . . was converted to serving the needs of city populations"[28] through research into urban hinterlands and trading networks. Their findings often need only "translation" into ecological terms, to identify concrete imprints of consumption and waste disposal by people in specific medieval cities. In metabolic terms— as Boyden, Luck, Woods, and others suggest—historians can identify the flow of materials and specific patterns of disturbance arising along the supply chain, gauge their order of magnitude, and, on rare occasions, measure them more precisely. The intent is to frame an indicative rather than comprehensive account of the phenomenon. Culturally based limits common to sources from the Middle Ages inhibit quantitative analysis (and so hamper any global indicator or comparative function); but the evidence establishes particular anthropogenic landscapes as resulting from material actions of medieval townspeople.[29]

Relationships we call urban metabolism, the intimate physical connection between medieval townsfolk's consumption and goods from outside, were well known to merchants, city authorities, and even some contemporary thinkers. After study at the cathedral school in Prague and the arts faculty at Padua, the Austrian monk Engelbert of Admont calculated in about 1287 that it took four regional agricultural producers to feed each nonfarmer.[30] From every town traders went out to get foods and raw materials they could sell to their neighbors: London corn mongers, for instance, bought wheat and oats in 1295 at manors and rural markets in Berkshire, Oxfordshire, Kent, and Essex.[31] Municipal rulers sought cheap abundance of food and fuel by actively encouraging flows from outside city walls. Governments of Cremona and Parma were subsidizing grain imports by the early thirteenth century, and anyone who brought grain to Orvieto was exempt from tax.[32] A 1408 ordinance opened Kraków's market to all who came with fish to sell, while Madrid contracted with wholesalers for exclusive shipment of fish and meat.[33] Such urban provisioning policies are a long-standing cliché of medieval economic history. The task here, however, is to combine written sources and material remains to pin down where certain towns actually drew essential inputs and to ascertain the effects these flows had on producing ecosystems. A subsequent section of the chapter then does the same with outflows of urban waste into surrounding landscapes. A comparative benchmark throughout will be current and careful scholarly estimates of urban populations and settled areas at their medieval maxima around 1300 and/or later troughs or distinctive points of further growth (fig. 10.2).

Feeding the Townspeople

Historians agree that medieval Europeans obtained most of their calories from cereals and that protein supplements, meat and fish, were more than otherwise consumed by elites and townspeople and generally during the post-1348 population trough when real income levels were higher than before. Acknowledging effects of social stratification, then, case studies of grain, meat, and fish consumption from several cities identify different patterns of impact on extramural landscapes.

Cereals comprised the largest continual flow of biomass into urban systems. Dietary studies from both sides of the Alps suggest mean annual consumption in the order of 300–500 liters (250–375 kilograms) per capita, with much of the variance arising from heavy consumption of ale, not wine, in northern regions. Findings include or exclude cereals for consumption by urban livestock, mainly horses, depending on locality.

The 80,000–100,000 inhabitants of London in about 1300 are thought by researchers in the Belfast-London "Feeding the City" project (whose findings I here exploit and reinterpret) to have consumed an annual 34,000–35,000 metric tons (165,000 quarters at 281.9 liters) of grain for food, drink, and animal feed.[34] Given production techniques in the surrounding ten-county area, this quantity represented a yield, after deduction for seed, of 43,000–65,000 hectares (106,000–170,000 acres), or some ten to fifteen percent of the land growing grain in that region each year.[35] As a benchmark for modern comparison, this footprint of land where London actually took grain covered 150–225 times the city's area.

Most of London's grain came to market through efforts of corn mongers in an extended but largely contiguous hinterland.[36] Price data, known contacts of corn mongers, and records of sales from demesne farms identify a grainshed of some 4,000 square miles (10,360 square

	Area (hectares)	Estimated Populations (in thousands) ca. 1300	later
London	288	80–100	50 ca. 1400
Paris	237–437 in 1364/80	200	100 ca. 1500
Ghent	644	56	25 ca. 1400
Bruges	430	30	20 ca. 1400
Antwerp	352	17	40–60 ca. 1500/20
Köln	320–97	40	
Strasbourg	270	25	
Nürnberg	138	14	36 by 1500
Vienna	170–80	20	
Florence	630	100	40 in 1427
Venice	324	100	85 in 1424, 105 in 1509

Sources: Josiah C. Russell, *Medieval Regions and Their Cities* (Bloomington: Indiana University Press, 1972); Jan de Vries, *European Urbanization 1500–1800* (Cambridge, Mass.: Harvard University Press, 1984), Bruce M. S. Campbell, James A. Galloway, Derek Keene, and Margaret Murphy, *A Medieval Capital and Its Grain Supply* (Belfast and London: Historical Geography Research Group, 1993), 43–45; David Herlihy and Christiane Klapisch–Zuber, *Tuscans and Their Families* (New Haven: Yale University Press, 1985); David Nicholas, *The Growth of the Medieval City from Late Antiquity to the Early Fourteenth Century* (London: Longman, 1997), 275–90; David Nicholas, *The Later Medieval City, 1300–1500* (London: Longman, 1997), 51–53.

Fig. 10.2. The scale of some medieval cities.

kilometers) (fig. 10.3), effectively delimited by the combined costs of production and transport (fig. 10.3). The area extended along the Thames from above the head of navigation at Henley some 250 kilometers to small ports in East Anglia and south Kent, but rarely more than 30 kilometers overland from the city or water access. In that space the London market exerted decisive influence—although Kent also shipped grain overseas—and caused agricultural intensification (applying additional labor and capital per land area) to modify ecosystems beyond what was required to support local lords and peasants. Since Londoners comprised 14 percent of the regional population but took 15–20 percent of the grain available for consumption there,[37] flows to the city could be held responsible for some 25 percent more grain production than was otherwise to be expected. Productivity levels achieved on demesne farms in southeastern England around 1300 suggest that London's consumption approached contemporary limits of sustainability. "Feeding the City" authors convincingly show that "ecology"—by which they mean soil type—was a minor factor compared to the urban market in shaping agricultural decisions.[38] The economic historians miss, however, the equally clear and almost measurable ecological effects of those market-

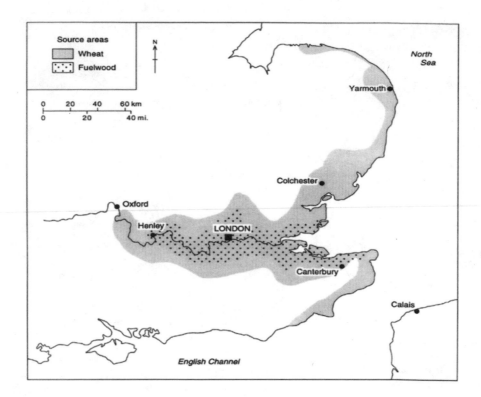

Fig. 10.3. Sources of supply for London, ca. 1300: wheat and fuelwood.

driven decisions that directed flows of biomass and nutrients well away from the arable fields and intensified human transformation of the land-scape.[39]

To the regionally formed footprint of cereal flows to London, people in northern Europe's densest medieval urban agglomeration in Flanders and Brabant added a long-distance component. Led by Ghent's 56,000 residents and the 30,000 or more at Bruges, well over 200,000 city dwellers filled that area around 1300. Rebound after a mid-fourteenth-century decline and then still further urbanization made for nearly a half million people in about 1500, forty percent of the population in Flanders, Brabant, and Holland. Published estimates of per capita grain consumption here vary greatly, but Richard Unger asserts that an annual total urban demand of 225,000 metric tons is "far from generous."[40] With allowance for seed, late medieval Flemish agriculture could grow this quantity from 625,000 hectares of arable land, much less than the land area of the three provinces. Still both before the mid-1200s and for a century again after the Black Death, urban consumers normally relied on a regional supply network reaching far into neighboring Artois, Picardy, and Hainault. Careful local research could likely recapture economic and environmental consequences of that steady relationship, a parallel to London's.

Between about 1250 and 1340, however, local shortfalls or marginal insufficiency evidently drew supplies from at least one distant landscape, for German merchants organized a flow of grain down the Elbe to Hamburg and thence coastwise to Flanders.[41] We cannot yet measure the share of Flemish needs so met nor its weight relative to regional production. But in the late thirteenth century rural landholders with easy access to the Elbe in Altmark Brandenburg replaced money rents from peasant tenants with dues in cereals and managed their own small demesne farms for the same export product.[42] Only after the 1350s, when shrunken Low Countries towns no longer needed more grain than the adjacent region could supply and cereal prices fell, did Altmark's landowners parcel out those demesnes to rent-paying tenants. And then interruptions in commercial traffic from Hamburg no longer affected prices and supply in Flanders.

There is little need here to detail the well-known post-1460 resurgence of northern grain shipments—now especially out of Poland's central Wisła basin via Gdańsk, which exported more than 10,000 tons a year by 1500—to revived urban markets of the Low Countries. At that time price correlations not earlier possible confirm the integration of cereal markets from the Baltic westward to Antwerp and its environs.[43] One market for a basic article of human diet and principal component of an agroecosystem linked ecologies hundreds of kilometers apart.

With due regard for different climatic and cultural expectations, Dante Alighieri's one hundred thousand fellow Florentines—and less than half so many in the 1420s—called, like their Flemish counterparts, on local and more distant sources of cereals. Early fourteenth-century reporters imply annual per capita consumption of about 256 liters of bread grain and sales of all cereals reaching about 315 liters per person.[44] Drinking wine instead of ale made a noticeable difference. Florentine totals thus came to 19,250 and 23,700 metric tons a year. While I am aware of no attempts to turn these figures into the output of agricultural acreage, present-day scholars and contemporary observers concur that domestic Tuscan production met but half of the city's needs[45] and the remainder (10,000 metric tons per annum?) came from Apulia and Sicily. Economic devolution of those regions into latifundia—vast agricultural enterprises hiring labor from peasant sharecropper families—since the mid-thirteenth century is commonly understood in part as a response to urban demand from the north.[46] Distinctive southern landscapes bore the imprint of urban consumption needs.

Distant rural ecosystems were even more plainly shaped by late medieval city dwellers' demand for meat, notably beef. Meat was never absent from medieval European diets, though it nowhere served as the principal source of calories and was eaten as much for reasons of taste and social prestige as for nutritional purposes. Large consumption of meat by the wealthy of the early and high Middle Ages spread down the social scale with increased per capita wealth after the 1350s. Towns-people in the fifteenth and early sixteenth centuries ate more meat per capita than Europeans would again before the late nineteenth century: 50 kilograms a year in Hamburg, 47 in southern German towns, and even 26 at Carpentras, for Mediterranean consumption was typically less than in the north. For Nürnberg or Vienna this came to 1,000 and more metric tons dressed weight. Köln's thirty thousand human inhabitants slaughtered six to eight thousand head of cattle each year in the 1490s.[47] Even with surplus arable land converted to pasture in the late fourteenth and fifteenth centuries, these numbers outran local production in the mixed farming regions of western Europe.

Urban demand in particular prompted export-oriented cattle production in three areas of eastern and northern Europe. Known even since the late thirteenth century were the droves from Hungary,[48] and they were the largest, too, with more than ten thousand head going yearly to Venice in about 1500 and more than fifty thousand to Austria and across southern Germany even so far as Strasbourg. As an anonymous Nürnberger said in 1518, from Hungary "the whole of Germany was provided with meat."[49] In fact, for most of the fifteenth century German consumers north of the Main were chiefly supplied by cattle producers in Masovia and parts of Great Poland, who shipped through Poznań. Meanwhile beef eaters in northwestern Germany, the Rhineland, and

Low Countries dined on animals from the open woodlands and pastures of southern Scandinavia. These moved through Schleswig to fatten in marsh pastures of northwestern Germany, then walked on to their fate. Insignificant Danish exports before 1450 went over ten thousand head by 1480 and later multiplied again. Central and western European urban populations thus depended on northern and eastern suppliers of beef.

Northern beef, like traditional western production, was mainly steers culled from peasant draft and dairy stock, but on the Hungarian *puszta* semiwild herds of distinctively large gray steppe cattle grazed an open range of natural semiarid continental grasslands. Yearly Hungarian exports around 1500 comprised only five to seven percent of a national herd estimated at three million head but earned more than half the country's export account.[50] At an average live weight over 300 kilograms, the sixty thousand head that left Hungary each year composed a biomass of more than 18,000 metric tons.

Flows of cattle to central European towns left physical footprints on drove routes and large metaphorical footprints on landscapes at their origin. As growing numbers of Danish animals shifted from traditional forest forage to open pasture and meadows, they occupied more land than did the country's arable but left it impoverished. The environmental historian Thorkild Kjærgaard blames overgrazing and the long-term transfer of nutrients away from pasture land (removal of animals, manure, hay, and turf) for the loss of fertility, sand drift, and bog formation that marked the deep ecological crisis of early modern Denmark.[51] On the Hungarian open range the animals themselves were changed. Recent archaeozoological findings indicate that distinctive Hungarian Grey cattle—long horned, rangy, pale in color—emerged only at the end of the Middle Ages as a consequence of large-scale grazing to meet rising export demand.[52] Sustaining carnivorous urban metabolisms set a strong imprint on distant ecosystems.

As much as medieval elites enjoyed eating meat, cultural rules of varying severity forbade this food some days every week and several whole weeks every year. On about 135 days, a third of the year, Latin Christians could eat fish in lieu of banned flesh. Then the same people who could afford regular meat reluctantly consumed relatively more expensive creatures from the water. Wealthy Paris, with two hundred thousand inhabitants in about 1300 the biggest urban market in western Christendom, makes a telling example of what this meant for aquatic

systems. Total or per capita consumption of fish is not now to be calculated, but medieval writers were astonished by the city's appetite for it:
one concluded simply, "Paris is a bottomless pit."[53] And the origins of
what people poured into that pit can be established.

Numbers of medieval recipe collections, menus, and cookbooks are
closely associated with Paris.[54] Used with caution they offer one perspective on what middle- and upper-class Parisians thought they might
eat. Dating between the 1280s and the Black Death (1347–51) are five or
more such documents (depending on how you count redactions), each
naming fourteen to forty-two fish varieties.[55] Unlike earlier dietary lists
(of nonurban origin), these are dominated by marine organisms (43–80
percent) but still include creatures from freshwater. Nearly all make several references to herring—both fresh and preserved in some way—and
to fresh cod, but varieties foreign to northwest European continental
and inshore waters are rare, with only occasional mention of carp (a
Balkan native) and one passing reference to dried cod (stockfish, a sub-
arctic product). Three further Parisian lists of fishes to eat date from the
late fourteenth to the mid-fifteenth century.[56] Their twenty-five to forty-
eight named taxa average two-thirds marine species and one-third those
native to or migratory in freshwater. In this second group of sources herring and cod, now often including stockfish recipes, are prominent.[57]

The later set of written records from Paris overlaps in time with rich
archaeological evidence, notably the fish remains recovered from
kitchen middens of rue Fromenteau, an elite urban neighborhood beside
the Louvre (fig. 10.4). Thousands of identified bones there fall into two
temporal periods, circa 1400 and circa 1525, and into several ecological
groups.[58] In the earlier time (coinciding with the second group of cookbooks and menus), fresh marine fishes (including cods) formed a solid
majority (about 55 percent), followed by herring, freshwater fishes
(including carp), and preserved cod. Just over a century later (when
there are no recipe collections *firmly* associated with Paris), remains of
preserved cod and of carp (each almost 30 percent) surpassed those of
fresh marine fishes (about 25 percent), herring remained common, and
wild freshwater fishes had nearly vanished. Dining expectations and
food wastes thus corroborate patterns of fish consumption at Paris
slowly shifting toward marine, even distant marine, habitats.[59]

The fishes named in recipes and scraped into the garbage mark the
engagement of late medieval Parisian consumers with distinct aquatic

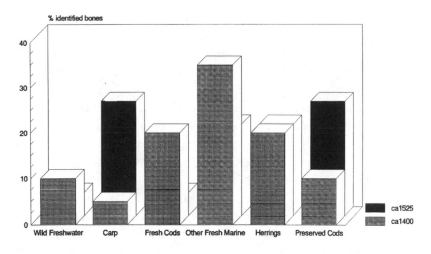

Fig. 10.4. Fishes eaten at late medieval Paris: remains from the rue Fromenteau.

and marine ecosystems, near and distant, natural and artificial, each tapped by a distinctive supply network. Wild freshwater and migratory fishes—gudgeon, pike, trout, shad—were taken from nearby royal or private waters by licenced artisans (*pescheurs du Seine, pêcheurs à verge,* and others). They or their wives peddled the fresh catch daily at designated locations in Paris.[60] The exotic carp, first known in northern France after 1200, were less likely wild than cultured in the confined or even fully artificial private ponds that had since the twelfth century proliferated in former wetlands along the Oise or Seine and in Sologne south of Orleans. Landholders, outside merchants, or domestic *poissonniers d'eau douce* transported these hardy animals alive in riverboats or wagons to the Paris market.

Getting fresh marine fishes to Paris, 150 kilometers from salt water, challenged medieval technical ingenuity and political clout. By sometime before 1250 a system of fast pack horse relays, the *chassé-marée,* outfitted with salt-filled panniers and protected by royal privileges, provided service overland in twenty-four to thirty-six hours from the nearest Norman ports. Complex brokerage schemes for distribution and price-fixing expedited a cargo that the *poissonniers de poisson de mer* then had one more day to sell in warm months and two days in cool ones.[61] Their shops offered wealthy customers a wide choice of inshore marine species native to the "Sleeve," including fresh cod, mackerel, and herring in season.

Herring are a pelagic fish that forms large seasonal spawning concentrations in certain estuaries and in open waters of the coastal Atlantic. Medieval Europeans devised methods for salting (eighth through tenth centuries) and brining (thirteenth through fourteenth centuries) to exploit abundant North Sea and Baltic stocks. By these means late summer and fall catches of these quick-spoiling oily creatures were kept and shipped for consumption in late winter as the quintessential Lenten food of the poor (including servants in households like those on rue Fromenteau). Preserved fish could save the expense of the *chassé-marée,* so bundled or barreled herring arrived overland by cart from Picard and Flemish ports and even more—some five tons or thirty million fish in 1321—by barge up the meandering Seine. Householders bought in bulk from *poissonniers de mer* or specialized salt-fish mongers, while hungry individuals might gulp down a single salty or sour little fish from a poor woman *harengère* hawking them on the street.

Dried cod, stockfish, came to Paris from what the 1390s author of the *Menagier de Paris* household manual called the *marces de la mer,* which was actually arctic Norway and Iceland. Oil-free flesh on the headless split carcases of large cod taken from late winter spawning concentrations dried without salt into a boardlike consistency suitable for long storage or shipment. Stockfish—as distinctive in the archaeological record as they were on the market—came south to consumers through a chain of Norwegian, German, and Flemish or French traders.

Parisian consumers thus tapped a range of local and far-off aquatic systems to dine on fish. Neither fish remains nor written records permit quantitative totals or good comparisons with other foodstuffs, whether in Paris or elsewhere. Towns elsewhere—London, those in Flanders, Kraków, Zurich, or Rome—exploited some of the same but also demonstrably different ecological connections and economically viable fisheries to supply their needs. Medieval urban Europeans, rich and poor, thus put their imprint on aquatic ecosystems in several ways.[62] I have elsewhere indicated reasons to believe that overfishing contributed to the deterioration of some freshwater and estuarine populations and the collapse of certain regional herring and cod stocks, clear signs of locally unsustainable demand.[63]

Energy Needs

Food supply is a culturally mediated consequence of biological needs for energy to sustain human organisms. Together with animal fodder, human food sustained the muscle power on which most medieval activities relied. In contrast the second essential energy source for medieval civilization, heat, was a cultural adaptation to environmental conditions. Absent major medieval use of fossil fuels, biomass energy, mainly from burning wood, supported domestic heating, cooking, and many manufacturing processes. Regions with little wine not only drank cereals as beer and ale, they also used much fuel for brewing. Urban concentrations of demand called up large flows of bulky, land-hungry fuel,[64] generating webs of economic activity and thoroughgoing manipulation of woodland ecosystems in the closest feasible proximity to consumers.

"Feeding the City" researchers estimated that around 1300 (and again by about 1550) each of London's eighty thousand inhabitants used the heat equivalent of some 1.76 tons of dry wood per year, so the whole city burned some 141,000 tons.[65] The smaller city of 1400 needed only 88,000 tons. By 1200 specialized wood sellers (*buscarii*) and colliers were evidently active in London.[66] Over the next century prices for wood in the city region rose more rapidly than did either general price levels there or those for wood elsewhere in England. Manorial accounts from around London document specialized production of brushwood (*subboscus*) for fuel. Woodland in the lord's control was managed for an annual crop of a marketable commodity. Self-regenerating coppice woods closed to grazing animals and unshaded by timber trees were then made to yield bundles of faggots or slightly larger "talwood" and "billets" every seven years, compared with eleven-year cycles elsewhere.

London absorbed the annual output from 29,000 hectares (70,000 acres) of such intensively managed woodland. A hundred times the area of the city, this figure approximates 11 percent of the land area of Middlesex and Surrey.[67] Heavier for its value than was grain, wood could economically enter London from as far as 27 kilometers (17.4 miles) over land, but cheaper movement by water narrowed the city's woodshed (fig. 10.3) into an elongate zone of about 160 kilometers along the Thames from Henley down to Foulness and Margate, with a possible extension to the channel coast of east Kent. Manorial woodlands in this river-oriented region were unusually common, valued, and well managed. The area's importance for fueling London is further confirmed by known shipments to elite London consumers such as Westminster Abbey and the Southwark residence of the bishop of Winchester. That same well-wooded zone could also serve overseas consumers. Marine transport made towns in Flanders and Zeeland closer to Kent than was London, so their fuel demand competed for firewood from east Kent and pulled more supplies out of the Kentish Weald through Winchelsea and Rye, which did not ship to London.

Supply of fuel to city consumers thus encouraged more, not less, woodland in southeastern England, but woodland artificial in form and process. Like agriculture, coppice woods speed up natural cycles, remove biomass, and change species composition. Coppicing eliminates conifers, degrades beech stands, and encourages regrowth of sun-tolerant over shade-tolerant species. There is no old growth habitat (ancient woodland).[68] Fast-growing shoots capture a high proportion of annual production for use as heat energy but probably approach limits to sustainability in the range of two tons of biomass per acre-year. Proximity to that production ceiling in woodland accessible to London's demand during high population decades around 1300 (and again after 1550) is suggested by experiment with sea coal, despite that fuel's famously noxious emissions and heavy transportation costs.

Steep inland Mediterranean mountain valleys little resemble rolling Kent, Surrey, and Sussex, but despite a milder climate and no brewing, one hundred thousand Florentines—as well as other townspeople in heavily urbanized Tuscany—pressed demand for fuel and other wood against regionally accessible woodlands. Florentine statutes of 1322/25 anticipated wood being floated down the Arno—even the hundred river kilometers from Montepulciano—for both construction and fuel and forbade its reexport from the city.[69] Even near the city's demographic nadir, the communal code of 1415 reiterated that ban while also taxing firewood (*ligna pro ardendi*) as it entered the city gates. Intensified fuel production is manifest in 1337 regulations from one rural commune, San Miniato al Tedesco, which mandate a four-year coppice cycle. Both during the pre-plague period and with renewed population growth after the mid-fifteenth century small rural communities tried to limit woodland use to local residents' subsistence needs, while for the sake of urban supply the city's laws challenged them.

Had each of the two hundred thousand Parisians in about 1300—wine drinkers in a climate more like London's—consumed only two-thirds the fuel of their English contemporaries, that still came to 240,000 tons annually, or the output of 48,000 hectares of coppice, more than a hundred times their city's area. Overseen by royal and municipal officers, Paris wood merchants received wood at designated points along the city's riverfront.[70] As with grain and fish, statutes discouraged intermediaries and sought to force quick sales at fixed prices, while ensuring a quality product. Some fuel of oak, box, and juniper floated down the Seine, Marne, Oise, and Yonne—and was missed in hard winters like 1459, when those rivers froze—but most firewood and charcoal was rafted *up* the Seine from the many woodlands that lined that river from Boulogne down to Poissy, the latter twenty-five kilometers from the city in a straight line but sixty kilometers by the meandering river. In emergencies like the war years of 1418–19 the Parlément de Paris permitted special cuts in the still closer and safely accessible royal forests of Laye, Sénart, Pommerage, and Bondy. French scholars have not attempted the close economic and spatial analysis of their English counterparts, but the importance of water transport and nearby regions is unmistakable.[71] City needs thus helped create especially wooded landscapes at the heart of the Île de France.

Late medieval Germany's second city, Nürnberg, lacked major water access, but its growing metallurgical industries demanded much fuel. While worries over deforestation in the naturally deciduous Reichswald nearby were being voiced by 1300, repeated efforts to limit the cut and reforest remained ineffective. By 1368, in an especially innovative response to the problem, the influential city merchant and landowner Peter Stromer had developed ways to reproduce pine trees from seed. By the early fifteenth century pine was becoming the dominant species in the Reichswald, supplying the city's fuel and construction needs from what was now an anthropogenic landscape. From Nürnberg the practice of plantation forestry spread to other urban centers, including Frankfurt and Vienna.[72]

Energy needs of cities in Flanders and Brabant drove environmental transformation to a still deeper level. Already by the twelfth century these cities were substituting for expensive local wood supplies regionally abundant peat, waterlogged deposits of decayed vegetation that when dug, cut, and dried yielded a fuel with about half the energy ratio of hardwood.[73] This first major form of fossil energy eventually served not only domestic needs but also brick and lime kilns, breweries, and dye- and saltworks.

The Flemish count Philip d'Alsace (1168–91) initiated large sales of peat land to urban abbeys, city hospitals, and eventually private entrepreneurs who supplied city markets.[74] The first heavily exploited peat deposits paralleled the south shore of the West Scheldt estuary in what is now Dutch Flanders, where a belt fifteen kilometers wide extended some fifty kilometers from northwest of Antwerp to northeast of Bruges and passed within twenty kilometers of the then largest market, Ghent. Northeast across the Scheldt, lords of Breda, North Brabant, opened up peat deposits in 1287 to supply Bruges, a hundred kilometers distant and farther by the cheapest, all-water route.[75] Further diggings begun in 1332 supplied Antwerp, which became the principal consumer by around 1500. In South Holland the price of peat for export to Antwerp rose during 1480–1530 half again faster than the general price level.[76]

Peat-digging villages combined subsistence farming with market production, taking a quarter *Last* per man day during the three-month spring cutting season. Peat dried through the summer, and then 90 percent was shipped to the towns in time for the heating season. On most soils removal of peat hampered future agricultural use of the land, turning marshy or boggy landscapes into sandy heaths or open-water lakes. Anthropogenic small lakes remain distinctive landscape features and ecosystems in the peat lands of North Flanders; South Holland's vast but equally artificial Haarlemmermeer between Haarlem and Leiden, not really drained until the nineteenth century, also resulted from late medieval peat exports for urban energy needs.[77]

Flows of fuels to meet concentrated energy needs of medieval cities changed producing landscapes. The radius of impact from urban energy consumption was set by regional interplay between production and transport costs and identification of technically exploitable resources. Most typically affected were woodlands accessible by cheap water routes, which tended to become intensively managed hardwood coppice. More ecologically intrusive conifer plantations remained a rare alternative. While wood fuel thus transformed but preserved wooded landscapes, peat energy destroyed wetlands or extensive agropastoral systems and left behind new aquatic or impoverished terrestrial ecologies.

Urban Effluents

Movement of materials to sustain urban metabolism left metaphorical footprints on the medieval environment. So, too, did a reverse flow of urban metabolic wastes. Outputs from urban activities sustained, indeed were, the life of the city, and economically productive towns exported value-added materials for use elsewhere, but these processes inescapably also generated human, consumption, and manufacturing waste. As today, some of this useless material was, purposely or not, sequestered for slow assimilation in urban sinks: medieval Europeans commonly buried human remains at sacred places within their communities, and a richly organic "black earth layer" is characteristic of soils on undisturbed medieval town sites.[78] While these accumulations help define distinctive urban ecosystems, another portion of medieval urban waste flowed into surrounding ecosystems. Research carried out to date seems more readily to confirm than to measure environmental consequences of medieval urban effluents. Nor is it yet possible to work through the entire flow of waste from a particular community into its own and neighboring ecosystems. Plainly, however, just as towns sought inputs from outside, they *purposely* directed their effluents out into their surroundings. Prevailing medical doctrine, accentuated after fearsome experience of mid-fourteenth-century epidemics, saw miasma, the stench of air corrupted by putrefaction, as a principal cause of human illness. Waste disposal and odor control were thus essential components of public health.

Human bodies generate a considerable waste stream, rich in plant nutrients and human endoparasites. If an average adult produces about 150 grams of feces and 1 to 1.5 liters of urine each day, a modest medieval urban center of five thousand had annually to dispose of some 250 tons of solids and 2,500 tons of liquid human wastes or sewage.[79] Consider then the masses that came from medieval Köln, Florence, or Paris and add the droppings of urban livestock, especially draft horses. By sometime in the thirteenth century most communities were trying to inhibit indiscriminate disposal of this material in the town itself.

Burial or flushing into a watercourse provided generally acceptable alternatives. Pit or barrel latrines at many urban dwellings contained household waste while the liquid component seeped into ground water and solids either slowly decomposed or had occasionally to be extracted and exported. Municipal regulations at Köln required the contents of cesspits to be emptied into the Rhine through downstream gates kept open overnight for that purpose. In Nürnberg domestic latrines without water access were cleared by members of the *Pappenheimer* or *Nacht-meister* guild, who carted the contents to the Pegnitz. Cleaning one Nürnberg latrine after seventeen years' use took three and a half nights to fill 108 cartloads at a cost of nearly one hundred *Pfund* in local currency.[80] While extramural gardeners and vineyard operators might eagerly recycle the nutrients from urban night soil,[81] expense alone made direct aquatic disposal the normal municipal preference. Rouen and Nürnberg placed latrines directly over natural watercourses and purpose-built channels, while elsewhere moats and canals left obsolete by urban growth became open receptacles for human and animal waste; the "shit hole" *(merderon),* so named at Troyes in 1208, was but the first to enter written record. Assiduous cleansing by regularly diverting local watercourses—the Seveso and Nirone in Milan, for instance—flushed the sewage into downstream ecosystems for assimilation.[82]

Had waste products of medieval material life relatively less environmental effect than do present-day equivalents? Medieval society reused and recycled many objects of material culture—building materials, clothing, animal by-products, and so forth.[83] Preindustrial technologies, including those from time to time mainly concentrated in towns, relied primarily on materials of organic, environmentally degradable, origin[84]—such as wood, animal and plant fibers, and ceramics. André Guillerme not only emphasizes efforts of municipal officials to control such wastes, but he also asserts that emissions of the tannic acid and alum so important in medieval leather and textile trades actually counteracted bacterial decomposition so that rivers could carry solid organic wastes "beyond city limits."[85] If so, we might at least hypothesize that fewer components entered the medieval waste stream and few of those persisted in the environment. Or were urban waste problems just pushed out of mind by washing them into wider peri-urban landscapes?

None would now deny what so far remains largely incidental evidence of effluents from urban manufactures and consumption flowing into nearby ecosystems. Production wastes from food and textile industries were among the more commonly noticed. In 1366 the university and colleges in Paris collectively complained that garbage from butchers subject to the Abbey of Ste.-Geneviève was corrupting the area's air and water.[86] Leather and cloth producers did use various chemicals to process their organic raw materials. Town governments—as at Strasbourg and Milan—commonly ordered the transportation of wastes from tanning, dyeing, fulling, and other manufactures to a designated disposal site, commonly in the local waterway at the *downstream* end of town. Acidic and corrosive effluents from Nürnberg's important metal industry were handled in the same way.[87] Emissions from burning mineral coal, meanwhile, fouled the air of London.[88] Recycled solid and liquid human waste enriched soils for suburban agricultural production around towns like Ghent, Paris, Milan, and Wrocław, sustaining enclaves of market garden or intensive fodder production on thoroughly modified soils. All these flows challenged the ecological resilience of regional landscapes.

Sometimes medieval urban effluents exceeded the assimilation capacity of receiving ecosystems. This is especially obvious when both material and written evidence identify environmental degradation downstream of medieval cities, even if time now obscures the relative roles of human, animal, and industrial sources. Recent archaeological work in the Pegnitz at Nürnberg recovered late medieval butchery waste and household refuse; the findings corroborate the stream's foul repute when each summer's low water left it long unflushed.[89] Likewise by the early 1400s effluent from Paris famously made the Seine below town *infectée et corrumpue* every summer.[90] Along the Bodensee shoreline at Konstanz, where, between the thirteenth and sixteenth centuries, a one-time lagoon gradually filled with town wastes, archaeobotanical study of plant remains in that deposit shows massive replacement of species native to clean waters by a filamentous algae closely associated with strongly eutrophic or polluted conditions.[91] As aquatic biologists might now expect, medieval cities seasonally and at Konstanz permanently caused nutrient overload (eutrophication) in downstream waters. What happened at Douai in 1452, however, looks more like toxic pollution: the clothier Barru Lourdel was taken to court for a fish kill caused by his retting flax and hemp in a brook, which drained into waters belonging to Anchin monastery: "and [the waters] have become so foul and infected that the fish which existed in the waters of my lords [the monks] are every one and in great numbers dead and others departed for waters elsewhere."[92]

Certainly, then, medieval urban metabolisms could force nearby ecosystems to assimilate their waste products. Assessing the volume and flow of waste from medieval cities into their surroundings should have high priority for future historical research, especially in places with voluminous administrative records such as Florence and other Italian cities, Paris, London, and the towns of Flanders and Brabant. How large and how widespread were the ecosystems dirtied by urban metabolic emissions?

Conclusion

Full specification and measurement of the marks that medieval European towns placed on the environment would account as well for such consumable inputs as water, wine, building timber, and stone and would assess outflows more closely.[93] But neither total coverage nor refinements are needed to conclude from what has already been learned that urbanization was a major source for environmental change in medieval Europe. Medieval cities had significant environmental impact. Whether imagined as organisms (metabolic processes) or as interaction among organisms and environment (ecosystem), cities played distinctive roles in mutual relationship with surrounding landscapes. Medieval cities were physically quite small, but concentration in them of distinctive populations and demand focused human transformation of ecosystems, with processual mechanisms and complex outcomes that transcend the overshoot paradigm. The metabolic approach drawing attention to flows of materials is an especially good guide for identifying resource use and tracing it to those sites of initial acquisition and eventual disposal where the environmental impacts become visible.

Consumption by inhabitants in specific, well-documented medieval cities drew flows of material that in turn drove large changes in land use. These processes had inherent, identifiable, and demonstrable ecological consequences, and not just in the immediate proximity of the consuming cities.

In fact the scale of medieval urban environmental impacts may slightly surprise, for cities measurably pulled both grain and wood from productive areas hundreds of times larger than they themselves covered. This is in part the simple consequence of low availability of biological surplus in natural systems and even less in ones that also provided peasant subsistence. It suggests as well that medieval urbanism was, on first approximation, ecologically sustainable, if only below limited thresh-holds *and* after or by means of the transformation of natural systems elsewhere. Neither long fallow agriculture nor coppicing is simply the gathering of a natural surplus, but rather they result from large and pur-poseful human intervention in natural processes and states. Urban foot-prints were no accident but rather inherent, sometimes even self-conscious, metabolic consequences of city living itself.

Environmental effects from medieval urbanism were not simply con-centric functions of distance and population but could also display dis-tinct spatial discontinuities. Sources of metabolic inputs were estab-lished first by transportation costs (economics) but second by available natural production (ecology). While regional production zones for each city's grain and fuelwood were shaped into the spatial rings of classic location theory, cattle, fish, and more grain flowed in from distant areas with special environmental endowments. Medieval townspeople ought thus to be considered pioneer "biosphere people," as geographer Ian Simmons termed present-day consumer cultures adapted not to a single ecosystem but rather to the entire globe.[94] And whether initially deter-mined by economic or ecological variables, all flows had ecological effects, leaving the producing ecosystems different than they otherwise would have been.

Environmental pollution from medieval urban effluents is more difficult to assess from research carried out to date. It unquestionably occurred, and with detectable effects on extraurban landscapes. Still the most probable conclusion would rank the impact of urban pollution below demand-induced changes in land use and as more limited in its spatial incidence.

Variations in environmental impact reflected long- and short-term changes in medieval urban metabolic relations. Quite durable regional differences in cultural and ecological adaptations lay behind, for instance, the lower energy and cereal demands of southern wine-consuming communities compared to northern beer drinkers. Major historical changes reflect complex differences between large, relatively impoverished European populations during the twelfth and thirteenth centuries—when many poor city people collectively consumed great total amounts of cheap cereal calories—and the demographic nadir but greater per capita wealth of the late fourteenth and fifteenth centuries—when arable landscapes retreated and more people could more often afford meat from cattle reared or fishes caught far away. Impacts on fisheries changed with the culturally defined seasonality of Lenten consumption, with development of techniques to preserve seasonally abundant catches for later use, and with long-term shifts of effort from depleted natural inland ecosystems to both aquaculture and distant marine resources. But, for all that cities were the largest consumers of most of these goods and so especially drove their production, at some point the widest effects might also be thought more generally market driven and less exclusively urban.

Some ecological effects of medieval land use changes and pollution have long been effaced or simply absorbed in a half millennium of subsequent history, but others persist, remaining physically visible to today's alert eye. Unerased "footprints" of medieval urban metabolism include pinewoods around Nürnberg and peat lakes on both sides of the Rhine-Maas delta, at least part of the eutrophication that still threatens the Bodensee, and both the continued presence of Hungarian Gray cattle (a protected heritage breed) and the continued absence of historic inshore spawning stocks of herring in the southernmost North Sea.

This chapter has tried to bring together two discourses that have for the most part been mutually unawares, namely, current environmental studies and research on medieval cities. Critical application of concepts and methodological approaches from present-day thinking about carrying capacity and sustainability to questions on consumption and waste disposal by medieval European townspeople suggested intriguing parallels and distinctions between then and now. These results may encourage environmental scientists to extend, test, and revise what is truly unique in current situations. They open the issue of sustainability in historical pasts and may stimulate medievalists more broadly to recognize the complex material forces and constraints operating in medieval civilization.

NOTES

This chapter has evolved through the challenge of presentation to several different kinds of audiences, each with its own interests. Earlier versions gained from discussion at the 2002 conference "City Limits: Urban Culture in the Middle Ages," sponsored by the Centre for Medieval Studies at the University of Toronto; a session on medieval landscapes organized by Christoph Sonnlechner for the European Society for Environmental History meeting at Charles University in Prague in 2003; the *Comparative Studies in Society and History* conference "Natures Past: Comparative Perspectives on Environmental Change" at the University of Michigan, Ann Arbor, in 2003; and a colloquium at the Zentrum für Umweltgeschichte of the Austrian interuniversity Fakultät für Interdisziplinäre Forschung und Fortbildung—Wien in 2004. I am especially grateful for critiques, ideas, and advice from Verena Winiwarter, Charlotte Masemann, Paolo Squatriti, Dolores Wilson, and Fridolin Krausmann, but all colleagues are absolved of responsibility for whatever I may here perpetrate.

1. Eric W. Sanderson et al., "The Human Footprint and the Last of the Wild," *Bioscience* 52 (2002): 891–904.

2. A conjunction of ecosystems that interact, though less directly than do the components of each, is called a landscape or region. Such normative definitions of an ecosystem are used, for instance, in Emily W. B. Russell, *People and the Land through Time: Linking Ecology and History* (New Haven: Yale University Press, 1997), 3; and Ian Simmons, *Changing the Face of the Earth: Culture, Environment, History,* 2d ed. rev. (Oxford: Blackwell, 1996), 12–27. Note that current ecological thinking no longer assumes ecosystems will tend toward stability or equilibrium.

3. This is conveniently summarized by David Nicholas in *The Growth of the Medieval City: From Late Antiquity to the Early Fourteenth Century* (London and New York: Longman, 1997), and *The Later Medieval City 1300–1500* (London and New York: Longman, 1997), both replete with bibliographical references.

4. Traditional issues and positions are compiled in Bert F. Hoselitz, "Generative and Parasitic Cities," *Economic Development and Cultural Change* 3 (1954–55): 278–94; and Gideon Sjoberg, *The Preindustrial City: Past and Present* (New York: Free Press, 1960), 87–92. For later examples, see Moses I. Finley, "The Ancient City: From Fustel de Coulanges to Max Weber and Beyond," in Brent D. Shaw and Richard P. Saller, eds., *Economy and Society in Ancient Greece* (New York: Viking, 1982), 1–23; or David R. Ringrose, *Madrid and the Spanish Economy, 1560–1850* (Berkeley: University of California Press, 1983). This debate is *not* the frame of reference for this chapter.

5. Thomas Glick, review of Peregrine Horden and Nicholas Purcell, *The Corrupting Sea* (Oxford: Blackwell, 2000), in *Speculum* 77 (2002): 555–57.

6. Fernand Braudel, *The Mediterranean and the Mediterranean World in the Age of Philip II,* trans. Siân Reynolds (New York: Harper, 1972), 1:312–53. Braudel's considerable attention to cities in his subsequent *Civilization and Capitalism 15th–18th Century* trilogy acknowledges no ecological perspective: see vol. 1, *The Structures of Everyday Life: The Limits of the Possible,* trans. Siân Reynolds (London: Collins, 1981), 479–558; and vol. 3, *The Perspective of the World,* trans. Siân Reynolds (London: Collins, 1984), 89–276.

7. Horden and Purcell, *The Corrupting Sea,* 90 (and 89–122 passim).

8. J. Donald Hughes, "Medieval Florence and the Barriers to Growth," *Capitalism, Nature, Socialism* 7, no. 1 (1996): 63–68, an essay essentially reproduced in J. Donald Hughes, *An Environmental History of the World: Humankind's Changing Role in the Community of Life* (London and New York: Routledge, 2001), 86–93.

9. *Environment and History* 7 (2001): 187–99.

10. J. Donald Hughes, "Classical Athens and Ecosystemic Collapse," *Capitalism, Nature, Socialism* 7, no. 3 (1996): 97–102, and re-presented in Hughes, *Environmental History,* 59–66.

11. J. Donald Hughes, "Ripples in Clio's Pond: The Pre-Industrial City as Ecosystem," *Capitalism, Nature, Socialism* 9, no. 1 (March 1998): 105–10. Hughes reworked ideas from this essay in his *Environmental History,* 30–33.

12. J. Donald Hughes and Yves Lenoir, "Ripples in Clio's Pond: Medieval Florence and the Barriers to Growth Revisited," *Capitalism, Nature, Socialism* 9, no. 3 (September 1998): 133–40.

13. As pointed out by, among others, Britta Padberg, *Die Oase aus Stein: Humanökologisch Aspekte des Lebens in mittelalterlichen Städten* (Berlin: Akademie Verlag, 1996), notably 41–80, based largely on traditional urban ecology and data from late medieval towns in northern Germany.

14. William E. Rees, "Ecological Footprints and Appropriated Carrying Capacity: What Urban Economics Leaves Out," *Environment and Urbanization* 4 (1992): 121–30; this special issue of the journal treated "sustainable cities."

15. Mathis Wackernagel, "Ecological Footprint and Appropriated Carrying Capacity: A Tool for Planning toward Sustainability," PhD diss., University of British Columbia, 1994, 68–78; William E. Rees and Mathis Wackernagel, "Ecological Footprints and Appropriated Carrying Capacity: Measuring the Natural Capital Requirements of the Human Economy," in AnnMarie Jansson et al., eds., *Investing in Natural Capital: The Ecological Economics Approach to Sustainability* (Washington, D.C.: Island Press, 1994), 362–90; Mathis Wackernagel and William E. Rees, *Our Ecological Footprint: Reducing Human Impact on the Earth* (Gabriola Island, B.C., and Philadelphia: New Society, 1996); Mathis Wackernagel and William E. Rees, "Perceptual and Structural Barriers to Investing in Natural Capital: Economics from an Ecological Footprint Perspective," *Ecological Economics* 20, no. 1 (1997): 3–24.

16. Lowrence J. Onisto, Eric Krause, and Mathis Wackernagel, "How Big Is Toronto's Ecological Footprint?" rev. ed. (Toronto: Centre for Sustainable Studies and the City of Toronto, 1998), 8–10. The originators and their disciples showed special interest in applying footprint methodology to urban communities. Besides Rees's original 1992 paper, which treated Vancouver, there are Mathis Wackernagel et al., "How Big Is Our Ecological Footprint" (Vancouver: UBC Task Force on Healthy and Sustainable Communities, 1993); William E. Rees and Mathis Wackernagel, "Urban Ecological Footprints: Why Cities Cannot Be Sustainable—And Why They Are a Key to Sustainability," *Environmental Impact Assessment Review* 16 (1996): 223–48; C. Folke, Asa Johnson, Jonas Larsson, and Robert Constanza, "Ecosystem Appropriation by Cities," *Ambio* 26 (1997): 167–72; Mathis Wackernagel, "The Ecological Footprint of Santiago de Chile," *Local Environment* 3 (1998): 7–25; and Kim Honey, "Cities Getting Too Big for the

Planet, Professor Says," *Globe and Mail* (Toronto), January 26, 1999, A10 (an interview with William Rees).

17. Jeroen C. J. M. van den Bergh and Harmen Verbruggen, "Spatial Sustainability, Trade, and Indicators: An Evaluation of the Ecological Footprint," *Ecological Economics* 29 (1999): 61–72.

18. Helmut Haberl, Karl-Heinz Erb, and Fridolin Krausmann, "How to Calculate and Interpret Ecological Footprints for Long Periods of Time: The Case of Austria, 1926–1995," *Ecological Economics* 38 (2001): 25–45.

19. Robert Costanza, "The Dynamics of the Ecological Footprint Concept," *Ecological Economics* 32 (2000): 341–45.

20. Richard York, Eugene A. Rosa, and Thomas Dietz, "Footprints on the Earth: The Environmental Consequences of Modernity," *American Sociological Review* 68 (2003): 279–301; at the opposite end of the scale, Manfred Lenzen et al., "Assessing the Ecological Footprint of a Large Metropolitan Water Supplier: Lessons for Water Management and Planning towards Sustainability," *Journal of Environmental Planning and Management* 46 (2003): 113–41, study one public utility in Sydney, Australia. Meanwhile the debate continues, with dissenting views of Swedish environmental analyst Bjorn Lomborg, reported in Natasha McDowell, "Ecological Footprint Forecasts Face Sceptical Challenge," *Nature* 419 (October 17, 2002): 656, promptly rebutted by Keith M. Vogelsang and William E. Rees, in letters to the editor of *Nature,* 420 (November 21, 2002): 267.

21. Matthew A. Luck, G. Darrel Jenerette, Jianguo Wu, and Nancy B. Grimm, "The Urban Funnel Model and the Spatially Heterogeneous Ecological Footprint," *Ecosystems* 4, no. 8 (December 2001): 782–96.

22. Richard Wood and Manfred Lenzen, "An Application of a Modified Ecological Footprint Method and Structural Path Analysis in a Comparative Institutional Study," *Local Environment* 8, no. 4 (August 2003): 365–86. Wood and Lenzen do not cite Luck et al., "The Urban Funnel Model."

23. The phraseology is reconfigured from Dolores Wilson, "The Environmental Cost of Medieval Cathedral Construction," a paper delivered at the Thirty-ninth International Congress of Medieval Studies, Western Michigan University, Kalamazoo, May 2004.

24. John R. McNeill, *Something New Under the Sun: An Environmental History of the Twentieth-Century World* (New York: Norton, 2000), 290.

25. Ibid., 291–94. Stephen Boyden et al., *The Ecology of a City and Its People: The Case of Hong Kong* (Canberra: Australian National University Press, 1981).

26. Stephen Boyden summarized his theory of urban metabolism within biotic and cultural systems in "Nature, Society, History, and Social Change," *Innovation: The European Journal of Social Science Research* 14 (2001): 103–16. Boyden there refers to Wackernagel and Rees, *Our Ecological Footprint,* but his work seems unengaged in the EF discourse.

27. McNeill, *Something New,* 281–94.

28. Ibid., 295.

29. This study is not, therefore, a broadly conceived examination of town-hinterland relations in medieval Europe; its focus is the mechanisms whereby medieval urban behavior had an effect on natural environmental (not human social, cultural, or economic) conditions outside the city.

30. Engelbert of Admont, *Compendium Politicorum,* ed. G. B. Fowler, "Admont 608 and Engelbert of Admont," *Archives d'histoire littéraire et doctrinale du moyen âge* 44 (1978): 201, as cited in Peter Biller, *The Measure of Multitude: Population in Medieval Thought* (Oxford: Oxford University Press, 2000), 325; compare Biller, *The Measure,* 279–81.

31. Bruce M. S. Campbell, James A. Galloway, Derek Keene, and Margaret Murphy, *A Medieval Capital and Its Grain Supply: Agrarian Production and Distribution in the London Region c.1300,* Historical Geography Research Series, no. 30 (London: Institute of British Geographers, 1993), 109 passim.

32. Hans C. Peyer, *Zur Getreidepolitik oberitalienischer Städte im 13. Jahrhundert* (Wien: Universum, 1950), 56–124 passim, esp. 68–71; Nicholas, *Growth of the Medieval City,* 182–84; Nicholas, *Later Medieval City,* 46. Compare Campbell et al., *Medieval Capital,* 2–4, or Raymond van Uytven, "L'approvisionnement des villes des anciens Pays-Bas au moyen âge," in his *Production and Consumption in the Low Countries, 13th–16th Centuries* (Aldershot: Ashgate, 2001), II:75–116.

33. Franciszek Piekosinski, ed., *Kodeks dyplomatyczne miasta Krakowa (1257–1506),* Monumenta medii aevi historica res gesta Poloniae illustrantia, vols. 5 and 7 (Kraków, 1879 and 1882), no. 299; Tomás Puñal Fernández, *El Mercado en Madrid en la baja edad media: Estructura y sistemas de abastecimiento de un concejo medieval castellano (s.XV)* (Madrid: Caja de Madrid, 1992), 126–216. For further discussion and examples, see Ronald E. Zupko and Robert A. Laures, *Straws in the Wind: Medieval Urban Environmental Law—The Case of Northern Italy* (Boulder: Westview, 1996), 75–79, 83–84.

34. Campbell et al., *Medieval Capital,* 32–36.

35. Ibid., 72, 37–38.

36. Ibid., 78–110.

37. Ibid., 76–77, 111–44.

38. Ibid., 171–83. See also Bruce M. Campbell, "Ecology Versus Economics in Late Thirteenth- and Early Fourteenth-Century English Agriculture," in Del Sweeney, ed., *Agriculture in the Middle Ages: Technology, Practice, and Representation.* (Philadelphia: University of Pennsylvania Press, 1995), 76–108. Simulation modeling with preindustrial input-output data of direct marketing regions around cities of various sizes convinced George W. Grantham that this was a general peri-urban phenomenon; see "Espaces privilégés: Productivité agraire et zones d'approvisionnement des villes dans l'Europe preindustrielle," *Annales ESC* 52 (1997): 695–726.

39. H. S. A. Fox, "Some Ecological Dimensions of Medieval Field Systems," in K. Biddick, ed., *Archaeological Approaches to Medieval Europe* (Kalamazoo:

Medieval Institute, 1984), 144: "Heavy transfers away from the arable fields . . . characterize all market-oriented systems of cereal production."

40. Richard Unger, "Feeding Low Countries Towns: The Grain Trade in the Fifteenth Century," *Revue Belge de Philologie et d'Histoire* 77 (1999): 329–31. The amount is six times that estimated for London.

41. Gerhard Theuerkauf, "Brandenburg, Böhmen und die Elberegion. Zur Handelsgeschichte des späten Mittelalters," in Norbert Angermann, ed., *Die Hanse und der deutsche Osten* (Lüneburg: Nordostdeutsches Kulturwerk, 1990), 67–78, confirms from commercial records on the Elbe what Wilhelm Abel (*Agricultural Fluctuations in Europe from the Thirteenth to the Twentieth Centuries* [London: Methuen 1980], 106–9), Walter Achilles ("Getreidepreise und Getreidehandelsbeziehungen europäischer Räume im 16 und 17 Jahrhundert," Diss., Universität Göttingen, 1957, 5–10), and Marie-Jeanne Tits-Dieuaide ("The Baltic Grain Trade and Cereal Prices in Flanders at the End of the Middle Ages," in Walter Michinton, ed., *The Baltic Grain Trade, Five Essays* [Exeter: Association for the History of the Northern Seas, University of Exeter, 1985], 11–19) had earlier surmised from western sources.

42. Evamarie Engel and Benedykt Zientara, *Feudalstruktur, Lehnbürgertum, und Fernhandel im spätmittelalterlichen Brandenburg* (Weimar: Bohlau, 1967), 147–87, 366–67.

43. Unger, "Feeding Low Countries Towns," 332–58.

44. G. Pinto, *Il libro del Biadaiolo: carestie e annona a Firenze dalla metà del 1200 al 1348* (Firenze: Biblioteca Storica Toscana, 1978), 77–78.

45. Ibid., 317.

46. Norman J. G. Pounds, *An Historical Geography of Europe 450 B.C.–A.D.1330* (Cambridge: Cambridge University Press, 1973), 425–28; Henri Bresc, *Un monde méditerranéen. Économie et société en Sicilie 1300–1450,* 2 vols. (Rome: École Française, 1986); S. R. Epstein, *An Island for Itself: Economic Development and Social Change in Late Medieval Sicily* (Cambridge: Cambridge University Press, 1992); Antonio Petino, *Aspetti e momenti di politica granaria a Catania ed in Sicilia nel Quattrocento* (Catania: Università di Catania, 1952); Marta Petrusewicz, *Latifundium: Moral Economy and Material Life in a European Periphery,* trans. Judith C. Green (Ann Arbor: University of Michigan Press, 1996), 7, 13–14, 149–57, 163, 174; Maurice Aymard, "Amministrazione feudale e trasformazione strutturali tra '500 e '700," *Archivio Storico per la Sicilia Orientale* 81 (1975): 17–42; Philip Jones, "Medieval Agrarian Society in Its Prime: Italy," in Michael M. Postan, ed., *The Agrarian Life of the Middle Ages,* 2d ed. rev., *The Cambridge Economic History of Europe,* vol. 1 (Cambridge: Cambridge University Press, 1966), 411, 413, 426.

47. Except as otherwise noted, information on the trade in cattle is from Ian Blanchard, "The Continental European Cattle Trades, 1400–1600," *Economic History Review* 2d series, 39 (1986): 427–60.

48. Zsigmond Pál Pach, *The Role of East-Central Europe in International*

Trade, 16th and 17th Centuries, Studia historica Academiae Scientiarum Hungaricae, no. 70 (Budapest: Akadémiai Kiadó, 1970), 223–46.

49. As quoted from Friedrich Lütge, *Strukturwandlungen im ostdeutschen und osteuropäischen Fernhandel des 14. bis 16. Jahrhunderts* (München: Verlag der Bayerischen Akademie der Wissenschaften, 1964), 6, in Blanchard, "Continental European Cattle Trades," 435n37.

50. István N. Kiss, "Agricultural and Livestock Production: Wine and Oxen: The Case of Hungary," and Jerzy Topolski, "A Model of East-Central European Continental Commerce in the Sixteenth and the First Half of the Seventeenth Century," both in Antoni Mączak, Henryk Samsonowicz, and Peter Burke, eds., *East-Central Europe in Transition from the Fourteenth to the Seventeenth Century* (Cambridge: Cambridge University Press, 1985), 88–91, 135–36; Eric Fügedi, "Der Aussenhandel Ungarns," in Ingomar Bog, ed., *Der Aussenhandel Ostmitteleuropas 1450–1650: Die ostmitteleuropäischen Volkswirtschaften in ihren Beziehungen zu Mitteleuropa* (Köln: Bohlau, 1971), 56–86.

51. Thorkild Kjærgaard, *The Danish Revolution, 1500–1800: An Ecohistorical Interpretation,* trans. David Hohnen (Cambridge: Cambridge University Press, 1994), 18–32.

52. László Bartosiewicz, "Animal Husbandry and Medieval Settlement in Hungary: A Review," *Beiträge zur Mittelalterarchäologie in Österreich,* 15 (1999): 148, and "The Hungarian Grey Cattle: A Traditional European Breed," *Animal Genetic Resources Information,* 21 (1997): 49–60. Correcting myths of an ancient steppe origin for these animals, recovered horn cores and bone from Hungarian cattle of the tenth through twelfth centuries conquest period lack the distinctive features that became visible by the sixteenth. Were these visible traits mere by-products of selection for growth and weight retention, or had they value as "trademarks" on foreign markets?

53. "Et est un abisme que Paris." Antoine J. V. Le Roux de Lincy and L. M. Tisserand, eds., *Paris et ses historiens aux 14e et 15e siècles: Documents et écrits originaux recueillis et commentés . . .* (Paris: Impr. impériale, 1867), 494.

54. Terence Scully, "Medieval France: The North," in Melitta W. Adamson, ed., *Regional Cuisines of Medieval Europe: A Book of Essays* (New York and London: Routledge, 2002), 48–50, discusses the use of cookbook and recipe sources.

55. The following fish catalogs, menus, and recipe collections, some of which exist in several redactions, reflect Parisian conditions and interests in and around Paris during the period from the mid-1200s to roughly 1320: Grégoire Lozinski, ed., *La Bataille de Caresme et de Charnage* (Paris: Champion, 1933), 121 passim; the earliest manuscript (VAL) of the collection later called the "Viandier de Taillevent," *The Viandier of Taillevent: An Edition of All Extant Manuscripts,* ed. and trans. Terence Scully (Ottawa: University of Ottawa Press, 1988); the recipe collection called *Enseignements* from Paris, Bibliothéque National, fonds latin 7131, published in Lozinski, *Bataille,* 181–87; the "Tractatus de modo preparandi et

condiendi omnia cibaria et potus," in Marianne Mulon, ed., "Deux traités inédits d'art culinaire médiéval," *Bulletin philologique et historique (jusqu'à 1610) du comité des travaux historiques et scientifiques,* année 1968 (Paris, 1971), 380–95; and the extensive description of a fish dinner in the "Roman de Comte d'Anjou," in Lozinski, *Bataille,* 192–93, subsequently repeated in the several revisions of the political satire *Le Roman de Fauvel in the Edition of Mesire Chaillou de Pesstain,* ed. Edward Roesner, François Avril, and Nancy Freeman Regalado (New York: Broude Brothers, 1990), ll. 116–41.

56. Of late fourteenth- to early fifteenth-century Parisian provenance are recipes and menus of fishes to eat in Jean Lefèvre, *La vieille ou, les derniéres amours d'Ovide: poême français du XIVe siècle. traduit du latine par Jean Lefèvre,* ed. H. Cocheris (Paris, 1861), ll. 956–1024; the late "Viandier" manuscript (VAT), ed. Scully, *Viandier;* and *Le Ménagier de Paris,* ed. Georgine E. Brereton and Janet M. Ferrier (Oxford: Clarendon, 1981), 231–43.

57. Cookbooks of English, German, or western Mediterranean (Spanish, Provencal, and Italian) origin display their own distinctive sets of fish varieties.

58. Jean Desse and Nathalie Desse-Berset, "Pêches locales, côtières ou lointaines: Le poisson au menu des parisiens du Grand Louvre, du 14ème au 18ème siècle," *Anthropozoologica* 16 (1992): 119–26.

59. High consumption of marine fishes in fourteenth-century Paris was unmatched, even in northern French towns closer to the sea, before the sixteenth century; see Benoît Clavel, *L'Animal dans l'alimentation médiévale et moderne en France du nord (XIIe–XVIIe siècles),* Revue Archéologique de Picardie, no. Spécial 19 (N.p.: CRAVO, 2001), 163–74.

60. André Bossuat, "La pêche en Seine au XVe siècle," *Bulletin de la Société de l'histoire de Paris* 90 (1963 [1965]): 60–81.

61. Caroline Bourlet, "L'Approvisionnement de Paris en poisson de mer aux XIVe et XVe siècles, d'après les sources normatives," *Franco-British Studies* 20 (1995): 5–22; Bernadette Auzary-Schmaltz, "Les Contentieux en matière d'approvisionnement, d'après les registres du parlement de Paris (XIVe–XVe siècles)," *Franco-British Studies* 20 (1995): 49–67. Compare Nicole Crossley-Holland, *Living and Dining in Medieval Paris: The Household of a Fourteenth-Century Knight* (Cardiff: Wales University Press, 1996), 80–85.

62. Richard C. Hoffmann, "Medieval Fishing," in Paolo Squatriti, ed., *Working with Water in Medieval Europe: Technology and Resource Use* (Leiden: Brill, 2000), 331–93.

63. Richard C. Hoffmann, "Frontier Foods for Late Medieval Consumers: Culture, Economy, Ecology," *Environment and History* 7 (2001): 152–53, and "Economic Development and Aquatic Ecosystems in Medieval Europe," *American Historical Review* 101 (1996): 648–52.

64. Wood for manufacturing and timber for construction are not discussed here.

65. Calculated from documented coal consumption in that city about 1600 by James Galloway, Derek Keene, and Margaret Murphy, "Fuelling the City: Production and Distribution of Firewood and Fuel in London's Region, 1290–1400," *Economic History Review* 49 (1996): 455–58. Margaret Murphy, "The Fuel Supply of Medieval London, 1300–1400," *Franco-British Studies* 20 (1995): 89, gave a slightly different estimate.

66. Galloway, Keene, and Murphy, "Fuelling the City," 451–55; Murphy, "Fuel Supply," 86–88.

67. Galloway, Keene, and Murphy, "Fuelling the City," 458–65; Murphy, "Fuel Supply," 89–95. If this figure is correct and so, too, that estimating the city's cereal needs as coming from 200 times its area (see the "Feeding the Townspeople" section of this essay), merely feeding and warming Londoners about 1300 required the product of 300 times their city's territory, already greater than the 290 times area estimated for all consumption by present-day Toronto (see the "From Metaphor to Method" section of this essay).

68. Oliver Rackham, *Trees and Woodland in the British Landscape,* rev. ed. (London: Dent, 1990), 1–25; R. Pott, "Impact of Human Influences by Extensive Woodland Management and Former Land-Use in North-Western Europe," in Fabio Salbitano, ed., *Human Influence on Forest Ecosystems Development in Europe* (Bologna: Pitagora, 1988), 271–74.

69. Francesco Salvestrini, "Law, Forest Resources, and the Management of Territory in the Late Middle Ages: Woodlands in Tuscan Municipal Statutes," in M. Agnoletti and S. Anderson, eds., *Forest History: International Studies on Socioeconomic and Forest Ecosystem Change* (Wallingford: CABI and IUFRO, 2000), 279–88.

70. Yvonne-Hélène Le Maresquier-Kesteloot, "L'Approvisionnement de Paris en bois (XIVe–XVe siècles)," *Franco-British Studies* 20 (1995): 69–83. See also Roland Bechmann, *Trees and Man: The Forest in the Middle Ages* (New York: Paragon House, 1990), 140–56, esp. 141–42.

71. When Venetians became aware of fuel shortages after 1440, they, too, thought first of riverine transport and riparian wood lots in their recently acquired mainland territories and only much later considered more fundamental issues of production and sustainability. See Karl Appuhn, "Politics, Perception, and the Meaning of Landscape in Late Medieval Venice: Marco Cornaro's 1442 Inspection of Firewood Supplies," in John Howe and Michael Wolfe, eds., *Inventing Medieval Landscapes: Senses of Place in Western Europe* (Gainesville: University Press of Florida, 2002), 70–88, and "Inventing Nature: Forests, Forestry, and State Power in Renaissance Venice," *Journal of Modern History* 72 (2000): 861–89.

72. Ursula Dötzer, "Der Reichswald—seine Bedeutung für die Stadt und seine Entwicklung vom Mittelalter bis in die frühe Neuzeit," in Birgit Friedel and Claudia Frieser, eds., *Nürnberg—Archaeologie und Kulturgeschichte* (Büchenbach: Verlag Dr. Faustus, 1999), 345–48. More generally on urban wood supply in medieval

Germany, see Rudolf Kieß, "Bemerkungen zur Holzversorgung von Städten," in Jürgen Sydow, ed., *Städtische Versorgung und Entsorgung im Wandel der Geschichte* (Sigmaringen: Thorbecke, 1981), 77–98, or Ernst Schubert, "Der Wald: wirtschaftliche Grundlage der spätmittelalterlichen Stadt," in Bernd Herrmann, ed., *Mensch und Umwelt im Mittelalter* (Darmstadt: Wissenschaftliche Buchgesellschaft, 1986), 257–74.

73. Vaclav Smil, *Energy in World History* (Boulder: Westview, 1994), 153, 219, rates peat at six to eight megajoules per kilogram, compared with sixteen to nineteen megajoules per kilogram for dry hardwood and twenty-eight to thirty megajoules per kilogram for charcoal. For more on peat as an energy source, see J. W. de Zeeuw, "Peat and the Dutch Golden Age: The Historical Meaning of Energy-Attainability," *A. A. G. Bijdragen* 21 (1978): 3–31, and Richard Unger, "Energy Sources for the Dutch Golden Age: Peat, Wind and Coal," *Research in Economic History* 9 (1984): 221–53.

74. B. Augustyn, "Traces of a Proto-Industrial Organization of the Medieval North Flemish Peat Region: Test-Case Kieldrecht, a Peat-Diggers Village ca. 1400," in H. J. Nitz, ed., *The Medieval and Early-Modern Rural Landscape of Europe under the Impact of the Commercial Economy* (Göttingen: Geographical Institute of the University of Göttingen, 1987), 61–74.

75. J. Renes, "Urban Influences on Rural Areas: Peat Digging in the Western Part of the Dutch Province of North Brabant from the Thirteenth to the Eighteenth Century," in Nitz, *Medieval and Early-Modern Rural Landscape,* 49–60.

76. Jan de Vries and Ad van der Woude, *The First Modern Economy* (Cambridge: Cambridge University Press, 1997), 37.

77. Petra J. E. M. van Dam, "Sinking Peat Bogs: Environmental Change in Holland, 1350–1550," *Environmental History* 6 (2001): 32–45, and *Vissen in veenmeren* (Hilversum: Historische Vereniging Holland, 1998), 58–81.

78. Romans, in contrast, cremated many bodies and kept their burials outside city walls, practices emulated (on other grounds) by modern Europeans. Fridolin Krausmann reminded me that cities also retained and stored their own waste.

79. Quantities suggested by Jean-Pierre Leguay, *L'eau dans la ville au Moyen Âge* (Rennes: Presses Universitaires de Rennes, 2002), 123.

80. Walter Lehnert, "Entsorgungsprobleme der Reichstadt Nürnberg," in Sydow, ed., *Städtische Versorgung und Entsorgung,* 152–56; Claudia Frieser, "Die spätmittelalterlichen Abwasserkanäle und heimlichen Gemächer Nürnbergs. Ein anrüchige Geschichte," in Friedel and Frieser, eds., *Nürnberg,* 195–98. More generally see Klaus Grewe, "Wasserversorgung und-entsorgung im Mittelalter—Ein technikgeschichtlicher Überblick," in Klaus Grewe, ed., *Die Wasserversorgung im Mittelalter,* Geschichte der Wasserversorgung, vol. 4 (Mainz: Phillipp von Zabern for the Frontinus Gesellschaft, 1991), 75–80; André E. Guillerme, *The Age of Water: The Urban Environment in the North of France, A.D. 300–1800* (College Station: Texas A&M University Press, 1988), 105–7.

81. Martin Illi, *Von der Schîssgruob zur modernen Stadtentwässerung* (Zürich, 1987), 24–28.

82. Ulf Dirlmeier, "Die kommunalpolitischen Zuständigkeiten und Leistungen süddeutscher Städte im Spatmittelalter (vor allem auf dem Gebiet der Ver- und Entsorgung)," in Sydow, ed., *Städtische Versorgung und Entsorgung,* 113–50; Guillerme, *Age of Water,* 105–7; A. Francesco La Cava, *Igiene e Sanità negli Statuti di Milano del Sec. XIV* (Milano: Hoepli, 1946), 64–66; Frieser, "Die spätmittelalterlichen Abwasserkanäle," 192–94; Till Lachmann, "Die Gewässer und ihre Nutzung," in Friedel and Frieser, eds., *Nürnberg,* 311–15. Generally on sewage in medieval French towns see also Leguay, *L'eau,* 247–75.

83. Padberg, *Oase aus Stein,* 46–47.

84. Zupko and Laures, *Straws,* 50.

85. Guillerme, *Age of Water,* 96–98.

86. Serge Lusignan, *"Vérité garde le roy": La construction d'une identité universitaire en France (XIIIe–XVe siècle)* (Paris: Sorbonne, 1999), 271.

87. Ulf Dirlmeier, "Zu den Lebensbedingungen in der mittelalterlichen Stadt: Trinkwasserversorgung und Abfallbeseitigung," in Bernd Herrmann, ed., *Mensch und Umwelt im Mittelalter* (Darmstadt: Wissenschaftliche Buchgesellschaft, 1986), 155–57; La Cava, *Igiene,* 44; Zupko and Laures, *Straws,* 36–37, 79–82, 86–87. Compare Illi, *Von der Schîssgruob,* 22. A quick review of the chemistry of medieval leather production is Rosita Nenno, "Gerbeverfahren, Lederverarbeitung und Ziertechniken," in Uta Lindgren, ed., *Europäische Technik im Mittelalter 800 bis 1400, Tradition und Innovation: Ein Handbuch* (Berlin: Gebr. Mann, 1996), 487–92.

88. William TeBrake, "Air Pollution and Fuel Crises in Preindustrial London, 1250–1650," *Technology and Culture* 16 (1975): 337–59.

89. Frieser, "Die spätmittelalterlichen Abwasserkanäle," 194–95.

90. As described in a waste disposal ordinance of 1415 cited from François A. Isambert et al., eds., *Recueil général des anciennes lois françaises depuis l'an 420 jusqu'à la Révolution de 1789,* vol. 8 (Paris, 1822), 565f, cap. 683, quoted in Ilja Mieck, "Die Anfänge der Umweltschutzgesetzgebung in Frankreich," *Francia* 9 (1981): 332. Later legislation (ibid., 335–36) dealt in particular with tanners' and potters' wastes.

91. Hansjörg Küster, "Mittelalterliche Eingriffe in Naturräume des Voralpenlandes," in Bernd Herrmann, ed., *Umwelt in der Geschichte: Beiträge zur Umweltgeschichte* (Göttingen: Vanderhoeck and Ruprecht, 1989), 72. Henry J. Regier, Robin L. Welcomme, Robert J. Steedman, and H. Francis Henderson, "Rehabilitation of Degraded River Ecosystems," in Douglas P. Dodge, ed., *Proceedings of the International Large River Symposium,* Canadian Special Publications in Fisheries and Aquatic Science, no. 106 (Ottawa: Queen's Printer, 1989), 88, specify this very botanical phenomenon as characteristic of an aquatic ecosystem under stress. Note further that where current speed and substrate prevent establishment of rooted aquatic vegetation, larger nitrate loads encourage suspended algae to grow and thus further increase turbidity.

92. "et ont esté si puantes et infectés que les pouissons qui estoient es yauwes de mesdis seigneurs sont les aulcuns et en grant nombre mors et les autres espars au loings en estranges yauwes." Leguay, *L'eau,* 292, from Pierre Plouchard, "La Scarpe et les gens de rivière," in R. Racine, ed., *Fleuves, rivières et canaux dans l'Europe occidentale et médiane* (Nancy: CRDP Lorraine, 1997), 850–51. Not all medieval fish kills should be taken as evidence of pollution. The legal cases and statutes extensively quoted in Richard Trexler, "Measures against Water Pollution in Fifteenth Century Florence," *Viator* 5 (1974): 455–67, concern neither waste disposal nor accidental or incidental emissions, but a well-known practice of catching fish with various chemical and herbal poisons that left the flesh still edible: Hoffmann, "Medieval Fishing," 324–26.

93. Besides the inputs examined previously, van Uytven, "L'approvisionnement," describes flows into Low Countries towns of wine, dairy products, salt, construction timber, building stone, bricks, wool, and dyestuffs, the latter two more for urban manufacturing than consumption. Historical application of metabolic analysis must at least consider the urban specificity of raw materials for and output from especially textile manufactures, whose huge economic (and hence ecological) role was differently distributed between town and countryside in various times and places. Perhaps the analytical limit for metabolic study would be the pattern of rural-urban migration, in which continual flows of young country people (human biomass) compensated for the higher mortality rates of urban populations.

94. Simmons, *Changing the Face,* 423.

Bibliography

WORKS CITED FOR CHAPTERS 1, 2, 3, 5, 6, 8, AND 9.

Abu-Lughod, L. 1990. "The Romance of Resistance: Tracing Transformations of Power through Bedouin Women." *American Ethnologist* 17 (1): 41–55.

Acheson, J. 1975. "Fisheries Management and Social Context: The Case of the Maine Lobster Fishery." *Transactions of the American Fisheries Society* 104 (4): 653–68.

———. 1988. *The Lobster Gangs of Maine.* Hanover, N.H.: University Press of New England.

———. 1989. "Where Have All the Exploiters Gone? Co-Management of the Maine Lobster Industry." In *Common Property Resources: Ecology and Community-Based Sustainable Development,* ed. F. Berkes, 199–217. London: Belhaven Press.

———. 1992. "Maine Lobster Industry." In *Climate Variability, Climate Change, and Fisheries,* ed. M. Glantz, 147–65. Cambridge: Cambridge University Press.

———. 1994. "Welcome to Nobel Country." In *Anthropology and Institutional Economics,* ed. J. Acheson, 3–35. Lanham, Md.: University Press of America.

———. 1997. "The Politics of Managing the Maine Lobster Industry: 1860 to the Present." *Human Ecology* 25 (1): 3–27.

———. 2003. *Capturing the Commons: Devising Institutions to Manage the Maine Lobster Industry.* Hanover, N.H.: University Press of New England.

Acheson, J., and R. Steneck. 1997. "Bust and Then Boom in the Maine Lobster Industry." *North American Journal of Fisheries Management* 17 (4): 826–47.

Acheson, J., and J. Wilson. 1996. "From the Bottom Up: A Maine Fishery Embarks on Co-Management and Everyone Is Watching." *Island Journal* 13:56–59.

Adas, M. 1983. "Colonization, Commercial Agriculture, and the Destruction of the Deltaic Rainforests of British Burma in the Late Nineteenth Century." In *Global Deforestation and the Nineteenth Century World Economy,* ed. R. Tucker and J. Richards, 95–110. Durham, N.C.: Duke University Press.

Administrative Center for China's Agenda 21. 1996. *Priority Programme for China's Agenda 21.* Beijing.

Agarwal, A. 1984. "Beyond Pretty Trees and Tigers: The Role of Ecological Destruction in the Emerging Patterns of Poverty and Peoples' Protests." *ICSSR Newsletter* 15 (1): 1–27.

———. 2002. "Common Resources and Institutional Sustainability." In *The Drama of the Commons,* ed. E. Ostrom et al., 41–85. Washington, D.C.: National Academy Press.

Agrawal, A., and K. Sivaramakrishnan, eds. 2000. *Agrarian Environments: Resources, Representations, and Rule in India.* Durham, N.C.: Duke University Press.

Agarwal, B. 1986. *Cold Hearths and Barren Slopes: The Woodfuel Crisis in the Third World.* London: Zed Books.

Alchain, A. 1950. "Uncertainty, Evolution, and Economic Theory." *Journal of Political Economy* 58: 211–21.

Alcorn, J. 1981. "Huastec Noncrop Resource Management: Implications for Prehistoric Rainforest Management." *Human Ecology* 9:395–417.

Alden, R. 1989. "Lobster Industry: Adapting to Meet the Challenges of the 1990s." *Commercial Fisheries News,* April 6.

Alter, P. 1985. *Nationalismus.* Frankfurt am Main: Suhrkamp.

Altermatt, U. 1999. *Katholizismus und Antisemitismus. Mentalitäten, Kontinuitäten, Ambivalenzen.* Frauenfeld and Stuttgart: Huber.

Anderson, B. 1991. *Imagined Communities: Reflections on the Origins and Spread of Nationalism.* London: Verso.

Anderson, P. 1979. *Lineages of the Absolutist State.* New York: Verso.

Anderson, R., and W. Huber. 1988. *The Hour of the Fox: Tropical Forests, the World Bank, and the Indigenous People of Central India.* Seattle: University of Washington Press.

Anderson, T., and R. Simmons. 1993. *The Political Economy of Customs and Culture: Informal Solutions to the Commons Problem.* Lanham, Md.: Rowman and Littlefield.

Anonymous, 1970. "Penertiban Tarah-Tanah Pengungsi Tijna di Kalimantan Barat." *Penyuluh Land Reform* 10(6): 13–14.

Appel, G. 1970. "Comparisons of Land Tenure Systems among the Dayak of Borneo." Manuscript.

Archer, W. 1974. *The Hill of Flutes: Life, Love, and Poetry in Tribal India: A Portrait of the Santals.* Pittsburgh: University of Pittsburgh Press.

Arnold, D. 1982. "Rebellious Hillmen: The Gudem Rampa Rebellions (1829–1914)." *Subaltern Studies* 1. Delhi: Oxford University Press.

———. 2000. *Science, Technology, and Medicine in Colonial India.* New York: Cambridge University Press.

———. 2006. *The Tropics and the Traveling Gaze: India, Landscape, and Science, 1800–56.* Seattle: University of Washington Press.

Aschmann, H. 1988. "Proprietary Rights to Fruit on Trees Growing on Residential Land." In *Whose Trees? Proprietary Dimensions of Forestry,* ed. L. Fortman and J. Bruce, 63–68. Boulder: Westview Press.

Axelrod, R. 1986. "An Evolutionary Approach to Norms." *American Political Science Review* 80 (4): 1095–111.

Baden, J., and G. Hardin. 1977. *Managing the Commons.* San Francisco: W. H. Freeman.

Baden-Powell, B. 1892. *The Land Systems of British India.* Oxford: Clarendon Press.

———. 1893. *Forest Law: A Course of Lectures on the Principles of Civil and Criminal Law and on the Law of the Forest.* London: Bradbury, Agnew.

Baden-Powell, B., and J. Gamble. 1875. *Report of the Proceedings of the Forest Conference, 1873–1874.* Calcutta: Superintendent of Government Printing.

Bailey, F. 1969. *Stratagems and Spoils.* New York: Schocken.

Baker, D. 1991. "State Policy, the Market Economy, and Tribal Decline: The Central Provinces, 1861–1920." *Indian Economic and Social History Review* 28 (4): 341–70.

Balee, W. 1989. "The Culture of Amazonian Forests." In *Resource Managements in Amazonia: Indigenous and Folk Strategies,* ed. D. Balee, 7: 1–21. New York: New York Botanical Garden.

Balling, J., and J. Falk. 1982. "Development of Visual Preference for Natural Environments." *Environment and Behavior* 14 (1): 5–28.

Bandhopadhyay, J., and V. Shiva. 1989. "Development, Poverty, and the Growth of the Green Movement in India." *Ecologist* 19 (3): 111–17.

Bangor Daily News. 1996. "Lobster Conservation Law Opposed." April 18, B1.

Barth, F. 1981. *Process and Form in Social Life.* London: Routledge and Kegan Paul.

Baxandall, R., and E. Ewen. 2000. *Picture Windows: How the Suburbs Happened.* New York: Basic Books.

Bayer, R., P. Daniel, and S. Vaitones. 1985. "Preliminary Estimate of Contributions of V-Notched American Lobsters to Egg Production along Coastal Maine Based on Maine Lobsterman's Association V-Notch Survey: 1981–1984." *Bulletin of the Department of Animal and Veterinary Sciences.* Orono: University of Maine.

Bayly, C. 1990. *Indian Society and the Making of the British Empire.* Cambridge: Cambridge University Press.

Beck, M. 1978. *Legende, Mythos und Geschichte. Die Schweiz und das europäische Mittelalter.* Stutttgart: Verlag Huber.

Beijing Daxue Zhongguo chixu fazhan yanjiu zhongxin. 1995. *Kechixu fazhan zhilu: Beijing daxue shouci kechixu fazhan kexue taolunhui wenji.* Beijing Shi: Beijing daxue chubanshe.

Bell, D. 2001. *The Cult of the Nation in France: Inventing Nationalism 1680–1800.* Cambridge, Mass.: Harvard University Press.

Berger, P., and T. Luckmann. 1966. *The Social Construction of Reality: A Treatise in the Sociology of Knowledge.* London: Penguin Books.

Bergier, J.-F. 1983. *Wirtschaftsgeschichte der Schweiz. Von den Anfängen bis zur Gegenwart.* Zurich: Orell Füssli.

Berkes, F. 1989. *Common Property Resources: Ecology and Community-Based Sustainable Development.* London: Belhaven Press.

Berlin, I. 1976. *Vico and Herder: Two Studies in the History of Ideas.* London: Hogarth Press.

———. 1981. *Against the Current: Essays in the History of Ideas.* Oxford: Clarendon Press.

Berman, M. 1982. *All That Is Solid Melts into Air: The Experience of Modernity.* New York: Penguin.

Bernard, P. P. 1978. *Rush to the Alps: The Evolution of Vacationing in Switzerland.* New York: Columbia University Press.

Berry, S. 1989. "Social Institutions and Access to Resources." *Africa* 59, no. 2: 1–5.

Bhatt, C. 1987. "Green the People." In *The Fight for Survival: Peoples' Action for the Environment,* ed. A. Agarwal, D. D'Monte, and U. Samarth. New Delhi: Centre for Science and Environment.

Bhattacharya, N., ed. 1999. "Forests, Fields, and Pastures." *Studies in History,* n.s., Special Issue, 14 (2).

Binswanger, H. 1989. *Brazilian Policies That Encourage Deforestation in the Amazon.* Environment Department Working Paper No. 16. Washington, D.C.: World Bank.

Birdwood, H. 1910. *Indian Timbers: The Hill Forests of Western India.* London: *Journal of Indian Art and Industry.*

Blaikie, P. 1985. *The Political Economy of Soil Erosion in Developing Countries.* London: Longman.

Blaikie, P., and H. Brookfield. 1987. *Land Degradation and Society.* London: Methuen.

Blanford, H. 1925. "Regeneration with the Assistance of Taungya in Burma." *Indian Forest Records* 11 (3). Calcutta: Government of India Press.

———. 1958. "Highlights of One Hundred Years of Forestry in Burma." *Empire Forestry Review* 37:33–42.

Bluntschli, J.-C. [1875] 1915. *Die schweizerische Nationalität.* Zurich: Verlag Rascher und Cie.

Boerlin-Brodbeck, Y. 1998. "Alpenlandschaft als politische Metapher. Zu einer bisher wenig bekannten 'Libertas Helvetiae.'" *Zeitschrift für Schweizerische Archäologie und Kunstgeschichte* 55:1–12.

Boom, B. 1987. "Ethnobotany of the Chacobo Indians." *Advances in Economic Botany* 4:1–68.

Bormann, F., D. Balmori, and G. Geballe. 2001. *Redesigning the American Lawn: A Search for Environmental Harmony.* 2d ed. New Haven: Yale University Press.

Boserup, E. 1981. *Population and Technology.* Oxford: Blackwell.

Botsford, L., J. Wilen, and E. Richardson. 1986. "Biological and Economic Analysis of Lobster Fishery Policy in Maine." Report Submitted to the Department of Marine Resources and the Maine Legislature. Manuscript.

Bourdieu, P. 1977. *Outline of a Theory of Practice.* Cambridge: Cambridge University Press.

Bovet, E. 1909a. "Réflexions d'un Homo Alpinus." *Wissen und Leben* 7 (January): 296–99.

———. 1909b. "Nationalité." *Wissen und Leben.* 21 (August): 431–45.

Boyden, S., 2001. "Nature, Society, History and Social Change." *Innovation: The European Journal of Social Sciences* 14, no. 2: 103–16.

Brandis, D. 1873. *The Distribution of Forests in India.* Edinburgh: McFarlane and Erskine.

———. 1875. *Memorandum on the Forest Legislation Proposed for British India.* Calcutta: Government of India Press.

———. 1876. *Suggestions Regarding Forest Administration in the Central Provinces.* Calcutta: Government of India Press.

———. 1881. *Suggestions Regarding Forest Management in Northwestern Provinces and Oudh.* Calcutta: Government of India Press.

———. 1883. *Suggestions Regarding Forest Administration in the Madras Presidency.* Madras: Government of India Press.

———. 1897. *Indian Forestry.* Woking: Oriental Institute.

———. [1906] 1971. *Indian Trees.* Dehradoon: Bishen Singh, Mahendrapal Singh.

Braudel, F. 1989. *The Identity of France.* Vol. 1. London: Fontana Press.

Braun, R. 1965. *Sozialer und kultureller Wandel in einem ländlichen Industriegebiet.* Stuttgart: Eugen Rentsch Verlag.

Brenner, R. 1976. "Agrarian Class Structure and Economic Development in Pre-Industrial Europe." *Past and Present* 70:30–75.

British Association for the Advancement of Science (BAAS). 1852. "Report of the Committee Appointed by the British Association to Consider the Probable Effects in an Economical and Physical Point of View of the Destruction of Tropical Forests." By Dr. Hugh Cleghorn, Madras Medical Establishment; Prof. Forbes Royle, King's College London; Capt. R. Baird Smith, Bengal Engineers; R. Strachey, Bengal Engineers. *Journal of the Agricultural and Horticultural Society of India* 8:118–49.

Bromley, D. 1989. "Property Relations and Economic Development: The Other Land Reform." *World Development* 17:867–76.

———. 1991. *Environment and Economy: Property Rights and Public Policy.* Cambridge: Basil Blackwell.

Brosius, P. N.d. "Landscape and Society in Borneo: Penan Hunter-gatherers of Sarawak." Manuscript.

Brubaker, R. 1992. *Citizenship and Nationhood in France and Germany.* Cambridge, Mass.: Harvard University Press.

————. 1996. *Nationalism Reframed: Nationhood and the National Question in the New Europe.* Cambridge: Cambridge University Press.

Bryant, R. 1992. "Political Ecology: An Emerging Research Agenda in Third-World States." *Political Geography* 11:12–36.

Bunker, S. 1985. *Underdeveloping the Amazon: Extraction, Unequal Exchange, and the Failure of the Modern State.* Chicago: University of Illinois Press.

Burke, N. 1955. *Jungle Child.* New York: W. W. Norton.

Canetti, E. [1960] 1971. *Masse und Macht.* Hamburg: Claassen Verlag.

Carleton, R. 1971. *Your Lawn: How to Make It and Keep It.* 2d ed. New York: Van Nostrand Reinhold.

Cator, W. 1936. *The Economic Position of the Chinese in the Netherlands Indies.* Chicago: University of Chicago Press.

Chafe, W. 1999. *The Unfinished Journey: America since World War II.* 4th ed. New York: Oxford University Press.

Chakrabarty, D. 1983. "Conditions of Knowledge for Working Class Conditions: Employers, Government and the Jute Workers of Calcutta, 1890–1940." *Subaltern Studies* 3. Delhi: Oxford University Press.

Champion, H., and S. Seth. 1968. *Forest Types of India.* Delhi: Government of India Press.

Chatterjee, P. 1982. "Agrarian Relations and Communalism in Bengal." *Subaltern Studies* 1. Delhi: Oxford University Press.

————. 1986. *Nationalist Thought and the Colonial World: A Derivative Discourse.* London: Zed Books.

Chemical Week. 1951. "Crabgrass Massacre Means Dollars." August 25, 28–29.

————. 1961. "Making a Killing in Crab Grass Control." April 1, 63–64, 66.

Chew, D. 1990. *Chinese Pioneers on the Sarawak Frontier, 1841–1941.* Singapore: Oxford University Press.

Clark, K. 1999. "Lawn and Order." *U.S. News & World Report,* May 3.

Claval, P. 1994. "From Michelet to Braudel: Personality, Identity, and Organization in France." In David Hooson, ed., *Geography and National Identity.* Oxford: Blackwell.

Clavien, A. 1993. *Les Helvétistes. Intellectuels et politique en Suisse romande au début du siècle.* Lausanne: Editions d'en bas.

Cleghom, H. 1860. *The Forests and Gardens of South India.* London: W. H. Allen.

Cobb, J. 1901. "The Lobster Fishery of Maine." *Bulletin of the United States Fish Commission* 19:241–65. Washington, D.C.: U.S. Government Printing Office.

Cohen, L. 2003. *A Consumers' Republic: The Politics of Mass Consumption.* New York: A. A. Knopf.

Cohn, B. 1966. "Recruitment and Training of British Civil Servants in India, 1600–1860." In *Asian Bureaucratic Systems Emergent from the British Imperial Tradition,* ed. R. Braibanti. Durham, N.C.: Duke University Press.

———. 1987. *An Anthropologist among Historians and Other Essays.* Delhi: Oxford University Press.

Cohn, B., and N. Dirks. 1988. "Beyond the Fringe: The Nation State, Colonialism, and the Technologies of Power." *Journal of Historical Sociology* 1 (2): 224–29.

Coleman, J. 1990. "Norm Generating Structures." In *The Limits of Rationality,* ed. K. Cook and M. Levi, 250–73. Chicago: University of Chicago Press.

Colfer, C., et al. 1993. *Shifting Cultivators of Indonesia: Marauders or Managers of the Forest?* Case Study Series No. 6. Rome: FAO Community Forestry.

Colfer, C., and H. Soedjito. 1995. "Food, Forests, and Fields in a Bornean Rainforest: Toward Appropriate Agroforestry Development." In *Borneo in Transition: People, Forests, Conservation and Development,* ed. C. Padoch. Kuala Lumpur: Oxford University Press.

Colley, L. 1992. *Britons: Forging the Nation, 1707–1837.* New Haven: Yale University Press.

Comaroff, J., and J. Comaroff. 1991. *Of Revelation and Revolution.* Vol. 1. Chicago: University of Chicago Press.

Cooper, R., and J. Uzmann. 1971. "Migration and Growth of Deep-Sea Lobsters." *Science* 171:288–90.

Coppel, C. 1983. *The Indonesian Chinese in Crisis.* Oxford: Oxford University Press.

Corber, R. 1997. *Homosexuality in Cold War America: Resistance and the Crisis of Masculinity.* Durham, N.C.: Duke University Press.

Correspondence of the Commissioner of Sea and Shore Fisheries. 1931a. Vernon Gould to Horatio Crie. February 16. Maine State Archives, Augusta.

———. 1931b. Llewellyn Crowley to Horatio Crie. February 2. Maine State Archives, Augusta.

———. 1931c. Alton Dobbins to Horatio Crie. February 9. Maine State Archives, Augusta.

———. 1931d. Draft of Speech Given by Horatio Crie. In folder for January 3. Maine State Archives, Augusta.

———. 1931e. Zenas Howe to Horatio Crie. November 20. Maine State Archives, Augusta.

———. 1933a. F. E. Peabody to Crie. February 27. Maine State Archives, Augusta.

———. 1933b. Horatio Crie to Russell Turner. September 23. Maine State Archives, Augusta.

———. 1933c. J. M. Jasper to Horatio Crie. May 1. Maine State Archives, Augusta.

———. 1933d. Horatio Crie to U.S. Representative E. C. Moran. May 31. Maine State Archives, Augusta.

———. 1933e. U.S. Rep. Edward Moran to Horatio Crie. April 10. Maine State Archives, Augusta.

————. 1933f. Henry J. Flint to Horatio Cree. July 13. Maine State Archives, Augusta.

————. 1933g. Horatio Crie to Alton Dobbins. December 16. Maine State Archives, Augusta.

————. 1933h. C. S. Beale to Horatio Crie. March 11. Maine State Archives, Augusta.

————. 1933i. Horatio Crie. "Speech to the Honorable Sea and Shore Fisheries Committee, Maine Legislature." Correspondence of the Commissioner of Sea and Shore Fisheries. Maine State Archives, Augusta. December 11.

————. 1934. Horatio Crie to Joseph Wallace. Telegram in box 54, n.d. (probably April or May). Maine State Archives, Augusta.

Cox, T. R., R. Maxwell, P. Thomas, and J. Malone. 1985. *This Well Wooded Land: Americans and Their Forests from Colonial Times to the Present.* Lincoln: University of Nebraska Press.

Cronon, W. 1983. *Changes in the Land: Indians, Colonists, and the Ecology of New England.* New York: Hill and Wang.

————, ed. 1995. *Uncommon Ground.* New York: W. W. Norton.

Crosby, A. 1972. *The Columbian Exchange: Biological and Cultural Consequences of 1492.* Westport, Conn.: Greenwood Press.

————. 1986. *Ecological Imperialism: The Biological Expansion of Europe, 900–1900.* Cambridge: Cambridge University Press.

Dahlmann, C. 1980. *The Open Field System and Beyond.* Cambridge: Cambridge University Press.

Daniels, S. 1993. *Fields of Vision: Landscape Imagery and National Identity in England and the United States.* Cambridge: Polity Press.

D'Arcy, W. 1898. *Preparation of Forest Working Plans in India.* Calcutta: Government of India Press.

Davidson, J. 2002. *Violence and Politics in West Kalimantan Indonesia.* Seattle: University of Washington Press.

Davidson, J., and D. Kamen, 2002. "Indonesia's Unknown War and the Lineages of Violence in West Kalimantan." *Indonesia* 73:1–31.

Davis, L., and K. Johnson. 1986. *Forest Management.* New York: McGraw Hill.

Dawson, M. 2003. *The Consumer Trap: Big Business Marketing in American Life.* Urbana: University of Illinois Press.

Denevan, W., and C. Padoch. 1987. *Swidden Fallow Agroforestry in Latin America.* Advances in Economic Botany 7. Bronx: New York Botanical Garden.

Dhanagare, D. 1983. *Peasant Movements in India, 1920–1950.* Delhi: Oxford University Press.

Dickens, C. [1842] 1985. *American Notes.* New York: St. Martin's Press.

Dirks, N. 1989. "The Invention of Caste: Civil Society in Colonial India." *Social Analysis,* Special Issue, 42–52.

————. 1990. "The Original Caste: Power, History, and Hierarchy in South Asia." In *India through Hindu Categories,* ed. M. Mariott. New Delhi: Sage.

Douglas, M. 1987. *How Institutions Think.* London: Routledge and Kegan Paul.

Dove, M. 1985. "The Agroecological Mythology of the Javanese and the Political Economy of Indonesia." *Indonesia* 39:1–36.

———. 1986. "Peasant versus Government Perception and Use of the Environment: A Case Study of Banjarese Ecology and River Basin Development in South Kalimantan." *Journal of Southeast Asian Studies* 17:113–36.

———. 1988. *The Real and Imagined Role of Culture in Development.* Honolulu: University of Hawaii Press.

———. 1996. "So Far from Power, So Near the Forest: A Structural Analysis of Gain and Blame in Tropical Forest Development." In *Borneo in Transition: People, Forests, Conservation, and Development,* ed. C. Padoch and N. Peluso, 41–58. Kuala Lumpur: Oxford University Press.

Dübi, H. 1900. "Die Erforschung der Alpen. Der Schweizer Alpenclub." In P. Seippel, ed., *Die Schweiz im neunzehnten Jahrhundert,* vol. 3. Bern: Schmid and Francke.

Dumont, L. 1970. *Homo Hierarchicus: The Caste System and Its Implications.* Chicago: University of Chicago Press.

Dyer, J. 1925. "Forestry in the Central Provinces and Berar." *Indian Forester* 51:345–56.

Edney, M. 1997. *Mapping an Empire: The Geographical Construction of British India, 1765–1843.* Chicago: University of Chicago Press.

Edwardes, S. 1922. "Tree Worship in India." *Empire Forestry Journal* 1 (1): 78–86.

Eley, G. 1980. *Reshaping the German Right: Radical Nationalism and Political Change after Bismarck.* New Haven and London: Yale University Press.

Eley, G, and R. G. Suny, ed. 1996. *Becoming National: A Reader.* Oxford: Oxford University Press.

Elster, J. 1989. *The Cement of Society.* Cambridge: Cambridge University Press.

Elton, A. 1933a. "Maine Lobster Law Remains Unchanged." *Atlantic Fisherman,* March 8.

———. 1933b. "Maine Lobster Fishermen Polled for Views: Asked Whether They Favor Present Law, Nine Inch Law, or Double Gauge." *Atlantic Fisherman,* February 9.

———. 1934. "Double Gauge Law Passed." *Atlantic Fisherman,* January 7.

Elvin, M., and Liu Ts'ui-jung, eds. 1995. *Sediments of Time: Environment and Society in Chinese History.* Cambridge: Cambridge University Press.

Elwin, V. 1936. *Leaves from the Jungle.* London: John Murray.

———. 1938. *The Baiga.* London: John Murray.

———. 1942. *The Agaria.* London: Oxford University Press.

———. 1945. "Saora fituris." *Man in India* 25 (4): 154–57.

———. 1950. *Bondo Highlanders.* London: Oxford University Press.

———. [1964] 1989. *The Tribal World of Verrier Elwin.* New York: Oxford University Press.

Embree, A. 1969. "Landholding in India and British Institutions." In *Land Control and Social Structure in Indian History,* ed. R. Frykenburg. Madison: University of Wisconsin Press.

Ensminger, J. 1992. *Making a Market: The Institutional Transformation of an African Society.* Cambridge: Cambridge University Press.

Ensminger, J., and A. Rutten. 1991. "The Political Economy of Changing Property Rights: Dismantling a Pastoral Commons." *American Ethnologist* 18 (4): 683–99.

Ernst, A. 1994. "Ethnos-Demos: Krise." In A. Ernst et al., eds., *Kontinuität und Krise. Beiträge zur Wirtschafts- und Sozialgeschichte der Schweiz.* Zurich: Chronos.

Ex, J. 1992. "Report on Social Forestry among Villagers in Saggau." Pontianak: GTZ. Manuscript.

Feagan, R., and M. Ripmeester. 1999. "Contesting Natural(ized) Lawns: A Geography of Private Green Space in the Niagara Region." *Urban Geography* 20 (7): 617–34.

———. 2001. "Reading Private Green Space: Competing Geographic Identities at the Level of the Lawn." *Philosophy & Geography* 4 (1): 79–95.

Feierman, S. 1990. *Peasant Intellectuals: History and Anthropology in Tanzania.* Madison: University of Wisconsin Press.

Fernandez, J. 1987. "Call to the Commons in Asturias." In *The Question of the Commons,* ed. B. McCay and J. Acheson. Tucson: University of Arizona Press.

Ford, K., and T. Creighton. 1951. *The American House Today.* New York: Reinhold.

Forsyth, J. 1889. *The Highlands of Central India: Notes on Their Forests and Wild Tribes, Natural History, and Sports.* London: Chapman and Hall.

Fortmann, L. 1985. "The Tree Tenure Factor in Agroforestry with Particular Reference to Africa." *Agroforestry Systems* 2:229–51.

———. 1988. "The Tree Tenure Factor in Agroforestry." In *Whose Trees? Proprietary Dimensions of Forestry,* ed. L. Bruce. Boulder, Colo.: Westview.

———. 1990. "Locality and Custom: Non-aboriginal Claims to Customary Usufructuary Rights as a Source of Rural Protest." *Journal of Rural Studies* 6:195–208.

Fortune. 1952. "Levitt's Progress." October.

Foucault, M. 1973. *The Order of Things: An Archaeology of the Human Sciences.* New York: Vintage.

———. [1978] 1991. "Governmentality." In *The Foucault Effect: Studies in Governmentality,* ed. G. Burchell, C. Gordon, and P. Miller. Chicago: University of Chicago Press.

———. 1980. *Power/Knowledge: Selected Interviews and Other Writings, 1972–77.* Ed. C. Gordon. New York: Pantheon.

Freeman, D. 1955. *The Methods of Land Usage Employed by the Iban of Sarawak in the Shifting Cultivation of Hill Rice.* Canberra: Australian National University.

Frei, D. 1964. *Das schweizerische Nationalbewusstsein. Seine Förderung nach dem Zusammenbruch der Alten Eidgenossenschaft 1798.* Zurich: Juris-Verlag.

———. 1967. *Neutralität—Ideal oder Kalkül? Zweihundert Jahre aussenpolitisches Denken in der Schweiz.* Stuttgart: Verlag Huber.

Freitag, S. 1985. "Collective Crime and Authority in North India." In *Crime and Criminality in British India,* ed. A. Yang. Tucson: University of Arizona Press.

French, W. 1989. "Crabgrass Wars: My Father's Surrender." *Commonweal,* August 11.

Frykman, J., and O. Löfgren. 1987. *Culture Builders: A Historical Anthropology of Middle-Class Life.* New Brunswick, N.J.: Rutgers University Press.

Gadgil, M. 1985. "Social Restraints on Resource Utilization: The Indian Experience." In *Culture and Conservation: The Human Dimension in Environmental Planning,* ed. J. McNeely and D. Pitt. London: Croon Helm.

Gadgil, M., and R. Guha. 1988. "State Forestry and Social Conflict in British India: A Study in the Ecological Bases of Agrarian Protest." *Past and Present* 123:141–77.

———. 1992. *This Fissured Land: An Ecological History of India.* New Delhi: Oxford University Press.

———. 1995. *The Use and Abuse of Nature in Contemporary India.* Delhi: Oxford University Press.

Gadgil, M., and K. Malhotra. 1983. "Adaptive Significance of the Indian Caste System: An Ecological Perspective." *Annals of Human Biology* 10 (5): 465–78.

Gadgil, M., and V. Vartak. 1976. "The Sacred Groves of Western Ghats in India." *Economic Botany* 30:152–60.

Geddes, W. 1954. *Report on the Land Dayaks of the First Division.* Kuching: Colonial Printing Office.

Geertz, C. 1963. *Agricultural Involution.* Berkeley: University of California Press.

———. 1973. "Ideology as a Cultural System." In *The Interpretation of Cultures: Selected Essays by Clifford Geertz,* 193–233. New York: Basic Books.

Gholz, H. 1987. *Agroforestry: Realities, Possibilities, and Potentials.* Dordrecht: Martinus Nijhoff.

Ghosh, A. 1973. *The Land Acquisition Act, 1894.* Calcutta: Eastern Law House.

Giddens, A. 1991. *Modernity and Self-Identity.* London: Polity Press.

Gilman, M. 1958. "Why They Can't Wait to Wed." *Parents,* November.

Glacken, C. J. 1967. *Traces on the Rhodian Shore: Nature and Culture in Western Thought from Ancient Times to the End of the Eighteenth Century.* Berkeley: University of California Press.

Goldstone, J. 1992. "Imminent Political Conflicts Arising from China's Environmental Crises." *AAAS Occasional Papers* (December 1992): 41–59.

Goodman, D. 2002. "The Politics of the West: Equality, Nation-Building, and Colonization." In *La Chine et son Occident: China and Its Western Frontier,* ed. F. Godement, 23–55. Paris: Centre Asie IFRI.

———. 2004. "Qinghai and the Emergence of the West." *China Quarterly* 178:379–99.

Gordon, R., and K. Gordon. 1959. "Psychosomatic Problems in a Rapidly Growing Suburb." *Journal of the American Medical Association* 170 (15): 1757–64.

Government of India. 1988. *National Forest Policy.* New Delhi: Ministry of Environment and Forests.

Greenfeld, L. 1992. *Nationalism: Five Roads to Modernity.* Cambridge, Mass.: Harvard University Press.

Greenlaw, L. 1978. "Act on Lobster Management." *Maine Commercial Fisherman,* October 1.

Greenough, P. 1982. *Prosperity and Misery in Modern Bengal: The Famine of 1943–1944.* New York: Oxford University Press.

———. 2001. "*Naturae Ferae:* Wild Animals in South Asia and the Standard Environmental Narrative." In *Agrarian Societies: Synthetic Work at the Cutting Edge,* ed. J. Scott and N. Bhatt. New Haven: Yale University Press.

Grosby, S. 1995. "Territoriality: The Transcendental, Primordial Feature of Modern Societies." *Nations and Nationalism* 1 (2): 143–62.

Grove, R. 1988. "Conservation and Colonialism: The Evolution of Environmental Attitudes and Conservation Policies on St. Helena, Mauritius and in Western India, 1660–1854." In *Changing Tropical Forests: Historical Perspectives on Today's Challenges in Asia, Australasia, and Oceania,* ed. J. Dargavel, K. Dixon, and N. Simple. Canberra: Center for Resources and Environmental Studies.

———. 1989. "Scottish Missionaries, Evangelical Discourses, and the Origin of Conservation Thinking in Southern Africa, 1820–1900." *Journal of Southern African History* 15:163–87.

———. 1993. "Conserving Eden: The (European) East India Companies and Their Environmental Policies on St. Helena, Mauritus and in Western India, 1660 to 1854." *Comparative Studies in Society and History* 36 (3): 318–51.

———. 1995. *Green Imperialism: Colonial Expansion, Tropical Island Edens, and the Origins of Environmentalism, 1600–1860.* Cambridge: Cambridge University Press.

———. 1997. *Ecology, Climate, and Empire: Colonialism and Global Environmental History, 1400–1940.* Cambridge: White Horse Press.

Grunebaum, J. 1987. *Private Ownership.* London: Routledge and Kegan Paul.

Gugerli, D., and D. Speich. 2002. *Topografien der Nation.* Zurich: Chronos.

Guha, Ramachandra. 1989. *The Unquiet Woods: Ecological Change and Peasant Resistance in the Himalaya.* New Delhi: Oxford University Press.

———. 1990. "An Early Environmental Debate: The Making of the 1878 Forest Act." *Indian Economic and Social History Review* 27 (1): 65–84.

———. 1991. "Dietrich Brandis and Indian Forestry: The Road Not Taken." Manuscript.

Guha, Ranajit. 1982. "The Prose of Counter-Insurgency." *Subaltern Studies* 1. Delhi: Oxford University Press.

———. 1983. *Elementary Aspects of Peasant Insurgency in India.* New Delhi: Oxford University Press.

———. 1987. "Chandra's Death." *Subaltern Studies* 5. Delhi: Oxford University Press.

———, ed. 1982–89. *Subaltern Studies: Writings on South Asian History and Society.* Vols. 1–6. Delhi: Oxford University Press.

Guha, S. 1999. *Environment and Ethnicity in Western India, c. 1200–1991.* Cambridge: Cambridge University Press.

———. 2002. "Claims on the Commons: Political Power and Natural Resources in Pre-colonial India." *Indian Economic and Social History Review* 39 (2–3): 181–96.

Guoli Gugong Bowuyuan, ed. 1982–88. *Gongzhongdang Qianlongchao Zouzhe.* 75 vols. Taibei: National Palace Museum Press.

Habib, I. 1985. "Studying a Colonial Economy without Perceiving Colonialism." *Modern Asian Studies* 19 (3): 355–81.

Hale, J. 1994. *The Civilization of Europe in the Renaissance.* London: Fontana Press.

Hardiman, D. 1987. *The Coming of the Devi: Adivasi Assertion in Western India.* Delhi: Oxford University Press.

Hart, G. 1922. "The Indian Forest Research Institute." *Empire Forestry Journal* 1:247–52.

———. 2002. *Disabling Globalization: Places of Power in Post-Apartheid South Africa.* Pietermaritzburg: University of Natal Press.

Hays, S. 1959. *Conservation and the Gospel of Efficiency: The Progressive Conservation Movement, 1890–1920.* New York: Atheneum.

Heath, A. 1976. *Rational Choice and Social Exchange.* New York: Cambridge University Press.

Hecht, S., and A. Cockburn. 1989. *The Fate of the Forest: Developers, Destroyers, and Defenders of the Amazon.* London: Verso.

Hecht, S., P. May, and A. Anderson. 1988. "The Subsidy from Nature: Shifting Cultivation, Successional Palm Forests, and Rural Development." *Human Organization* 47:25–35.

Hecht, S., and D. Posey. 1989. "Preliminary Results of Soil Management Techniques of the Kagapó Indians." *Advances in Economic Botany* 7:174–88.

Hechter, M. 1990. "On the Inadequacy of Game Theory for the Solution of Real-World Collective Action Problems." In *The Limits of Rationality,* ed. K. Cook and M. Levi, 240–49. Chicago: University of Chicago Press.

Heidhues, M. 2003. *Goldiggers, Farmers, and Traders in the "Chinese Districts" of West Kalimantan, Indonesia.* Ithaca: Cornell University and Southeast Asian Program Publications.

Helbling, B. 1994. *Eine Schweiz für die Schule. Nationale Identität und kulturelle Vielfalt in den Schweizer Lesebüchern seit 1900.* Zurich: Chronos.

Henley, P. 1982. *The Panare: Tradition and Change in the Amazonian Frontier.* New Haven: Yale University Press.

Herrick, F. 1911. "Natural History of the American Lobster." *Bulletin of the Bureau of Fisheries* 19:153–440. Washington, D.C.: U.S. Government Printing Office.

Hilty, C. 1875. "Die schweizerische Nationalität." In Carl Hilty, ed., *Vorlesungen über die Politik der Eidgenossenschaft.* Bern: Max Fiala's Buch- und Kunsthandlung.

Hirsch, E. 1995. "Landscape: Between Place and Space." In E. Hirsch and M. O'Hanlon, eds., *The Anthropology of Landscape: Perspectives on Place and Space.* New York: Oxford University Press.

Hobsbawm, E. J. [1990] 1993. *Nations and Nationalism since 1780: Programme, Myth, Reality.* Cambridge: Cambridge University Press.

Hooson, D., ed. 1994. *Geography and National Identity.* Oxford: Blackwell.

Hope Nicolson, M. 1959. *Mountain Gloom and Mountain Glory: The Development of the Aesthetics of the Infinite.* Ithaca, N.Y.: Cornell University Press.

Horkheimer, M. 1947. *Eclipse of Reason.* New York: Oxford University Press.

Hoy, S. 1995. *Chasing Dirt: The American Pursuit of Cleanliness.* New York: Oxford University Press.

Huber, M. [1916] 1947. "Der Schweizerische Staatsgedanke." In *Heimat und Tradition. Gesammelte Aufsätze.* Zurich: Atlantis Verlag.

———. [1934] 1947. "Vom Wesen und Sinn des Schweizerischen Staates." In *Heimat und Tradition. Gesammelte Aufsätze.* Zurich: Atlantis Verlag.

———. 1947. *Heimat und Tradition. Gesammelte Aufsätze.* Zurich: Atlantis Verlag.

Hurd, J. 1975. "Railways and the Expansion of Markets in India, 1861–1921." *Explorations in Economic History* 12:260–85.

Im Hof, U. 1991. *Mythos Schweiz.* Zurich: Verlag Neue Zürcher Zeitung.

Imperial Forest College (IFC). 1906. *A Manual of Forest Law.* Calcutta: Government of India Press.

Isaacman, A. 1990. "Peasants and Rural Social Protest in Africa." *African Studies Review* 33:1–120.

Jackson, J. 1970. *Chinese in the West Borneo Goldfields: A Study in Cultural Geography.* Hull, U.K.: University of Hull.

Jackson, K. 1985. *Crabgrass Frontier: The Suburbanization of the United States.* New York: Oxford University Press.

Jain, S. 1981. *Glimpses of Indian Ethnobotany.* New Delhi: Oxford and India Book House.

Jenkins, V. 1994. *The Lawn: A History of an American Obsession.* Washington, D.C.: Smithsonian Institution Press.

Ji Yun. 1937. *Wulumuqi Zashi.* Shangai: Shangwu Yinshuguan.

Joshi, H., ed. [1921] 1980. *Troup's Silviculture of Indian Trees.* Dehradoon: Forest Research Institute.

Jost, H.-U. 1988. "Nation, Politics, and Art." In Swiss Institute for Art Research on Behalf of the Coordinating Commission for the Presence of Switzerland Abroad, ed., *From Liotard to Le Corbusier: 200 Years of Swiss Painting, 1730–1930.* Bern: Coordinating Commission for the Presence of Switzerland Abroad.

———. 1992. *Les Avant-Gardes Réactionnaires. La naissance de la nouvelle droite en Suisse 1890–1914.* Lausanne: Editions d'en bas.

Judd, R. 1988. "Saving the Fisherman as Well as the Fish: Conservation and Commercial Rivalry in Maine's Lobster Industry: 1872–1933." *Business History Review* 62:596–625.

Kapferer, B. 1976. *Transactions and Meaning: Directions in the Anthropology of Exchange and Symbolic Behavior.* Philadelphia: Institute for the Study of Human Issues.

Kaufmann, E. 1998. "'Naturalizing the Nation': The Rise of Naturalistic Nationalism in the United States and Canada." *Comparative Studies in Society and History* 40 (4): 666–95.

Kelly, B. 1993. *Expanding the American Dream: Building and Rebuilding Levittown.* Albany: State University of New York Press.

Kelly, K. 1990. "A Summary of Maine Lobster Laws and Regulations: 1820–1990." Lobster Informational Leaflet No. 19. Augusta: Maine Department of Marine Resources.

Kelly, W. 1991. "Directions in the Anthropology of Contemporary Japan." *Annual Review of Anthropology* 20:395–431.

Kirby, W. 1990. "Continuity and Change in Modern China: Economic Planning on the Mainland and Taiwan, 1934–58." *Australian Journal of Chinese Affairs* 24:121–41.

Knight, J. 1992. *Institutions and Social Conflict.* Cambridge: Cambridge University Press.

Knight, R. 1950. "I Love Crab Grass." *Saturday Evening Post,* August 19.

Kreis, G. 1987. "Die besseren Patrioten. Nationale Idee und regionale Identität in der französischen Schweiz vor 1914." In F. de Capitani and G. Germann, eds., *Auf dem Weg zu einer schweizerischen Identität 1848–1914.* Freiburg: Universitätsverlag Freiburg.

———. 1988. "Das Festspiel—ein antimodernes Produkt der Moderne." In B. Engeler and G. Kreis, eds., *Das Festspiel: Formen, Funktionen, Perspektiven.* Willisau: Theaterkultur-Verlag.

———. 1991. *Der Mythos von 1291. Zur Entstehung des schweizerischen Nationalfeiertages.* Basel: Friedrich Rinhardt Verlag.

———. 1992. "Der 'homo alpinus helveticus'. Zum schweizerischen Rassendiskurs der 30er Jahre." In Guy P. Marchal and A. Mattioli, eds., *Erfundene Schweiz. Konstruktionen nationaler Identität.* Zurich: Chronos.

Krouse, J. 1972. "Size at First Maturity for Male and Female Lobsters Found along the Maine Coast." Lobster Information Leaflet No. 2. Augusta: Maine Department of Marine Resources.

———. 1973. "Maturity, Sex Ratio, and Size Composition of the Natural Population of American Lobster, *Homarus Americanus,* along the Maine Coast." *Fishery Bulletin* 71:165–73.

Krouse, J., and J. Thomas. 1976. "Effects of Trap Selectivity and Some Population Parameters on Size Composition of American Lobsters Catch along the Maine Coast." *Fishery Bulletin* 73 (4): 863–71.

Kumar, D. 1995. *Science and the Raj, 1857–1905.* Delhi: Oxford University Press.

Lahjie, A., and B. Seibert. 1988. "Agroforestry: Untuk Tembanguanan daerah Pedesaan di Kalimantan Timur." Proceedings of a seminar held September 19–22, 1988, at Fakultas Kehutanan, Universitas Maluwarman, Samarinda and GTZ (German Forestry Group).

Lan Dingyuan. 1958. *Pingtai Jilue.* Taibei: Taiwan Yinhang.

Larrabee, E. 1948. "The Six Thousand Houses That Levitt Built." *Harper's Magazine,* September, 79–88.

Lasserre, A. 1992. "Le peuple des bergers dans son 'Réduit national.'" In G. P. Marchal and A. Mattioli, eds., *Erfundene Schweiz. Konstruktionen nationaler Identität.* Zurich: Chronos.

Laws of Maine. 1874. *An Act for the Better Protection of Lobsters in the Waters of Maine.* Chapter 210, 146–47. Augusta: Office of the Secretary of State of Maine.

———. 1879. *An Act for the Protection of Lobsters.* Chapter 96, 114. Augusta: Office of the Secretary of State of Maine.

———. 1883. *An Act for the Protection of Lobsters.* Chapter 138, 115–16. Augusta: Office of the Secretary of State of Maine.

———. 1885. *An Act to Amend Chapter Forty of the Revised Statutes, Relating to Fish and Fisheries.* Chapter 275, 224–26. Augusta: Office of the Secretary of State of Maine.

———. 1889. *An Act for the Regulation of the Lobster Industry.* Chapter 292, 258–60. Augusta: Office of the Secretary of State of Maine.

———. 1907. *An Act to Amend Section Seventeen of Chapter Forty-one of the Revised Statutes Relating to Measurement of Lobsters.* Chapter 49. Augusta: Office of the Secretary of State of Maine

———. 1935. *An Act Relating to Measurement of Lobsters.* Chapter 294. Augusta: Office of the Secretary of State of Maine.

———. 1947. *A Law to Revise the Sea and Shore Fisheries Laws.* Chapter 332, 408. Augusta: Office of the Secretary of State of Maine.

———. 1978. *An Act to Revise the Laws Concerning Marine Resources.* Chapter 661, Section 6433. Augusta: Office of the Secretary of State of Maine.

Leach, E. 1977. *Political Systems of Highland Burma.* London: Athlone Press.

Leach, M. 1995. *Rainforest Relations: Gender and Resource Management among the Gola of Sierra Leone.* Washington, D.C.: Smithsonian Press.

Leach, T. A. 1988. "Date Trees in Halfa Province." In *Whose Trees? Proprietary Dimensions of Forestry,* ed. L. Bruce, 43–48. Boulder, Colo.: Westview.

Leaman, D., Y. Razali, and H. Sangat-Roemantyo. 1991. *Kenya Dayak Forest Medicines.* Jakarta: World Wide Fund for Nature/Indonesia Programme.

Lefebvre, H. 1979. *The Production of Space.* Cambridge: Blackwell.

Legislative Department. 1890. *The Indian Forest Act, 1878, as Modified up to 1890.* Calcutta: Government of India Press.

Legislative Document. 1872. *An Act to Protect the Spawn or Egg Lobsters in the Waters of Maine.* House No. 54.

———. 1935. *An Act Relating to Measurement of Lobsters.* House No. 503, February 12.

———. 1995. *An Act to Establish a Management Framework for the Lobster Fishery within State Waters.* House No. 782.

Legislative Record. 1915a. Senate, March 30, 1165.

———. 1915b. Senate, March 30, 1160.

———. 1915c. House of Representatives, March 25, 1070.

———. 1915d. Senate, March 25, 1070.

———. 1917. House of Representatives, March 8, 486.

Lev, D. 1985. "Colonial Law and the Genesis of the Indonesian State." *Indonesia* 40:57–75.

Lévi-Strauss, C. 1972. *The Savage Mind.* London: Weidenfeld and Nicolson.

Levitt, A. 1948a. "Chats on Gardening." *Levittown Tribune,* April 8, 13.

———. 1948b. "Chats on Gardening." *Levittown Tribune,* June 17, 7.

———. 1949. "Chats on Gardening." *Levittown Tribune,* May 12, 12.

———. 1951. "Chats on Gardening." *Levittown Tribune,* April 5, 8.

———. N.d. *The Care of Your Lawn and Landscaping.* N.p.: Levitt and Sons.

Levitt, W. 1964. "A House Is Not Enough: The Story of America's First Community Builder." In *Business Decisions That Change Our Lives,* ed. S. Furst and M. Sherman, 59–71. New York: Random House.

Levittown Tribune. 1948. "All Lawns To Be Renovated By Company, Levitt Announces." April 1, 1.

Lewis, D. 1969. *Convention: A Philosophical Study.* Cambridge, Mass.: Harvard University Press.

Life. 1958. Lawn Boy advertisement. April 21, 86.

Lobster Bulletin of the University of Maine. 1995. "V-notching: Then, Now and around the World." Vol. 8 (2): 3.

Lowenthal, D. 1978. "Finding Valued Landscapes." *Progress in Human Geography* 2 (3): 373–418.

———. 1994. "European and English Landscapes as National Symbols." In David Hooson, ed., *Geography and National Identity*. Oxford: Blackwell.

Lowood, H. 1990. "The Calculating Forester: Quantification, Cameral Science, and the Emergence of Scientific Forestry Management in Germany." In *The Quantifying Spirit in the Eighteenth Century*, ed. T. Frangsmyr, J. Heilbron, and R. Rider. Berkeley: University of California Press.

Maine Commercial Fisheries. 1978. "Retain Measure, Heed Our Experience—Fishermen Say." October, 1.

Maine Commission of Sea and Shore Fisheries. 1926. *Fourth Biennial Report of the Commission of Sea and Shore Fisheries of the State of Maine*. Rockland: Maine Commission of Sea and Shore Fisheries.

Maine Department of Marine Resources. 1995. *Summary of the Maine Lobster Industry*. Hallowell: Maine Department of Marine Resources.

Maine Department of Sea and Shore Fisheries. 1936. *Ninth Biennial Report of the Department of Sea and Shore Fisheries of the State of Maine*. Thomaston: Maine Department of Sea and Shore Fisheries.

Majeski, S. 1990. "An Alternative Approach to the Generation and Maintenance of Norms." In *The Limits of Rationality*, ed. K. Cook and M. Levi, 273–81. Chicago: University of Chicago Press.

Mao Qiling. [ca. 1700] 1997. *Xianghu Shuilizhi*. 3 vols. Jinan: Qilu shushe chubanshe.

Marchal, G. P. 1986. "Die Ursprüngen der Unabhängigheit." In *Geschichte der Schweiz und der Schweizer*, ed. U. Im Hof, B. Mesmer, 109–214. Basel and Frankfurt: Helbing and Lichtenhahn.

———. 1990. "Die Alten Eidgenossen in Wandel der Zeiten. Das Bild der frühen Eidgenossen im Traditionsbewusstsein und in der Identitätsvorstellung der Schweizer vom 15. bis ins 20. Jahrhundert." In Historischer Verein der Fünf Orte, ed., *Innerschweiz und frühe Eidgenossenschaft. Jubiläumsschrift 700 Jahre Eidgenossenschaft*, vol. 2. Olten: Walter-Verlag.

———. 1992a. "Das 'Schweizeralpenland': eine imagologische Bastelei." In Guy P. Marchal and A. Mattioli, eds., *Erfundene Schweiz. Konstruktionen nationaler Identität*. Zurich: Chronos.

———. 1992b. "La naissance du mythe du Saint-Gothard ou la longue découverte de l' 'homo alpinus helveticus' et de l'Helvetia mater fluviorum' (Xve s.–1940)." In J.-F. Bergier and S. Guzzi, eds., *La découverte des Alpes*, Actes de Colloque Latsis 1990. Basel: Schwabe.

Marks, R. 1998. *Tigers, Rice, Silk, and Silt: Environment and Economy in Late Imperial South China*. Cambridge: Cambridge University Press.

Marling, K. 1994. *As Seen on TV: The Visual Culture of Everyday Life in the 1950s*. Cambridge, Mass.: Harvard University Press.

Martin, K., and N. Lipfert. 1985. *Lobstering and the Maine Coast*. Bath: Maine Maritime Museum.

Marx, K. [1852] 1990. *The 18th Brumaire of Louis Bonaparte.* New York: International.

———. 1973. *Grundrisse: Foundations of the Critique of Political Economy.* Trans. M. Nicolaus. Harmondsworth, U.K.: Penguin.

Massey, D. 1994. *Space, Place, and Gender.* Cambridge: Polity.

Mathieu, J. 1998. "Die Bevölkerung des Alpenraums von 1500 bis 1900." *Schweizerische Zeitschrift für Geschichte* 48:1–24.

Mattioli, A. 1996. "Die Moderne und ihre Kritiker. Zur seismographischen Qualität antimodernistischer Einstellungen im Kanton Fribourg." In A. Ernst et al., eds., *Die Neue Schweiz. Eine Gesellschaft zwischen Integration and Polarisierung (1910–1930).* Zurich: Chronos.

May, E. 1999. *Homeward Bound: American Families in the Cold War Era.* Rev. ed. New York: Basic Books.

Mayaram, S. 1991. "Criminality or Community: Alternate Constructions of the Mev Narrative of Darya Khan." *Contributions to Indian Sociology* 25 (1): 75–84.

Mazumdar, S. 1998. *Sugar and Society in China: Peasants, Technology, and the World Market.* Cambridge, Mass.: Harvard University Press.

McCay, B., and J. Acheson, eds. 1987. *The Question of the Commons.* Tucson: University of Arizona Press.

McCormack, G. 2001. "Water Margins: Competing Paradigms in China." *Critical Asian Studies* 33 (1): 5–30.

McFarland, R. 1911. *A History of the New England Fisheries.* Philadelphia: University of Pennsylvania Press.

McGoodwin, J. 1990. *Crisis in the World's Fisheries.* Stanford: Stanford University Press.

Menzies, N. 1988. "Three Hundred Years of Taungya." *Human Ecology* 16 (4): 361–76.

Merchant, C. 1990. *Ecological Revolutions: Nature, Gender, and Science in New England.* Chapel Hill: University of North Carolina Press.

Merki, C. 1995. *Und wieder lodern die Höhenfeuer. Die Schweizerische Bundesfeier als Hoch-Zeit der nationalen Ideologie.* Zurich: Chronos.

Metcalf, T. 1964. *The Aftermath of Revolt: India, 1857–1870.* Princeton: Princeton University Press.

———. 1979. *Land, Landlords, and the British Raj.* Berkeley: University of California Press.

Michon, G., and F. Michon. 1994. "Conversion of Traditional Village Gardens and New Economic Strategies of Rural Households in the Area of Bogor, Indonesia." *Agroforestry Systems* 25:31–58.

Mills, C. 1961. *First in Lawns: O. M. Scott & Sons.* New York: Newcomen Society of North America.

Mitch, L. 1988. "Crabgrass." *Weed Technology* 2:114–15.

Mizoguchi Yuzo. 1980. "Chugoku ni okeru ko, shi gainen no tenkai." *Shiso* 669:19–38.

Moore, S. 1986. *Social Facts and Fabrications: "Customary" Law on Kilimanjaro, 1880–1980.* New York: Cambridge University Press.

Mosse, G. L. 1964. *The Crisis of German Ideology.* New York: Grosset and Dunlap.

Nadkami, M. 1989. *The Political Economy of Forest Use and Management.* New Delhi: Sage.

Nasgaard, R. 1984. *The Mystic North: Symbolist Landscape Painting in Northern Europe and North America 1890–1940.* Toronto: University of Toronto Press.

Nepstad, D., and S. Schwartzman. 1992. *Non-Timber Forest Products as Sustainable Management Strategies.* Bronx: New York Botanical Garden.

Neumann, R. 1992. "The Political Ecology of Wildlife Conservation in the Mount Meru Area of Tanzania." *Land Degradation and Rehabilitation* 3:85–98.

New York Times. 1915. "What Is a Weed?" November 7, Sec. 7, 5.

———. 1950. "The Family Lawn." Editorial. April 10, 18.

———. 1992. "Plenty of Fish in the Sea? Not Any More." March 25, Sec. A, 14.

Nigam, S. 1990a. "The Making of a Colonial Stereotype: The Criminal Tribes and Castes of North India." Part 1 of "Disciplining and Policing the 'Criminals by Birth.'" *Indian Economic and Social History Review* 27 (2): 131–64.

———. 1990b. "The Development of a Disciplinary System, 1871–1900." Part 2 of "Disciplining and Policing the 'Criminals by Birth.'" *Indian Economic and Social History Review* 27 (3): 257–87.

Nora, P. 1996. "General Introduction: Between Memory and History." In *Realms of Memory: Rethinking the French Past.* New York: Columbia University Press.

Nordhaus, W. 2000. "New Directions in National Economic Accounting." *American Economic Review* 90 (2): 259–63.

North, D. 1990. *Institutions, Institutional Change, and Economic Performance.* Cambridge: Cambridge University Press.

O'Brien, J., and W. Roseberry. 1991. "Introduction." In *Golden Ages, Dark Ages: Imagining the Past in Anthropology and History.* Berkeley: University of California Press.

O'Hanlon, R. 1988. "Recovering the Subject: Subaltern Studies and Histories of Resistance in Colonial South Asia." *Modern Asian Studies* 22 (1): 189–224.

Okoth-Ogendo, H. 1989. "Some Issues of Theory in the Study of Tenure Relations in African Agriculture." *Africa* 59 (1): 6–17.

Olson, M. 1965. *The Logic of Collective Action: Public Goods and the Theory of Groups.* Cambridge, Mass.: Harvard University Press.

Orlove, B. 1980. "Ecological Anthropology." *Annual Review of Anthropology* 9:235–73.

Ortner, S. 1984. "Theory in Anthropology since the Sixties." *Comparative Studies in Society and History* 26 (1): 126–66.

―――. 1989. *High Religion: A Cultural and Political History of Sherpa Buddhism.* Princeton: Princeton University Press.

Osborne, A. 1994. "The Local Politics of Land Reclamation in the Lower Yangzi Highlands." *Late Imperial China* 15 (1): 1–46.

―――. 1995. "Highlands and Lowlands: Economic and Ecological Interactions in the Lower Yangzi Region under the Qing." In *Sediments of Time: Environment and Society in Chinese History,* ed. M. Elvin and Liu Ts'ui-jung, 203–34. Cambridge: Cambridge University Press.

Ostrom, E. 1990. *Governing the Commons: The Evolution of Institutions for Collective Action.* Cambridge: Cambridge University Press.

―――. 2000a. "Reformulating the Commons." *Swiss Political Science Review* 61 (1): 29–52.

―――. 2000b. "Collective Action and the Evolution of Social Norms." *Journal of Economic Perspectives* 14 (3): 137–58.

Ozinga, J. 1940. *De economische ontwikkeling der Westerafdeeling van Borneo en de bevolkingsrubbercultuur door.* Wageningen: Zomer en Keuning.

Paasi, A. 1996. *Territories, Boundaries, and Consciousness: The Changing Geographies of the Finnish-Russian Border.* New York: Wiley.

Padoch, C., 1983. *Migration and Its Alternatives among the Iban of Sarawak.* The Hague: Martinus Nijhoff.

―――. 1994. "The Woodlands of Tae: Traditional Forest Management in Kalimantan." In *Forest Resources and Wood-Based Biomass Energy as Rural Development Assets,* ed. W. Gowen. New Delhi: Oxford and IBH Publishing.

Padoch, C., and C. Peters. 1993. "Managed Forests of West Kalimantan, Indonesia." *Perspectives on Biodiversity: Case Studies of Genetic Resources for Conservation and Development.* Washington, D.C.: American Association for the Advancement of Science.

Paehlke, R. 1989. *Environmentalism and the Future of Progressive Politics.* New Haven: Yale University Press.

Pandey, G. 1980. "A View of the Observable: A Positivist Understanding of Agrarian Society and Political Protest in Colonial India." *Journal of Peasant Studies* 7 (3): 375–83.

Pant, G. 1922. *The Forest Problem in Kumaon.* Nainital: Gyanodaya Prakashan.

Parker, R. 1923. "The Indian Forest Department." *Empire Forestry Journal* 2 (1): 34–41.

Pearson, R., and H. Brown. [1932] 1981. *The Commercial Timbers of India.* Delhi: Researchco Reprints.

Peluso, N. 1991. "The History of State Forest Management in Java." *Forest and Conservation History* 35 (2): 65–75.

―――. 1992a. "The Ironwood Problem: (Mis-)Management and Development of an Extractive Rainforest Product." *Conservation Biology* 6:210–19.

―――. 1992b. "The Political Ecology of Extraction and Extractive Reserves in East Kalimantan, Indonesia." *Development and Change* 23:49–74.

————. 1992c. *Rich Forests, Poor People: Resource Control and Resistance in Java.* Berkeley: University of California Press.

————. 1993a. "Coercing Conservation: The Politics of State Resource Control." *Global Environmental Change* 4, no. 2: 199–217.

————. 1993b. *The Impacts of Social and Environmental Change on Indigenous People's Managed Forests of West Kalimantan, Indonesia.* Rome: Food and Agriculture Organization.

————. 2003a. "Territorializing Local Struggles for Resource Control." In *Environmental Discourses in South and Southeast Asia,* ed. P. Tsing and A. Tsing, 231–52. Durham, N.C.: Duke University Press.

————. 2003b. "Weapons of the Wild: Strategic Uses of Wilderness and Violence in West Kalimantan." In *In Search of the Rainforest,* ed. C. Slater. Durham, N.C.: Duke University Press, 284–340.

————. 2006. "Passing the Red Bowl: Creating Community through Violence in West Kalimantan, Indonesia." In *Violent Conflict in Indonesia,* ed. Charles Coppel. New York: Routledge.

Peluso, N., and E. Harwell. 2001. "Territory, Custom, and the Cultural Politics of Ethnic War in West Kalimantan, Indonesia." In *Violent Environments,* ed. N. Peluso and M. Watts, 83–116. Ithaca: N. Y.: Cornell University Press.

Peluso, N., and C. Padoch. 1995. "Changing Resource Rights in Managed Forests of West Kalimantan." In *Borneo in Transition: People, Forests, Conservation, and Development,* ed. C. Padoch and N. Peluso, 121–36. Singapore: Oxford University Press.

Perdue, P. 1982. "Water Control in the Dongting Lake Region during the Ming and Qing Periods." *Journal of Asian Studies* 41 (4): 747–65.

————. 1987. *Exhausting the Earth: State and Peasant in Hunan, 1500–1850.* Cambridge, Mass.: Harvard University Press.

————. 1990. "Lakes of Empire: Man and Water in Chinese History." *Modern China* 16 (1): 119–29.

————. 2005. *China Marches West: The Qing Conquest of Central Eurasia.* Cambridge, Mass.: Harvard University Press.

Peters, P. 1987. "Embedded Systems and Rooted Models." In *The Question of the Commons: The Culture and Ecology of Communal Resources,* ed. B. McCay and J. Acheson. Tucson: University of Arizona Press.

————. 1992. "Manoeuvres and Debates in the Interpretation of Land Rights in Botswana." *Africa* 62:413–34.

————. 1994. "The Erosion of Commons and the Emergence of Property: Problems for Social Analysis." Paper presented at the Society for Economic Anthropology.

Piccard, A. 1994. *Die Schweiz und die Juden 1933–1945.* Zurich: Chronos.

Pinchot, G. 1947. *Breaking New Ground.* New York: Harcourt, Brace.

Pinkerton, E. 1989. *Co-operative Management of Local Fisheries: New Directions for Improved Management and Community Development*. Vancouver: University of British Columbia Press.

Polanyi, K. 1957. *The Great Transformation*. Boston: Beacon Press.

Pollan, M. 1991. *Second Nature: A Gardener's Education*. New York: Atlantic Monthly Press.

Pomeranz, K. 2000. *The Great Divergence: China, Europe, and the Making of the Modern World Economy*. Princeton: Princeton University Press.

Portland Sunday Telegram. 1933. "Machiasport Lobster Fishermen in Favor of Double Gauge Law." December 31, A2.

Posey, D. 1985. "Indigenous Management of Tropical Forest Ecosystems: The Case of the Kayapo Indians of the Brazilian Amazon." *Agroforestry Systems* 3:139–58.

———. 1989. "Forest Islands." In *People of the Tropical Rain Forest*, ed. J. Padoch. Berkeley: University of California Press.

Potter, L. 1987. "Degradation, Innovation, and Social Welfare in the Riam Kiwa Valley, South Kalimantan, Indonesia." In *Land Degradation and Society*, ed. P. Brookfield, 164–76. London: Methuen.

Potts, A. 1989. "Constable Country between the Wars." In R. Samuel, ed., *Patriotism: The Making and Unmaking of British National Identity*. London: Routledge.

Prabhakaran, G. 2004. "Silent Valley: Another Battle in the Offing." In *Survey of the Environment, 2004*. Chennai: Hindu.

Prakash, G. 1990. "Writing Post-Orientalist Histories of the Third World: Perspectives from Indian Historiography." *Comparative Studies in Society and History* 32 (2): 383–408.

Pringle, R. 1970. *Rajahs and Rebels: The Ibans of Sarawak under Brooke Rule, 1841–1941*. Ithaca: Cornell University Press.

Radhakrishna, M. 1989. "The Criminal Tribes Act in Madras Presidency: Implications for Itinerant Trading Communities." *Indian Economic and Social History Review* 26 (3): 269–95.

Ramseyer, R. 1987. "Berna und Helvetia. Der Wandel des Begriffs 'Vaterland' im Spiegel des Intelligenzblattes für die Stadt Bern um die Mitte des 19. Jahrhunderts." In F. de Capitani et al., eds., *Auf dem Weg zu einer schweizerischen Identität 1848–1914*. Freiburg: Universitätsverlag.

Rangarajan, M. 1992. "Forest Policy in the Central Provinces, 1860–1914." PhD diss., Oxford University.

———. 1994. "Imperial Agendas and India's Forests: The Early History of Indian Forestry, 1800–1878." *Indian Economic and Social History Review* 31 (2): 147–67.

———. 2002. "Polity, Ecology, and Landscape: New Writings on South Asia's Past." *Studies in History*, n.s, 18 (1): 135–47.

Rathbun, R. 1887. *The Lobster Fishery: The Fisheries and Fishery Industries of the*

United States. In *History and Methods of the Fisheries,* Sec. 5, vol. 2 ed. G. Brown Goode. Washington, D.C.: U.S. Government Printing Office.

Ravi Rajan, S. 1997. "The Ends of Environmental History." *Environment and History* 3 (2): 245–52.

Rawski, E. 1972. *Agricultural Change and the Peasant Economy of South China.* Cambridge, Mass.: Harvard University Press.

Reed, K. 1997. "Early Hominid Evolution and Ecological Change through the African Plio-Pleistocene." *Journal of Human Evolution* 32:289–322.

Repetto, R., and T. Holmes. 1983. "The Role of Population in Resource Depletion in Developing Countries." *Population and Development Review* 9 (4): 609–32.

Reports. 1900–1930. *The Forest Administration of the Central Provinces.* Nagpur: Central Provinces Administration.

Ribbentrop, B. 1900. *Forestry in British India.* Calcutta: Government of India Press.

———. 1902. *Termes Taprobanes—White Ants as Pests of Trees.* Nagpur: Department of Land Records and Agriculture, Central Provinces.

Ribot, J., and N. Peluso. 2003. "A Theory of Access." *Rural Sociology* 68:153–81.

Richards, J., and M. McAlpin. 1983. "Cotton Cultivating and Land Clearing in the Bombay Deccan and Kamatak: 1818–1920." In *Global Deforestation and the Nineteenth Century World Economy,* ed. R. Tucker and J. Richards. Durham, N.C.: Duke University Press.

Riesman, D. 1958. "The Suburban Sadness." In *The Suburban Community,* ed. W. Dobriner. New York: G. P. Putnam.

Ritter, A., and J. Bondanella, eds. 1988. *Rousseau's Political Writings.* New York: W. W. Norton.

Rodger, A. 1925. "Research in Forestry in India." *Empire Forestry Journal* 4:45–53.

Rome, A. 2001. *The Bulldozer in the Countryside: Suburban Sprawl and the Rise of American Environmentalism.* New York: Cambridge University Press.

Roseberry, W. 1991. "Potatoes, Sack, and Enclosures in Early Modern England." In *Golden Ages, Dark Ages: Imagining the Past in Anthropology and History,* ed. J. O'Brien and W. Roseberry. Berkeley: University of California Press.

Rosen, C., and H. Zerner. 1984. *Romanticism and Realism: Mythology of Nineteenth Century Art.* London: Faber and Faber.

Ross, L. 1988. *Environmental Policy in China.* Bloomington: Indiana University Press.

Rousseau, J. 1990. *Central Borneo: Ethnical Identity and Social Life in a Stratified Society.* New York: Oxford University Press.

Rowe, W. 2001. *Saving the World: Chen Hongmou and Elite Consciousness in Eighteenth-Century China.* Stanford: Stanford University Press.

Ruddle, K., and T. Akimichi, ed. 1984. *Maritime Institutions in the Western Pacific.* Senri Series in Ethnology No. 17. Osaka: National Museum of Ethnology.

Russell, E. 2001. *War and Nature: Fighting Humans and Insects with Chemicals from World War I to* Silent Spring. New York: Cambridge University Press.

Rustomji, N. 1990. *Verrier Elwin: Philanthropologist.* New Delhi: Oxford University Press.

Rutschmann, V. 1994. *Fortschritt und Freiheit: Nationale Tugenden in historischen Jugendbüchern der Schweiz seit 1880.* Zurich: Chronos.

Sabean, D. 1984. *Power in the Blood: Popular Culture and Village Discourse in Early Modern Germany.* Cambridge: Cambridge University Press.

Sahlins, M. 1981. *Historical Metaphors and Mythical Realities: Structure in the Early History of the Sandwich Island Kingdom.* Ann Arbor: University of Michigan Press.

Said, E. 1979. *Orientalism.* New York: Vintage.

Salafsky, N., O. Dugelby, and J. Terborgh. 1993. "Can Extractive Reserves Save the Rainforest? An Ecological and Socio-economic Comparison of Non-timber Forest Product Extraction Systems in Peten, Guatemala, and West Kalimantan Indonesia." *Conservation Biology* 7:39–52.

Sandner, G. 1994. "In Search of Identity: German Nationalism and Geography, 1871–1910." In David Hooson, ed., *Geography and National Identity.* Oxford: Blackwell.

Santschi, C. 1991. *Schweizer Nationalfeste im Spiegel der Geschichte.* Zurich: Chronos.

Sarkar, S. 1984. "The Conditions and Nature of Subaltern Militancy: Bengal from Swadeshi to Non-cooperation." *Subaltern Studies,* 3. Delhi: Oxford University Press.

Sather, C. 1990. "Trees and Tree Tenure in Paku Iban Society: The Management of Secondary Forest Resources in a Long-Established Iban Community." *Borneo Review* 1:16–40.

Saxena, N. 1987. *Social Forestry in the Hill Districts of Uttar Pradesh.* Kathmandu: International Center for Integrated Mountain Development.

Schabel, H. 1990. "Tanganyika Forestry under German Colonial Administration, 1891–1919." *Forest and Conservation History* 34 (3): 130–43.

Schama, S. 1995. *Landscape and Memory.* London: Fontana Press.

Scheiben, O. 1987. *Krise und Integration. Wandlungen in den politischen Konzeptionen der Sozialdemokratischen Partei der Schweiz 1928–1936.* Zurich: Chronos.

Schieder, T. 1991. *Nationalismus und Nationalstaat. Studien zum nationalen Problem im modernen Europa.* Göttingen: Vandenhoeck and Ruprecht.

Schlich, W. 1925. "The Indian Forester, 1875–1925." *Indian Forester* 51 (7): 291–301.

Schneider, W. 1973. "The Social Organization of the Selako." PhD diss., University of North Carolina.

Schoppa, K. 1989. *Xiang Lake: Nine Centuries of Chinese Life.* New Haven: Yale University Press.

Schultz, W. 1999. *A Man's Turf: The Perfect Lawn.* New York: Three Rivers Press.

Scott, F. 1870. *The Art of Beautifying Suburban Home Grounds of Small Extent.* New York: D. Appleton.

Scott, J. 1976. *The Moral Economy of the Peasant: Rebellion and Subsistence in Southeast Asia.* New Haven: Yale University Press.

———. 1990. *Domination and the Art of Resistance: Hidden Transcripts.* New Haven: Yale University Press.

Sewell, W. H., Jr. 1996. "Three Temporalities: Toward an Eventful Sociology." In Terence J. McDonald, ed., *The Historic Turn in the Human Sciences.* Ann Arbor: University of Michigan Press.

Shapiro, J. 2001. *Mao's War against Nature: Politics and the Environment in Revolutionary China: Studies in Environment and History.* Cambridge: Cambridge University Press.

Shepherd, J. 1993. *Statecraft and Political Economy on the Taiwan Frontier, 1600–1800.* Stanford: Stanford University Press.

Shipton, P., and M. Goheen. 1992. "Understanding African Landholding: Power, Wealth, and Meaning." *Africa* 62:307–27.

Shiva, V. 1988. *Staying Alive: Women, Ecology, and Development.* London: Zed Books.

———. 1991. *Ecology and the Politics of Survival: Conflicts over Natural Resources in India.* New Delhi: Sage.

Short, J. R. 1991. *Imagined Country: Society, Culture, and Environment.* London: Routledge.

Shreeve, J. 1996. "Sunset on the Savanna." *Discover* 17 (7): 116–25.

Siegenthaler, H. 1990. "Die Rede von der Kontinuität in der Diskontinuität des sozialen Wandels—das Beispiel der dreissiger Jahre." In S. Brändli et al., eds., *Schweiz im Wandel. Studien zur neueren Gesellschaftsgeschichte.* Basel: Helbing and Lichtenhahn.

Singh, C. 1986. *Common Property and Common Poverty: India's Forests, Forest Dwellers, and the Law.* New Delhi: Oxford University Press.

Sivaramakrishnan, K. 1987. "Forests in Development." *Seminar* 330:27–32.

———. 1992. "Persistent Elites and Social Change: Agrarian Relations in Colonial Bengal, 1750–1950." *Yale Graduate Journal of Anthropology* 4 (1): 1–15.

———. 1995. "Situating the Subaltern: History and Anthropology in the Subaltern Studies Project." *Journal of Historical Sociology* 8 (4): 395–429.

———. 1999. *Modern Forests: Statemaking and Environmental Change in Colonial Eastern India.* Stanford: Stanford University Press.

Skud, B., and H. Perkins. 1969. "Size Composition, Sex Ratio, and Size at Maturity of Offshore Northern Lobsters." *U.S. Fish and Wildlife Service Special Scientific Report 598,* 1–10.

Smil, V. 1992. "Environmental Change as a Source of Conflict and Economic Loss in China." *American Association for the Advancement of Science Occasional Papers.*

————. 1993. *China's Environmental Crisis: An Inquiry into the Limits of National Development.* Armonk, N.Y.: M. E. Sharpe.

Smith, A. D. 1976. "Neo-Classicist and Romantic Elements in the Emergence of Nationalist Conceptions." In A. D. Smith, ed., *Nationalist Movements.* London: Macmillan.

————. 1984. "National Identity and Myths of Ethnic Descent." *Research in Social Movements, Conflict, and Change* 7:95–130.

————. 1986. *The Ethnic Origins of Nations.* Oxford: Blackwell.

————. 1991. *National Identity.* Harmondsworth: Penguin.

————. 1995. *Nations and Nationalism in a Global Era.* Cambridge: Polity.

Smith, N. 1984. *Uneven Development: Nature, Capital, and the Production of Space.* Oxford: Basil Blackwell.

Snell, D. 1962. "Snake in the Crab Grass." *Life,* October 12.

Somanathan, E. 1991. "Deforestation, Property Rights, and Incentives in Central Himalaya." *Wastelands News* 7 (1): 14–27.

Sonnenberg, L. 1991. "Me Lobster Gauge Bill Moving, Scallops on Hold." *Commercial Fisheries News,* March, A22.

Spigel, L. 1992. *Make Room for TV: Television and the Family Ideal in Postwar America.* Chicago: University of Chicago Press.

Spitteler, C. 1915. *Unser Schweizer Standpunkt.* Vortrag gehalten in der NHG. Gruppe Zürich, December 14, 1914. Zurich: Verlag Rascher und Cie.

Stebbing, E. 1922. *The Forests of India.* Vol. 1. London: John Lane.

————. 1926. *The Forests of India.* Vol. 3. London: John Lane.

Stein, B. 1983. "Idiom and Ideology in Early Nineteenth Century South India." In *Rural India: Land Power and Society under British Rule,* ed. P. Robb. London: Curzon Press.

————. 1990. *Thomas Munro: The Origins of the Colonial State and His Visions of Empire.* Delhi: Oxford University Press.

Stein, S. 1993. *Noah's Garden: Restoring the Ecology of Our Own Back Yards.* Boston: Houghton Mifflin.

Steinberg, T. 2002. *Down to Earth: Nature's Role in American History.* New York: Oxford University Press.

Stettler, P. 1969. *Das aussenpolitische Bewusstsein der Schweiz (1920–1930).* Zurich: Buchdruckerei Leemann AG.

Stokes, E. 1959. *The English Utilitarians and India.* Cambridge: Cambridge University Press.

————. 1986. *The Peasant Armed.* Oxford: Clarendon Press.

Sugden, R. 1986. *The Economics of Rights, Cooperation, and Welfare.* London: Basil Blackwell.

Suparlan, P. 1998. "Konflik Antara Orang Dayak da Orang Madura di Kalimantan Barat." *Wacana Antropologi* 2:7–9.

Swidler, A. 1986. "Culture in Action: Symbols and Strategies." *American Sociological Review* 51 (April): 273–86.

Taylor, M. 1990. "Cooperation and Rationality: Notes on the Collective Action Problem and Its Solutions." In *The Limits of Rationality*, ed. K. Cook and M. Levi, 222–40. Chicago: University of Chicago Press.

Teng, E. 2004. *Taiwan's Imagined Geography: Chinese Colonial Travel Writing and Pictures, 1683–1895*. Cambridge, Mass.: Harvard University Press.

Teyssot, G., ed. 1999. *The American Lawn*. New York: Princeton Architectural Press.

Thapar, R. 1978. *Ancient Indian Social History: Some Interpretations*. Delhi: Orient Longmans.

———. 1989. "Imagined Religious Communities: Ancient History and the Modern Search for Hindu Identity." *Modern Asian Studies* 23 (2): 209–31.

Thomas, K. 1983. *Man and the Natural World: Changing Attitudes in England, 1500–1800*. London: Penguin.

Thompson, E. 1963. *The Making of the English Working Class*. London: Victor Gollanez.

———. 1975. *Whigs and Hunters: The Origins of the Black Act*. London: Allen Lane.

———. 1978. "Eighteenth Century English Society: Class Struggle without Class." *Social History* 3 (2): 133–65.

Time. 1959. "The Wicked Weed." September 7, 72, 74.

———. 1961. "Weed 'Em & Reap." May 12, 34.

Tinker, H. 1966. "Structure of the British Imperial Heritage." In *Asian Bureaucratic Systems Emergent from British Imperial Tradition*, ed. R. Braibanti. Durham, N.C.: Duke University Press.

Trevor, C. 1923. "Review of Indian Forest Management." *Empire Forestry Journal* 2 (2): 243–48.

Troup, R. [1921] 1980. *Sylviculture of Indian Trees*. Dehradoon: Forest Research Institute.

———. 1940. *Colonial Forest Administration*. London: Oxford University Press.

Tsing, A. 1993. *In the Realm of the Diamond Queen: Marginality in an Out-of-the-Way Place*. New Jersey: Princeton University Press.

Tsing, P., and A. Tsing. 2003. *Environmental Discourses in South and Southeast Asia*. Durham, N.C.: Duke University Press.

Tucker, R. 1983. "The British Colonial System and the Forests of the Western Himalayas." In *Global Deforestation and the Nineteenth Century World Economy*, ed. R. Tucker and J. Richards. Durham, N.C.: Duke University Press.

———. 1989. "The Depletion of India's Forests under British Imperialism: Planters, Foresters, and Peasants in Assam and Kerala." In *The Ends of the Earth*, ed. D. Worster. Cambridge: Cambridge University Press.

Umney, J. 1896. *Report on Carica Papaya*. Calcutta: Government of India Press.

United States Census Bureau. 2002. *Statistical Abstract of the United States: 2002.* Washington, D.C.: Government Printing Office.

Von Furer-Haimendorf, C. 1943. *The Chenchus: Jungle Folks of the Deccan.* London: Macmillan.

———. 1945a. "Aboriginal Rebellions in the Deccan." *Man in India* 25 (4): 208–16.

———. 1945b. *The Reddis of the Bison Hills.* London: Macmillan.

———. 1948. *The Raj Gonds of Adilabad.* London: Macmillan.

———. 1982. *Tribes of India: Struggle for Survival.* Berkeley: University of California Press.

Von Greyerz, H. 1980. "Der Bundesstaat seit 1848." In *Handbuch der Schweizer Geschichte.* Zurich: Berichthaus Verlag.

Wachter, D. 1995. *Schweiz. Eine Moderne Geographie.* Zurich: Verlag Neue Zürcher Zeitung.

Wade, R. 1988. *Village Republics.* London: Routledge and Kegan Paul.

Walter, F. 1989. "Attitudes towards the Environment in Switzerland." *Journal of Historical Geography* 15 (3): 287–99.

———. 1990. *Les Suisses et l'environnement. Une histoire du rapport à la nature du 18e siècle à nos jours.* Genève: Editions Zoé.

———. 1992. "Lieux, paysages, espaces. Les perceptions de la montagne alpine du XVIIIe siècles à nos jours." In J.-F. Bergier and S. Guzzi, eds., *La découverte des Alpes.* Actes de Coloque Latsis 1990. Basel: Schwabe.

Washbrook, D. 1981. "Law, State, and Society in Colonial India." In *Power, Profit, and Politics,* ed. C. Baker, G. Johnson, and J. Gallagher. Cambridge: Cambridge University Press.

Washington Post. 1939. "The Post Impressionist and Crab Grass." July 14, 12.

Watt, G. [1889–96] 1972. *A Dictionary of the Economic Products of India.* 7 vols. (1889–96); 10 vols. (1972). New Delhi: Cosmo Publications.

Watts, M. 1983. *Silent Violence: Food, Famine, and Peasantry in Northern Nigeria.* Berkeley: University of California Press.

Weigert, A. 1994. "Lawns of Weeds: Status in Opposition to Life." *American Sociologist* 25 (1): 80–96.

Weinstock, J. 1983. "Rattan: Ecological Balance in a Borneo Rainforest Swidden." *Economic Botany* 37:58–68.

Weishaupt, M. 1992. *Bauern, Hirten und "frume edle puren." Bauern- und Bauernstaatsideologie in der spätmittelalterlichen Eidgenossenschaft und der nationalen Geschichtsschreibung der Schweiz.* Basel: Helbing and Lichtenhahn.

Weston, M. 1960. "Suburban Neurosis: Crabgrass." *New York Times,* July 24, Sec. 6, 21.

Wharton, D. 1986. "Lawns May Hark to Man's Origin." *Los Angeles Times,* August 7, 20.

Whitcombe, E. 1972. *Agrarian Conditions in North India, Uttar Pradesh: 1860–1900.* Berkeley: University of California Press.

White, L. 1967. "The Historical Roots of our Ecological Crisis." *Science* 155:120–27.

Widmer, T. 1992. *Die Schweiz in der Wachstumskrise der 1880er Jahre.* Zurich: Chronos.

Wigger, E. 1997. *Vom Burgfrieden zum Bürgerblock: Krieg und Krise in der politischen Kommunikation 1910–1922.* Zurich: Seismo.

Williamson, O. 1985. *The Economic Institutions of Capitalism.* New York: Free Press.

Wilmsen, E. 1989. *Land Filled with Flies: A Political Economy of the Kalahari.* Chicago: University of Chicago Press.

Winter, R. 1967. "O. M. Scott Thrives by Enticing Families to Beautify Lawns." *Wall Street Journal,* May 8, p. 1.

Wozniakowski, J. 1987. *Die Wildnis. Zur Deutungsgeschichte des Berges in der europäischen Neuzeit.* Frankfurt am Main: Suhrkamp.

Yuan, B. (2000). *Chinese Democracies: A Study of the Kongsis of West Borneo (1776–1884).* Leiden: Research School of Asian, African and Amerindian Studies, Universiteit Leiden.

Zaidi, S. 1989. "The Mughal State and Tribes in Seventeenth Century Sind." *Indian Economic and Social History Review* 26 (3): 343–62.

Zhongguo Huanjingbao. 1984. 1:33 (Fakansi [inaugural issue]).

Zimmer, O. 1993. "Zur Typisierung der Juden in der Schweizer Tagespresse der Jahre 1933 und 1934: Aspekte eines Fremdbildes im Prozess nationaler Identitätskonstruktion." In K. Imhof et al., eds., *Zwischen Konflikt und Konkordanz. Analyse von Medienereignissen in der Vor- und Zwischenkriegszeit.* Zurich: Seismo.

———. 1996. "Die 'Volksgemeinschaft.' Entstehung und Funktion einer nationalen Einheitssemantik in den 1930er Jahren in der Schweiz." In K. Imhof et al., eds., *Konkordanz und Kalter Krieg. Analyse von Medienereignissen in der Schweiz der Zwischen- und Nachkriegszeit.* Zurich: Seismo.

———. 2003. *A Contested Nation: History, Memory, and Nationalism in Switzerland, 1761–1891.* Cambridge: Cambridge University Press.

———. 2004. "'A Unique Fusion of the Natural and the Man-Made': The Trajectory of Swiss Nationalism, 1933–1939." *Journal of Contemporary History* 39, pp. 5–24.

———. 2006. "Circumscribing Community: Swiss Nationhood in the Long Nineteenth Century." In Mark Hewitson and Timothy Baycroft, eds., *Nationalism in Europe: Civic and Ethnic Traditions.* Oxford: Oxford University Press, 100–119.

Contributors

PROFESSOR JAMES ACHESON has a joint appointment within the University of Maine's Department of Anthropology and its School of Marine Sciences. He is a cultural anthropologist with an acute interest in Maine lobstering.

PROFESSOR RICHARD C. HOFFMANN teaches medieval European history at York University in Canada. He has a long list of publications on the history of medieval environments, not just aquatic ones, to his credit.

NICHOLAS HOWE was Professor of English at the University of California, Berkeley. His research revolved around Anglo-Saxon literature and, more recently, landscape.

PROFESSOR JAMES C. MCCANN teaches African history at Boston University. His interests and publications have ranged across agricultural and environmental histories of the continent.

J. R. MCNEILL is Professor of History and also has an appointment in the Walsh School of Foreign Service at Georgetown University in Washington, D.C. His interest in modern environmental history has led to several publications on the subject.

PROFESSOR NANCY LEE PELUSO specializes in environmental sociology and resource policy in the Department of Environmental Science, Policy & Management at the University of California, Berkeley.

PETER C. PERDUE is Professor of History in the Massachusetts Institute of Technology's history department. His research on early modern and modern China has focused on frontiers, minorities, and environments.

K. SIVARAMAKRISHNAN is Professor of Anthropology at the University of Washington. His specialties include environmental anthropology, agrarian studies, and South Asian culture.

ASSOCIATE PROFESSOR PAOLO SQUATRITI teaches medieval European and most types of Italian history in the Departments of History and Romance Languages and Literatures at the University of Michigan.

TED STEINBERG is Professor of History at Case Western Reserve University. He specializes in nineteenth- and twentieth-century U.S. history and has published extensively on environmental change.

OLIVER ZIMMER is Lecturer in Modern History at University College, University of Oxford, in England. He specializes in German history 1760–1914 and is interested in issues of identity formation.